PC Magazine Guide to Connectivity

PC Magazine Guide to Connectivity

Frank J. Derfler, Jr.

Ziff-Davis Press
Emeryville, California

Development Editor: Eric Stone
Copy Editor: Glen Becker
Technical Editor: Marvin Schwartz, Ph.D.
Project Coordinator: Sheila McGill
Proofreader: Katja Amyx
Front Cover Concept: Gerard Kunkel
Back Cover Concept: Laura Lamar, MAX Design
Cover Design: Gary Kaplow and Rob Smith
Book Design: Paper Crane Graphics, Berkeley
Technical Illustration: Cherie Plumlee
Photography: Robert Sondgroth
Photographic Design: Paper Crane Graphics, Berkeley
Page Layout: Kevin Shafer & Associates
Indexer: Julie Kawabata

This book was produced on a Macintosh IIfx, with the following applications: FrameMaker, Word, MacLink*Plus*, and FreeHand. Imagesetting of film negatives was produced on a Compugraphic 9400PS.

Ziff-Davis Press
5903 Christie Avenue
Emeryville, CA 94608

ISBN 1-56276-001-7
Manufactured in the United States of America
10 9 8 7 6 5 4 3

To Marlene, Shandra, and Steve: a small family, but growing!

■ Contents at a Glance

■ Table of Contents

Chapter 6:   Cables and Adapters: The Hardware Heart of the LAN

Chapter 7:   The Big Three LAN Standards: Ethernet, Token-Ring, and ARCnet

■ Foreword

No other area of computer technology, or computer applications, draws such incredibly hard-headed, closed-minded and often utterly incorrect statements as networking.

I have often joked to audiences that networks must be more theology than technology, because the arguments those charged with planning, designing, buying, installing and supporting them use are so often cast in terms of dogma. I have spent days and days of high-priced consulting time sitting at tables surrounded by people making the most foolish statements about networks, and about what they *know* about networks. I wondered, often, if I was really there to give advice, or rather to serve as a referee . . . and perhaps, as a confessor.

Worse, we get drawn into these dogmatic arguments over the most amazing details: network protocols, network topologies, even network cabling. Can you imagine any other business in which a roomful of adults would sit around arguing for hours about *wiring?!?*

I have heard otherwise sensible people say the most remarkable things about wiring systems. "Only coax will do—we want the best." "Twisted pair is the most up to date cabling system around." "I won't let fiber optics on the premises around here: no one can make it work." "The real difference in cost in putting in a network is the cabling system we use—it all depends on what kind of wire we're going to pull."

Amazing.

You will not be surprised that the louder and angrier these things are said, the more certainty attached to the claims in speakers' minds, the likelier they are to be wrong.

In networking, people know what they know, by God—but often don't know what they're talking about at all.

In this swamp of misinformation, Frank Derfler stands out like a light atop a rocky headland, shining clearly through the fog on a treacherous sea.

First, Frank really *does* know what he's talking about: a commodity rare enough among consultants in general, and one particularly valuable in the morass of networking options available today. Second, Frank doesn't drag theology into the fray: he likes to find specific answers for specific problems, and doesn't much care who came up with those answers. Third, Frank has actually Been There and Done It: his professional opinions carry the weight of someone who has had to make this call before, and live with the results.

Maybe best of all, despite his clear-headed analysis of connectivity needs and products, he doesn't feel the need to bash people's heads in when his answer is different from theirs.

Bernie Hoffman, a famous Life magazine photographer in the 40s, used to grow weary of young hotshots in Life's ranks telling him how good they were. When a flavor-of-the-month kid tossed his head to the side and said, haughtily, something like "All *I* use is 35MM, you know," or "I refuse to shoot with anything but an 8x10," Bernie would nod, say "Yes"—then a split second later add "Because of course that's the limit of your knowledge and experience."

Though he has the credentials to do so, Frank never follows that path. He hears out even the most air-headed schemes, then nods and says in his best (and, I'm convinced, entirely unconscious) Jack Benny style, "Well. (*pause*) What *I'd* do is . . . ."

And he's always got the better idea.

Frank has also somehow avoided the idiocy of status issues in networking. He's perfectly happy to recommend a data switch when that's the right answer. Or a zero-slot LAN, when it's the cost-effective solution. Even though both are considered declasse by many networking purists.

And while many consultants and networking gurus sneered at multiuser DOS systems, Frank not only recommended them, but helped that small industry pull itself together around some standards. There wasn't anything in that for Frank Derfler . . . but there was a lot in it for his readers and clients.

Networks are enormous investments, and as much as we talk about throw-away technology and three-year life cycles, the truth is that the network you put in today is the one you're going to be living with for a long time to come. You may add more servers, stretch it with gateways, bridges and repeaters, piggyback voice or video or God knows what else on top. But that underlying conceptual and physical structure—design, layout, cabling, topology, protocols, adapter cards—is going to be there for years to come.

Which is what makes it so important to get networking decisions right the first time.

Learning about networking starts right here. For most readers, this book will take them as far as they want to go. And even for network experts—real ones, as well as the Konnectivity Klowns—this book has a lot of value.

The effective networking of business PC users is clearly going to be the single biggest issue in computing in the 1990s. This book is your guide to that world.

Jim Seymour
March, 1991

■ Introduction

My goal in writing this book is to make you a hero. I want to help you solve problems in your company or organization, improve productivity, and save money. That's the stuff of modern heroes. With the information I've given you in this book, you can amplify, release, and focus the power that is available in modern PCs when you connect them together to synthesize and distribute information.

I've written this book with managers in mind, not just technicians or PC power users. I assume you're "PC-savvy" enough to understand DOS subdirectories and that you know how to plug a printer into the parallel port of a PC, but otherwise you don't need any special information, background, or experience to use this book.

The book you have in your hands is different from most books, because it is more than just printed pages of text. The diskettes, the diagrams, and the Connectivity Decision Tree chart bound into the back of the book lead you to important information and recommendations that can help you make decisions without forcing you to wade through oceans of words.

The first chapter introduces the concept of information as the raw material, inventory, and finished product of many organizations. Chapter 2 takes you through the Connectivity Decision Tree. Its questions and recommendations can help you find economical and effective ways to design, install, and operate a connectivity system.

Chapters 2 through 4 of this book discuss a variety of ways you can link computers together to share printers, exchange files, and use networked applications.

The connectivity field is broad. No other logical division of the computer industry encompasses so many different technologies. The world of local area networks—only one portion of the connectivity galaxy—includes many specialized elements such as cables, connectors, interface adapters, connecting software, and management tools. Chapters 5 through 11 give you an overview, specific details, and practical hints about all these different network elements.

Chapters 12 and 13 explore a rapidly evolving aspect of the connectivity market: interoperability. This deals with the problems of connecting computers that use different architectures and operating systems, often in different locations. An arena of challenges, interoperability draws in some of the most arcane leading-edge technologies used in the computer industry.

The Appendix contains a database of connectivity products and vendors, and the diskettes include a variety of programs you can use. The diagrams show important principles and describe how things work.

Near the back of the book you'll find an extensive glossary covering topics ranging from modems to the definitions of the IEEE 802.X standards.

Throughout this book, I've clustered information together into related areas—sometimes allowing overlap between those subject areas—to make the concepts and hints as readily available to you as possible. You don't have to read this book from cover to cover or even from front to back. It's designed to act as a quick reference, a tutorial, and a friendly consultant. Please enjoy it.

■ Acknowledgments

My sincere thanks to Glen Becker, Dr. Marvin Schwartz, and Eric Stone for their humor, encouragement, and technical skills. Kimberly Maxwell, Gerard Kunkel, Ames Kanemoto, Bob Sondgroth, Kim Haglund, Cherie Plumlee, Sheila McGill, Katja Amyx, and Jeff Green provided the outstanding "look and feel" of this book.

CHAPTER

1

Society + Commerce = Connectivity

- Connectivity Is Dead

- An Open World and Everybody's World

- Networks and LANs

- Layers of a Structured Market

- The Future of Connectivity

You don't have to be a corporate networking guru to be interested in linking computers to each other. As the Workgroup Systems Editor of *PC Magazine,* I receive any number of letters from people who work in offices with five or six PCs and want to know the best way to connect their computers in order to share data or printers.

Similarly, you don't have to be a power programmer to install a printer-sharing device or even a full network for a dozen or more PCs. Modern networking products make it easy and economical to install powerful and flexible networking systems.

From surveys of the readers of *PC Magazine,* I know that more than half of the PCs our readers own are connected to modems, mainframes, or local area networks (LANs). Market Intelligence Research Company predicts that the percentage of microcomputers that are connected to PC LANs worldwide will rise to more than 43 percent by 1995. The interconnected organization that relies on a flow of information is the commercial role model for the 1990s.

Commerce and society in the United States and in many other countries is increasingly based on information. Information replaces the need for inventory in the "just-in-time" production lines. In the bustling city of Atlanta, Georgia, the airport is the largest employment center. But without the information grid underlying the airline, air traffic control, car rental, and metropolitan transportation systems, the entire operation and the peripheral businesses it supports would grind to a halt in an hour.

In some organizations, information is a necessary lubricant for trade. In others, information is both a raw material and a crafted output product.

Computers hold and sort information, and communications networks transport information between computers. Computers and their networks form the manufacturing and transportation infrastructure of modern organizations and societies.

At certain stages in the development of a society, the majority of the people need practical skills in such areas as agriculture, herding, or fishing. As societies industrialize, a large percentage of the populace must learn how to drive a car, and many people master mechanical trades. In the United States, we are now at the stage when many people must master the information trades. The majority of people have to know how to use information-delivery tools such as television sets, and an increasing number have to be able to put information into and take information from a computer. The need to use a computer connected to a communications network follows quickly after that.

Not every member of society will need the skills taught in this book to select, install, and manage connectivity systems, but someone in practically every commercial office and workgroup must have these skills in order for the enterprise to run efficiently and effectively. A hundred years ago, commercial organizations relied on horsepower and the skills of teamsters and farriers as they moved their products by horse-drawn wagons. Fifty years ago commerce was based on the train and the truck, and on the skills of drivers and mechanics. Today, commerce is increasingly dependent on computers and their communications systems and on the skills of the professionals who create, install, and maintain them. Now is the right time for you to learn about computer connectivity systems.

■ Connectivity Is Dead

I used to begin my speeches to groups of PC users and managers by announcing, "Connectivity is dead!" Since I carried the title of Connectivity Editor of *PC Magazine* at the time, my audiences thought this was a strange thing to say. My point was that Connectivity, with a capital *C,* is an IBM term describing a method of interconnecting computers that inexorably laced people into IBM's proprietary web. Once you connected using Big Blue's signaling, cabling, and software systems, it was difficult to integrate products from other manufacturers into your network.

That type of Connectivity is dead. The new world of connectivity, with a little *c,* allows interconnection between computer systems made by many different manufacturers. Today, you can shop for components on the basis of features, price, service, support, and availability and generally know that the software and hardware products you buy will work together.

■ An Open World and Everybody's World

The escape from the "closed" meaning of Connectivity was an upstream trek. Many companies, institutions, and even governments took thousands of small steps to reach a system of "open" connectivity. In 1977, the International Standards Organization (ISO) established a subcommittee to define standards for products used to link heterogeneous computers.

The world of open connectivity specifications or "protocols" is a paradise with rules, where all products work together in harmony because they conform to published standards for interoperability. The first real footsteps of mortals echoed in this paradise in 1987, when companies like AT&T, Digital Equipment Corp., and others began announcing and releasing products conforming to certain sections of the ISO specification for Open Systems Interconnection (OSI). Digital, at least, won't field a full OSI suite of products until the mid-1990s.

An interesting thing happened on the way to paradise. Many companies learned to get along with each other even without conforming exactly to the ponderous ISO OSI model. While companies learned how to create products for the structure of the open systems, they also learned that it was relatively easy to create products for each others' systems. So aggressive companies such as D-Link Systems and 3Com Corp. created software that lets their network operating systems interoperate with Novell's popular NetWare. Novell fielded software allowing networks that use NetWare to interoperate with those using Microsoft Corp.'s LAN Manager and with computers running the Unix operating system.

Modern network managers can mix network pieces and parts from different companies in a variety of ways. The open world, designed to be open according to certain guidelines, became everybody's world. Particularly in the United States, but also in other pragmatic countries, following the rules of openness became less important than working together directly.

■ Networks and LANs

An organization usually takes some time to evolve to the point where it needs large open systems, or at least cooperative computer systems made up of pieces supplied by many vendors. The need for connectivity often begins with a simple desire to share a single printer between two PCs or to move a file from one person to another without writing it to a diskette and walking it down the hall. These modest problems don't always require solutions with miles of wire and megabytes of programs. Some connectivity problems cry out for local area networks, but others yield to simpler solutions.

The word *network* and the phrase *local area network* (LAN) are both overused and abused, so we should be sure we have the same frame of reference. A network is any type of interactive information-carrying system. There are networks of sensors and nerve fibers in your body, and there are information and entertainment networks displayed on your television set. The information-carrying aspect of networking is important. Information-carrying networks are the infrastructure—the roads and highways—of modern societies. Computer communications networks carry information between different computers and between computers and their peripherals.

A LAN is a computer communications network that spans a limited geographical area—usually no more than a few miles, and often much less. Other types of computer communications networks include the *metropolitan-area network* (MAN) and the *wide-area network* (WAN). Technical factors force these computer communications networks to trade speed for distance. In a LAN, the data moves at tens or even hundreds of megabits per second—and you will note that the text in this book represents only about 5 megabits of data—within an office, throughout a factory, or across a campus. By contrast, data in a WAN typically moves at 1 megabit per second or less, but this kind of network can span continents and oceans. This book will focus primarily on local-area-network connectivity alternatives, but we will also consider networking over longer distances in Chapter 13.

■ Layers of a Structured Market

Overall, buyers of connectivity products seem to fall into four categories, based primarily on the complexity of the systems they need. Figure 1.1 illustrates how these layers overlap.

Figure 1.1

The buyers of LAN systems divide themselves among those with simple resource-sharing needs, people who need to link 2 to 20 PCs in a network, managers of larger networks with 20 to 200 nodes or even more, and the new priests of computing who practice the arts of interoperability.

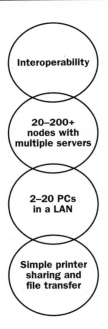

The first level of connectivity buyers are innovators who see a need to link computers and share information, usually in a small organization or workgroup, and who take action to fill that need. These buyers often include PC-savvy managers and people who are genuinely enthusiastic about personal computers. They often shop with a limited budget and look for practical solutions that don't involve a lot of training or support. Usually they don't have to coordinate their decisions with a lot of technical specialists. These people often buy the products they use through catalogs or directly from magazine ads. They can buy printer-sharing and simple file-transfer systems and have them installed and operational in just a few hours.

The second level of buyers are those who know they need a high-speed network for a group of 2 to 20 users. These people are often engaged in what has been called "guerilla networking." They bring in small networks in an underground guerilla operation, sometimes under the noses of unresponsive corporate data-processing professionals.

The networking hardware and software for a group of 2 to 20 PCs runs about $300 per PC. This is within the discretionary limits of a middle manager, so these buyers aren't strapped for cash, but they must carefully account for what they spend. There are several good networking products, including Invisible Ethernet NET/30, LANsmart, and LANtastic, that allow these people to install a network for 2 to 20 PCs in one afternoon, spend a couple of hours configuring the applications and batch files, and enjoy a functional network on the third day.

This class of network doesn't need a full-time person dedicated to the job of network management. But someone usually emerges or is appointed as the caretaker of the LAN.

The next category of connectivity buyers includes many graduates of the guerilla school of networking and some of the corporate data-processing professionals who understand the importance of networked PCs. These folks need a multiserver network for 20 to 200 users or more. They operate from funds specially budgeted for the network, and they worry about speed, reliability, and support much more than cost.

Buyers of networks with 20 to 200+ nodes might hire professional system integrators to supply and install their networks, but the buyers typically dictate the brands and components of a system. Increasingly, organizations with networking requirements on this scale have a professional staff dedicated to maintaining and expanding the network.

Interestingly, contributions to the budget for the operation of larger networks often come from managers of the business side of an organization. In a growing number of organizations, the business managers control line items in their budgets for services such as copy machines, telephones, and the LAN. This gives business managers an important input into the activities of the technical staff.

Finally, at the top of the stack are those managers who must integrate multivendor networks. The people involved in this sphere of *interoperability,* as I've named it, come from several different disciplines. First, there are the PC-savvy zealots who have climbed a long trail and learned many lessons. Second, there are people who specialize in communications systems, often schooled more in telephone networks than in corporate computing networks. There are corporate data-processing managers and people whose whole line of work depends on computers, like structural or mechanical engineers who use computers as tools every day. They have to learn the technology of their tools in order to use them well.

In many ways these people are today's priests of computing, and they chant a litany that would be lost on managers and buyers of the lower-level systems. There is a much bigger step into the technology of interoperability than the one from small- to medium-size networks. The words are different, the concepts are sometimes arcane, and the arguments between factions supporting different protocols, architectures, and vendor-backed systems are fierce. Yet once you master this technology of openness and interoperability, it really works.

The priests of interoperability often control their own budgets, but they must work with network systems servicing and financed by business managers, so they worry about productivity and economy more than the corporate data-processing professionals of the 1960s and '70s ever did. They usually write the specifications for their own systems and often buy directly from manufacturers.

All of these consumers of connectivity products are trying to solve the problem of how to tap their organizations into the volume and type of information they need for successful operation. Working in and building up the infrastructure for modern commerce and society are the role of the modern connectivity worker.

Whatever category you fall in, when you are ready to make your buying decisions you look for products. These products will conform to certain protocols and follow certain technical strategies, but the buying process finally comes down to a company name, product name, and price.

■ The Future of Connectivity

It's easy to predict the future, but making those predictions come true is often much more difficult. Here are some of today's connectivity trends and some projections of where I think they will take us.

- Interoperability: Interoperability will continue to replace "openness" as companies deliver an increasing number of products pragmatically designed to work together.

- Distributed processing: In distributed-processing systems, a program executes tasks on many processors spread around the network. In several ways, this architecture makes more sense than the use of "super servers" with multiple processors in one box as they are marketed today.

- Diversity: The industry will continue to offer a variety of alternative ways to share information and resources. There won't be a single big winner among the competing wiring schemes and network operating systems, but rather a rich blend of offerings.

- Wireless connections: There are many problems, including overcrowding the radio frequency spectrum, but you'll see an increase in the number of wireless alternatives for LAN, MAN, and WAN connectivity.

- Direct sales: The majority of buyers will be sophisticated enough to bypass higher-cost sales channels for the purchase of everything from cables to software in favor of buying direct. As the products become more interoperable, people will shop primarily for price, differentiating features, and availability.

The 1990s will be a rich time for people who manage and use computer networks. Many new personal careers will be launched. But the technology will continue to multiply in its complexity. The *PC Magazine Guide to Connectivity* is designed to help newcomers get started and to help more experienced people stay current in the critically important field of connectivity.

More than a Dozen Good Ways to Connect Computers

- Connection = Sharing

- More than Mail

- Distance Makes the Difference

- The Multiuser DOS Alternative

- Media-Sharing LANs

- Making Outside Connections

- Linking LANs

- LAN-Management Tools

- Making the Right Choices

I designed this chapter for folks who know (or perhaps just suspect) that they need to link their PCs together, gain access to mainframe computer systems, or simply share printers, but aren't sure how to do it. You've probably heard about local area networks (LANs), and you might even use one now. Yet, beyond what you'll learn to call media-sharing LANs, there are lots of different ways to link PCs to each other, to other kinds of computers, and to shared devices such as printers and modems. Some of the alternatives cost less than traditional LANs and provide more flexibility. This chapter will lead you through the alternatives and guide you toward other references in this book and on the Connectivity Guide diskettes that came with it.

The heart of this chapter is a chart called the Connectivity Decision Tree, bound at the back of the book. The chart consists of a series of yes-or-no questions leading to recommendations. At each branch of the Connectivity Decision Tree, I suggest an alternative connection scheme or service. Boxed comments indicate the major advantages and drawbacks of each alternative. I'll give you a brief explanation of the major connectivity alternatives in this chapter; later chapters contain detailed explanations of nearly all of the alternatives.

As we examine those alternatives, you can use the Appendix near the back of the book to find companies offering products in each category I describe. The Appendix includes phone numbers and addresses so that you can contact the companies for further information.

■ Connection = Sharing

The need to share inspires all of the connectivity systems, techniques, and alternatives discussed in this book. You link computers together to gain shared access to resources such as printers, files, and communications gateways.

The most common initial reason for linking computers is to share printers. Even though the prices of very capable laser printers have declined in recent years, it still makes economic sense to share printers among PCs if you can do this without too much technical and managerial overhead.

Connecting to Print

Let's start with the question in the upper-left corner of the Decision Tree: "Need to share more than printers?" If you answer no to this question, it means that sharing printers is all you need to do. Several kinds of products give you low-cost printer sharing.

You can share printers among a few people using a manual switch to route the printer connection from one PC to another. Typically, however, you would automate the process through a *printer-sharing buffer*. Such devices—usually small boxes roughly the size of this book (see Figure 2.1)—can give up to ten people shared access to the same printer at a cost of about $75 per connection.

Figure 2.1

The Logical Connection from Fifth Generation Systems is a popular printer-sharing buffer. In its typical configuration, it can accept print jobs from six PCs and route them to either of two printers.

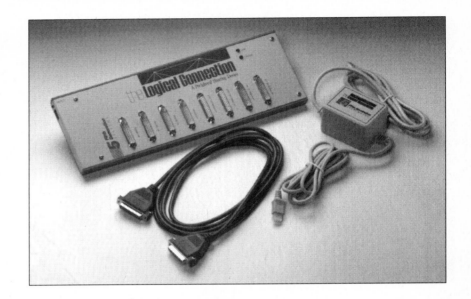

When a PC has something to print, the printer-sharing buffer routes the job to the printer. The person using that PC simply invokes an application program's print function in the usual way, and the buffer does all the work. Buffers often include their own internal memory to hold or *spool* print jobs until the printer can handle them. Some printer-sharing buffers include a small pop-up terminate-and-stay-resident (TSR) program allowing you to select the desired printer, but others use no software in the PCs.

Printer-sharing buffers attach to serial or parallel ports on each PC and to one or more printers. When you buy one of these products, you have to choose a model with the appropriate types of ports for the PCs and printers you want to link. The dealers and manufacturers of these devices have a good handle on the technical specifications of any devices you are likely to have, so do ask for help in selecting the right buffer.

Refer to the Appendix near the back of this book for a list of companies offering these products, and see Chapter 3 for more detailed information on printer-sharing techniques.

Sending the Mail

After printer sharing, the most common reason people report they want to link PCs together is to exchange files and to send electronic mail (e-mail). Surveys of *PC Magazine*'s readers have revealed that electronic mail will soon equal printer sharing as a justification for local area network installations. As you have seen, you don't need to invest in a full LAN to share printers; savvy managers also know that they don't need a sophisticated network to establish a first-class electronic-mail system, either.

Electronic-mail programs are relatively simple pieces of software. Primarily, they transfer files (messages) from one subdirectory (mailbox) to another. Programs that let people share database files simultaneously or that provide shared access to mainframe computers are complex pieces of software, but e-mail packages are simpler programs that don't need a lot of sophisticated shared resources or network support.

Since e-mail programs primarily transfer small files, they will work over a wide variety of connection schemes. Simple cables connected to a PC's serial port, modems connected to telephone lines, and high-speed LAN cables all can carry e-mail messages. Later branches of the Decision Tree will help you make more decisions about your connection options.

■ More than Mail

Look at the next question on the Decision Tree: "Need to share databases too?" This question helps you decide whether you need a sophisticated network system that can support database sharing, or whether simpler and less expensive alternatives will work for you.

If you need printer-sharing, file-transfer, and electronic-mail services, but not multiple, simultaneous access to the same data files, then you should look at two types of products that link personal computers (including those from Apple Computer and other companies) through their serial and parallel ports. These products, zero-slot LANs and data switches, don't require the installation of complex, expensive networking adapters, cables, and software.

Zero-Slot LANs

A *zero-slot LAN* uses software to link two or three PCs together over a maximum of 50 to 100 feet of cable. Simple software that runs on each PC makes it possible to transfer files and exchange electronic mail. Some products allow PCs to connect through their serial ports, and others provide for faster parallel-port connections. In all cases, the maximum file-transfer rate is about 30 kilobits per second. This is much faster than a telephone modem, which typically operates at a transfer rate of less than 2 kilobits per second, but much slower than a LAN, which typically moves data to each client station with a *through-put* (or effective transfer rate) of 500 kilobits per second.

The primary advantage of a zero-slot LAN is its low cost—about $80 per connection—for printer sharing, file transfer, and electronic mail. The primary disadvantage is slow speed and inefficiency, because the processors in the connected computers must divide their attention between the tasks of communicating and running the application programs you want to use.

While most of the zero-slot LAN products allow you to connect more than two computers together, I don't recommend it. The communications workload is too high in a three- or four-way system, and the alternative we'll consider next—the data switch—does a better job in a multiconnection environment.

Refer to the Appendix for a list of companies selling these products, and see Chapter 3 for more information.

Data Switches

The other alternative for printer-sharing, file-transfer, and electronic-mail tasks is a *data switch*. A data switch (Figure 2.2) is a small device, about the size and mass of a desktop telephone, that can accept connections from multiple computers, printers, and modems. It works exactly like the regular telephone switching center in your community. All of the devices—PCs, Macs, modems, and printers—connect to the data switch through cables attached to their serial or parallel ports. On request, the switch creates an electronic connection between any two devices, just as when you make a voice telephone call. When the two devices are through with the "call," they disconnect and become available for another connection.

Through a data switch, you can connect your PC to any of several printers, to expensive high-speed modems, or to other computers. Simple file-transfer and electronic-mail software runs on each PC, but unlike a zero-slot LAN, the data switch itself handles a lot of the communications functions for each connected device. This configuration lessens the load on the PC and improves throughput.

The primary advantage of a data switch is its moderate cost: about $100 per port. The least expensive media-shared LAN costs $200 per node, but $400 per node is a more typical price. Data switches also provide more flexibility than the slightly less expensive zero-slot LANs and permit connections over greater distances (several hundred feet of cable). Likewise, data switches typically have slightly faster throughput than a zero-slot LAN— about 40 to 50 kilobits per second—but they still don't equal a media-sharing LAN in data-transfer capability.

Figure 2.2

Digital Products'
NetCommander is a
powerful and flexible data
switch offering both device
and resource sharing,
along with PC-to-PC file-
transfer capabilities.
Options include access to
IBM 3270 computers and
automated tape backup.
The unit's maximum speed
of 115,200 bits per
second gives it excellent
throughput.

Refer to the Appendix near the back of this book for more information on companies offering these products. We will cover them more thoroughly in Chapter 3.

■ Distance Makes the Difference

When you get to the question "All within 1,000 feet?" in the Decision Tree, we've established your commitment to the concept that you need a connectivity scheme fast enough to provide multiuser, concurrent access to the same data files. Only the question of the distance between devices remains.

The laws of physics make it much more difficult—and therefore expensive—to send a fast signal over a long distance than to send a slow signal over a long distance or a fast signal over a short distance. If you want high-speed service over a mile or more, you'll have to pay for special signaling techniques and circuits, but it is relatively easy and economical to maintain a signaling rate of 10 megabits per second over 1,000 feet.

ISDN Moves Data over Distances

One technique you can use to link PCs over a distance is called the *Integrated Services Digital Network*, or ISDN. The ISDN program, supported by funds from many governments and international companies, has the goal of digitizing the analog telephone systems of the world. You'll find ISDN available in the major cities of North America, Europe, and Japan.

The links between ISDN and personal computers are still emerging, but as new hardware and software reaches the market, ISDN promises to provide 128-kilobit-per-second computer-to-computer communications across thousands of miles at reasonable prices.

Refer to the Appendix to see a list of companies selling ISDN products and services. Read Chapter 12 for more detailed information.

The PBX Alternative

If you want to link computers over a distance of a mile or so, then a digital *private-branch telephone exchange*, or PBX, is a good alternative. One of these devices will often serve as the voice telephone switch for an organization, but they also have the ability to move data between computers at 128 kilobits per second across a "campus" or large installation.

Refer to the Appendix near the back of this book for a list of companies making telephone switches with computer data-switching capabilities. See Chapter 12 for more information.

If ISDN and digital PBX systems don't meet your needs for high-speed long-distance computing, don't despair. You can divide your resources into several local area networks and then link the networks at high speed over long distances. If you are interested in this technique, continue on through the Decision Tree to select your local network alternatives, and then refer to Chapter 13, where we'll discuss how to link your LANs across the miles.

■ The Multiuser DOS Alternative

Answering no to the Decision Tree question "More than five users of the same files?" leads you to a recommendation to try a *multiuser DOS* system. In the multiuser DOS approach, a special operating system splits the attention of a computer with an 80386 or 80486 processor among four or five people with inexpensive terminals on their desks. The programs they run are the standard DOS applications many people already own and know how to use.

Multiuser DOS systems offer significant economy (a cost of less than $1,000 "per seat" for full computing and networking capabilities), excellent security, and attractive equipment. In a multiuser DOS system, people don't have disk drives at their stations, so they can't walk out the door with a diskette full of data; they each have only a small and noiseless terminal on their desktops.

The one drawback to such systems is that they don't serve more than five users for database and word processing applications, and they are even more limited if you want to use computer-aided design programs, which consume a lot of processor time. But even this drawback is mitigated by the ability of these systems to link up to larger media-sharing LANs.

The multiuser DOS solution for workgroup connectivity is largely unknown and certainly underappreciated. If you have a small organization, multiuser DOS systems provide an excellent way to meet all of your computer and networking needs. Refer to the Appendix near the back of this book for a list of companies in this business, and see Chapter 4 for more information.

■ Media-Sharing LANs

Fasten your seat belt and tug on your helmet strap; we're about to enter the fast lane. When you decide you need shared databases and access to communications services such as mainframe links, and you need more "seats" than you can get from a multiuser DOS system, you're in the world of *media-sharing LANs*. These networks use special adapter cards to let each computer on the network share access to high-speed cables or *media* connecting them together.

The next stops on the Connectivity Decision Tree involve the selection of cabling schemes, adapter cards, and LAN software. (Figure 2.3 shows examples of some typical networking products.) Soon you'll have to be familiar with terms such as *ARCnet, Ethernet, DOS-based operating systems*, and *gateways*, but don't worry; you'll find the information you need in Chapter 5. That chapter gives you an introductory overview of media-sharing LANs. Later chapters cover topics such as adapter boards in even more detail.

Cables for Mainframe Connections

One important question is whether the PCs on your network will need access to an IBM mainframe; hence the question "Need IBM mainframe connections?" in the Connectivity Decision Tree. You should make this decision early, because IBM designed one cabling and access scheme—Token-Ring—as the primary way to link mainframes to a network. If you choose not to use Token-Ring (as well you might, because it is ugly and expensive), there are other good ways to link PCs to mainframes, but Token-Ring is clearly the primary route IBM wants you to use for this purpose. If your organization will ever need connections between PCs and

IBM mainframes, choosing a Token-Ring architecture now gives you the option to use special IBM connection equipment later. Chapter 6 describes LAN wiring alternatives.

Figure 2.3

Media-sharing LANs use internal adapter circuit boards, cables, and wiring hubs. These products from Thomas-Conrad Corp. provide connections for networks using Token-Ring wiring.

If Token-Ring access to IBM mainframes is not critically important to you, the two other wiring schemes you should consider are ARCnet and a general family of standards known as Ethernet.

Your choice will depend largely on your answer to the Decision Tree question "Need to follow IEEE standards?" Many organizations and government agencies buy only electrical and connectivity systems conforming to national and international standards. Unfortunately, the ARCnet cabling and media-access scheme never became a standard accepted by the Institute of Electrical and Electronics Engineers (IEEE). To be sure, ARCnet works well, many companies make ARCnet adapters, and compatibility between ARCnet products is seldom a problem, yet the potential for incompatibility and changes in product design remains because of the lack of standards. Action is underway to make ARCnet a standard, but in the absence of certain unique factors such as a large installed base of ARCnet cable, I suggest you first consider any of the many wiring alternatives available under the IEEE 802.3 (Ethernet) standard.

You have many factors to consider when you select LAN cabling. The construction of the building, existing wiring, the experience and knowledge of the people doing the installation, and other factors all influence this decision. In later chapters, we'll discuss other, less critical aspects of different LAN wiring systems, but the questions in the Decision Tree show you the most important considerations.

On to Software

The next question on the Decision Tree is "More than a dozen users of the same files?" The number of people simultaneously sharing the same data files is a rough indicator of the workload placed on the computer that acts as a file server. Heavily loaded servers—those handling more than a dozen simultaneous users running word processing, spreadsheet, and accounting applications—need an operating system that is able to handle several tasks at a time. Lightly loaded servers can run efficiently using the single-tasking operating system MS-DOS.

Multitasking Server Operating Systems

A server carrying the load of many busy client stations can receive hundreds of requests for file actions per second. The operating systems in these servers need special multitasking techniques to queue and satisfy these requests. The three most widely used server operating systems are Novell's NetWare, Microsoft's LAN Manager, and Banyan Systems' VINES. These high-quality products have comparable prices, capacities, and performance ratings, so choosing between them is largely a matter of selecting the product with the right features for your organization, bearing in mind the expertise of the local installers and support people.

DOS-Based Servers

Lightly loaded servers—those handling only a few simultaneous users—can run effectively with DOS as their operating system. Because the PC acting as a server runs DOS, it can also perform as a local workstation for someone running applications. The server tasks and the local workstation tasks interact to slow each other down, but this arrangement works in organizations with light network loads or with many computers configured as servers.

When you choose between multitasking server operating systems and DOS-based servers, you can base your decision on a number of factors, including cost and the question of centralized versus distributed structure.

But the primary difference between these types of server operating systems is in the number of simultaneous users of the same files they can support.

The Appendix lists companies providing both multitasking and DOS-based server operating systems. You'll find a lot more information on these operating systems in Chapters 5, 8, and 9.

■ Making Outside Connections

The next series of questions in the Connectivity Decision Tree deals with extending the network beyond the limits of its local high-speed cable. Extended links can go to mainframe computers, to other local networks, and to unlikely-sounding devices like distant facsimile machines.

Mainframe Links

At this point in the Decision Tree, we again raise the question, "Need mainframe connections?" If you selected IBM's Token-Ring wiring scheme when this question came up earlier, you have a path to the mainframe already.

If you don't have Token-Ring wiring, there are several other LAN-to-mainframe-connection alternatives. If the computers follow the IBM 3270 communications architecture, you can establish a network gateway, or give each PC the ability to emulate a 3270 terminal and connect directly to the mainframe through coaxial cable or over modem-equipped telephone lines. Some of these terms may be new to you, but Chapter 12 contains detailed information on linking to mainframe computers. The Appendix provides listings of companies selling LAN gateway products under the menu selection "mainframe links."

A negative reply to the question "Only IBM mainframes?" opens a path to the subject of linking computers with architectures designed by many companies through the *TCP/IP protocol services.* TCP/IP (Transmission Control Protocol/Internet Protocol) is a standard set of communications protocols developed by the U.S. government and adopted by many companies and institutions around the world. If you properly select communications software designed to meet the TCP/IP standards, you can link computers with many different kinds of operating systems and internal architectures. TCP/IP utilities let you exchange files, send mail, and store data on different types of computers connected to local and extended networks.

Talking Fax

People operating LAN client stations can use the network to link to distant facsimile machines. One PC on the network acts as a special type of communications server called a *fax gateway,* which can send and receive the images of fax documents. People working at individual client PCs can view fax messages on their screens and send files created by word processing software as fax messages.

Chapter 8 contains more information on network fax servers. You can refer to the Appendix near the back of this book to find a list of companies offering these products.

■ Linking LANs

Organizations with offices in many locations quickly face the problem of linking widely separated local area networks. The Decision Tree question "Want to link LANs?" introduces more questions relating to how far apart the LANs are and how much data will flow between them. Solutions range from connections made over fiber-optic links (Figure 2.4) to the use of ISDN.

Figure 2.4

Fiber-optic cabling provides long-distance connections between PCs and between discrete networks of PCs using more typical copper wiring.

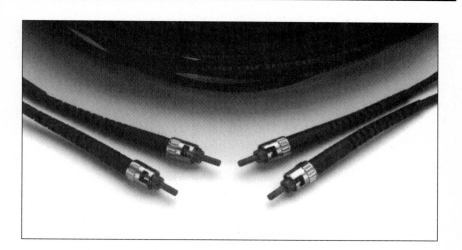

Those of you looking for ways to connect networks together or to connect remote and portable PCs into a LAN should seriously consider using modems and *remote-control software.* The ability to remote-control one PC from another effectively integrates distant computers into a local area network.

Chapter 8 covers the subject of communications servers, and the companies marketing these products are listed under "communications servers" in the Appendix.

■ LAN-Management Tools

LAN administrators in large and small organizations are increasingly coming under pressure to back up their budgets, to monitor LAN operations in real time, and to safeguard against network abuse. Network management is a high-priority topic for anyone responsible for the tens of thousands of dollars invested in the typical network. Several categories of network-management software provide administrators with strong tools to prevent abuse, collect statistics, and provide reports on network operations. Chapter 10 contains more information on these products, and they are listed in the Appendix near the back of this book.

Traffic Monitoring

If you answer yes to the question about being the network troubleshooter, then you need some special tools. Network troubleshooters can use two types of traffic-monitoring systems. *Media-monitoring software* gathers statistical data from a centralized wiring hub and provides second-by-second control over the connections that servers and client stations make to the network. *LAN protocol analyzers* capture the packets of data flying across a network and decode them into more-or-less plain English.

Application-Metering Software

The question "Need to limit the number of application users?" refers to the need to keep the number of people simultaneously using an application within the limits of the software license. LAN *application-metering software* controls the number of people who can simultaneously access a networked application. This type of software helps you buy only as many copies of an application as you really need while eliminating the fear of abusing software licenses. *Statistical-reporting LAN-management software* produces printed reports that administrators can use to plan LAN growth and justify expenditures.

■ Making the Right Choices

The Connectivity Decision Tree won't replace a good consultant, but it will help you to organize your needs and to make some important early decisions about the approach to take. An investment in a media-sharing LAN can pay big dividends in workgroup productivity, but such a complex system requires a great deal of investment, planning, and management. Less complex alternatives and techniques might work well for you. The Connectivity Decision Tree and the Appendix can help you manage the growth and operation of your network for years to come.

CHAPTER

3

Connecting PCs for Printer Sharing and File Exchange

Sharing relatively expensive printers among several people has always been a primary objective of PC connectivity. In the mid-1980s, even dot-matrix printers with "near-letter quality" were expensive. As the cost of letter-quality printers declined, printers able to produce the special fonts needed for desktop publishing came on the horizon as high-cost items. Now, as the cost of printers suitable for basic desktop publishing declines, printers that can use large sheets of paper or print in color populate the high-end market. Similarly, large-format plotters carry high price tags. Since one person probably won't keep a modern printer busy, it makes sense to share printers among as many people as possible.

■ Simple Switches

To many people, printer sharing means having a box with a switch on the front and cables running to the PCs and printer. When you turn it, the switch establishes a connection to the printer from one of two or three PCs.

Manual printer switches (Figure 3.1), often called *A-B boxes* after the designation of the switch positions, are simple to operate, but you can only use a maximum of about 25 feet of parallel cable to each computer. Additionally, several printer manufacturers, including Hewlett-Packard, warn against using manual switches with shorting contacts that make one connection before they break the other, as this could cause an excessive voltage spike to damage your printer when someone changes the switch setting.

Figure 3.1

An A-B box, like this Hard-switch from Rose Electronics, provides a simple way of sharing a printer between two PCs. Lights on the switch's front panel show the status of activity. The unit pictured is for serial printer connections, but units for parallel connections are also available.

The next section introduces media-sharing LANs, a very capable—perhaps overly capable—printer-sharing technique. The rest of the chapter will describe three alternative printer-sharing techniques that provide more flexible and capable services than a manual switch box without the expense of a media-sharing LAN. They reduce the hassle for the user and still have competitive prices. In turn, we will examine economical software packages called zero-slot LANs, inexpensive printer-sharing buffers, and a versatile printer-sharing alternative called a data switch.

■ Media-Sharing LANs

Traditional LANs:

👍 **Fast**

👎 **Expensive**

👎 **Complex**

The wide-ranging capabilities of media-sharing LANs are a major factor behind their popularity. Before we learn about lower-cost alternatives to media-sharing LANs, let's briefly examine how these popular connection systems function. Chapters 5 and 6 will provide more detailed information.

Media-sharing LANs carry messages simultaneously from multiple stations over a shared high-speed medium. The most common medium is coaxial copper cable, but new advances in fiber-optic cable and twisted-pair copper wire continue to improve the popularity of these media alternatives. The media-sharing LANs use signaling and sharing schemes with names like ARCnet, Ethernet, and Token-Ring. *Adapter boards* for these networks occupy a slot in each PC and perform the data handling and precise timing chores that become necessary when the media are shared among hundreds of stations.

Because the shared-cable system moves data 5 to 15 times as fast as the rate at which a PC can accept it, network designers have enough headroom to create elegant network operating systems that fool DOS into thinking that distant disk drives and printers, residing on computers acting as servers, are really on the local computer. The redirection of DOS service requests to the network allows standard applications to use resources like the network server for file storage, but the special interface cards and sophisticated software these systems require also make them costly and challenging to install and maintain.

When you put together a card-carrying LAN, you need space in each PC and some technical skill to install the LAN adapter card, and you also need a good budget for the cabling and for special LAN software. The hardware and software for these networks have a minimum price of about $275 per station, and they can cost four or more times that amount. Managing a media-sharing network with a dozen stations or more can employ the talents of a PC support person full-time. You get what you pay for, because these LANs provide more functionality and speed than any other connectivity alternative, but then again you might not need all the functionality of a media-sharing LAN.

Print Servers

One or more PCs on a media-sharing LAN can take on the role of a *print server*. A print server makes its attached printers available to all other devices on the network. Software resident in each PC using the network intercepts the print jobs that standard applications create and sends them to a network print server.

The PC acting as a print server might simultaneously act as a file server or as a personal workstation. There are no special hardware requirements for the print server aside from having enough serial or parallel ports for the attached printers. An old cast-aside IBM PC with a slow 8088 processor works just fine as a dedicated network print server. Modern LAN operating systems provide ways for any PC attached to the network to fill this function.

The print server accepts print jobs from client PCs on the network and queues these jobs until the attached printers can accept them. Utility software included in LAN packages gives network users and administrators control over the priority of jobs in the queue.

LAN Printing Problems

The concept behind shared LAN printing is simple, but the administrative details involved in making everything work correctly are often complex. Downloading fonts to the printer for desktop publishing often requires several carefully executed steps. Because applications don't always reset the printer mode before and after executing a print job, people can find their text produced in compressed form, with strange fonts, or sideways because one of these attributes was used in a previous print job.

On the Bottom Line of LAN Printing

You get the best value in a media-sharing LAN when you use it to provide simultaneous access to the same files for many people. Media-sharing LANs shine when you use them to provide accounting services, inventory control, and any other database applications. They also provide good value when you use them to share expensive communications links to distant locations or to different computer systems such as mainframes. But most people use these complex LANs just to share printers. If you merely want to share printers and similar peripherals such as plotters, read on.

■ Overview: Zero-Slot LANs, Buffers, and Switches

You don't have to use internal adapter boards and expensive cable to get most of the sharing benefits of media-sharing LANs. Zero-slot LANs, printer-sharing buffers, and data switches can do the job with reasonable speed and potentially at a lower cost and with less complexity.

Systems called *zero-slot LANs* exchange files and share resources such as printers and other peripherals without adapter cards or expensive cabling. A zero-slot LAN system transmits data through cables attached to the existing serial or parallel ports on your PCs, so you don't have to sacrifice an expansion slot for an adapter board.

A zero-slot LAN package consists of software on a diskette and thin telephone-type cables that link two or more PCs. Figure 3.2 shows a simple zero-slot LAN installation.

Figure 3.2

Zero-slot LAN systems offer an inexpensive way to link two or three PCs together for printer sharing or file transfers. Parallel or serial hookups connect the computers. Each PC runs some combination of client and host software.

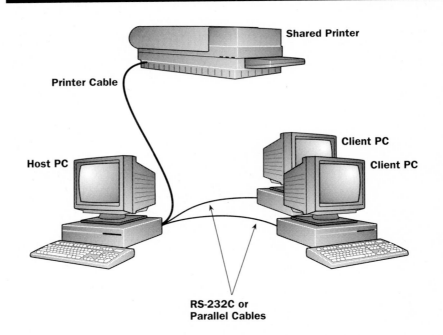

Because a zero-slot LAN package normally links a small number of PCs, you don't get the benefit of dividing the cost over many stations. The lowest-priced zero-slot network costs about $50 for each connected PC, but $100 per PC is more typical.

Printer-sharing buffers and data switches don't use an adapter in the PC, and they communicate through cabling attached to the serial port, but they require another piece of hardware—a centrally connected switch—to control the communications over the wire.

Printer-sharing buffers and data switches share a common architecture. A data switch is basically a printer-sharing buffer with a better processor and more capable software, giving it more flexibility.

A printer-sharing buffer is connected between two or more PCs and a printer. The PCs connect to the buffer through their serial or parallel ports, as Figure 3.3 shows. The PCs don't need special software; standard applications send the print jobs out the port in the normal way. The printer-sharing buffer queues the print jobs in its own RAM and sends them to the printer in the order received. You can buy a printer-sharing buffer with up to 8 megabytes of RAM for print job storage.

Figure 3.3

Printer-sharing buffers provide the simplest method of connecting computers and a shared printer. These devices require little setup and no special software in the PCs.

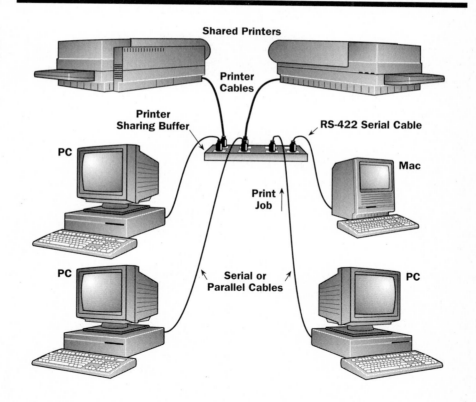

Data switches connect many kinds of different devices like laptops, modems, and printers, while zero-slot LANs are PC-to-PC systems, and printer-sharing buffers only move jobs from PCs to printers. As Figure 3.4 illustrates, data switches can connect many different types of intelligent devices, including Apple Macintosh computers, and link dumb terminals to minicomputers or mainframes.

Figure 3.4

Data switches allow you to connect many different kinds of computers to each other and to shared printers and modems. These devices offer great flexibility and a low cost per port, and they require only a small software program in each client computer.

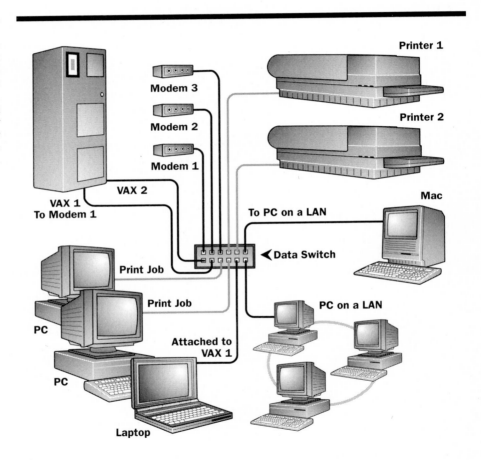

The investment in hardware makes data-switched LANs slightly more expensive than zero-slot LANs—just over $125 per node, on the average—but they can service many more nodes with much greater flexibility.

Zero-slot LANs:

👍 **Simple**

👍 **Effective**

👍 **Inexpensive**

👎 **Limited**

👎 **Slow**

■ Zero-Slot LANs

I coined the phrase "zero-slot LANs" in a 1987 *PC Magazine* review of these low-cost but highly functional PC-connection products. To create a zero-slot LAN, you simply take two PCs, connect one cable between their serial or parallel ports, and load a small piece of software in each PC. The software lets the people using each PC share each other's printers, exchange files, and even simultaneously access the same data file.

The up-front advantage of a zero-slot LAN is that it doesn't take up an expansion slot for network adapter hardware, but it still allows you to share disk drives and printers between PCs like its more hardware-hungry cousins. Zero-slot LANs don't just pinch the pennies, they make them scream. Prices range from about $100 to $395 for products that can connect two or three stations together.

On the downside, zero-slot LANs don't deliver the performance of media-sharing networks that use special adapters to carry their data. I recommend them only for networks of two or at most three computers. Today's zero-slot LAN products can provide connections to more than two PCs, but they suffer significant speed degradation when several PCs make simultaneous use of the connection.

The cables connecting the earliest zero-slot LANs were thick, cumbersome, and not easy to hide in a professional office environment. The makers of modern zero-slot LAN products learned the lesson that appearances count, and they now use thin and flexible wires similar to those that run between your telephone and the wall plate. Additionally, the sleek software installs more easily than its predecessors, and it operates almost invisibly.

Shared Printers

The zero-slot LAN software lets each PC make printers and drives available for the other attached PCs to use. The person running a PC without a connected printer uses standard application programs to print files using the regular commands. The zero-slot LAN software intercepts the print job (which the application is trying to send to a local printer) and sends it over the cable to another PC.

Zero-slot LAN software in the print server handles the job of accepting print jobs from other computers and moving them to the printer. These jobs often pass through a queue maintained on a hard disk in the print server. Print jobs from each of the PCs wait in the queue for the printer to take them. You can typically assign queue priorities to specific jobs or to those coming from a particular station.

The primary drawbacks of this printer-sharing arrangement are the need for a hard disk to hold the print queue in the print server and the loss of some processing power in the print server. While the print server's CPU moves data from the serial or parallel port to the queue and from the queue to the printer, the CPU has less time available to compute a spreadsheet or to index a database for the local operator. You have to strike a balance between the number of print jobs moving through a zero-slot LAN system and the need to run large and important application programs on the PC acting as a print server.

Many products let you adjust the amount of time the CPU gives to host duties and the amount of time it devotes to running local applications. By adjusting the time slicing, you can favor local applications or devote practically all of the host PC's efforts to servicing connected clients.

The low cost of zero-slot LANs makes them appealing as printer-sharing devices, but only for a few PCs in the right setting. Read the description of data switches later in this chapter for a more flexible, low-cost, printer-sharing alternative.

The Virtue of Virtual Drives

Modern zero-slot LAN products give you an important capability we call *virtual disk drives*. With virtual drives, you can access a drive on another PC as though it were on your own system. For example, the C drive on your PC may become the D drive on the machine linked to it. The person who uses that machine can issue standard DOS commands to move and access files on your PC by addressing commands to the redirected D drive.

When you understand the concept of virtual disk drives, questions of file integrity and data security should light up in your head. Can another person on your zero-slot LAN access the file you're working on simultaneously? Can you lock other people out? The answers to these file safety and security questions vary with the products. Some products, like LAN-Link 5X and LANtastic/Z, give you setup menus allowing you to specify the system configuration and to create rules for security. Printer LAN supplies a more limited menu for controlling access to and from your disk drives and shared peripherals. There are many approaches to security in zero-slot LANs as well. In MasterLink, you can lock out the other PCs through a configuration program or at the command line. The designers of DeskLink weren't concerned with drive and file security, since there can only be two computers in their network configuration.

Technically, the availability of virtual drives means you can use multiuser programs like database managers that allow multiple stations to access the same files at the same time. These software packages know how to tell DOS to open data files in a shared mode. Practically, however, multiple simultaneous file access involves the exchange of a great deal of DOS information. This complex exchange bogs down over the relatively slow data communications links that zero-slot LANs provide. You can get useful performance from multiuser systems over zero-slot LANs that use parallel ports, but the serial-port systems are not a good choice for shared-database applications.

Having virtual drives makes it easy to issue file-transfer and other DOS commands, but because it can take 15 to 17 seconds to transfer a 50k file between two PCs over the relatively slow links that zero-slot LAN systems use, modern packages need the ability to transfer files in background mode. This capability takes the frustration out of waiting for a large file to move between PCs. It lets the PC's foreground processing take care of your next immediate need without waiting for the transfer to be finished. For the same reasons, background printing is another useful feature. DeskLink and Printer LAN allow you to print jobs on a remote shared printer in the background. We all know that nothing is free, and the cost of this feature is paid in the amount of RAM these programs use and in some slowdown of the foreground processing task.

Serial and Parallel Cable Connections

Transmission of data through a parallel port, available in products like LAN-Link 5X and LANtastic/Z, provides a much faster throughput rate than a serial-port connection. The results of the benchmark tests conducted at PC Magazine LAN Labs show that the throughput of products using parallel transmission is several times greater than that of products using serial transmission. Parallel transmission ranges from about 12 kilobits per second to over 123 kilobits per second.

The diversity of ports and connectors available on PCs makes getting the proper cables a challenge. Many PCs have 9-pin connectors for their serial ports, but others use 25-pin connectors. Serial- and parallel-chassis connectors differ, and each type of cable has special requirements. The zero-slot LAN product you buy should include the right cables for the PCs you have to connect.

Other Network Services

Many zero-slot LAN products we see at PC Magazine LAN Labs respond to *NetBIOS* calls from application programs. The NetBIOS interface provides a standard way for programs to communicate between stations on a media-sharing LAN. The availability of this interface lets you use the zero-slot links between PCs to access gateways to mainframe computers and certain electronic-mail packages.

The relatively slow speed of zero-slot LAN products isn't a limitation for these applications, because most of them rely on even slower modem communications to get the job done. An SNA gateway, for example, connects to a mainframe over a 19.2-kilobit-per-second data line, so the typical 115.2-kilo-bit-per-second zero-slot LAN connection between PCs is not a bottleneck. Using a zero-slot LAN is a practical way to give two or three people access to an SNA gateway. Terminal-emulation programs that exchange screen images and keystrokes with a mainframe aren't hampered by the relatively slow RS-232C network signaling speeds that serial transmissions use.

Flexibility and Features

Just because you simply want to connect one PC to another today doesn't mean that next week you won't want to connect eight more. Although we have painted a scenario for connecting one PC to another, you can do much more with a zero-slot LAN package. Products like LANLink 5X and Master-Link can expand to include hardware giving a single PC up to 16 parallel ports. Thus you can set up one machine as a centralized server with many client stations.

Several of the packages allow you to connect client stations to more than one serial port on a PC acting as host. Keep in mind, however, that when multiple connections operate simultaneously, no one gets fast service. Low-priced media-sharing LANs with adapter cards will serve the needs of most people in multistation installations better than zero-slot LANs extended to multistation configurations.

A Chat or Dialog feature can be a big bonus for two people with comput-ers linked through a zero-slot LAN. Through Chat, a receptionist can notify people in a busy office of incoming phone calls and visitors without using the telephone. You can also have a running discussion concerning files you want to share or transfer. DeskLink is the only package with a Chat feature. Printer LAN's E-Mail feature has a quick NotePad, offering the simplicity of a Chat feature without the real-time response.

Some packages, such as DeskLink, MasterLink, and Printer LAN, set themselves apart as TSR (terminate-and-stay-resident) programs, which you can easily load and unload from memory. Zero-slot LAN programs generally take between 40k and 143k of RAM, depending on the design of the pack-age, the resources shared, and the utilities you load.

Overall, zero-slot LANs involve a consistent trade-off between cost and performance. If you don't have heavy requirements for data and printer shar-ing, then a zero-slot LAN can be a good choice for your installation. These LANs serve admirably in small offices, where they simplify the tasks of trans-ferring files and sending jobs to a shared printer.

What to Consider when You Buy a Zero-Slot LAN

* Do you want to use faster parallel-port connections?
* Are the appropriate cables included?
* Do you need 9-pin serial-port connections?
* Do you need security for shared disk drives?

■ Printer-Sharing Buffers

Printer-sharing buffers:

👍 **Moderate in cost**

👍 **Simple to install and use**

👎 **PC-to-peripheral only**

Printer-sharing buffers and data switches automate the concept of the manual printer switch. Both of these types of devices connect to each PC and printer and switch print jobs and connections from the PCs to the printers.

When using a printer-sharing buffer or data switch, each person who shares the printer sends print jobs just as if the printer were attached directly to the PC. The device receives the jobs, checks for the printer's availability, and either passes the job to the printer or stores it until the printer can accept it.

Printer-sharing buffers come in models that can handle a wide number of PCs. You can find models with up to 64 ports. The price of these products typically stays at slightly more than $100 per port.

Although printer-sharing buffers come in a variety of sizes and shapes, each device typically has a cabinet just big enough for all the connectors mounted on it and a separate power supply molded into the wall plug. You can often fit a printer-sharing buffer inconspicuously next to the printer. Some companies even design them to fit inside popular printers like the Hewlett-Packard LaserJet.

Certain models of printer-sharing buffers will handle problems such as mismatched speed between the PC and printer serial ports, or the need to convert between PC serial connections and printer parallel connections. Figure 3.5 shows one popular printer-sharing buffer.

The cables required for attaching PCs to printer-sharing buffers are limited in terms of the distance they can cover, particularly if you use a faster parallel-cable connection. You can count on a good connection using up to 50 feet of parallel cable, but the distance between the printer and the most distant PC can't be much more than that. Several products in this market can carry serial-port connections to printers over several thousand feet of cable.

Printer-sharing buffers are practical devices. They don't do anything more than move print jobs to the printer efficiently, but if that is all you need, your worries are over. Check the Appendix for the makers of printer-sharing buffers.

Figure 3.5

The Caretaker Plus from Rose Electronics is a printer-sharing buffer with excellent expansion capabilities. The front-panel lights show the status of incoming print jobs, and the buttons provide manual control over the routing of jobs from PCs to printers.

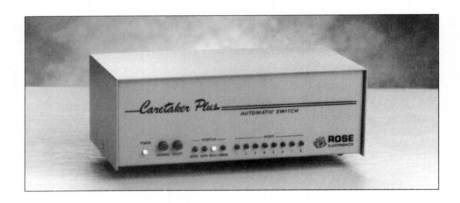

What to Consider when You Buy a Printer-Sharing Buffer

- How many PC and printer ports do you need?

- How much RAM is available for the print job queue?

- Do you want serial or parallel connections?

- Do the cables come with the unit?

- Does the unit allow PCs and printers at different speeds to be connected?

- What are the size of the unit and the type of cable connectors?

- Where will you get technical support?

■ Data Switches

Data switches:

👍 **Inexpensive**

👍 **Flexible**

👍 **Able to link Macs, PCs, and laptops**

👎 **Not for file sharing**

As reliable and easy to use as a telephone, the data switch (Figure 3.6) is a data- and peripheral-sharing facilitator that seems primitive when compared with even low-cost media-sharing LANs. Nonetheless, data switches are increasingly being recognized as an efficient way to make flexible connections.

A data switch is an external box that works like a telephone system for PCs; through data switches, PCs make connections with each other and with external devices such as modems and printers over standard serial links. The PCs use simple software that typically takes only a few kilobytes of RAM and doesn't affect the performance of application programs.

Although data switches might seem low-tech in comparison with full-scale media-sharing LANs (like those using Token-Ring hardware combined with Novell's NetWare), a growing number of companies successfully sell them. Data switches are beginning to be taken seriously as a simple and effective way to interconnect small groups of PCs and printers.

Attractively inexpensive and simple, data switches cost a little more than $100 per workstation, compared with about $275 per station for even the lowest-cost media-sharing LANs, or about twice that much for a full-featured media-sharing LAN. While data switches are most suitable for small networks (most of them handle from 8 to 24 connections), with the proper software you can chain them together to form networks with hundreds or even thousands of nodes. And because they use standard serial- or parallel-port connections, you can integrate a wide variety of different types of computers into a single network, from PCs, laptops, and Macintoshes to minicomputers and mainframes.

Figure 3.6

The Logical Connection Plus from Fifth Generation Systems is a data switch with full capabilities for PC-to-PC, PC-to-modem, or PC-to-printer connections. Generally, data switches provide a relatively inexpensive and highly functional alternative to media-sharing LANs.

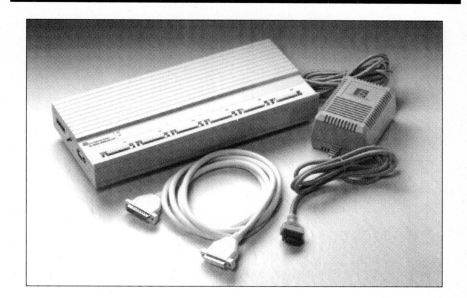

The trade-off is in speed and power. Most data switches are limited to a speed of 19,200 bits per second—far below the 10 megabits per second supported by media-sharing Ethernet systems, for example—and they require a dedicated cable connection to each workstation. Moreover, they cannot manage simultaneous accesses to the same data file, so you can't run complex multiuser databases on PCs linked through a data switch.

Features and Capabilities

For the basic tasks of sharing printers and exchanging files, it's hard to beat the capabilities of a data switch. The big difference between printer sharing through a data switch and through either a zero-slot or media-sharing LAN is that with a data switch you don't need a PC to act as a print server. The switch holds and queues the print jobs and can route them to multiple printers. The flexibility of modem sharing and the ability to connect different types of computers make these switches even more appealing as computer-connection devices.

In fact, if you have a minicomputer, you can even get around the data switch's inability to allow multiple, simultaneous access to the same data by running your accounting, inventory, and other multiuser systems on that computer, using the data switch to give your PCs access to it as if they were terminals. This architecture offers good performance at a cost comparable to that of a multiuser LAN system, but without the latter's complexity. And as a bonus, you'll get the full security and data-management features of the minicomputer operating system.

What Makes It Tick?

From the outside, a data switch is just a box, ranging from the size of a clothbound novel to that of an AT-compatible PC. Inside, you'll find a number of ports—usually between 8 and 24, though the Commix 32 from Infotron Systems Corp. can take up to 32 ports, and the INC-64 Intelligent Network Controller from Western Telematic can handle as many as 64. An internal microprocessor handles the port control and switching tasks, giving the data switch enough processing power to handle the traffic of all the ports at once. You connect the switch to the workstations and other devices using dedicated serial cables. You normally do not need to install special interface cards in your workstations, as most PCs today come equipped with at least one serial port.

A data switch is equally straightforward in its operation. When it's running, the switch constantly listens for commands from the workstations. When a workstation signals the switch for a connection to another port, the switch makes the link and then leaves it alone until the workstation receives a signal to disconnect. This lets the workstations use modems or printers as if they were local devices.

If you make a link between one workstation and another, the two machines can exchange files over the wire using the appropriate communications software. And if the other port is connected to a minicomputer, the workstation can load terminal-emulation software and sign on to the remote system. In all cases, the data switch is transparent once it's connected.

Available Features

The data switches on the market offer several elaborations of this basic scenario. For print buffering, most of the switches come with a substantial amount of RAM installed—often as much as 8Mb. A number of them support parallel ports, allowing easy connection to parallel printers, and handle the serial-to-parallel conversions automatically. Others, such as the Alternet from Equinox Systems, let you use parallel printers attached to remote workstations. If the switch does not support parallel ports, you can connect your parallel printers through an external serial-to-parallel converter.

Many switches can run their serial links faster than 19,200 bps, the maximum speed allowed within the RS-232C specification, but this extra speed makes the cable more susceptible to electrical interference. Some even support RS-422 serial connections, which can run reliably over longer distances than the RS-232 links and allow speeds of up to 38,400 bps. In either case, most of them can translate between serial devices running at different baud rates, letting you use high-speed links to your workstations without having to downshift when connecting to slower serial printers and modems.

If your switch supports parallel ports, you can often connect your PC's parallel port to the switch. This makes for a very high-speed link, though you're limited by the 15-foot length of the average parallel-printer cable.

Installation Aids

If you've ever installed a modem or a serial printer, you know that the ostensibly "simple" and "standard" RS-232C interface is, in fact, neither of these. Since designers of equipment and software can implement the RS-232C wiring scheme in many different ways, variations in the configurations of the wires that transmit data and the presence or absence of various status signals often conspire to make successful communications very difficult. For this reason, setting up the physical wiring of the network is usually the hardest part of installing a data switch. The ability of a product such as the 1082 Main-Street from Newbridge Networks to sense the configuration of the cable and adapt to it is a significant help.

Fortunately, finding the cabling to go between these units is not much of a problem with serial networks of this type. Often, you can use twisted-pair telephone wiring already in the walls to connect your workstations with the switch, provided that the wire doesn't run more than a few hundred feet. If you can't use the wiring in your walls, almost all of the data switches on the market can use telephone-type wiring with small RJ-11 or RJ-45 telephone-type connectors.

If your installation requires eight wires for a PC-to-switch connection, you can use unobtrusive serial cables that are easy to install under a carpet, through a false ceiling, or around wallboard. Small converter boxes are available to link the DB-25 or DB-9 connectors on your PCs to modular telephone plugs.

Once the data switch has been wired in, you use the manufacturer's configuration program to set it up. The program tells the switch which devices are attached to which ports, and sets the speed and other communications parameters for each one. Once the switch is configured, the information is held in battery-backed RAM, so it will be safe for a time even if you turn the switch off.

If the data switch has a security system, you'll also set this up. Though data-switch systems are often run without passwords, almost all the switches we reviewed can be programmed to ask for an entry password, and some can password-protect specific resources such as modems connected to long-distance lines.

For even easier use, you can often set up "hunt groups" that let users take advantage of the first available port among several ports attached to identical devices. For example, you might connect four ports of a 32-port switch to 9,600-bps V.32 modems. When a user requests a V.32 modem, the switch will then find the first open V.32 port. Hunt groups are also an excellent way to control contention for a few expensive minicomputer ports.

Control Software

Once you've set up the switch, you can control it through software. Most switches come with memory-resident utilities that let users make port connections and control their print jobs through menus. In many cases, these programs can read the configuration information from the switch, so that users can connect to printers or other workstations without having to know the port number or other technical details of the connection. But if you prefer to set up batch files to control the connections, all of the switches will respond to commands sent to the ports or embedded in print jobs.

Once the connection has been made, printing is a simple matter. Nearly all programs that drive printers have serial- and parallel-port options, and your software won't care if the printer is in the next room or the next building. Most data switches dynamically allocate the memory in their print buffers as needed, and some offer software that spools jobs to a user's own hard disk or to the hard disk on a remote workstation.

Moving Files

Some switches come with software that lets you transfer files from workstation to workstation in background mode. This is a desirable feature because it allows you to send files without disturbing the recipient. Sometimes you even get e-mail and terminal-emulation software thrown into the bargain.

But these functions don't require special programs. You can always make your connections through the switch using the menu program or batch files, then load a communications program or a file-transfer program such as The Brooklyn Bridge or Lap-Link to do this work. Similarly, you may prefer a full-fledged third-party electronic-mail system to the rather limited versions that come with the data switches.

The most sophisticated switches, such as the NetCommander NC16 from Digital Products and the Master Switch (N Series) from Rose Electronics, offer true networking software as an option. These programs support virtual drives just like media-sharing network operating systems, making file transfers much simpler. You simply assign a drive letter to the remote workstation's hard disk, then use the DOS COPY command to transfer the file over.

Though they'll never replace the true media-sharing LANs, data switches are hard to beat for many connectivity duties. Their low prices and their versatility make them attractive alternatives to large installations; for a small office, a data switch may be all you need. The advanced features of today's models go a long way toward defusing the often frustrating problems of serial connections.

What to Consider when You Buy a Data Switch

- How many PC and printer ports do you need?

- Do you need software for Macintosh computers?

- Do you want to use serial or parallel connections for PCs?

- Do you want to use serial or parallel connections for printers?

- How many wires are needed in the connecting cable?

- Does the switch accommodate differences in transmission speed?

- Does the switch recognize and automatically accommodate the cable-configuration differences between computers and peripherals such as modems?

- Does the PC software make it easy to share printers and connect PCs for file sharing?

■ Summary: Printer-Sharing Alternatives

In this chapter we have explored several excellent ways to share printers among a group of users. It isn't necessary to install complex and expensive media-sharing networks when zero-slot LANs, printer-sharing buffers, and data switches can do the job nicely.

Printer sharing is an important part of workgroup productivity. You should install a system that can provide you with all the capabilities you need, but don't pay for more than you are going to require.

Slicing the Power of the 386 with Multiuser DOS Systems

- A Quick Look at Media-Sharing LANs

- Time Slicing Revisited

- Sharing the Processor

- Multiuser DOS Systems

- Growing Fast

Workgroup computing means using computers connected together to exchange files and electronic mail, share printers and modems, access shared data files, and use workgroup scheduling and other productivity-enhancing programs. While several effective and economical linking schemes can give a group of people these connected-computing features, the most common choice is to buy low-cost PCs and link them together with a low-cost network. This chapter describes a much-overlooked alternative to media-sharing LANs called *multiuser DOS systems* (Figure 4.1). Multiuser DOS installations let you use standard DOS applications on desktop terminals connected to a shared PC. Special operating systems share the power of a single 80386 or 80486 processor among these terminals. This shared-CPU architecture yields a low cost per user, high security, low noise and heat, and excellent performance for many categories of DOS application programs. Let's begin by looking at two common technologies for workgroup computing: media-sharing LANs and time-sharing systems.

Figure 4.1

Multiuser DOS systems share the power of a 386- or 486-based computer among as many as five attached monochrome or color terminals. This solution provides effective, low-cost computing services for practically all DOS applications. (Technical support and equipment on this photo courtesy of THEOS Software Corporation, Walnut Creek, California.)

■ A Quick Look at Media-Sharing LANs

The media-sharing LAN alternative for workgroup computing gives each person the services of a dedicated desktop PC—at a price. If you shop carefully, you can put together a network of five workstation PCs with 80286 processing power, a separate 80386 server, monochrome graphics, and network interfaces, for as little as $1,700 per user. Putting together this configuration with low-cost 80386 machines can cost as little as $3,200 per user—including the server and all network hardware and software.

For the individual user, the media-sharing LAN architecture is nice from the perspective of performance and personal independence, but LANs can be tricky to install and maintain. Typical network problems include memory limitations, I/O address conflicts, and improper application-software configurations. PC-based LANs also threaten the security of the data in your organization because people can download files to their own floppy diskettes and walk out the door with them. Finally, PCs can be big, hot, noisy pieces of furniture in a small office. Small and noiseless desktop terminals have a lot of appeal.

■ Time Slicing Revisited

The oldest workgroup-computing architecture, the one used in on-line mainframes, shares the time of a single processor among several users, who communicate with the processor through display terminals. But this solution to the workgroup problem typically doesn't allow you to use popular DOS application programs except as tasks running under special control environments, like VPix under Unix. And while Unix, PIC, Theos, and VMS are multiuser operating systems, you can't pick up a copy of software written for a DOS PC, like WordPerfect or Lotus 1-2-3, and run it on them efficiently.

■ Sharing the Processor

Paradoxically, the oldest architecture is also the newest. Developments in processor and operating-system technologies make it practical to share a single 80386 processor, running DOS applications, among four to six people equipped with inexpensive terminals consisting of a display monitor but no local processor. In many applications, this configuration makes it look as if each user had the dedicated power of an 80386 processor running standard DOS applications in 8086 CPU mode.

Monochrome Terminals

Many organizations don't need color display screens—or even want them (because of concerns about the health hazards of long-wave radiation). Multiuser DOS systems lend themselves particularly well to monochrome terminals and applications, particularly database entry and accounting. The monochrome terminals used with these systems are small, quiet, and diskless. Their cost depends on the capabilities you need, but a nice-looking terminal with a good keyboard and that displays only ASCII characters (no graphics) costs about $400. If you must add serial ports to the host computer to communicate with the terminals, an RS-232C four-port board can cost several hundred dollars, but it communicates with four terminals. As we'll see later, more expensive, color monitors are available.

Low Cost Per Seat

The cost for a multiuser 386-based system can be very low on a per-person basis. A shared 80386 machine requires 3 to 4 megabytes of RAM and a large hard disk, so $6,000 is a realistic estimate for the price of the computing hardware. The operating system will be under $1,000, and each RS-232C monochrome terminal is about $500, so a five-node system costs about $1,900 per node, compared with the $1,700 to $3,200 cost of a media-sharing LAN. This configuration will run DOS applications with monochrome text, and will provide excellent response times under typical use by four to six terminals.

■ Multiuser DOS Systems

Multiuser DOS systems:

👍 **Low cost**

👍 **High security**

👍 **Low heat and noise**

👎 **Limited number of users**

👎 **Perceived lack of status**

As you can see from the Appendix near the back of this book, at least six companies market multiuser operating systems that allow several DOS applications to share the same CPU and files. They work in two different ways. Products like Quick Connect/386, 386/MultiWare, and VM/386 MultiUser are multiuser operating environments that work with standard DOS to give it multitasking capabilities. By contrast, Concurrent DOS 386 and PC-MOS/386 are complete operating systems that replace DOS. The DOS replacements emulate MS-DOS, and their manufacturers claim that they are compatible with any application program that uses standard DOS calls.

In their present form, these multiuser operating systems and environments carry out the basic network functions of file exchange, printer sharing, and file sharing. But these systems don't have all of the bells and whistles accepted as standard in LANs. Only Quick Connect/386 comes with its own electronic mail. The lack of NetBIOS services in these operating systems and environments means that many of the popular third-party mail packages won't run under the multiuser operating systems. Similarly, shared gateways to SNA and other computing environments are not available under some of these architectures.

The processing power allocated to any one task varies dynamically either with the task or with human management control. This means that you can mix different tasks, and you can mix "power" users and occasional users very effectively.

Shared Peripherals

Multiuser DOS systems typically let users share printers attached directly to the host computer. Standard DOS applications send the print jobs to a queue maintained by the operating system. The operating system moves the print jobs to the printer and provides some queue-management utilities.

Because the host computer may sit some distance from the desktop terminals, the printer might not be in a convenient location. Some terminal products let you connect another printer to your terminal so you can get local printouts, just as if you had your own dedicated PC and printer. The same terminal port also lets you put a modem at your elbow for convenient operation.

Links to LANs

You don't have to make an either/or choice between multiuser DOS systems and media-sharing LANs. Several products, including PC-MOS/386, give people running terminals the ability to become clients on a NetWare network. A single LAN adapter card in the PC with the shared CPU serves all the users. Our experience at PC Magazine LAN Labs shows that this kind of connection offers good performance and excellent utility.

The ability to link to LANs gives you room for growth. You can start with a multiuser DOS system and grow into a media-sharing LAN, or you can use a multiuser DOS system to extend a media-sharing LAN into a special workgroup. The link to the media-sharing LAN gives full LAN file, printer, and communications services to everyone who has a terminal. Choose the right software and you won't foreclose your options.

Security

PC-MOS/386 has a good security system providing different levels of privileges. 386/MultiWare and Quick Connect/386 provide a way to make subdirectories private, and Concurrent DOS 386 has some password-level protection. But these three products don't provide the read/write/create security that is standard in even the least expensive LAN software. Under VM/386, for example, any user can access all of the files that aren't open or protected in some way by an application program.

Desktop Color Graphics

One persistent problem is the need to have high-resolution graphics available in a multistation workgroup at a low cost per workstation. You need a big checkbook if you want to set up a LAN of individual PCs equipped to run color graphics applications, such as computer-aided design (CAD) systems or image databases. But there are many organizations, ranging from architects' offices to security-guard forces, that need to use these applications. If you want a network of 80386 PCs with VGA graphics and the services of a LAN, you'll spend a minimum of $3,000 per node plus the cost of another computer to act as a server.

Until recently, multiuser DOS systems haven't been the answer for workgroup CAD and similar applications. The slow communications link (usually RS-232C) between the host and typical terminals limits the ability to show color graphics on the terminals. To create a simple CGA screen, 16 kilobytes of data have to be transmitted. At the usual serial-terminal transmission speed of 19.2 kilobits per second, it would take 6 to 7 seconds to paint a color CGA screen.

Fortunately, things have changed. New technologies, shown in Figure 4.2, give terminals on shared CPU systems the ability to display VGA-level graphics. At least three systems can put color EGA and VGA terminals on multiple desktops. On a per-node basis, these systems cost between $1,200 and $2,600. That's much less than the cost of a PC-based LAN with similar capabilities.

But a single CPU can do only so much. A PC with a 33-MHz 80386 CPU can reasonably support four heavy-duty graphics users. If you add any more graphics terminals, the system response time starts to go down. On the other hand, if some stations don't run graphics applications, the PC can carry a bigger load.

There are two basic types of color monitor systems. The first high-performance color graphics terminal on the market—and one using a unique technology—comes from SunRiver Corp. (Figure 4.3). SunRiver Fiber Optic Stations use a "bus extension" architecture that extends the PC data bus from the host computer to the local workstation. Communication between the host and the workstation takes place via a fiber-optic link operating at 32 megabits per second.

The second technology uses special integrated circuits to extend the keyboard, video, parallel, and serial port cables far beyond their normal limits. This "long cable" architecture combines all of the graphics, keyboard, and serial ports of the workstation into circuits contained on an adapter card in the host PC. The integrated signals then go out over a multiconductor copper cable to a small station-controller box at each desktop, with connections for a keyboard, a monitor, and a serial port. The AMR Video Graphics Network

Adapter from Advanced Micro Research and the VPT System 2000 from Viewport Technology use this approach.

Figure 4.2

Multiuser DOS systems leverage the power of modern 80386 and 80486 processors to provide a low cost per seat, even for applications requiring the use of graphics. Different types of terminals use RS-232C serial connections, "long cable" hookups, and fiber-optic cable links. Each type of terminal has its own cost and feature trade-offs.

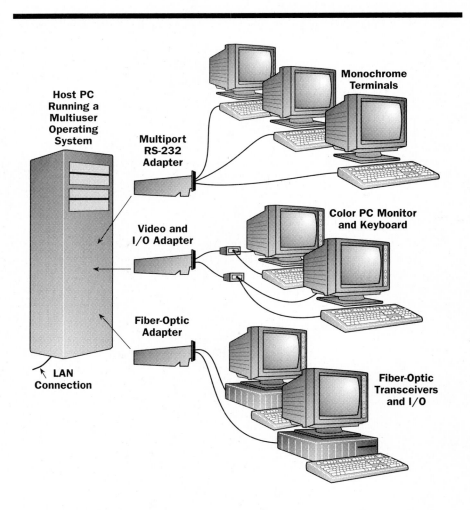

An advantage of the fiber-optic technology is that the workstations can be up to 1,000 feet from the host. Fiber-optic cable has further advantages such as small size, immunity to radio-frequency interference from fluorescent lights or AC wiring, and a potentially high data rate. Its disadvantages include a large minimum bend radius (usually about 1 inch), a greater fragility than coaxial cable, and a higher cost. A 100-foot fiber-optic cable costs $199, versus $147 for a 13-twisted-pair cable. At 250 feet, the costs are $369 for the fiber-optic and $282 for the twisted-pair.

Figure 4.3

The SunRiver Fiber Optic Station extends the data bus of the shared computer to a VGA color terminal over fiber-optic cables.

The twisted-pair cables used for the "long cable" systems are about the diameter of your parallel printer cable. You might find them bulky to weave around the nooks and crannies of your office. This type of cable is not totally immune to interference, so plan carefully before you run it next to motors, relays, or radio-frequency-producing devices. The maximum cable length is 250 feet for the Viewport system or 100 feet for the AMR. That may limit where you place your workstations.

The AMR system, like the SunRiver, lets you connect existing PCs into your multiuser system as terminals.

How Much Work Can It Do?

For our benchmark tests at PC Magazine LAN Labs, we ran each hardware system on a Dell System 325 with the VM/386 operating system marketed by Intelligent Graphics Corp. We chose VM/386 simply because that product has drivers for all of the hardware platforms.

While the different hardware products will perform far differently with other operating systems, we can make some generalizations. Normally, even the busiest AutoCAD shop will be happy with a four-node system running on a single 386 PC. Measured objectively, none of these systems gave quite the throughput of a single user on the 386 machine running under DOS. Subjectively, however, our team was hard-pressed to see the difference. The only time we really noticed a slowdown was when more than one terminal used the host's hard disk at the same time. And a slowdown due to disk I/O is a situation common to all multiuser systems—even LANs and mainframes.

Your system choices depend on the question of what kind of job you need to accomplish. If you have a small team of heavy graphics users and want to equip them with the most economical yet workable system, a "long cable" arrangement may be just what you need. If you've got an environment that demands the noise immunity of fiber-optic cable, or its ability to cope with longer distances, then the SunRiver system has distinct advantages.

But It Isn't a PC

Technically, these multiuser DOS systems provide high-performance computing power. You should note, however, that the psychology of computing can be as powerful as the technology. Some people perceive a multiuser terminal as less powerful and therefore less desirable than a standalone PC. Multiuser DOS terminals and diskless PCs share a reputation for being somehow less than equal with PCs.

If you emphasize the shared power, small size, and low heat and sound output of these products, it's easy to overcome the perception of inequality. Sensitivity to the potential for this problem can stop it from appearing.

■ Growing Fast

These are young products. It is fair to expect a fast influx of new products and new versions with many added features. Yet for certain specialized applications, for small offices where the security of personal files is not a concern, and for people who are concerned mainly with cost, a multiuser operating system running on an 80386 processor can already be an excellent way to gain the advantages of workgroup computing while keeping familiar DOS applications.

What to Consider when Buying a Multiuser DOS System:

- Will the operating system run the application software you want to use?

- If you need color graphics, will the operating system support the color terminals you like?

- How far apart are your terminals going to be?

- How much RAM and disk space will you need in the shared PC?

- Do you need security restrictions for different users?

- Do you need links to NetWare LANs?

- Do you need NetBIOS services for gateways or other LAN functions?

- Who will install the hardware and software?

- Where will you get technical support?

CHAPTER

5

A Field Guide to LANs

- Networking's Necessary Hardware

- The Soft Side

- The Future

- Networking Acronyms and Buzzwords

Because the PC-based LAN is such an important connectivity alternative, I've written this chapter to give you an overview of the pieces and parts in a media-sharing LAN system and to describe the important considerations in stringing together those pieces and parts.

Later chapters deal with the features and foibles of specific cabling schemes and operating systems in more depth. This chapter gives you the strategic view, the buzzwords, and the background you'll need to get the most out of the material in later chapters.

Local area networks have many complex and interrelated parts. This guide explains those parts, how they fit together, and the pros and cons of the different combinations.

As a first step in explaining these systems, we'll divide them into hardware and software. Even this seemingly simple division isn't clean, because some hardware elements have software on board in read-only memory (ROM), but it's a good way to start to examine the pieces of the LAN puzzle. After we examine the real pieces and parts, we'll move from the material to the ethereal and introduce a number of networking acronyms and concepts.

■ Networking's Necessary Hardware

Servers, client PCs, adapter cards, and cables are the dry-bones hardware into which networking and application software breathe life. Because modern hardware products follow international standards, you can often mix and match hardware products from different vendors within the same network. Similarly, the hardware you buy does not determine your selection of application software for the network. But the selection of the right hardware isn't simple. You have to make up-front decisions with long-term consequences.

Servers and Clients

In a PC-based network, computers act in the functional roles of *servers* and *client stations*. The servers make their attached disk drives, printers, modems, and unique communications links (such as fax) available to the client stations. Software running in the client PCs gives network users access to the data and devices available on one or more servers. The networking software running on a server determines whether the server is dedicated to its service role or whether it also runs local application programs in what is termed a "peer-to-peer network."

Practically any 80286-, 80386-, or 80486-based computer can act as a server. Organizations with as many as a dozen users find 80286-based servers adequate. Powerful LAN operating systems like Microsoft's LAN Manager and Novell's NetWare 386 can use the power and memory-addressing capabilities of 80386 and 80486 processors. An increasing number of new network applications run partly in the server, so an investment in a powerful processor today will pay future dividends. Considering the reasonable price of 80386-based PCs, I recommend buying 386 PCs as servers.

Many companies sell computers with multiple expansion slots and disk drive bays as servers, but simply designing a computer with a lot of internal space, a fast processor, and a vertical mounting pedestal doesn't make it a good server. In the real-estate business, they say the three most important things about a piece of property are location, location, and location. Similarly, the three most important things about a server are disk drive speed, disk drive speed, and disk drive speed. Spend your money on large, fast hard drives for your server. This is the most important investment you'll make in LAN hardware.

You'll hear many arguments in favor of using a Micro Channel Architecture (MCA) bus or an Extended Industry Standard Architecture (EISA) bus as a server. Tests at PC Magazine LAN Labs show no practical differences between these advanced bus architectures and the IBM PC AT's Industry Standard Architecture (ISA) bus in the server role. The type of hard disk drives you use does make a difference. The type of network adapter cards used in the server makes a difference, but the bus architecture itself does not guarantee high performance as a server.

Here is our advice on servers: First, price a good set of hard drives with triple the capacity you think you'll ever need, plus a fast caching disk controller, and a PC with a processor in the 80386 25-MHz class or better. Then see whether your budget will stand the expense of an EISA- or MCA-bus computer and the extra cost of adapter cards for that bus. You won't see the benefits of investing in an EISA or MCA server anytime soon, but eventually the theoretical throughput advantage of these architectures will be realized.

Interface Cards

The most frequent investment you make in LAN hardware is in *network interface adapters* (generally called *interface cards* or *adapter cards*). Companies such as National Semiconductor Corp., Standard Microsystems Corp., and Texas Instruments market chip sets for Ethernet, ARCnet, and Token-Ring network interface cards. In 1987, a typical network interface card cost $600. Today, the increased availability of these chip sets has turned interface cards into commodity products, with current prices for no-frills Ethernet and ARCnet cards in the low $200 range.

Every computer on the network needs one of these printed circuit boards to move the serial signals on the network cables, or media, into the parallel data stream inside the PCs. These adapters can also change the format of the data from parallel to serial and amplify the signals so they can travel over the necessary distances. In some cases, you will put two or more adapters in a server to split the load; this technique helps overcome any limitation of the ISA bus.

These adapters also have the important job of controlling access to the media. This *media-access control* (MAC) function takes three general forms: listen-before-transmitting, sequential station number, and token-passing.

Media-Access Control

The listen-before-transmitting scheme, called *carrier sense multiple access* (CSMA), operates like a CB, police, or other two-way radio system. A station with a message to send listens to the LAN cable. If it doesn't hear the *carrier* or transmitted signal of another network node, the station broadcasts its message. Various techniques (detailed in Chapter 6) handle the problems when more than one station hears the empty channel and starts to transmit.

ARCnet uses a different media-access scheme, which assigns a station number (0 to 255) to each node on the network. The stations with messages to send simply wait for their number to come up in turn.

The other popular media-access control scheme, token-passing, involves a special message called a *token*, passed from node to node by active stations on the network. This token grants the receiving station permission to transmit.

LAN scientists and the people marketing different LAN products can argue for days over the theoretical advantages of the CSMA, token-passing, and ARCnet media-access protocols. My advice is not to worry about the question. Other factors, such as the type of wire you want to pull in the walls, are much more important than the type of media-access protocol used by the adapters you choose. But you do need to know what people mean when they talk about the media-access scheme or MAC protocol.

Wire, Wire Everywhere, and Not an Inch to Link

The most important question associated with the adapter board is what kind of cable or wire to use for the network. Modern Ethernet and ARCnet adapters, and to some degree Token-Ring adapters, give you a wide variety of wiring choices.

The network interface card determines the type of cabling you'll need to connect the servers and the client stations. Choices include twisted-pair telephone wire, data-grade (shielded) twisted-pair wire, coaxial cable, and fiber-optic cable. If one of these types of wire is already installed in your building, you'll want to select an interface card that can work with the existing wiring. Figure 5.1 shows the major types of network wiring.

Figure 5.1

The major types of network wiring are (from left to right): a thin coaxial cable with BNC connector, fiber-optic cable and connectors, shielded twisted-pair wire with an IBM Token-Ring connector attached, and unshielded twisted-pair wire with a modular connector attached.

Coaxial Cable

Coaxial cable, particularly the thin RG-58 or RG-62 type, is easier to install than shielded data-grade twisted-pair cable and has many of the same noise-resistance advantages. Thin Ethernet and ARCnet schemes typically use coaxial cable. One version of Ethernet uses a thick coaxial cable—particularly, for example, as a backbone between workgroups on different floors of a building. Thick Ethernet cable, known in the trade as "frozen yellow garden hose" because of its stiffness and color, is difficult to install, and its popularity is diminishing.

Fiber-Optic Cable

Though it does not improve transmission speed, fiber-optic cable allows for greater distance between stations and provides total immunity to electrical noise. A fiber-optic link can run for several kilometers without the need for repeaters to regenerate the signal. Radio transmitters, arc welders, fluorescent lights, and other sources of electrical noise have no effect on the light pulses traveling inside this kind of cable. Many vendors offer versions of their network interface cards adapted for fiber-optic transmission.

Fiber-optic cabling can account for the most significant costs of the network. Depending on local labor rates and building codes, installing cable can cost as much as $1,000 per workstation. But as the results of a *PC Magazine* Interactive Reader Service survey indicate, many companies are reducing costs by installing the cable themselves, even if they have systems integrators install the networking cards and software.

Data-Grade Twisted-Pair Wire

Data-grade twisted-pair wire has a name similar to the unshielded twisted-pair wiring used in 10BaseT, but it has a very different construction. Data-grade twisted-pair wire is bound in an external aluminum-foil or woven-copper shield specifically designed to reduce electrical noise absorption. Different companies have their own specifications for such cables, although IEEE standards apply to systems like IBM's Token-Ring.

Shielded twisted-pair cables are expensive and difficult to work with, and they require custom installation. Still, IBM has successfully marketed a wiring plan that uses these cables for Token-Ring installations. The IBM plan adds reliability (and substantial cost) by using a separate run of cable between each server or workstation and a central wiring hub. This wiring plan significantly increases the amount of cable used, but it also ensures against the total failure of the network in the event that one cable is broken or shorted. See Chapter 6 and check the Appendix for more information on Token-Ring wiring.

Twisted-Pair Wire

Twisted-pair telephone wire is typically installed in buildings to carry voice telephone traffic. Many organizations find that this wire is an excellent way to carry LAN data, too. A subspecification of the IEEE 802.3 standard describes a twisted-pair wiring scheme called 10BaseT. Testing at PC Magazine LAN Labs has shown that 10BaseT twisted-pair wiring carries data quickly and has several advantages over other wiring schemes in terms of reliability and the cost of installation. Some companies also market ARCnet cards that can use twisted-pair wiring.

When you find them already installed, twisted-pair telephone wires can have the significant advantage of economy. Yet because the wires carrying LAN traffic have more stringent installation criteria than those carrying voice, you must often install more twisted-pair wire for data even if you have spare voice pairs in the walls.

See Chapters 6 and 7 for more detailed information on twisted-pair wiring and the 802.3 10BaseT specification. Refer to the Appendix for a list of companies marketing these products.

Network Topology

A *physical topology* is a description of the route the network cables take as they link nodes. The *logical topology* describes how the messages flow to the stations. As Chapters 6 and 7 will explain, the physical form and the logical path can be two different things.

ARCnet typically uses a wiring plan or topology in which every station links directly into a central wiring hub, a scheme that reduces the vulnerability of the overall network. Token-Ring uses a similar hub in its physical topology. Thin Ethernet, on the other hand, uses a station-to-station wiring scheme that is economical because it uses less cable than a hub-type scheme, but it runs the risk of total network failure if any one link is severed or shorted.

■ The Soft Side

Because of the current de facto standards and protocols, you can mix and match these pieces—servers, network interface cards, cables, and software—in myriads of ways to form an optimally productive and cost-effective network.

Many people worry more about network interface cards and cabling than about operating systems. While they can usually specify that they want a server with fast disk drives and a fast processor, they don't know how to quantify, describe, or select networking software. But software can make or break a network.

Networking operating systems make distant resources local. If you are interested in files residing on a computer down the hall, the networking software enables you to access those files as if they resided on disk drives in your own machine. It lets you use printers located thousands of feet away—or even miles away—as if they were snugly attached to your own LPT1 port. And it allows you to use network modems or minicomputers as if they were cabled to your own COM1 port.

Network operating systems have a multitasking and multiuser architecture; in that respect, they're more like minicomputer and mainframe-computer operating systems than like Microsoft's DOS for the PC (MS-DOS). Your PC's DOS takes requests from application programs and translates them, one at a time, into actions to be performed by the video display, disk drives, and other peripheral devices. Network operating systems, on the other hand, take requests for services from many application programs at the same time and satisfy them with the network's resources—in effect, arbitrating requests for the same services from different users.

Invisible and Modular

Ideally, networking software is invisible to the users. When you use it, you know you have additional resources available, but you usually don't care where the resources are or how you attach to them.

Structurally, networking software has many modules. Most of them reside in the machine that acts as the server for data, printer, or communications resources. But, as Figure 5.2 shows, several important program modules must be installed in every workstation, or sometimes in devices posed between the workstation and the network.

Figure 5.2

Network software/
hardware interaction

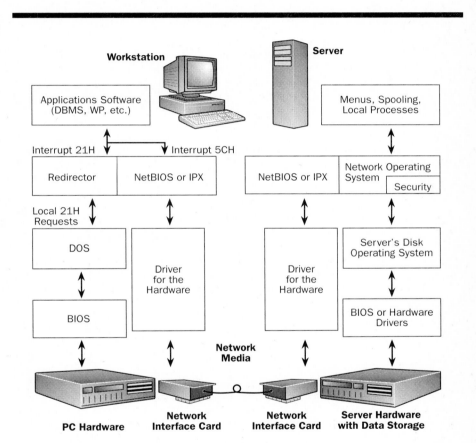

Figure 5.2 diagrams how the operating software interacts with the hardware and software on the workstation (left) and the server (right). For both workstation and server, the hardware is the bottom level of the diagram; everything above that is software. Arrows represent the flow of messages—requests for services and data and the responses.

The workstation is only a "client," with no capabilities for contributing resources to other network stations. It has the same PC hardware (disk drives, monitor, keyboard, and so forth), BIOS (Basic Input/Output System, the software that links the hardware to DOS), and operating system (DOS) that all PCs have, whether networked or not.

For LAN operation, several additional elements are necessary, both hardware (the interface cards and cables) and software (the redirector, NetBIOS, and driver software). The application program running on the workstation may have certain added network attributes, such as the ability to issue record- and file-lock commands automatically through DOS. (This software enhancement is not strictly necessary, since even application programs not designed with a LAN in mind can run on a network.)

The redirector module is added to intervene between the application program and DOS. It intercepts software calls from an application program asking DOS for services such as file access. Each PC's redirector is programmed to switch certain calls out through the network for service (for instance, requests for data from drives that don't exist in the local PC's hardware). Thanks to the redirector, a PC application can easily use network resources just by addressing the correct disk drive.

Another added software module, the interface card driver, moves data between the redirector and the workstation's network interface card. This driver software is specifically designed for network interface card hardware. Some card vendors supply it in a format that from the redirector's view looks like the NetBIOS program that IBM and Sytek developed to link their network hardware and software. If the driver is wrapped in a NetBIOS interface, it fits the Microsoft redirector supplied with IBM's PC LAN and many other operating systems.

If the interface card driver doesn't perform the communications functions associated with NetBIOS, another software module such as IPX must perform those functions. Application programs are written to make a special call for session-level communications services from the NetBIOS emulator or conforming NetBIOS software.

The network interface card sits in the expansion bus of the workstation. In modern networks, the wiring and media-access protocol are almost always independent of the networking software. The interface card includes programs in read-only memory that manage the creation and transmission of packets over the network.

At the other end of the cable from the workstation interface card is the server, with additional specialized LAN software and its own interface card. After the server's interface card does its job, a NetBIOS module or emulator watches for packets containing NetBIOS information. Other messages pass on to the security and multiuser software modules.

Like any other computer, the server runs an operating system—sometimes DOS, but often a unique system or one derived from the Unix system. If the system is DOS, you can almost always run local application programs and use your computer as a network terminal. But remember, all server software requires a lot of processor RAM and attention.

Finally, network utility programs run on the server, offering print spooling, auditing, and other LAN features.

Working together, these program modules perform the basic actions of networking software. In a nutshell, networking software recognizes users, associates their preprogrammed privileges with their identities, and then reroutes their DOS requests to the appropriate server for action. The operating-system software in the server frequently is not a variety of MS-DOS, but it must emulate DOS and respond properly to DOS requests routed from the workstations.

Different Species

Darwin's method of categorizing strange critters according to species can also be applied to operating systems, which occur in two different species, each having different ancestors and largely different attributes. One species is derived from MS-DOS; the other has roots in minicomputer operating systems like Unix.

The MS-DOS Species

MS-DOS is a weak basis for a network operating system, since it was not designed to run multiple programs and satisfy many users simultaneously. Companies marketing DOS-based network software use patches and shell programs that intercept multiple requests, buffer them, and divide processor time among tasks. Some companies, such as Artisoft, DCA 10NET Communications, and TOPS, have developed their own programs to modify DOS and give stations network capabilities. These programs represent separate branches evolving along parallel lines.

The largest number of DOS-derived operating systems, however, are the work of Microsoft. That company has developed a set of programs for DOS-based network operating systems called MS-Net, and many vendors license pieces of MS-Net for their use. AT&T, Digital Equipment Corp. (DEC), IBM, and 3Com, for example, incorporate some part of MS-Net in their networking systems, adding their own menus and user interfaces. Some, like DEC and 3Com, add significant pieces of their own code, using only small parts of MS-Net.

These DOS-based network operating systems share a number of characteristics. The most evident one is *peer-to-peer resource sharing*—the ability to allow any PC on the network to contribute resources such as printers and disk drives. The DOS add-on programs that offer multifunction capabilities work in the background mode, so someone else on the network can use your disk drive or printer, for example, while you are running PC application programs on your machine.

Peer-to-peer resource sharing is both a capability and a limitation. On the positive side, it allows great flexibility and makes these systems economical in installations having as few as two PCs. Since the operating systems in question can run on any of the Intel processors used in the PC family, even IBM PC-XTs or Model 30s can share their resources with other PCs. On the negative side, peer-to-peer resource sharing typically will slow response times; it can stifle the network's growth and make the network more difficult to manage. When files and printers are spread among many machines acting as servers, the administrative problems multiply.

DOS-based systems (with the exceptions of 10NET and LANtastic Network Operating System) share another trait: RAM hunger. It isn't unusual to lose 120k or 140k of RAM to the networking software in a workstation. Often, buffers and code loaded on boot-up in the CONFIG.SYS file use some of this space, so it's lost to DOS applications whether the network is in use or not.

If your workstation is configured to share resources with the network, some programs—like IBM's PC Local Area Network Program (PC LAN)—can occupy nearly 400k of RAM. True, there are ways to compensate. A few specialized memory add-on products might allow the use of RAM outside of DOS's 640k for at least part of the networking software modules in some programs. Likewise, some adapter cards are designed to reduce some of the pressure on RAM by storing more program code on the networking card. But generally you'll lose RAM space for application programs with almost all types of networking software.

MS-Net–based programs have another similarity: They share a common command syntax. Some members of this species, like TOPS and Tapestry, evolved separately from DOS and use very different command-line statements and syntax (icons, in the case of Tapestry). Because the MS-Net syntax is used so widely, DCA 10NET adopted it for the 10NET operating system, and Western Digital Corp. merged it with ViaNet by simply adding the MS-Net commands to the company's older command languages.

The standard features of the DOS-based operating systems vary widely. They all have menus and some kind of print-job spooling and queuing capability, but most do not include electronic-mail or network-management functions. 10NET, with its standard library of features such as mail, chat, and network statistics, is a notable exception. Artisoft includes a powerful e-mail capability in LANtastic, but many of these programs include only the basics needed for resource sharing. If you want electronic mail, group calendaring, or other productivity tools, you must buy them from third-party vendors.

Evolution from MS-DOS to OS/2

The evolution of MS-DOS–based LAN operating systems isn't over. Systems like Artisoft's LANtastic keep pushing the boundary of what MS-DOS machines can do. But the main branch of this product line, Microsoft's MS-Net, has stopped evolving. Instead, Microsoft has turned its energies to developing LAN Manager, a network operating system based on the multitasking operating system OS/2. LAN Manager splices the MS-DOS and Unix roots together into a new strain of networking products.

The Unix Species

The other root of today's network operating systems is the minicomputer world. Minicomputer operating systems such as Unix were designed from the beginning with multitasking capabilities. Non-DOS operating systems for networked PCs don't need patches or added modules to give them the ability to do more than one thing at a time. But they still must respond appropriately to DOS calls for services.

LAN operating systems derived from minicomputer stock clearly include Banyan's VINES and Novell's NetWare. The link between Unix and OS/2 isn't as clear, but as OS/2 evolves, every new release makes it look more like Unix with a modern face.

VINES bears the greatest external resemblance to a minicomputer operating system. When you turn on a VINES server, the operating system describes step by step the programs it is initializing and running. Together, these programs constitute the network operating system on the server. The hard disk uses the Unix file structure, and Unix controls the server's I/O ports. While even the network administrator never directly addresses the Unix operating system underlying VINES, Unix is there performing the multiuser and multitasking functions so important to server operation.

In Novell's NetWare family of operating systems, the file structure of the server is unique to Novell, but the operating system incorporates many Unix structures, including an internal communications process called *streams*. MS-DOS limitations on memory space and I/O port limitations don't apply to a NetWare server. Novell's Advanced NetWare 286 runs the 80286 processor in its protected mode, allowing efficient internal processing and external memory addressing. The special techniques in NetWare 386 take advantage of the address space and internal processing capabilities of 80386 and 80486 processors.

Microsoft's network operating system LAN Manager includes multitasking capabilities, and a special High-Performance File System (HPFS) gives it the ability to queue and service requests from many client stations simultaneously. LAN Manager was designed as an OS/2 application, but several companies including AT&T now run it on top of the Unix operating system.

LAN Manager's MS-Net ancestry shows up in the ability to run LAN Manager as one task on a PC that is also running local applications. VINES and NetWare servers are dedicated to the task of LAN management, but LAN Manager servers can be servers and local workstations at the same time.

All of these operating systems—VINES, NetWare, and LAN Manager—use functionally similar software in the client stations. Software modules (NetWare calls them *shells*) running in each workstation communicate with the networking software on the server to pass along requests for service. Application programs or DOS command-line entries on the workstations generate the requests.

The server software accepts the requests, checks the identity and the authority of each requester, translates the requests into messages the server operating system understands, and passes them along to that operating system. The server software then sends back the requested data and issues appropriate error codes to the workstations.

The major difference between this Unix-based species of operating system and the MS-DOS–based species is that the server software in the Unix-based species takes care of mediating simultaneous requests for the same data, and it also runs multiple programs. The result is typically much faster performance. In addition, workstations in these systems are not able to contribute resources to the network. Only one or a few dedicated computers perform the role of server—filing, printing, or running communications. (A special version of NetWare designed for small installations lets the server also operate as a workstation—but a workstation cannot function as a server without the appropriate software.)

This type of network operating system is typically rich in accessories and management tools. You can expect to find network bridging, electronic mail, print spooling, remote-workstation support, and other software modules, either in the standard release of the software or in the form of inexpensive add-on modules supplied by the original manufacturer.

Operating-System Features

With the two broad species of networking operating systems in mind, you'll want to consider the following features when selecting a particular system.

- *Dedicated servers versus a shared solution.* MS-DOS–based network operating systems such as LANtastic, PC LAN, 10NET, and TOPS allow any workstation to contribute drives, printers, and other resources to the network. Microsoft's LAN Manager has the same capabilities. Other operating systems, such as Novell's NetWare and Banyan's VINES, require a computer dedicated to the server role.

The shared solution (also called *peer-to-peer resource sharing*) is appealing in small installations where the cost of a dedicated machine is a factor. Sharing a workstation's resources always slows down the operation of local programs, while dedicated servers give faster network performance, but many PCs with 80386 and 80486 processors have enough power to support both server and local processing tasks.

- *Fault tolerance.* If critical business, security, or safety operations run on a network, the operating system software can help improve survivability. So-called *fault-tolerant* operating systems mirror the operation of a disk drive or even an entire server on a duplicate resource. If the first drive or server fails, the mirror image takes over. Novell's comprehensive *system fault-tolerant* (SFT) packages provide a wide variety of options and seamless takeover by the mirror-image resource.

- *Server-based applications.* In the typical PC-based network, application programs run on the workstations, and the servers run special programs dealing only with security and resource sharing. This arrangement is usually efficient, but sometimes performing certain disk-intensive tasks on the network file server is more efficient; these tasks include indexing a database or compiling program source code. Some modern operating systems, like NetWare and LAN Manager, can run appropriate application tasks on the server, increasing the efficiency (and complexity) of operation for installations that are busy with disk-intensive applications.

- *Server software memory.* The amount of RAM the server software uses is important if you want to use PCs as both workstations and servers in peer-to-peer networks.

- *Workstation memory.* Some network operating systems, like PC LAN, use more than 100k of RAM on each workstation for the redirection software. Some, like 10NET and LANtastic, require much less RAM. Others, like VINES and 3Com's 3+Open LAN Manager, can hide their workstation programs in special blocks of memory provided in optional cards.
  The significance of losing memory in the workstations depends on the kinds of programs you use. Some people might demand access to everything DOS allows, while others might never miss a few hundred kilobytes of RAM. The option of hiding most of the networking code in memory away from the RAM used by DOS could be important.

- *CONFIG.SYS program loading and command-line loading.* Some network operating systems load driver modules through the CONFIG.SYS program when the computer is booted. Those modules always take up RAM, even when the network is not in use. Other systems load everything from the command line, so no RAM is used when the operating-system software is not loaded.

- *Network administration.* Every successful network has someone who officially or unofficially becomes the system administrator. What kinds of information does your system administrator have to see in order to control who is using the network and what the workload is? Reporting system usage by user is standard in minicomputer systems but rare in LAN operating systems. Yet on a LAN with many stations, knowing who causes the heaviest workload could be important.

- *Diagnostic utilities.* Some network operating systems give the network supervisor certain utilities to use in finding problems and in configuring the server for optimum operation. These utilities can supply reports of bad packets and network errors, and they include tools for the operation of disk-cache programs.

- *Security.* Security is usually provided through the use of passwords. The best systems have different levels of access giving users various privileges (including read, write, modify, create, and erase). Another form of security is the ability to provide password protection to facilities such as a disk drive, subdirectories, or even selected files.

- *Electronic mail.* A good electronic-mail system alone might justify your investment in a LAN. It should store and forward messages, allow for direct replies and forwarding, and give the status of messages. Quite a few modern operating systems include a store-and-forward mail system.

- *Print spooling.* When several LAN stations use a printer attached to a central server, the print jobs are saved in a special file called a *spool*. The print jobs are then queued for printer access. Users should have a way to see the position of their jobs in the queue and to kill jobs sent there by mistake. The network administrator should be able to change the priorities of jobs in the print queue and to assign specific priorities to certain users.

■ The Future

Interoperability is the key trend for the future of PC-based networks and their operating-system software. Computers running under DOS, Apple's Finder, OS/2, Unix, Xenix, and other operating systems such as DEC's VMS can all interact as peers on the network.

The differences between minicomputers and LAN servers will continue to erode. Machines based on 80386 and 80486 processors will act as both at the same time. AT&T and DEC have taken the lead in this area, and now it seems that practically every minicomputer manufacturer is offering "DOS support" that makes the mini a server. At the same time, companies like Novell and Microsoft are rehosting their software to run over Unix and DEC's VMS operating system.

Another clear trend is improvement in the tools provided to the LAN administrator in new operating systems. Many companies offer improved reporting and better ways to manage security, costs, administration, and operational control of networks. Novell, Banyan, and Microsoft each provide a rich menu of statistical utilities and management tools in their latest operating systems. The importance of this area is shown in the number of third-party companies marketing add-on products with even more capabilities.

Essentially, the future of networking is based on greater cooperation among computers. Tomorrow's "enterprise LAN" (a network serving an entire business group, organization, or enterprise) will have many servers running different operating systems. Specialized machines will perform specific I/O-intensive tasks, and powerful computers will split their resources in many ways. Multiple solutions will be available to handle every task. As is true today, no one solution will be perfect for every requirement, but every environment will have one ideal solution.

■ Networking Acronyms and Buzzwords

Before you can fully understand networking, you've got to speak the language. At the very least, the next time your boss asks whether you think the company should migrate to SAA, you should know that this doesn't mean moving corporate headquarters south of the border. The following guide will help demystify the acronyms and buzzwords that industry insiders toss around so glibly.

ISO's OSI Model

Since you need a structure to hang the acronyms and buzzwords on, you first have to know about the ISO and its OSI model. The International Standards Organization (ISO), based in Paris, develops standards for international and national data communications. The U.S. representative to the ISO is the American National Standards Institute, or ANSI. In the early 1970s, the ISO developed a standard model of a data communications system and called it the Open Systems Interconnection (OSI) model.

The OSI model, consisting of seven layers, describes what happens when a terminal talks to a computer or one computer talks to another. This model was designed to facilitate creating a system in which equipment from different vendors can communicate.

The other data communications models are IBM's Systems Network Architecture (SNA) and Digital Equipment Corp.'s DEC Network Architecture (DNA), which both predated the OSI model. These companies now equate their systems more or less with the OSI model (DEC more and IBM less), and they promise OSI compatibility.

Protocols

Most of the buzzwords we will describe are *protocols*. Like the signals that a baseball catcher and pitcher exchange for pitches, protocols represent an agreement among different parts of the network on how data is to be transferred. Though you aren't supposed to see them and only a few people understand them, their effect on system performance can be spectacular. A poorly implemented protocol can slow data transfer, but software following standard protocols can make communications possible between dissimilar systems. For instance, the TCP/IP protocol allows you to transfer data between computers with different architectures and operating systems.

The key elements of a protocol are syntax, semantics, and timing. The *syntax* specifies the signal levels to be used and the format in which the data is to be sent. *Semantics* encompasses the information structure needed for coordination among machines and for data handling. *Timing* includes speed matching (so that a computer with a 9,600-bit-per-second port can talk to one with a 1,200-bit-per-second port) and the proper sequencing of data in case it arrives out of order.

Protocols describe all these functions. Since protocols are implemented in real products, though, often they don't fit the full description of the OSI model, either because a product predates the model or because its engineers couldn't resist adding that extra little tweak.

Layer Cake

Think of the OSI model as a layer cake like the one in Figure 5.3. At the bottom, holding everything else up, is the physical layer—the wiring, the cables.

The Physical Layer

The physical layer furnishes electrical connections and signaling. Subsequent layers talk through this physical layer. Twisted-pair wiring, RS-232C cable, fiber-optic strands, and coaxial cable are all part of the physical layer.

Probably the most common standard in the physical layer is RS-232C, a wiring and signaling standard that defines which pin does what, and when a voltage level on a wire represents a 1 or a 0. A new standard called RS-449 is supposed to replace RS-232C eventually. Europeans use an international standard called V.24, which is a lot like RS-232C. All of these are physical-layer standards.

Figure 5.3
Layers of the OSI model

7) Application layer: At this level, software follows standards for look and feel. 6) Presentation layer: Here, data is formatted for viewing and use on specific equipment. 5) Session layer: This layer provides a standard way to move data between application programs. 4) Transport layer: This layer of software is particularly important to local area networks. Transport-layer software provides for reliable and transparent transfer of packets between stations. 3) Network layer: Software operating at this layer provides an interface between the physical and data-link levels and the higher-level software. This software establishes and maintains connections. 2) Data-link layer: This layer provides for the reliable transfer of information across the physical link. It synchronizes the blocks of data, recognizes errors, and controls the flow of data. 1) Physical layer: The most fundamental layer is concerned with transmitting a stream of data over the physical cables and wires. Hardware and software operating at this level deal with the types of connectors, signaling, and media-sharing schemes used on the network.

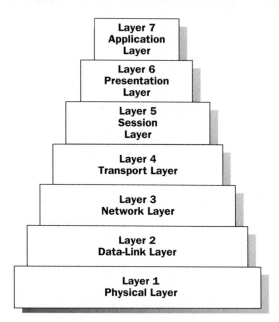

The physical layer carries the signals for all the higher layers. Pull the plug and you won't communicate at all. But without the higher layers, you won't have anything to say. The higher in the OSI model you go, the more meaningful the communication is to the end user.

The Data-Link Layer

Once you make the physical and electrical connections, you must control the data stream between your system and the one at the other end. The data-link layer of the OSI model works like the overseer of a railroad yard putting cars together to make up a train. This functional level strings characters together into messages and then checks them before putting them on the tracks. It may also receive an "arrived safely" message from the overseer in the other yard, or work with the other yard to reconstitute a message when a data disaster strikes. Routing trains between yards is the job of the network layer.

The data-link layer uses many protocols, including High-level Data Link Control (HDLC), bisynchronous communications, and Advanced Data Communications Control Procedures (ADCCP). But you don't need to know the details of any of these protocols; just picture them putting data trains on the right tracks and making sure they arrive safely. In PC-based communications systems, special integrated circuits on interface cards (instead of separate software programs) typically perform the functions of the data-link layer.

Certain programs in PC communications act like data-link-layer protocols. If you use Xmodem or Crosstalk for error detection and retransmission during a file exchange, you're using an application program that acts like a data-link-layer protocol while it is transferring a file.

The Network Layer

Larger wide-area networks typically offer a number of ways to move a string of characters (put together by the data-link layer) from one geographic point to another. The third layer of the OSI model—the network layer—decides which physical pathway the data should take, based on network conditions, priority of service, and other factors.

The network-layer software usually resides in switches out in the network, and the interface card inside your PC must put the train together in a way that the network software can recognize and use in routing. In traditional PC-to-PC networks, the network layer isn't important. But if you use Northern Telecom's powerful Meridian LANStar PC network or value-added carriers like Accunet, CompuServe, Telenet, or Tymnet, they're providing such network-layer services for you.

The Transport Layer

The transport layer—layer 4 of the OSI model—does many of the same jobs as the network layer, but it does them locally. Drivers in the networking software perform the transport layer's tasks. This layer is the railroad yard dispatcher who takes over if there is a wreck out in the system. If the network goes down, the transport-layer software will look for alternative routes or perhaps save the transmitted data until the network connection is reestablished. It handles quality control by making sure that the data received is in the right format and in the right order. This formatting and ordering capability becomes important when transport-layer programs implement connections among dissimilar computers.

The data-link layer can count boxcars to see whether they are all there. The transport layer opens them up to see whether anything is missing or broken.

Networks of dissimilar computers can use several transport-layer protocols. One of the most common is the Transmission Control Protocol (TCP), developed by the Department of Defense and now adopted and marketed by many companies as part of the TCP/IP protocol suite. Because TCP does not exactly match the ISO model, companies are moving to a new ISO-compliant protocol called TP4.

Three commonly used software products that perform transport-layer functions in PC networks are NetBIOS, Named Pipes, and NetWare's Internetwork Protocol Exchange (IPX). We will describe these products later on; for now, all you need to know is that these pieces of software reside in every network station and pass calls between application programs on the network. The primary applications that make use of transport-layer communications are network gateway programs.

The Session Layer

Layer 5, the session layer, is often very important in PC-based systems. It performs the functions that enable two applications (or two pieces of the same application) to communicate across the network, performing security, name recognition, logging, administration, and other similar functions.

Programs like NetBIOS and Named Pipes often jump the ISO model and perform both transport-layer and session-layer functions, so I can't name a piece of commonly used software that is unique to this layer. But the ISO has developed ISO 8327, the Connection-Oriented Session Protocol Specification, so that companies will have separate software programs performing these functions.

The Presentation Layer

As soon as you start using blinking characters, reverse video, special data-entry formats, graphics, and other features on the screen, you get into the presentation layer. This layer may also handle encryption and some special file formatting. It formats screens and files so that the final product looks the way the programmer intended.

The presentation layer is the home of control codes, special graphics, and character sets. Its software controls printers, plotters, and other peripherals. Microsoft Windows and IBM's Presentation Manager are two program environments that perform the presentation-layer functions.

The Application Layer

The top of the layer cake—the application layer—serves the user. It's where the network operating system and application programs reside—everything from file sharing, print-job spooling, and electronic mail to database management and accounting. The standards for this top layer are new, like IBM's Systems Application Architecture (SAA) and the X.400 Message Handling specification for electronic mail. Yet this layer is the most important one, because the user controls it directly.

Some functions, such as file-transfer protocols, work from the application layer but do jobs assigned to a lower layer. This is something like the president of a railroad sometimes having to sweep out boxcars.

That's it—the top of ISO's OSI model. The concepts are pretty easy, but dozens of committees are working to define standards for little pieces of each layer, and great political fights are being waged over whose ideas should prevail. Let's go on to hang some buzzwords on the model and see where they fit.

IEEE 802.X Standards

The Institute of Electrical and Electronics Engineers (IEEE) has developed a set of standards describing the cabling, physical topology, electrical topology, and access scheme of network products. The committee structure of the IEEE is numbered like the Dewey decimal system. The general committee working on these standards is 802. Various subcommittees, designated by decimal numbers, have worked on different versions of the standards.

These standards describe the protocols used in the lower two layers of the OSI model. They don't go above those layers; thus, using the common name of an IEEE standard (like Token-Ring) is an incomplete response to the question, "What network do you use?" Your reply should also specify the network interface, including the media and access protocol as well as the networking software.

IEEE 802.3 and 802.5

Let's look at two IEEE 802 committee standards that relate to PC-based LANs: 802.3 and 802.5. I'll describe the work of the 802.6 committee a few paragraphs later.

IEEE standard 802.5 describes the Token-Ring architecture. The work of a committee that received a lot of attention and leadership from IBM, this standard describes a token-passing protocol used on a network of stations connected together in a special way, combining an electrical ring topology (where every station actively passes information on to the next one in the ring) with a physical hub topology.

IBM's Token-Ring system is becoming more important to corporate data-processing managers because IBM supports an increasing number of mainframe-computer Token-Ring interfaces. Under IBM's Systems Application Architecture (SAA), mainframes and PCs share data as peers on networks.

An increasing number of vendors, like Proteon, make Token-Ring interface cards for popular minicomputers. These allow easy interaction without resorting to complex and expensive micro-to-mainframe links and gateways.

IEEE 802.3, on the other hand, describes a standard that owes a lot to the earlier Ethernet system. It uses carrier sense multiple access (CSMA) signaling on an electrical bus topology. The standard leaves room for several wiring options.

The 802.3 committee is currently a hotbed of activity. Vendors such as AT&T, Hewlett-Packard (HP), SynOptics Communications, and 3Com have developed standards for 10-megabit-per-second service on 10BaseT twisted-pair wiring.

Meanwhile, the 802.3 standard (particularly as represented by slightly variant Ethernet systems from DEC, HP, 3Com, and Xerox) is extremely popular. You can buy 802.3 interface cards for the PC from a dozen or more manufacturers. Similar cards designed for popular minicomputers are widely available. IBM even includes an optional Ethernet port on its mini/mainframe computer, the 9370.

IEEE 802.6

Metropolitan-area networks or MANs make up a subcategory of the IEEE 802 standards project called 802.6. Metropolitan networks can take many forms, but the term usually describes a backbone network of fiber-optic cables that could span hundreds of square miles. Local exchange carriers (the local telephone companies) provide a great deal of MAN connectivity, as do a growing number of cable television companies. While some organizations install their own microwave systems for MAN circuits, the majority lease circuits from local carriers. State utility commissions may regulate the tariffs for MAN services.

MAN carriers usually offer services in 1.544-megabit-per-second increments, and their backbone services provide throughput in the range of 80 megabits per second. The 802.6 MAN standard calls for a Distributed Queue Dual Bus topology with drops at each service location. This topology uses multiple fiber-optic cables with special equipment at each service location to interleave messages into the cable.

Wide-area networks (WANs) generally link cities. Specialized long-distance carriers lease circuits to organizations and communications companies to construct WANs. You can buy service at any speed, but speeds of 56 and 64 kilobits per second are the most economical, and 1.544-megabit-per-second service is common. The Federal Communications Commission has authority over the rates the long-distance carriers charge.

Eight-Oh-Two-Dot-Something

While the 802.X standards don't describe every popular network cabling and access protocol scheme (ARCnet, for instance, is not a perfect fit), "eight-oh-two-dot-something" is a frequently used expression that you should know.

IBM's Cable Plan

Another shorthand used by LAN writers and speakers is derived from IBM's cabling scheme. The major vendors—AT&T, DEC, Northern Tele-com, and others—have their own wiring schemes. These vendors all want you to wire your buildings in certain ways that are advantageous for their equipment and that will keep the competing vendors away from your door.

The IBM cabling plan, like most things IBM, is comprehensive, capable, and expensive to install. IBM has developed standards for certain types of cables, and it certifies certain manufacturers as meeting those standards. Here's a quick rundown:

- Type 1 Cable (Figure 5.4): Shielded cable with two twisted pairs made from solid wire (as opposed to the stranded wire used in Type 6, below). Used for data transmission, particularly with Token-Ring networks.

Figure 5.4

Many companies sell cable that follows IBM's Type 1 specification. This cable combines two separately shielded pairs of solid twisted wire. PVC and Teflon jackets provide different degrees of fire resistance.

- Type 2 Cable (Figure 5.5): Four unshielded pairs of solid wire for voice telephone and two shielded data pairs in the same sheath.

- Type 3 Cable: Four unshielded, solid, twisted pairs of wire for voice or data. IBM's version of modern twisted-pair telephone wire.

- Type 4 Cable: No specification published. Must be used to connect PS/2 Model 40s together.

- Type 5 Cable: Two fiber-optic strands.

Figure 5.5

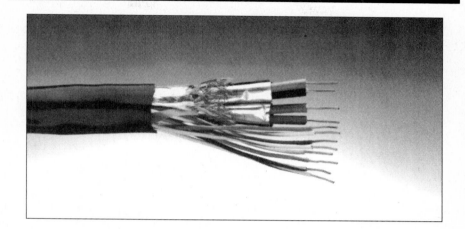

Cables that follow IBM's Type 2 cable specifications are used primarily to combine telephone and Token-Ring wiring within the same cable installation. Two pairs of shielded twisted-pair wiring are joined with four unshielded twisted pairs.

- Type 6 Cable: Shielded cable with two twisted pairs made from stranded wire. More flexible than Type 1 cable. Designed for data transmission; commonly used between a computer and a data jack in the wall.

- Type 7 Cable: No specification published.

- Type 8 Cable: A special "under-the-carpet" shielded twisted-pair cable designed to minimize the lump in the carpet that covers it.

- Type 9 Cable: Plenum cable. Two shielded, twisted pairs covered with a special flame-retardant coating for use between floors in a building.

Linking LAN Segments

Signals can travel only limited distances before losing power. For instance, on an Ethernet network, a signal can typically travel up to 1,000 feet; on a Token-Ring system, up to about 600 feet. Networks use repeaters, bridges, routers, and gateways to relay and regenerate signals traveling long distances and to talk to other LANs or wide-area networks.

Repeaters do what their name says: They repeat electrical signals between sections of networking cabling. You won't find many of these relatively simple devices in new networks. Repeaters relay signals in both directions with no discrimination. More modern devices, like bridges and routers, look at the messages the signals carry to determine whether they really need to pass each message to the next segment.

Bridges allow you to join two local area networks, and they allow stations on either network to access resources on the other. Bridges use media-access control (MAC) protocols in the physical layer of the network. They can link dissimilar types of media such as fiber-optic cable and thin 802.3 coaxial cable.

Routers operate at the network layer of the OSI model. They examine the address of each message and decide whether the addressee lies across the bridge. If the message doesn't need to go across the bridge and create traffic on the extended network, they don't send it. Routers can translate between a wide variety of cable and signaling schemes. For example, a router could take your messages from Ethernet and put them out on a packet-switched network operating through modems connected to high-speed leased telephone lines.

Gateways, which run on the OSI session layer, allow networks running totally incompatible protocols to communicate. In PC-based networks, gateways typically link PCs to host machines such as IBM mainframes. You'll find more information on bridges, routers, and gateways in Chapter 13.

Higher-Level Protocols

Moving up through the OSI model's layers, let's look at the techniques (and buzzwords) that different LAN software suppliers use for the transport-layer and session-layer protocols.

If you don't specify the transport-layer protocols you want to use, you'll get whatever the vendor includes in its standard "protocol stack." Those protocols may or may not be available for the various mainframes or minicomputers in your network. For managers of large corporate networks, selection of the proper higher-level protocols is a complex, important task.

TCP/IP

The earliest large network systems were fielded by the Department of Defense (DoD). The DoD financed the development of interactive network communications software for many different mainframes and minicomputers. The standard core of the DoD-specified software consists of programs that implement two protocols, called Transmission Control Protocol (TCP) and Internet Protocol (IP). The availability of TCP/IP software and the DoD's continuing enforcement of the protocols (through software certification) make them attractive to managers who face the challenge of integrating dissimilar computer systems.

TCP and IP perform primarily what the OSI model terms layer-3 (network) and layer-4 (transport) functions. Particularly important is the ability to communicate and to order data among two or more different computer systems.

Companies like Chi Corp., ftp Software, and The Wollongong Group sell TCP/IP software customized for specific computers and controller cards. These software modules communicate through the network, recognize each other, and pass messages in a common format generated by the higher-level session-layer and application programs.

TCP/IP software is popular with managers of large networks because it works and is available for many computers. Banyan, Novell, 3Com, and other vendors of networking software offer various options, ranging from standalone interface boxes to TCP/IP LAN gateways.

NetBIOS

Another institutional solution now enjoying grass-roots support is NetBIOS. NetBIOS started as an interface between the IBM PC Network Program (PCNP, superseded by PC LAN) and network interface cards provided by Sytek. When the IBM/Sytek team designed the interface, they also made it a programmable entryway into the network, allowing systems to communicate over network hardware without going through the networking software.

A grass-roots movement of large-network users is now pushing a combination of NetBIOS (operating at the OSI session layer) and TCP/IP. In this combination, application programs make calls to NetBIOS. Vendors like Banyan, Novell, and 3Com don't actually use NetBIOS to drive network interface cards, but their operating systems can run NetBIOS emulators to furnish the same session-layer communications services that NetBIOS offers.

NetBIOS modules establish virtual communications sessions with each other across the network. But NetBIOS uses a simple naming scheme that doesn't work well between networks or in a wide variety of operating systems. The Internet Protocol portion of TCP/IP envelops the NetBIOS modules so that they travel intact through multiple levels of network names and addresses.

Layer 4 and Above

If you don't use TCP/IP and NetBIOS—or some rare layer-4 (network-layer) protocol complying with the ISO model—you enter a maze of vendor-specific protocols. If you use PCs only, working together in a network, or perhaps using a gateway for mainframe file sharing, you won't care what protocols the networking software uses. But if you want computers from DEC, HP, IBM, and other vendors to treat each other as peers on the network, and if you want to access files on the DEC from your PC's D drive and files on the HP from your PC's H drive, the network protocols you use become very important. (One caveat: These protocols don't make otherwise incompatible application files compatible; they just move them across the network and offer access to them.)

Each vendor engages other vendors to support its protocol in their products. What's important is that the set of vendors supporting a specific protocol matches the set of vendors whose equipment is used on your network.

IBM's SNA and APPC

IBM would like to wrap you in the Big Blue web called Systems Network Architecture. IBM's answer to the OSI model, SNA describes how IBM thinks a communications system should work.

Advanced Program-to-Program Communications (APPC) is a protocol within the SNA model that establishes the conditions enabling programs to communicate across the network. APPC is analogous to the session layer of the OSI model. According to IBM, APPC is the communications basis for all of the corporation's future applications and systems products. Two other hot buzzwords from IBM—APPC/PC and LU 6.2—are the names of products that actually implement the APPC specifications. These programs, however, are large and cumbersome and have not caught on quickly.

IBM's SAA

You can think of IBM's Systems Application Architecture (SAA) as a stack of documents describing how things should be done. SAA describes application program interfaces (that look just like OS/2's Presentation Manager), screen and keyboard standards, and protocols that govern communications to operating systems and to facilities like APPC.

DECnet

The other company that can drown you in a sea of acronyms is Digital Equipment Corp. DEC has developed its own protocol stack for interconnecting DEC systems, both locally and over wide-area networks. The DECnet protocols are supposed to be heading toward compatibility with the ISO standards. It seems likely that DEC will adopt certain ISO protocols (as will many other vendors) to beat the drum for their compatibility.

Apple

Apple Computer has its own set of protocols in the AppleTalk family. The AppleTalk Filing Protocol (AFP) is the one that allows distributed file sharing across the network. AFP is attached to the Hierarchical File System (HFS) in the Macintosh operating system.

Distributed File Systems

SMB, RFS, NFS, and XNS are acronyms for some of the contending distributed-file-system network protocols. *Distributed file systems*, which are a part of every network, allow one computer on a network to use the files and peripherals of another networked computer as if they were local. The two operating systems link so that a subdirectory made available on the host is seen as a disk drive or as a separate subdirectory on the user's computer. Thus, application programs running on the user's computer can access the files and resources on the host without requiring special programming.

These protocols operate in approximately the same way, but they are not interchangeable. Typically, a major vendor develops a protocol for use within a product line, and other vendors license it to achieve compatibility.

SMB stands for *Server Message Block*, a protocol developed by IBM and Microsoft for use in the PC LAN program and in LAN Manager. AT&T, DEC, HP, Intel, Ungermann-Bass, and others all support or accommodate it to some degree.

RFS is the *Remote File Service* developed by AT&T. Since RFS is integral to Unix V, Version 3, vendors in the Unix market support it in their products. RFS is implemented in Unix System V.3 using the powerful "streams" facility, which allows applications to open a stream to or from a device (in Unix everything is a device: serial port, disk, and so forth) across any defined transport-level interface (TLI). The TLI can be the default Unix transport services, or TCP, or some other protocol.

NFS stands for *Network File System*, an architecture developed by Sun Microsystems. Sun's PC-NFS is a complete but no-frills network operating system for the PC. This memory-resident module gives you access to files stored on Unix-based minicomputers. Companies in the professional workstation market, including Harris Corp., HP, Texas Instruments, and many others, support the NFS architecture in their products.

Largely because of its leading role in selling Ethernet products, Xerox has been successful in promoting its own *Xerox Network Services* (XNS). 3Com uses XNS in its 3+Share software, and Novell uses a subset of XNS (called IPX) in its popular NetWare.

■ Now I Know My ABCs

Although this primer on buzzwords and acronyms just scratches the surface of networking terminology, it should help you gain a better understanding of the strange new language of connectivity.

Cables and Adapters: The Hardware Heart of the LAN

- Network Adapters

- Cables for Network Connections

- Topologies

- Putting It All Together

This chapter provides detailed information on the adapters and cables that link together the computers in a local area network. I've structured this information to help you buy the best adapters and make the right wiring choices for your installation.

In this chapter, I'll describe the small piece of hardware a computer needs to link it to the LAN: the network adapter card. Then we'll follow the path of the network cables and also explore how to send signals using light. In Chapter 7 you'll learn about the big three LAN cabling and signaling schemes: Ethernet, ARCnet, and Token-Ring, but here in Chapter 6 I'll give you the details of the pieces and parts those schemes use.

■ Network Adapters

Inside a computer, the low-powered electrical signals representing digital data travel on 8, 16, or 32 thin, parallel conductors, which are collectively called a *data bus*. The data bus carries signals between the central processor, random access memory (RAM), and the input/output (I/O) devices. Modern computer designs put I/O devices such as serial and parallel ports both on the main board of the computer and in the expansion interface slots connected to the data bus.

A local area network *adapter card* (Figure 6.1), also called a *network interface card* or *NIC*, fits into an expansion interface slot and changes the low-powered parallel signals on the data bus into a robust stream of electrical 0's and 1's marching in single file through a cable connecting the stations on the network.

The concept of putting a special adapter inside the computer to communicate with devices outside the computer isn't new. In the early personal computers, the serial and parallel port connections were always provided by separate extra-cost adapter cards. In about 1984, companies such as Zenith and Tandy began including serial and parallel ports in their computers to add more value.

The industry-wide acceptance of PC serial ports configured according to the IEEE RS-232C standard, and of parallel ports following the de facto standard established by Centronics, encouraged manufacturers to include these ports in their PCs. Designers knew these standard ports would be compatible with a wide variety of products such as modems and printers.

Because of the variety of possible network connections, companies making PCs have not included network interfaces in their products. A PC manufacturer can't include interfaces for even the three most common network schemes and still market a reasonably priced product. You must buy separate adapters and match them to the computer and cabling scheme you want to use. The list of connectivity vendors in the Appendix near the back of this book contains the names of many companies that offer different types of network adapter cards.

Figure 6.1

Artisoft's LANtastic Ethernet adapter uses the 16-bit expansion slot in a PC AT and provides the interface between the network and the PC's internal data bus.

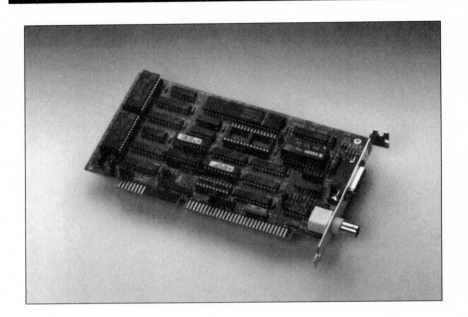

Linking the Adapter and the PC

I'll spend a large part of this chapter describing how the cables and other external LAN connections work. But the most important network connections are inside the PC. The best cabling and signaling schemes become unimportant if the data can't move quickly between the adapter and the PC. This is particularly true when the PC acts as a file or communications server on the network. A bottleneck in a server slows down the entire network's performance.

Bottlenecks can occur both in the software that integrates the adapter into the computer and in the way the adapter and computer electrically exchange information.

Hot Drivers

Our tests at PC Magazine LAN Labs clearly show the importance of a small piece of software loaded into every networked computer called the network interface card *driver*. We'll discuss how this software integrates into the total networking software package in Chapters 8 and 9, but for now you should understand the driver's role in adapter performance.

While Novell and 3Com sell both network adapter boards and network operating systems, like all other LAN software vendors they want their operating systems to work with adapter boards from many different companies. A software company gains a significant market advantage by offering a network operating system that can work with hardware from many different companies.

Some LAN operating system developers include the integrating software, or drivers, for many adapters in their installation packages; Novell puts drivers for over 30 different adapters in NetWare. But the operating system vendors typically can't keep up with every change and every new product released by the adapter vendors. Therefore, many adapter vendors include drivers that will work with different network operating systems on a diskette shipped with each adapter.

Programmers use different techniques to create the driver software. Certain ways of moving data and using data storage buffers move the bits quickly between the adapter and the PC. Some programmers write small and efficient code using highly detailed assembly language, while others take the easier route and write less efficient drivers in the C programming language. Quite simply, some programmers write faster and more robust adapter-board drivers than others, and some companies spend more resources developing driver software than others.

While network adapter boards from different companies are alike in many ways, your safest bet is to buy adapters from name-brand companies. Typically, the drivers for these adapters are field-tested and incorporated in the installation packages of the major software vendors.

Some smart adapter-board vendors clone the adapter interface specifications of products known for their proven driver software. Artisoft, for example, sells excellent Ethernet adapters with interface characteristics identical to Novell's popular NE-1000 and NE-2000 adapters. You can pay less for the Artisoft adapters and run them using the carefully crafted drivers for the NE-1000 or NE-2000 contained in Novell's NetWare and other operating systems.

Gateway Communications, Novell, and 3Com all have proven reputations for producing quality adapters and software, but no company can top the variety of drivers provided for Western Digital's large family of adapters.

I/O Options

The PC and adapter can communicate across the data bus using several techniques. You need to understand the different input/output options in order to balance performance, complexity, and cost when you select adapters.

Modern network adapters use one of four techniques to move data between the board and the PC's RAM: programmed I/O, direct memory access (DMA), shared memory, and bus-mastering DMA. Unfortunately, not every interface scheme works in every PC; for this reason, many adapters allow you to select between at least two different schemes. So, in preparation for the challenge of interfacing adapters to PCs, here are the details of the four I/O techniques.

Programmed I/O

A technique called *programmed I/O* provides an efficient way to move data between the PC and the adapter. In this technique, the special-purpose processor on the adapter board controls a shared 8k, 16k, or 32k block of memory. The adapter's processor communicates with the PC's central processor through this common I/O location.

Both devices move data quickly by reading and writing to the same block of memory—which functions like the window between the kitchen and the counter in a fast-food diner. And, just as in the diner, the processor on either side of the shared window rings a bell to signal the presence of something in the window. The bell in this case is a signal called *I/O Ready*.

The programmed I/O technique uses less memory than some other data-transfer strategies. For this reason, many LAN adapters, such as Artisoft's AE-2, D-Link Systems' DE-250, and Novell's NE1000 and NE2000 use programmed I/O as their primary operating mode.

On the downside, to use programmed I/O the host PC must have a processor more powerful than the Intel 8088 and 8086 used in the IBM PC and PC-XT, because the processor must execute a specific command to read the memory address, a command that is unique to the 80286 and later chips. Also, older PCs generate a wait-state signal for each I/O operation, and this reduces throughput. But if you have the right processor, programmed I/O is the right choice for an adapter interface technique.

Direct Memory Access

Many adapters use a technique called *direct memory access (DMA)* to signal between the processor in the PC and the processor on the adapter. This alternative is particularly useful for older PCs with 8086 and 8088 processors. When it receives a DMA request from an adapter or interface card, the PC's processor halts other operations to handle the data transfer.

In early PCs, the DMA signaling channel used a 4.77-MHz timing clock. Newer PCs still use the same clock rate to maintain compatibility with older adapters, so DMA is an inefficient data-transfer technique for modern PCs, and I recommend that you use it with care.

Shared Memory

Shared memory is a method devised to overcome the shortcomings of the programmed I/O and DMA techniques. A *shared-memory adapter* contains memory that the host PC's processor can access directly at full speed with no wait states. You can buy such adapters with both 8- and 16-bit-wide interfaces to the PC's data bus, but the 16-bit adapters often run into memory conflicts with other devices in the PC. Shared memory offers the fastest way to move data to and from an adapter, but installing a shared-memory adapter in a PC crowded with VGA video and other memory-hungry interfaces can be a frustrating job. You may run into memory conflicts that only manifest themselves when the LAN adapter and some other device try to use the same location at the same time.

Bus Mastering

A special technique, used primarily on Micro Channel Architecture (MCA) and Extended Industry Standard Architecture (EISA) computers, provides an adapter board with the ability to send data to and receive data from the computer's memory without interrupting the processor. *Bus-mastering DMA* adapters take over control of the data bus and move data directly between the network adapter and the PC's RAM while the processor continues its operations. Figure 6.2 shows a PureData Token-Ring bus-mastering adapter.

Figure 6.2

PureData's PDuC8025 is a software-configurable, 16-bit bus-mastering Token-Ring adapter for Micro Channel file servers and client stations. It supports both shielded and unshielded twisted-pair wiring. (PureData is a registered trademark of PureData, Inc.)

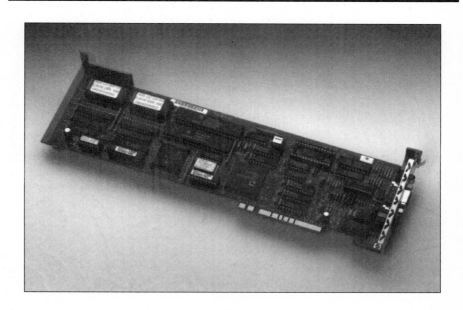

Only a few companies market bus-mastering adapters because they're difficult to develop and carry high price tags. Typically, you would buy bus-mastering adapters only for LAN file servers, although their fast throughput might enhance some workstations used for computer-aided design, because graphics workstations frequently move large files.

Features and Options

One option that's become almost a standard feature among LAN adapter manufacturers is an open socket for a *remote boot ROM*. This special ROM forces the host station to take its DOS start-up files from the server. PCs equipped with a remote boot ROM don't need local floppy or hard disk drives. Diskless PCs eliminate the potential for someone stealing data files or programs on a diskette; this concept also reduces costs and reduces the minimum size of the computer. Other useful features include LEDs indicating operational status, dual in-line package (DIP) switches that make it easy to change the card configuration, and different kinds of connectors.

Some buyers will want to note whether their Ethernet adapters include an attachment unit interface (AUI) port. The AUI port connects to a device called a *transceiver*, with connections for thick and thin Ethernet coaxial cables and fiber-optic cables (some companies call a transceiver a medium attachment unit (MAU), although that acronym has other meanings). If a board has an AUI, it gives you more flexibility and potential for reuse on other wiring schemes. Boards equipped with an AUI might cost a few dollars more, but they offer a wider variety of connection options.

Finding Space in Crowded PCs

PCs have only a limited number of expansion interface slots, memory addresses, IRQ lines, and DMA channels. High-density video adapters, mouse ports, and other communications boards all consume these resources in their host PCs. Table 6.1 shows some of the IRQ lines and I/O addresses that standard PC devices use; these IRQ lines and memory addresses commonly interfere with the operation of LAN adapters.

Some professional installers consider the techniques they use to avoid interrupt and memory address conflicts as "trade secrets," but the real secret is organization. Smart network administrators record the I/O and interrupt address of every device in every networked PC. You don't need a fancy database program; a three-ring binder works nicely to record the data pertaining to each PC. But having a quick reference to the I/O and interrupt addresses used in each machine can avoid frustration and save hours of installation time.

Table 6.1

Commonly Used IRQ Lines
and Memory Addresses

IRQ LINE	MEMORY	DEVICE
2	—	Use with care in a PC AT
3	2F8h	COM2
3	2E0h	COM4
4	3F8h	COM1
4	2E8h	COM3
5	280h	Tape controller
5	3F0h	PC-XT hard disk controller
5	278h	LPT2
6	3F0h	Floppy disk controller
7	378h	LPT1

My first advice about network adapter installation is to use the defaults recommended by the manufacturer of your adapter. The company chose those defaults to avoid typical problems.

If the adapter doesn't work at the default memory and I/O address, its installation manual will typically list at least two alternatives. Adapters designed for the standard IBM PC AT expansion bus (the Industry Standard Architecture or ISA bus) usually use slide-on jumpers to determine the shared RAM address and IRQ line. Adapters designed for the Micro Channel Architecture (MCA) and Extended Industry Standard Architecture (EISA) change all parameters through special configuration programs provided on a diskette shipped with each adapter.

One important point to remember: You must change the network driver software to match the memory address and IRQ line set on the board. The software can't find the adapter if it doesn't know where to look.

The first installation trick you should know concerns IRQ3. The COM2 serial port on all PCs uses this IRQ line. But many LAN adapters come with the same IRQ line set as the default. Most PCs use electrical techniques to avoid a conflict as long as both devices don't send signals on the same IRQ line at the same time. This means you usually can use a LAN adapter at

IRQ3 even if a COM2 is in the machine, as long as you don't try to use the COM2 serial port and the network at the same time—as you might, for example, with a serially attached printer or modem.

Many manufacturers of PCs provide a method in either software or hardware to disable an on-board COM2 port, but there is no single standard technique. A smart LAN administrator asks how to disable COM2 whenever a new PC comes into the office. Getting this information early can save problems later.

Because so many IBM PC AT clones come equipped with an internal COM2, installers often use IRQ5 whenever they put LAN adapters in these computers. But don't try this setting in an IBM PC-XT, because its hard disk controller will conflict with IRQ5 every time. Similarly, the LPT2 port used in many PCs acting as network print servers also uses IRQ5.

Selecting IRQ2 for an 8-bit LAN adapter often works on AT-type machines. However, this IRQ is actually served by IRQ9, so you can encounter conflicts if any devices in the AT use this higher-numbered interrupt. IRQ2 conflicts often sneak up on you when you try to add an internal device to a PC AT that has been happily operating with a LAN adapter at IRQ2.

You'll have to set an I/O address for the general operation of the board and perhaps one for a special auto-boot ROM. Many adapters use I/O addresses at 2A0h and 300h with success. Auto-boot ROMs let you use diskless workstations to boot from the server. The auto-boot ROMs use higher addresses, and they can conflict with the ROMs in modern video adapters. At PC Magazine LAN Labs, we've successfully used CC00h as the boot ROM address in many computers with VGA video systems.

If you must install an adapter using a DMA channel, try DMA3 as the default on an AT-style machine. On an XT, slip down to DMA2 to avoid the XT's hard disk. But all PCs use DMA2 for the floppy disk drive controller, so someone simultaneously trying to use the floppy disk drive and a LAN adapter set to DMA2 will experience problems.

You usually won't have a problem setting up a LAN adapter in a typical client workstation if you use the defaults. The challenge comes when you want to put a LAN adapter in a PC equipped with a special adapter for a mainframe connection or with a tape drive controller. These devices (and to a lesser extent, internal mouse adapters) often default to the same IRQ lines and memory locations used by LAN adapters. Some conflicts are insidious. You might not see a problem, for example, until you try to perform a tape backup and pull files across the network at the same time. In this case, one of the conflicting products must move—usually to IRQ5 with an I/O address of 320h in an AT. Figure 6.3 shows the jumpers used to select IRQ lines and memory locations, along with other important components of the adapter.

Figure 6.3

This diagram identifies the major components on a DCA 10Net Ethernet network adapter board. This board is typical of modern adapter design. (Photo copyright © 1990 National Semiconductor Corp.)

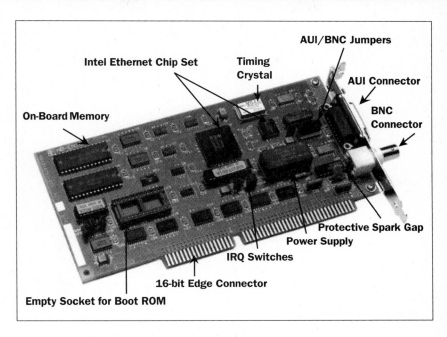

Getting multiple boards to work together in tricky installations is often a matter of experience and luck. That's why many system integrators support only product lines with a proven ability to work together. The craft of LAN installation involves some art, but it is primarily a skill, with specific rules and a road map of the PC's architecture you can follow.

External Adapters

A LAN adapter normally resides in one of the PC's expansion slots. But laptops typically don't have standard expansion slots, and some PCs are already crowded with add-in options. If you don't have a spot for an internal adapter, or if you simply don't want to open up the PC, you can use an external adapter to link the PC to the LAN. Several companies, including D-Link Systems and Xircom, sell external network adapters that connect to your PC's parallel printer port. With special software, the parallel port—normally a one-way device—becomes a two-way path to the PC. These devices don't have the same fast throughput as an internal adapter, but they are adequate for 99 percent of all network client station tasks. Figure 6.4 shows Xircom's popular external adapter.

Figure 6.4

The Xircom external adapter attaches to the parallel port of a PC and provides connections for Ethernet or Token-Ring networks. This kind of product is particularly useful for laptop PCs and those with limited internal expansion slots.

The Need for Speed

There are several possible choke points in any network. The speed of the file server's hard disk has the biggest influence on the server's response time. But after you install a fast hard disk drive and controller, the server's LAN adapter card becomes the next likely choke point. Busy client stations can ask the server to provide 3 to 7 megabits of data a second over a heavily loaded network. This transfer rate taxes the whole data bus, driver software, and adapter system.

The easiest way to improve server performance in a busy network, after you're sure you have the best hard disk system you can afford, is to split the network load among two or more LAN adapters in the server, as shown in Figure 6.5. NetWare and VINES can host up to four adapters in the same server, while other operating systems can use at least two adapters at the same time. It often takes some juggling to find an open combination of IRQ line, memory address, and DMA channel for more than one adapter, but it's worth the effort.

When you split the network load among adapters, you give each adapter interface a chance to make an orderly transfer of its data. This trick can allow you to postpone the installation of another server in a growing network, and can ensure fast response times in stable networks. As a side benefit, if one cable run or adapter fails, the stations on the other side of the network will still have the use of the server.

Figure 6.5

This diagram shows how the network load can be split among two or more adapters in the server. Testing at PC Magazine LAN Labs proves that splitting the load in the server among multiple network adapters significantly increases the throughput on heavily loaded networks—if the hard disk subsystem can carry the load.

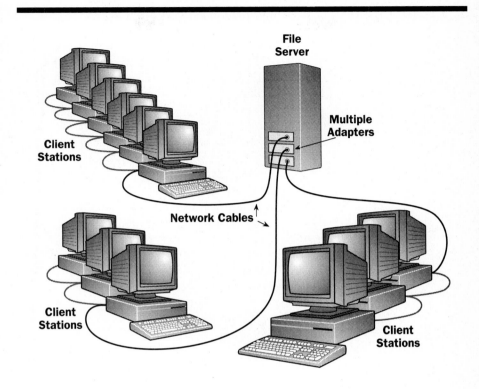

The First Things to Consider When You Buy Network Adapter Cards:

- What kind of bus is in the computer?
  - 8-bit Industry Standard Architecture (ISA) (PC bus)
  - 16-bit ISA (AT bus)
  - Micro Channel Architecture (MCA)
  - Extended Industry Standard Architecture (EISA)

- Can you use bus mastering in the server?—Must be MCA or EISA

- What other devices occupy memory and IRQ lines in the PCs?

■ Cables for Network Connections

The type of adapter you buy dictates the possible types of cable in the network, the physical and electrical form of the network, the type of electrical signaling on the network, and how the networked PCs share access to the connecting cable. People in the network business generally refer to the path of the cables as the *physical topology* and the route of the messages on those cables as the *logical topology* of the network. There is no fancier turn of phrase to describe *electrical signaling*, but sharing the cable becomes *media-access control*.

In the remainder of this chapter, I'll discuss the general characteristics of cables, their physical topologies, and the signals they carry. At the end of the chapter, I'll briefly describe the two logical topologies. In the next chapter I'll get into the logical topologies and media-access control schemes specifically associated with the Ethernet, Token-Ring, and ARCnet networking systems.

Three types of wiring are used to connect computers together in a network: coaxial cable, twisted-pair wiring, and fiber-optic cable. They differ significantly in cost, installation techniques, and electrical characteristics.

If you start from scratch, the cost of LAN wiring is divided between the costs of material and labor. While prices vary with the amount of cable you buy, here are some general estimates: When bought in reels of 1,000 feet or more, typical fiber-optic cable should cost just under $2 a foot. The shielded twisted-pair wiring used for Token-Ring runs about 40 cents a foot, the thin coaxial cable used for Ethernet costs about 25 cents a foot, and four-pair twisted wire costs 10 cents a foot. The prices for shorter hunks of cable skyrocket.

A lot of contractors know how to install twisted-pair wiring. And the cable television industry took away the mystery of installing coaxial cable. But there are very few good fiber-optic contractors or people who know how to wire Token-Ring networks. Labor costs for cable installations vary widely, driven by locale and the availability of knowledgeable contractors, but expenses of $1,000 per networked PC are frequently reported in major metropolitan areas.

Companies often elect to have their own computer resource people plan and even install LAN cabling with the help of a licensed electrical contractor. Involving your own people in LAN wiring can save money, avoid mistakes, and facilitate expansion. Several companies, including AT&T, Cabletron Systems, Northern Telecom, and SynOptics Communications, provide courses in wiring techniques.

The Harmonics of Square Waves

The signals on LAN cables are electrical square waves. A signal rising quickly to a level of 15 volts represents a binary 0, and a signal falling rapidly to a negative 15 volts represents a binary 1. The voltage transition from 0 to the positive or negative level signals the transmission of the bit to the receivers on the network.

This signaling scheme works well, but it has two problems: radiation and interference. The different network cables take different approaches to these problems.

The first problem comes from the harmonics generated by the rising and falling voltages. A simple rule of physics states that the harmonics of square waves are infinite. This means that the square waves generate radio signals all the way up the radio-wave spectrum. The radio-frequency emissions generated by the data signals on a LAN cable can cause interference with a wide range of radio and television devices located miles away. So LAN cables and equipment must somehow prevent radiation of the unwanted harmonics.

Government organizations set limits on the degree of allowable radiation for all computer products. The U.S. Federal Communications Commission sets two standards, Class A and Class B, for office and home use, respectively. Class B requirements are more stringent than Class A.

Organizations engaged in commercial or international espionage can use the radiated electrical signals to intercept the data moving across LAN cables. Some cable systems meet a stringent set of specifications called the Transient Electromagnetic Emanations Standard, or TEMPEST, designed to make it very difficult for any unauthorized party to receive signals from the cable.

The second problem that cable designers must deal with is outside interference. The effect of electrically radiated signals works in the other direction, too. Electrical signals from motors, power lines, fluorescent lights, radio transmitters, and many other sources can distort and override the desired signals on the LAN cable. LAN cables must somehow protect the signals they carry from disruption by such outside electrical interference. Fortunately, the same techniques work to cut down unwanted radiation and to reduce incoming interference.

Coaxial Cable

Coaxial cable consists of a center copper wire—either solid wired or stranded—surrounded by an external shield of woven copper braid or metallic foil. The braid and center conductor have the same axis, and that's where the term *coaxial cable* comes from. Flexible plastic insulation separates the inner and outer conductors, and another layer of insulation covers the outer braid. Figure 6.6 shows the shielding on thin and thick Ethernet cabling.

The outer conductor shields the inner conductor from outside electrical signals and reduces the radiation of interior signals. The distance between the two conductors, the type of insulation, and other factors give each type of cable a specific electrical characteristic called *impedance*. Different LAN signaling schemes, such as Ethernet, ARCnet, and IBM's 3270 cabling scheme, use cables with specific impedances, and they aren't interchangeable. You can't judge a coaxial cable's impedance by looking at it unless you read its type on the outside of the cable. The cables follow a letter and numeric designation scheme. If you just remember that Ethernet uses a cable called RG-58 and that ARCnet uses a cable called RG-62, you have as much knowledge as you'll probably ever need.

Figure 6.6

These pieces of thick and thin coaxial cable have multiple layers of braid and foil shielding.

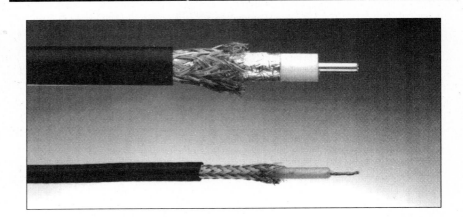

It takes a little experience and practice to install the connectors on coaxial cable, but the skill is important because one bad connection can halt the operation of an entire network. It pays to invest in good connectors that are plated with silver, not tin. It also pays to invest in a good crimping tool to install the connectors. Figure 6.7 shows a BNC connector attached to a piece of coaxial cable.

Figure 6.7

The connectors on the ends of this coaxial cable are typical of those used for thin Ethernet.

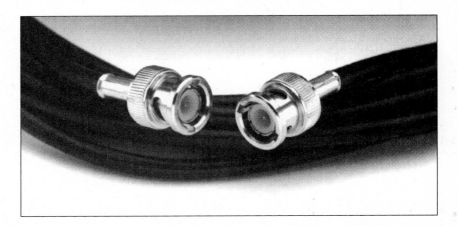

Watch particularly for cheap Ethernet T-connectors. Use only connectors meeting military specification UG-274. If a T-connector meets this specification, it will say so on the body of the barrel or on the lip of the male connector; look for that mark before you accept or install Ethernet T-connectors. I recommend replacing unmarked "generic" connectors. With good connectors retailing for $35 each and crimping tools for $50, you'll feel an urge to scrimp, but it's a bad gamble. Figure 6.8 shows two T-connectors.

Figure 6.8

The quality of the T-connectors you use can have an important impact on the reliability and efficiency of your Ethernet network. The connector on the left shows its MIL SPEC numbers and has a reinforced junction at the center. Experience at PC Magazine LAN Labs shows that connectors like the one on the right fail at the junction due to mechanical stress from the cable. Such failures are often difficult to detect.

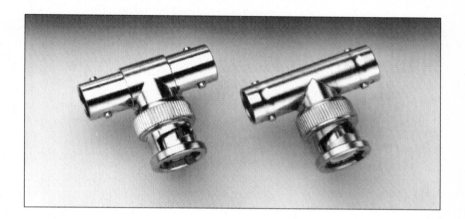

Similarly, don't scrimp on the cable itself. Markings on thin Ethernet cable should identify it as RG-58/A-AU or as conforming to IEEE 802.3 specifications. Don't confuse the 53-ohm-impedance RG-58/A-AU cable with the 73-ohm RG-62/A-AU used in ARCnet, IBM's 3270, and other systems.

The radio industry is being plagued by low-quality coaxial cable that presents unacceptable power losses at high frequencies. LAN cables aren't asked to carry high frequencies, so the problem might not show up for a few years until the insulation breaks down and the cable changes electrical characteristics. Insist on brand-name cable clearly labeled with the standards it meets. An investment in good connectors, tools, and cable will pay dividends for years.

Unshielded Twisted-Pair

As the name implies, *twisted-pair wiring* is made up of pairs of wires insulated from each other and twisted together within an insulating sheath. The twisting of the wire pairs produces a mutual shielding effect. This effect cuts down on the absorption and radiation of electrical energy, but it is not as effective as an external wire braid or foil.

Unshielded Telephone Wire

People often associate the term *twisted-pair wiring* with telephone wiring, but not all telephone wiring is twisted-pair. There are many types of telephone wire. *Quad*, the wiring found in residences, has four parallel wires in one cable. The telephone wiring plants in many older buildings were designed for a key system—one using phones with multiple line buttons and thick multiconductor cables. A few modern buildings were wired with something the industry calls *silver satin*. Silver satin cable is flat and typically has a silver vinyl jacket. None of these wiring systems—quad, multiconductor, or silver satin—is adequate for modern LAN data services.

Buildings wired for modern private branch exchange (PBX) systems in the last 5 to 7 years usually have a cabling system of high-quality twisted-pair wiring. Each pair of wires in these cables is twisted together, so the electromagnetic fields in the wires cancel each other and reduce the amount of induced electrical interference and radiation. Figure 6.9 shows unshielded twisted-pair wire; Figure 6.10 shows the most common terminator for unshielded twisted-pair wiring, the RJ-45 connector.

Figure 6.9

Unshielded twisted-pair wire offers an economical alternative for both Ethernet and Token-Ring networks. The twist of the wire provides a degree of shielding from external electromagnetic currents.

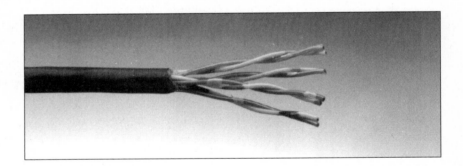

This wire will work for LAN transmission, but, to quote a Western Digital White Paper on installations that use unshielded twisted-pair wire, "The arrangement of twisted pairs at the wall jack in a typical telephone installation is usually not acceptable for network signal transmissions." In other words, the wires don't go to the right pins in the wall jack to complete the connection to the PC adapter.

Additionally, most PBX wiring installations provide four pairs of wires to the wall jack. The PBX telephone typically uses two pairs. The network connection needs two pairs, so there should be enough. But if you have an intercom or some other special telephone feature, this uses another pair and you have no room for the LAN. Also, a rule of thumb says that 2 to 3 percent of the wire pairs in an installation are bad. When the number of available pairs is already marginal, attrition takes a big toll.

Finally, the twisting of the wires affords some shielding from electromagnetic interference, but elevator motors, fluorescent lights, special telephone options, and many other devices emit signals strong enough to get into the wire and interrupt digital signals. Unshielded wires installed for networks should avoid areas of high electromagnetic noise. PBX wire runs seldom follow the same rule.

Figure 6.10

Unshielded twisted-pair wiring typically terminates in the RJ-45 modular connectors shown in this photo.

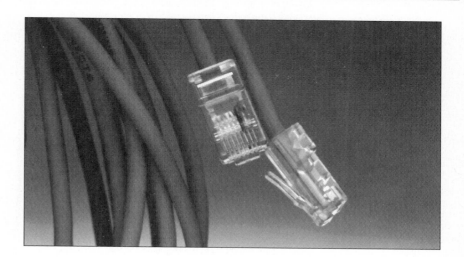

So, on the bottom line, you will probably have to pull more telephone wire for a new network installation. Expect to pay about 10 cents a foot, in bulk, for the wire—plus the cost of labor and parts such as connection blocks and wall jacks. Also, budget about $3,000 for a wiring hub that can accommodate 20 nodes. This $150-per-port hardware expenditure lays waste to arguments in favor of unshielded twisted-pair wiring based solely on installation cost.

By comparison, thin coaxial cable is about 25 cents a foot, but you can easily use less than half as much as if you were using twisted-pair, because thin Ethernet uses a point-to-point wiring scheme instead of the 10BaseT star wiring plan. Your hardware cost is about $5 per station for coaxial cable connectors, assuming the LAN card vendor supplies the needed T-connector for each card. On close inspection, low cost and the chance to use existing wiring aren't strong advantages of a twisted-pair setup. Let's examine its real benefits.

Even if you must pull additional twisted-pair wiring to install a LAN, at least it is the same wiring used for the telephone system. The technology of twisted-pair wiring, unlike coaxial Ethernet alternatives and Token-Ring's shielded twisted-pair, is familiar to technicians you already have on staff or under contract. If an installer abides by a few rules (for example, keeping to a maximum wire length of 330 feet between computer and hub and avoiding sources of electrical noise), the installation is simple. Choosing unshielded twisted-pair wiring doesn't introduce complex and ugly cabling, wall jacks, and desktop attachments into your office.

Avoiding Twisted-Pair Problems

Telephone system suppliers such as AT&T, Northern Telecom, the regional Bell operating companies, and other PBX companies have standards for telephone wiring systems. Their standards, and the resultant wiring systems, are not identical, but they are close enough that you can usually assume their wiring systems can carry your data—if there are enough vacant wire pairs in the cables.

The heart of all of the systems is the same: a wiring closet with rows of *punch-down blocks*. Some companies call them *telco splice blocks,* and veterans know them from the old AT&T monopoly days as *Type 66 blocks*. Whatever their name, these central wiring points often become central failure points in wiring plants.

A punch-down block gets its name from the act of using a special hand tool to punch a wire down between the jaws of a retaining clip. The clip slices through the wire's PVC insulation and makes electrical contact. Punch-down blocks make installations and modifications simple while avoiding the major problem of telephone systems—short circuits.

Still, the quality of the electrical connection made by the punch-down process varies considerably. The contact area between the clip and the wire is small, and moisture, crystallization, electrolysis, and corrosion all can degrade the electrical connection. On a voice system, the bad connection manifests itself in lower volume and perhaps frying or popping sounds. The human ear and brain deal with those problems admirably. Unfortunately, computer data systems have less-than-human flexibility.

AT&T and other companies have new wire-splice blocks. AT&T calls its design the *Type 100*; it uses wire-wrap techniques and gold contacts for better connections. If you have transmission problems using unshielded twisted-pair wire and "repunching" or wiggling the wires on the existing splice block changes the condition, you should consider retiring the old punch-down block in favor of more modern (and higher-priced) wire connection alternatives.

I've devoted a lot of space to unshielded twisted-pair wire as a LAN connection scheme because this method of connecting network nodes is becoming increasingly important. Another twist on twisted-pair, however, is making some important inroads of its own. Shielded twisted-pair wiring is growing in popularity because it is IBM's choice for its Token-Ring network system.

Shielded Twisted-Pair

Telephone twisted-pair wiring has no external shield. By contrast, *data-grade twisted-pair wire* carries an external aluminum-foil or woven-copper shield specifically designed to reduce electrical noise absorption. Thus, it combines the shielding properties of both coaxial cable and telephone twisted-pair wire. Different companies have their own specifications for such cables; the IEEE standards apply to systems like IBM's Token-Ring. Figure 6.11 shows the foil and braid shielding on shielded twisted-pair wire.

Figure 6.11

Shielded twisted-pair wiring combines the shielding of coaxial cable with the twisting of unshielded twisted-pair wire. On the other hand, this kind of wiring is bulky and expensive, and it requires care to install properly.

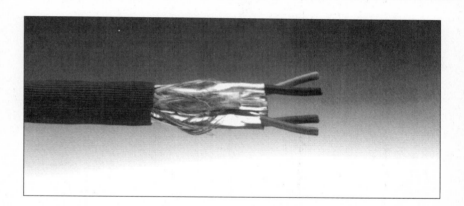

Shielded twisted-pair cables are relatively expensive and difficult to work with, and they require custom installation. Still, IBM has successfully marketed a wiring plan using these cables for Token-Ring installations. The IBM plan adds reliability (and substantial cost) by using a separate run of cable between every server or client station and a central wiring hub. This wiring plan significantly increases the amount of cable used, but it also ensures against the total failure of the network in the event that one cable is broken or shorted. IBM uses special connectors, shown in Figure 6.12, for connection to the central wiring hub.

Coaxial cable, particularly the thin RG-59 or RG-62 type, is easier to install than shielded, data-grade, twisted-pair cable, and it has many of the same noise-resistance advantages. But if you want real data security and immunity from noise, you can't beat signals sent with light.

Figure 6.12

The D-shell connector shown in this photo connects the cable to the Token-Ring adapter card. The larger, darker connector is an IBM Data Connector, which attaches the two twisted pairs of wire and shielding to an IBM medium attachment unit.

Fiber-Optic Cables

Fiber-optic cables—cables made of glass fibers, as shown in Figure 6.13, rather than wire—run many channels of stereo sound to airline passengers' seats, eliminating hundreds of pounds of wiring. Certain automobiles (such as Chevrolet's Corvette) rely on fiber-optic strands to route light from exterior lights to the dashboard for monitoring safety conditions. Now even PC-based local area networks can use fiber-optic cables.

A couple of years ago, the big promise of fiber-optic systems came from their bandwidth. Hundreds of simultaneous telephone conversations or high-speed data transmissions can travel down a single fiber of glass a couple of times the diameter of a human hair. The telephone companies are making good use of fiber technology in this way as they expand and replace their systems.

Most people imagine data moving through fiber-optic cables at a never-before-possible speed. But speed is not one of the advantages of PC-based fiber-optic local area networks. The fibers that LANs use to hook PCs together are not faster than similar coaxial or twisted-pair wiring. The packets of data don't travel in parallel motion through the fiber. In fact, electrical signals move through coaxial cable practically as fast as light travels through glass.

Why, then, are fiber-optic local area networks something to crow about? Because distance and reliability are the primary assets most people value, and because security is equally important to many users.

Figure 6.13

Fiber-optic cable consists of a glass fiber surrounded by a Teflon coating. Kevlar or even stainless steel fibers often surround the Teflon for added strength. The lower photo shows two types of connectors attached to the fiber cables.

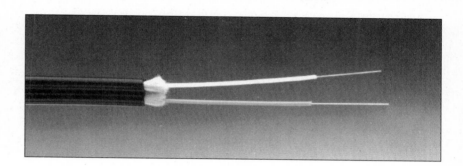

Distance

Signals on a copper cable and light in a glass fiber travel at approximately the same speed, but the light meets less resistance as it moves along. Therefore, light signals go farther with less attenuation. Fiber-optic links from simple PC-based LAN systems can run without a repeater to distances of more than 3.5 kilometers. This is more than 11 times the maximum distance for coaxial cable, and 15 times the distance for twisted-pair systems such as StarLAN. (Architectural criteria other than the media limit Ethernet networks to 2.5 kilometers overall.)

Reliability

The primary reason for the reliability of fiber systems is that they don't pick up electrical signals and impulses. Despite shielding, bypassing, and grounding, copper cables become antennas. The longer they are, the more energy they absorb from sparking motors, radio transmitters, power wires, and other electrical devices. Additionally, metal cables can develop different voltage potentials to the electrical ground. This leads to electrical "ground loops" that can induce interference and even sparking from metal cables. The energy from all these sources modifies and smothers the data signals in the metal cable, causing bad packets and sometimes transient unreliability. Fiber cables are immune to all electrical fields, so they carry clean signals and never spark or arc.

The physical topology of fiber LANs also adds to their reliability. All fiber-optic LAN systems use a physical hub topology. This means that cables run from each workstation to a central hub, like the one shown in Figure 6.14. If one cable breaks, the network remains operational. This is in contrast to station-to-station wiring schemes or even some coaxial hub systems, where if one cable is shorted or one connector is open, the entire network fails. The hub also serves as a point for translation between fiber and copper cable links.

Figure 6.14

Thomas-Conrad Corp. manufactures a full line of fiber-optic products. This photo shows a fiber-optic hub and adapter. The Thomas-Conrad TCNS family of products breaks the typical mold by increasing the signaling speed to 100 megabits per second.

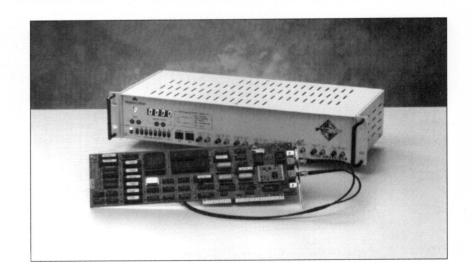

Security

Fiber LANs have improved security because they carry light, and that light is precisely controlled. If I can put my hands on a coaxial cable LAN, I can tap into it and read all of the data passing over it, including passwords. Some coupling techniques let me intercept the signals without even piercing the cable; this is because copper cables radiate signals as well as picking them up. Fiber-optic cables often play a major role in voice and data communications systems approved under TEMPEST criteria because they radiate their light only at the ends of connectors.

If the amount of light going through the cable is precisely adjusted, the insertion of an unauthorized device to tap off some of the light causes the entire link to fail. System failure indicates that something unusual has happened to the cable. Since they don't leak, and it's difficult or impossible to insert a physical tap, fiber-based systems are practically immune to interception.

Who's Buying

The people buying fiber-optic LANs, or fiber-optic links for their LANs, aren't necessarily computer scientists and engineers with huge amounts of data to send. Instead, they are likely to be stockbrokers, bankers, medical technicians, and people in the fields of security and intelligence who need extended-distance coverage, absolute reliability, and perhaps confidentiality for their networks.

Fiber optics has moved quickly from a young technology with great promise to a set of mature, practical products with significant advantages over other methods of connecting computers. At the same time, fiber systems bring some unique installation problems, and they cost more than alternative systems using copper cables.

Our experiences show that anyone who can install a regular coaxial or twisted-pair-wire LAN can install a fiber LAN with preattached connectors after about 1 minute of additional training. If long fiber runs with connections are needed, then a 1-day training course on attaching connectors to fiber is in order. Such a course is available from many manufacturers.

Fiber networks are no longer mysterious high-tech curiosities. They provide practical ways to move data with security and reliability.

Wiring Standards

There are many companies that would like to help you wire your walls. AT&T, DEC, IBM, and Northern Telecom all have standard building wiring plans. Some of these plans are expensive to implement. Several of the others don't provide connections for equipment outside a given company's own product line, but they all include good rules for installing wiring in a building.

From everything I can see, AT&T's Premise Distribution System makes the most sense. AT&T's plan is heavy on twisted-pair wiring (of course), but it also uses fiber in the right places. The fiber AT&T specifies is compatible with the developing Fiber Distributed Data Interface (FDDI) specifications.

■ Topologies

You can't always judge how the messages flow by looking at the physical layout of the cables; the physical and logical topologies of a network are relatively independent. But both topologies can affect your network's reliability, economy, and resistance to interruption.

Logical Topologies

The nodes on a LAN handle messages in one of two logical ways. Either they relay messages from node to node in a *sequential* logical topology or they send the messages out to all stations simultaneously in a *broadcast*. Ethernet and ARCnet use a broadcast topology, while Token-Ring uses a sequential technique.

Physical Topologies

Theoretically, there are several ways of physically running the cables connecting a group of computers. But in the real world, you can only buy products conforming to one of two different physical topologies: the *daisy chain* and the *star*. Figure 6.15 shows how fiber-optic cables are laid out in a typical installation.

Figure 6.15

Fiber-optic systems always use a physical star topology. Some adapters connect directly to the fiber-optic cables, while others use an external transceiver or medium attachment unit (MAU). Many manufacturers market fiber-optic wiring hubs that can accept fiber, coaxial, and twisted-pair wire at the same time.

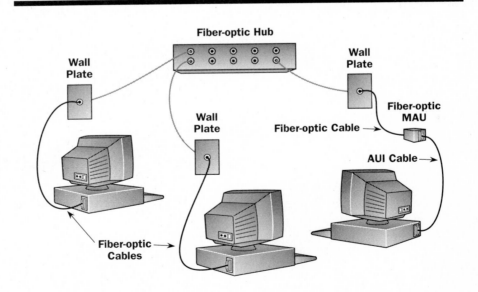

The Daisy-Chain Topology

In a physical daisy-chain topology, the cable takes the shortest path from one network node to the next. Another common name for this is *bus* topology, presumably because the cable follows a direct route from stop to stop.

This topology is typically associated with Ethernet, a complete signaling and media-sharing scheme described in the next chapter. A version of ARCnet marketed by several companies also uses this general node-to-node cable topology.

The cable goes from PC to PC, but it doesn't go into each PC and come back out again. Instead, a coaxial T-connector provides a tap into the cable at each network node.

Because of the electrical characteristics of a daisy-chain topology, if the cable breaks at any point the entire network fails. The cable does have many connection points, and a bad connection at any point spells failure.

Figure 6.16

The LAN-Line Thinnet Tap system from Amp, Inc. provides an answer to the difficult task of making a neat installation with thin Ethernet cabling. (LAN-Line is a trademark of Amp, Inc.)

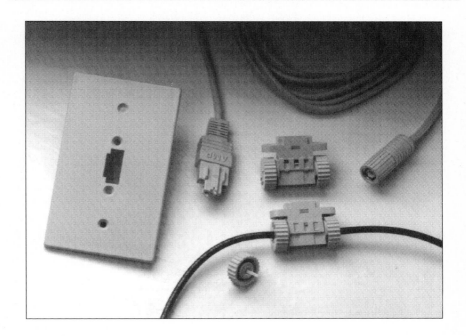

Daisy-chain cable installations are often messy because two cables run from the CPU to the back panel of each computer and then go off along the floor in separate directions. You can create neater installations by using an interesting product called the LAN-Line Thinnet Tap from Amp, Inc., a well-known connector manufacturer. This system, shown in Figure 6.16, costs about $9 in large quantities. It terminates the two cables in a single wall connector and eliminates the twin-cable clutter of typical thin Ethernet installations.

The Star Topology

The second physical arrangement is the star or hub topology. In this arrangement, the network wires run between the network nodes and a central wiring hub, usually located in the building's wiring closet. Figure 6.17 shows a wiring hub for combining 10BaseT, Token-Ring, and fiber-optic systems.

Figure 6.17

SynOptics' LattisNet Model 3000 Concentrator allows you to configure a combination of wiring schemes in a physical star topology. This concentrator combines fiber-optic cable, 10BaseT wiring, and Token-Ring cabling. (Equipment and technical support courtesy of SynOptics Communications, Inc.)

As previously indicated, the primary advantage of the star wiring topology is operational survivability. The wiring hub isolates the runs of network cabling from each other. Even if a wire between a station and the wiring hub breaks or develops a bad connection, the rest of the network remains operational.

Because the wire in a star topology runs from the wall plates to a central point, like telephone wiring, it is typically easier to install than cable running from point to point. The overall installation is usually neater because fewer wires run to each node. This topology also makes it easier to move PCs and change connections. But the star topology uses more wire than the daisy chain, and you'll have to pay for the wiring hub. In some cases, the hub devices can cost $500 to $600 for eight connections, and many of them need 120-volt AC power, so this isn't a small consideration.

■ Putting It All Together

The next chapter describes the combinations of these physical topologies, cables, and adapters used in three standard network architectures. As you'll see, these architectures continue to evolve and expand to include a variety of alternatives. If you understand the underlying features, you can master the array of options provided in each alternative.

Here are some of the advantages of each physical topology:

Daisy chain:

- Uses less cable.

- Does not require room or power for a wiring hub as the star configuration does.

Star:

- Provides a neater installation.

- Does not allow total outages to be caused by a break or short at any one point in the cable, while one bad connection takes the whole daisy-chain network down.

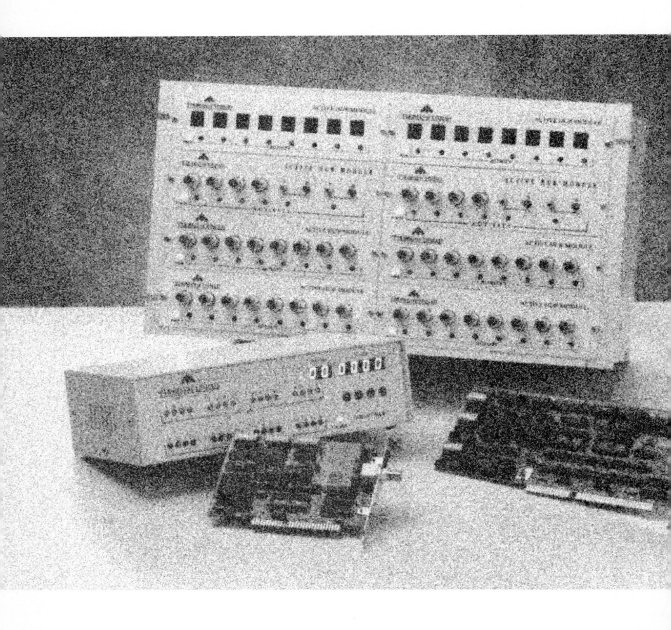

The Big Three LAN Standards: Ethernet, Token-Ring, and ARCnet

- How the Standards Got That Way

- Ethernet the Elder

- Token-Ring: The IBM Way

- ARCnet: Low-Cost Performance

- Networking Alternatives

The physical elements of LAN cabling—the adapters, cables, and physical topology—merge with the semi-mystical concepts called *standard protocols* to make a real operational network.

Protocols are agreements describing how systems will work. Committees established by such organizations as the Institute of Electrical and Electronics Engineers (IEEE), the Electronic Industries Association (EIA), and the International Consultative Committee on Telephone and Telegraph (CCITT in French) typically labor for years to develop agreements on how electronic devices should signal, exchange data, and handle problems. Committees develop protocols, but companies develop products conforming to those protocols. Some companies, particularly IBM, used to establish their own proprietary protocols and products (at least partly because they wanted to lock customers into their technology), but today, "open systems" built around protocols established by national and international committees prevail.

In theory, if any company develops a product operating according to a standard protocol, it will work with products from all other vendors meeting the same standard. In practice, companies often implement the protocols in such different ways that the products don't work together without a lot of adjustment on both sides. But the concept is sound, and constant efforts to improve compatibility among LAN products are succeeding.

There are three standard protocols for LAN cabling and media-access control that should interest you: Ethernet, Token-Ring, and ARCnet. A few companies, usually in the low-cost-LAN market, still sell adapters following protocols that aren't approved or even de facto standards. Generally, I urge you not to buy nonstandard LAN cabling systems. The small cost savings opens you to the risk of owning an orphan system without support and without the ability to expand.

Each LAN protocol combines physical and logical topologies, signaling, and media-access control techniques in different ways. We'll describe the important features of each one.

■ How the Standards Got That Way

The IEEE assigns numbers to its active committees. Committee 802 is a very large organization, with members from industry and academia interested in a broad range of wide-area and local-area network systems. Subcommittees of Committee 802 develop and maintain standards for several different LAN topologies. The subcommittees use decimal numbers to identify their work. The glossary describes many 802 committee standards in addition to 802.5 and 802.3, which I will discuss here.

IEEE standard 802.5 covers the Token-Ring architecture. This standard describes a token-passing protocol used on a network of stations connected in a special way, combining a logical ring topology (where every station actively passes information on to the next one in the ring) with a physical star topology.

IEEE 802.3 describes a standard that owes a lot to the earlier Ethernet system. Networks conforming to IEEE standard 802.3 use a carrier sense multiple access (CSMA) media-access control scheme on an electrical bus topology. The standard leaves room for several wiring options, including thin coaxial cable and unshielded twisted-pair wiring.

ARCnet is not an IEEE standard, but it is an accepted industry standard. So many companies sell equipment meeting the ARCnet specification developed by Datapoint Corp. that you can install ARCnet adapters with full assurance of continued support and interoperability.

■ Ethernet the Elder

Ethernet was one of the first LAN architectures. This network cabling and signaling scheme came onto the market in the late 1970s and is still a respected standard. The reason for Ethernet's longevity is simple: The standard provides high-speed transmission at an economical price, offering a broad base of support for a variety of LAN and micro-to-mainframe applications. Companies marketing Ethernet adapters have kept their products up to date, and Ethernet is still a wise network choice.

These days you can buy an adapter card that will let you plug your PC into an Ethernet network for as little as $200, although retail prices are usually slightly over $300. Figure 7.1 shows an Ethernet adapter for laptop PCs. Over 20 companies market comparable adapters for other computers. Since most adapters are made from the same set of function-specific chips—usually from National Semiconductor Corp.—you'll find them quite similar. Some of them, however, are better for plugging into a server than into a PC workstation. And there are other important differences in terms of features, performance, and cost.

Definitive Ethernet

People often associate Ethernet with network elements beyond the scope encompassed by the cabling and signaling scheme coinvented by Robert Metcalfe and David Boggs at Xerox's Palo Alto Research Center (PARC). According to Metcalfe, the name *Ethernet* derives from "the luminiferous ether thought to pervade all of space for the propagation of light" (a.k.a. electromagnetic waves).

Actually, Ethernet is a specification describing a method for computers and data systems to connect and to share cabling. Ethernet encompasses what the International Standards Organization calls the physical and data-link layers of data communications. (See "Networking Acronyms and Buzzwords" in Chapter 5 for a more detailed explanation of the ISO's OSI architecture.)

Figure 7.1

This Ethernet adapter from PureData fits inside a variety of Toshiba laptop computers and gives them the ability to connect directly to thin Ethernet cable. On some models the T-connector is a tight fit!

The IEEE 802.3 family of standards includes the specifications of the older Ethernet protocols, but the committee's work also includes changes to the basic structure of the data packets, so technically the term *Ethernet* doesn't include all of the options outlined under 802.3. "Eight-oh-two-dot-three" is a more complete description of the standard, but more people understand the term *Ethernet*.

The primary characteristics of the physical Ethernet link include a data rate of 10 megabits per second, a maximum station separation of 2.8 kilometers, a shielded coaxial cable connecting the stations, and a specific kind of electrical signaling on the cable called *Manchester-encoded digital baseband*. The latter specification describes the electrical signals that make up the digital 0's and 1's that are constantly passing over the network.

The major part of the data-link layer specification for Ethernet describes the way stations share access to coaxial cable through a process called *carrier sense multiple access with collision detection* (CSMA/CD). CSMA/CD is the kind of operational scheme that modern standards committees call a *media-access control* (MAC) protocol. The medium is the coaxial cable connecting the network nodes, and the MAC protocol determines how nodes on the network share access to the cable.

Ethernet the Perennial

For many years Ethernet was the fastest-growing network system and the first choice of many data managers and system integrators. But many people now buying networks choose IBM's Token-Ring cabling and media-sharing plan instead. Token-Ring performs well, and IBM continually dangles new ways of using it to connect PC and mainframe computers as bait for prospective buyers.

Token-Ring installations, however, are very expensive compared with those of Ethernet. And Ethernet offers efficient ways to connect to DEC, Hewlett-Packard, IBM, Xerox, and many other kinds of computer systems.

As befitting a network scheme with its tenure, Ethernet has had many offspring. Ethernet adapters using fiber-optic cable are available from Codenoll Technology Corp. and DCA 10Net Communications. The latest growth area is in Ethernet adapters operating over twisted-pair telephone wire at data rates of 10 megabits per second.

The "coax" cabling scheme found most often in installations of PC-based networks uses a thin, 52-ohm coaxial cable between each pair of network stations. This cable, commonly called *thin Ethernet* and sometimes called "cheapernet," is typically limited to 305 meters (1,000 feet) between repeaters, although an IEEE specification limits it to 600 feet. The network interface card in each station usually attaches to this cable through a T-connector, which facilitates connecting and disconnecting stations on the network without breaking the continuity of the cable (see Figure 7.2).

The oldest Ethernet cabling scheme is more frequently found in installations with larger computers. This scheme uses heavily shielded coaxial cable (informally named "frozen yellow garden hose," which aptly describes its size, color, and ease of installation), which serves as a backbone among the clusters of nodes scattered around a building. Here the maximum length of cable between repeaters is 500 meters (1,640 feet), and the cable attaches to devices called *transceivers*, which transform the cable's connections into something more suitable for a PC or terminal. A flexible transceiver cable made up of a shielded twisted-pair wire runs between the transceiver and the AUI port on the network adapter. Transceiver cables can be up to 15 meters (45 feet) long; they connect to the network card through a 15-pin D-connector (see Figure 7.3).

Packaging and Moving Data: The Ethernet Way

Ethernet uses a communications concept called *datagrams* to get messages across the network. The CSMA/CD media-access technique makes sure that two datagrams aren't sent out at the same time, and it serves as a method of arbitration if they are.

Figure 7.2

The thin Ethernet coaxial cable runs from PC to PC in a physical daisy-chain topology. The cable connects to each node through a coaxial T-connector. The terminating resistors at each end of the cable are critical to proper operation. You should use only Ethernet T-connectors meeting military specification UG-274.

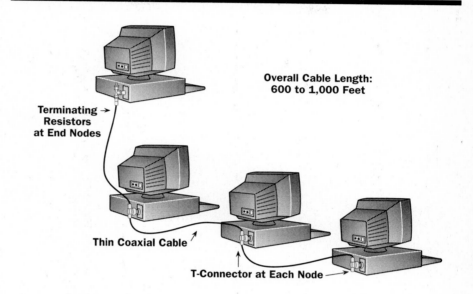

Overall Cable Length: 600 to 1,000 Feet

Terminating → Resistors at End Nodes

Thin Coaxial Cable ↗

T-Connector at Each Node →

Ethernet's datagram concept is supported by the simple premise that a communicating node will make its best effort to get a message across. The datagram concept, however, does not include a guarantee that a message will arrive at any specific time or that it will be free of errors or duplications; it does not even guarantee that delivery will occur. If you want any of these assurances, you have to implement them in higher-level software.

The Ethernet datagrams take the form of self-contained packets of information. These packets have fields containing information about their destination and origin and the sort of data they contain, not to mention the data itself. Because the data field in each packet can be no larger than 1,500 bytes, large messages must traverse the network in multiple packets. (Articles statistically describing the efficiency of packet-transmission systems have been the favorite filler of professional journals since Bob Metcalfe published his Harvard Ph.D. thesis, "Packet Communications," in 1973.)

One element of the Ethernet packet structure shown in Figure 7.4 is different from that codified by the IEEE 802.3 committee. The 802.3 committee saw a need for a user ID in the packet; thus, its specification trades the *byte count* field for a *user ID* field. Fortunately, the network interface cards don't care. They take their data from higher-level software that sets up the packets. Ethernet and 802.3 packets can traverse the same network, but nodes operating under one format can't exchange data with nodes designed for the other without software translation at some level.

Figure 7.3

Standard Ethernet cable is a thick coaxial cable that usually remains hidden behind walls. Transceivers connect directly at the cable and then extend the connection to each node through AUI cable.

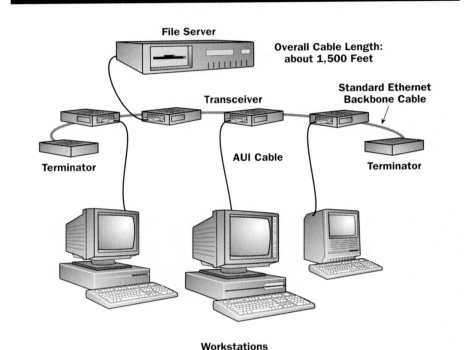

Listen Before Transmit

Before packets can traverse the coaxial cable of the Ethernet network as datagrams, they must deal with CSMA/CD, the media-access protocol that determines how nodes on the network share access to the cable.

CSMA/CD works in a listen-before-transmitting mode: If the network adapter receives data to send from higher-level software, it checks to see whether any other station is broadcasting on the cable. Only when the cable is quiet does the network adapter broadcast its message.

CSMA/CD also mediates when the inevitable happens—when two or more nodes simultaneously start to transmit on an idle cable and the transmissions collide. The adapters can detect such collisions because of the higher electrical-signal level that simultaneous transmissions produce. When they detect a collision, the network adapter cards begin transmitting what is called a *jam signal* to ensure that all the conflicting nodes notice the collision. Then each adapter stops transmitting and goes to its internal programming to determine a randomly selected time for retransmission. This "back-off" period ensures that the stations don't continue to send out colliding signals every time the cable grows quiet.

Figure 7.4

In the Ethernet protocol, messages are sent between workstation nodes in the form of "packets," or frames. Each packet measures 72 to 1,526 bytes long and contains six fields, five of which are of fixed length. The *preamble* field allows the receiving station to synchronize with the transmitted message. The *destination* and *source address* fields contain the network ID of the nodes receiving and initiating the message. The *type* field indicates the type of data in the *data* field which contains the actual data. The *CRC* field helps the receiving node perform a cyclical redundancy check—an error-checking analysis of the total packet.

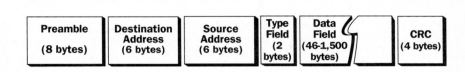

IEEE 10BaseT

In late 1990, after three years of meetings, proposals, and compromises, an IEEE committee finalized a specification for running Ethernet-type signaling over twisted-pair wiring.

The IEEE calls the new 802.3 standard *10BaseT*. The IEEE 802.3 family of standards generally describes carrier sense multiple access signaling, like Ethernet, used over various wiring systems. The name *10BaseT* indicates a signaling speed of 10 megabits per second, a baseband signaling scheme, and twisted-pair wiring in a physical star topology (see Figure 7.5).

The theoretical—and widely touted—appeal of the 10BaseT standard is that it gives LAN managers the option of using installed telephone wiring, thus saving installation problems and costs. But many organizations don't have enough existing high-quality wiring to support a network installation, so LAN planners find they must pull more wire anyway. On the other hand, the technology of twisted-pair wiring, unlike coaxial Ethernet alternatives and Token-Ring's shielded twisted-pair, is familiar to technicians you probably have on staff or under contract already. As we found during testing at PC Magazine LAN Labs, the strong practical appeal of 10BaseT products is in their commonality. You can safely mix and match 10BaseT adapter cards and wiring hubs from many companies and use them together on the same network. This commonality provides you with multiple sources of supply, competitive pricing, and confidence in long-term support.

Our tests also proved that you don't pay a performance penalty for using 10BaseT twisted-pair. Our throughput tests showed consistent performance, on a par with that of coaxial-cable Ethernet wiring.

For a network manager, the biggest potential advantage of a 10BaseT wiring installation comes from the star wiring scheme, which provides both reliability and centralized management. Like the spokes of a wheel, the wires go from a central wiring hub, like the one shown in Figure 7.6, out to each node. If one wire run is broken or shorted, that node is out of commission but the network remains operational. In Token-Ring or thin Ethernet wiring schemes, one bad connection at any point takes down the entire network.

The central wiring hub is an ideal place to install a monitoring microprocessor and network management software. I'll discuss that management facility more fully in Chapter 10.

Figure 7.5

10BaseT is the IEEE designation for Ethernet running on unshielded twisted-pair (UTP) wire in a physical star topology. The UTP can run directly to the adapters in each node or to an unshielded twisted-pair medium attachment unit (MAU) connected to the node through AUI cable.

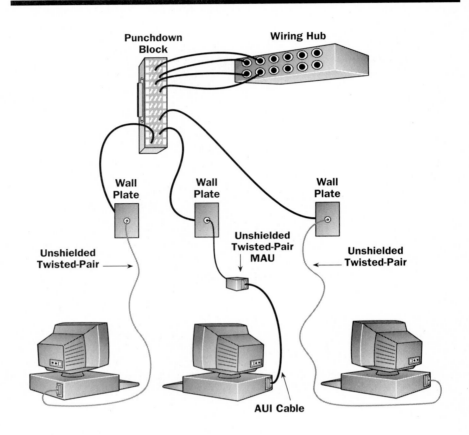

Commodity Products

I'll probably make a few companies angry by sticking the label "commodity products" on the 10BaseT market. I don't mean to imply that there are no technical differences, but the differences between 10BaseT adapters won't matter much to most buyers. After weighing a few technical considerations, you can safely buy 10BaseT adapters based on price, availability, brand name, and the factors that usually influence commodity purchases.

In keeping with the commodity label, the prices of these products continue to fall as companies maneuver for position. The products on the market vary in terms of a few technical points, such as the number and types of diagnostic lights on each adapter and whether it sets communications parameters using jumpers or software. The diagnostic lights are valuable (we avoided several time-consuming troubleshooting sessions during our testing just by looking at the lights showing connection status and activity), but most people will focus on two factors that differentiate among these adapters.

Figure 7.6

The 10BaseT twisted-pair wiring system gains reliability and flexibility through the use of a wiring hub like this one marketed by Gateway Communications. Note that such 10BaseT hubs require AC power.

The first important factor is the availability of the right software driver interface for whatever LAN file-server software you use. All of the adapters we reviewed support NetWare, and many companies now support the Network Driver Interface Specification (NDIS), a Microsoft specification for writing hardware-independent drivers; this provides compatibility with all versions of LAN Manager and certain other operating systems, including VINES.

Western Digital has the best set of adapter card interfaces, including an excellent implementation of NetBIOS. If you're buying LAN hardware for an organization using different LAN file-server systems, you should look at Western Digital's adapters first. Using its adapters lets you standardize on one type of hardware. But if you need only an interface to NetWare, 10BaseT is a commodity market for you.

The second important consideration is the availability of appropriate adapters for a server, such as 16-bit ISA, 32-bit Micro Channel, bus-mastering, or 32-bit EISA devices. But because you can mix and match 10BaseT and other standard adapters, you don't have to use adapters from the same vendors for the servers and workstations.

Note that the designers of these products seem to have faith in their quality. Warranties of 3 years are common, and many companies cover their boards for as long as 5 years.

Not Less Expensive, But...

Installing a wiring system according to the 10BaseT standards might not initially save you money in comparison with other LAN wiring alternatives. But 10BaseT's LAN management advantages and the ability to stay operational despite physical wire problems make it a good option for any modern network installation.

Logical Topology

IEEE 802.3 Ethernet can have either of the two common physical topologies: the daisy chain and the star. Regardless of how the wires run, the logical topology remains the same. This is a broadcast system; each station broadcasts data into the network for all other stations to hear. The CSMA/CD media-access control plan is based on the assumption that all stations on the cable will receive some part of the packet at the same instant, so no station starts sending its own packet while other stations are still receiving an older packet.

How Fast Does It Go?

The fact that Ethernet's 10-megabit-per-second throughput specification is much faster than IBM's original Token-Ring specification (4 megabits per second) and ARCnet's (2.5 megabits per second) can be misleading, because these figures describe the transmission rate over the cable. What they fail to reflect is the factors that limit effective throughput on a PC-based LAN—things like the data transfer rate of a hard disk, the transfer rate of the computer's data bus, and the efficiency of the networking software. Ethernet was designed to handle traffic in bursts, and that is exactly what it gets in real-world PC-based LANs.

To share access to the coaxial or twisted-pair cable effectively, Ethernet adapter cards must follow the CSMA/CD protocol. The "back-off" algorithm that CSMA/CD generates in the event of packet collisions has a tiny, practically immeasurable effect on the performance of any one client PC on the network.

Adapter Chip Sets

All Ethernet adapters on the market are designed using chip sets that contain the basics of the Ethernet protocols. Currently, the majority of the cards use the set created by National Semiconductor Corp., although some use Fujitsu, Intel, and Western Digital chip sets.

The Ethernet adapter cards available from different manufacturers differ in the way they use the chip set and in the features the designers add. Companies have designed different implementations to improve performance and to incorporate value-added features, but the adapters remain very similar.

On the cable side of the network, these adapter cards are interchangeable. Adapters from 3Com will happily exchange packets over a shared cable with an adapter from Novell or any of the other vendors. They all conform to the same electrical signaling, physical connection, and media-access protocol specifications.

■ Token-Ring: The IBM Way

The IEEE 802.5 subcommittee, with a firm lead from IBM's representatives, developed a set of standards describing a token-passing network in a logical ring topology. IBM also put identical standards into place within the structure of the European Computer Manufacturers' Association.

The Token-Ring network is to networks what the Boeing 747 is to airplanes. It makes strange noises and requires special handling, but it can carry heavy loads. It offers power and flexibility, but it demands skilled management and control. It is one of the fastest things flying—but not one of the prettiest.

The Token-Ring structure is the keystone of IBM's wide-area and local area network architecture. IBM provides optional Token-Ring connections on its mainframe computer hardware and software to make PCs and mainframes act as peers on the same network. But don't assume that you must use only IBM hardware and software on networks with Token-Ring adapters. Madge Networks, Thomas-Conrad, 3Com, and many other companies sell Token-Ring adapters. You can use networking software from Banyan, Microsoft, Novell, and other companies on adapters from IBM or from the other Token-Ring hardware manufacturers.

IBM didn't invent the concept of tokens or the idea of the ring configuration. Indeed, IBM paid a fee—allegedly in the area of $5 million—to clear a patent on Token-Ring networking filed by Olof Soderblom of the Netherlands. Other companies in the Token-Ring business have to decide whether to fight or accommodate Soderblom's claim of proprietary rights.

The multiple standards and IBM backing apparently nurtured the faith of the semiconductor companies. Texas Instruments leads a pack of companies who sell relatively inexpensive chip sets like the TMS 380 that can perform all the functions of the 802.5 standard. Companies such as Madge, 3Com, and Ungermann-Bass use these chips to market network adapters following the 802.5 standard.

Token Technique

In a token-passing ring network, a stream of data called a *token* circulates like a freight train through the network stations when they are idle. This technique defines both the sequential logical topology and the media-access control protocol. A station with a message to transmit waits until it receives a free token. It then changes the *free* token to a *busy* token. The station transmits a block of data called a *frame* immediately following the busy token. The frame contains all or part of the message the station has to send. The system does not operate by having one station accept a token, read it, and then pass it on. Instead, the stream of bits that make up a token or a message might be passing through as many as three stations simultaneously.

When a station transmits a message, there is no free token on the network, and so other stations wishing to transmit must wait. The receiving station copies the data in the frame, and the frame continues around the ring, making a complete round trip back to the transmitting station. The transmitting station purges the busy token and inserts a new free token on the ring. The use of the token-passing media-access control system prevents messages from interfering with one another by guaranteeing that only one station at a time transmits.

This streaming of data makes Token-Ring networks better suited to fiber-optic media than broadcast-type systems like Ethernet or ARCnet are. Optical media typically carry one-way transmission, and the token travels in only one direction around the ring, so there is no need for optical mixers that divide power, or for expensive active repeaters.

Ring Around a Star

The physical topology of a Token-Ring network isn't what you might expect. Although the tokens and messages travel from node to node (client station, gateway, or server) in a sequential logical topology, the cables actually use a physical star topology, as shown in Figure 7.7.

Token-Ring systems use a wire center (hub) that houses electromechanical relays to make the physical star into a logical ring. (Note that IBM's name for the Token-Ring wiring hub is *Multistation Access Unit*, or MAU. Don't confuse this MAU with the medium attachment unit—a transceiver connecting to the AUI port on an Ethernet adapter.)

When a station tries to join the ring, a voltage goes from the adapter board, through the cable, and to the hub, where it activates the relay for that wire run in the hub. The action of the relay reconfigures the ring in milliseconds and adds the new station. Token-Ring networks are the only networks you can hear operating, because there is an audible click from the relay in the wire center whenever a station joins the ring.

Figure 7.7

Token-Ring uses shielded wire to connect each node to a central Multistation Access Unit (MAU). This diagram also shows two-port hubs, used to reduce wiring costs. Wiring hubs can connect through optional fiber-optic cable links.

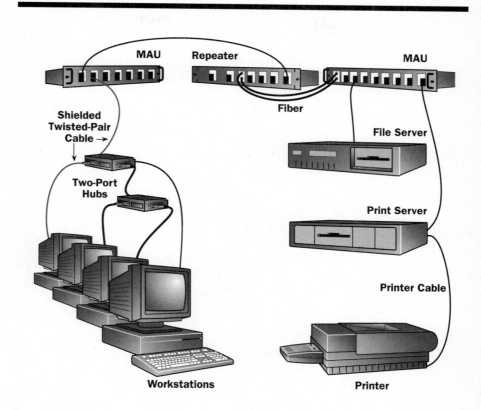

If the cable from the station breaks, or the wires in the cables short together, or the station loses power, then the relay opens and the station drops out of the ring. This arrangement prevents one bad cable from taking the entire system down (a major selling point for Token-Ring, ARCnet, and 10BaseT systems using a physical hub topology).

The typical Token-Ring wiring hub (Figure 7.8) accommodates eight nodes. The hubs stack on top of one another in a rack, and they are connected by patch cords running from one hub's "out" port to the next hub's "in" port. These cables extend the logical ring from one hub to another, so nodes are on the same ring even if they are attached to different wiring hubs. Provisions are available for linking the hubs through fiber-optic cable. Figure 7.9 shows a hub for small workgroups that can extend connections to other hubs.

When the Ring Stops

While the hub topology improves the network's chances of surviving a disrupted cable, the token-passing media-access protocol has its own unique survivability problem. If one adapter fails in an Ethernet or ARCnet system, only that node loses network access. But the malfunction of one adapter in a Token-Ring network can bring the whole network down, because every node in the ring must actively pass every token and message. If the receiver or transmitter in one Token-Ring adapter fails, the token stops there.

Figure 7.8

This photo shows an unshielded twisted-pair wire Token-Ring wiring hub on top of a wiring hub for shielded twisted-pair wire. The RING-IN and RING-OUT connectors used to link hubs together are clearly visible.

Figure 7.9

This Token-Ring wiring hub economically connects four nodes together using unshielded twisted-pair wiring. Its RI and RO jacks can be used to make connections to other hubs located several hundred feet away.

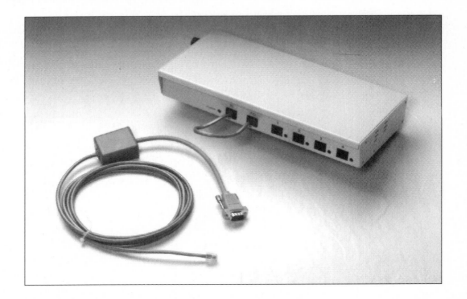

While this type of failure is not common, it is catastrophic. For this reason, and because active management at the network hub makes sense, several companies (including Proteon and Thomas-Conrad) market Token-Ring hubs with active management capability and controlling software for a monitoring PC. These products immediately alert a manager to problems such as malfunctioning adapters, and they provide a way of forcibly disconnecting nodes from the ring. Management hubs cost more—in the vicinity of $1,100 each, as opposed to $600 dollars for an eight-port hub with no management capabilities—but each management hub can also report on activities in less capable units.

IBM's MAU has no management/control capabilities, but then it doesn't require primary and backup 120-volt AC power in the wiring closet as the management hubs do.

Cables for the Ring

The typical cable recommended for Token-Ring installations contains two pairs of twisted wire covered by a foil shield. The maximum length of cable between the Token-Ring hub and the attachment point for the network node can't exceed 150 feet (45 meters). You can have another 8 feet of cable between the attachment point (for example, a jack in a wall plate) and the node itself. The cables are connected to the hub using a special data connector that requires some experience to attach to the cable.

It is possible to install a special device in the cable coming from the LAN adapter that allows the use of unshielded twisted-pair wiring. But I don't recommend this technique. I've heard too many stories of problems caused by electrical interference absorbed through the unshielded twisted-pair cable. Because the token must circulate through each station, a single noise problem on one leg of the network cable can halt the operation of the entire network.

Ring Speed

The original IBM Token-Ring product uses a 4-megabit-per-second signaling speed on the network cable. In 1989, IBM released a Token-Ring version using 16-megabit-per-second signaling. The 16-megabit adapters also work at 4 megabits on networks with the slower adapters. Other companies tried to follow IBM's high-speed lead, but they took over a year to get their products to market.

Although the signals representing 0's and 1's move faster across the wire, don't assume that 16-megabit-per-second Token-Ring will provide faster responses on your network than the 4-megabit-per-second variety. On the other hand, don't assume that 4-megabit-per-second *Token-Ring* gives slower responses than 10-megabit-per-second *Ethernet*. Many factors other than the network signaling rate limit throughput—particularly the speed of the server's hard disk and the interface between the adapter and the server's data bus. Few organizations will see an improvement in overall network throughput by changing from 4- to 16-megabit-per-second Token-Ring systems. But if the plans for your network include hundreds of network nodes, multiple servers, and mainframe equipment on the LAN, then an investment in a 16-megabit-per-second Token-Ring network makes good sense.

Caught in the Ring

Many companies, spurred by IBM's sponsorship, choose Token-Ring as their wiring and media-access control architecture. While the operational benefits of Token-Ring over Ethernet are still the subject of esoteric debate, you need to look for the real benefits—particularly the potential for direct mainframe attachments—and weigh them against the cost of installing Token-Ring adapters, cables, and wiring hubs. As I'll explain in Chapter 12, there are other effective ways to interface with mainframe computers that don't require a Token-Ring installation.

■ ARCnet: Low-Cost Performance

Using tokens or messages to regulate when a station can transmit over a shared wire isn't unique to IEEE 802.5. The ARCnet system, originated by Datapoint and fostered in the microcomputer world by Standard Microsystems, uses "transmission permission" messages addressed to specific stations to regulate traffic. The acronym *ARC* stands for Datapoint's Attached Resource Computing architecture. You can buy ARCnet adapters through the mail for under $75, yet the throughput and reliability of these adapters is generally excellent.

If the ARCnet technology had the backing of an IEEE 802 subcommittee, it would certainly limit the popularity of both Token-Ring and Ethernet architectures. At PC Magazine LAN Labs, we like ARCnet, and we consider it a safe bet for your data despite its lack of IEEE acceptance.

ARCnet Topologies

ARCnet uses a broadcast-type logical topology, which means that all stations receive all messages broadcast into the cable at approximately the same time. The ARCnet scheme traditionally uses RG-62 coaxial cable in a physical star topology. The ARCnet star topology allows for a hierarchy of hubs. Small two- or four-port wiring hubs can feed other large and small hubs in an economical wiring scheme that retains the resistance to total outage inherent in a star topology. Modern versions of ARCnet can also use coaxial cable or unshielded twisted-pair wire in a station-to-station physical topology. Figure 7.10 shows a variety of ARCnet products.

Figure 7.10

ARCnet adapters and wiring hubs are available for both coaxial cable and unshielded twisted-pair wiring. Interchangeable modules in the Thomas-Conrad Smart Hub provide the needed connections. These adapters are intended for 8- and 16-bit ISA and MCA Computers.

A complex set of rules regulate how big an ARCnet network can be. Generally, the maximum length of cable from one end of the network to the other is 20,000 feet. The maximum cable length between *powered* or "active" hubs that can regenerate signals is 2,000 feet. The length between a powered hub and a network node is also 2,000 feet. Unpowered "passive" hubs can connect to nodes over 100 feet of cable. As you can see, ARCnet systems can cover a large geographical area.

The RG-62 cable specified for ARCnet is the same cable that IBM uses in its 3270 wiring plan, which links terminals to mainframe terminal controllers. Since this plan also uses a physical star topology, many companies find it easy to install ARCnet when they downsize their computer systems from IBM mainframes to networks of PCs.

High-impedance ARCnet adapters allow a physical daisy-chain topology identical to that of thin Ethernet networks. The daisy-chained nodes can also connect to active powered hubs, for an overall network of 20,000 feet of cable.

Several companies, including PureData and Standard Microcomputer Systems, offer fiber-optic versions of ARCnet systems. These systems have the typical fiber-optic characteristics of low electrical emissions, low absorption of electrical noise, and extended distance.

ARCnet Access Control

The technical literature describes ARCnet as a token-passing system, but ARCnet operates very differently from IEEE 802.5 Token-Ring. Instead of having a token passed from station to station, it has one station broadcast the transmission permission message to the others on the network.

Each Ethernet and Token-Ring adapter has a unique adapter identifier assigned by the manufacturer and drawn from a common pool established by industry associations. ARCnet adapters, however, don't come with identification numbers assigned. You set an identification number, from 1 to 255, using switches located on each adapter. The identification numbers have no relationship to the position of the nodes on the cable or to other physical relationships.

When activated, the adapters broadcast their numbers, and the lowest-numbered active station becomes the controller for the network. This controller sends a token to each active station granting permission to transmit. When each station receives the permission token, it either sends its waiting message or remains silent. Then the controlling station sends a permission token to the next station in numeric sequence.

When a new station enters the network, the stations all rebroadcast their station numbers in what is called a reconfiguration or "recon." Like the collisions in Ethernet, the concept of a recon bothers people who worry about esoteric matters of network efficiency. In reality, a recon takes no longer than 65 milliseconds, at worst, and scarcely disturbs the flow of traffic on a network.

Here are a couple of practical hints for all ARCnet installers:

- There are two things you can't afford to lose: the instruction manual telling you how to set the adapter numbers and the list of adapter numbers active on the network. If you know what station numbers have been assigned, it's easy to add more stations. If you don't know what station numbers are active, you face a frustrating session of research or trial-and-error installation.

- Keep your assigned station numbers close together, and put PCs with the most powerful CPUs in the low-numbered slots. The polling task takes a tiny bit of CPU power, so put your husky servers and other fast PCs in position to take on that role.

Speed

Traditional ARCnet operates at a signaling speed of 2.5 megabits per second. While many installations will never find this signaling speed a limitation, it doesn't really keep up with the capability of modern servers to deliver data. But you can divide the ARCnet network into sections by installing several adapters in the server and splitting the output into multiple channels. This is an economical solution that also improves overall network reliability.

ARCnet Futures

Standard Microsystems and other companies are working to make a 10-megabit-per-second ARCnet system an IEEE 802 standard. Theoreticians argue that the sequential logical topology of the ring eliminates the overhead of addressing individual tokens. Similarly, proponents of both Token-Ring and ARCnet argue that their *deterministic protocols* are less wasteful than the *colliding protocols* of Ethernet. But in practice, many other factors—including the quality of the driver software for the adapters—have much more impact on network throughput than the media-access control scheme.

At PC Magazine LAN Labs, our tests with adapters from many different manufacturers consistently prove the value of ARCnet. Choosing ARCnet adapters is an economical, smart, and safe move for many organizations.

■ Networking Alternatives

To a large degree, the type of network adapter you choose dictates the logical and physical topologies, the type of media, and the access protocol scheme your network uses. These choices do not, however, dictate the type of networking software you use. The LAN hardware and the network operating-system software are two important but separate decisions. The next two chapters describe the operation and selection of LAN operating-system software.

The Structure of Network Operating Systems

- LAN Software Functions

- Software in the Client PC

- Types of Servers

This chapter reviews and elaborates on the concepts behind network operating-system software described in Chapter 5. We'll explore the functions of server software, client workstation software, and the underlying communications protocols.

Chapters 6 and 7 detailed the basic hardware portions of a local area network: the cabling scheme and network adapters. There are other pieces you might think of as hardware—primarily servers, bridges, and gateways—but these are usually PCs acting in particular functional roles rather than unique pieces of hardware designed for networks.

One interesting and useful feature of LAN hardware like the Ethernet, ARCnet, and Token-Ring systems described in the previous chapters is its complete independence from the networking software. If you stick with IEEE- and industry-standard hardware and avoid proprietary cable and signaling schemes, you can choose practically any network operating system for your client workstations, servers, and other functional elements. Your decision on cabling and your decision on LAN software are separate.

■ LAN Software Functions

Two concepts you've encountered in earlier chapters are worth repeating:

- The primary purpose of networking software is to let you share resources such as printers, hard disks, and communications links among client stations.

- The primary function of networking software is to make distant resources appear local.

A network operating system is not one program but rather a series of programs. Some of these programs run in the PCs acting as servers of various types, and others run in PCs acting as client workstations. The networking software in servers provides and controls multiple simultaneous access to disk drives, printers, and other devices such as modems and facsimile boards. The networking software in client stations intercepts and redirects the requests for service that application programs generate and sends each of them to the appropriate server for action.

Terms like *server* and *client station* describe the *function* of a computer on the network; they don't tell you anything about the power or capacity of the PC acting in that role. Also, they aren't mutually exclusive terms; a PC will often act as a server of some kind—particularly as a print server—and as a client workstation at the same time.

■ Software in the Client PC

We call computers using a network's resources *clients*. A client PC uses hard disks, communications lines, and printers on a server as if these things were part of each user's own workstation. That redirection capability is the prime power of networks. Under some network operating systems, client stations can also act as servers, but most computers on the LAN typically serve only as clients.

Here are some important concepts to understand about how the networking software does its job:

- Client PCs use shared resources provided by servers.
- You don't always need special applications on client PCs.
- Redirection software routes requests to servers.
- Transport-layer software carries data across the cable.
- There are many different kinds of servers.

The following sections explain these points in much more detail.

The Redirector

The redirection software in each client computer makes the resources available on the network look like local DOS or OS/2 devices to the programs and people using them. Commands sent from the keyboard and from programs to drives with names like D, E, and F are redirected over the network to the appropriate file servers. Similarly, programs sending output to a network printer address a local LPT port just as they normally do. The print jobs are redirected to the shared printer and queued on the PC acting as a print server until the printer is ready to take the job.

Operating-system modules in the client stations include the redirector and the software elements that carry the redirector's output through the network. The redirector modifies the DOS or OS/2 operating system in the client stations so that certain requests made by applications go out through the network adapter for action instead of going to local disk drives or I/O ports. The network administrator programs the redirector through a menu or a command-line prompt to route all requests addressed to a specific drive letter or I/O port to a selected network resource.

For example, in a network using Novell's NetWare you would enter the following command to route requests sent to the F drive out to a subdirectory called ACCOUNTS in a disk volume called VOLUME1 residing on a server named SERVER1:

```
MAP F: = SERVER1/VOLUME1: ACCOUNTS
```

Commands like this are usually part of the log-on script for an individual user, giving each person a customized view of the network resources. Network administrators have the important task of creating and maintaining customized log-on scripts and batch files for each user.

Transport-Layer Software

Additional layers of networking software in the client move an application's request for service from the redirector to the network adapter and onto the network cable. This software has three parts:

- An application program interface (API)

- A network communications section that follows a specific protocol

- Drivers customized for the LAN adapter

Figure 8.1 shows the relationship of the redirector and transport-layer software.

Figure 8.1

Novell calls its redirection software a "shell" to indicate that it wraps around the MS-DOS operating system and intercepts all data requests and commands coming from application programs and the keyboard. The Microsoft redirector, licensed by IBM and many other companies, modifies MS-DOS so that it routes appropriate requests to the redirector. The NetWare shell and the Microsoft redirector move the messages they receive to the network adapter card through transport-layer software such as NetBIOS or Novell's SPX/IPX. Each driver is configured specifically for the brand and model of LAN adapter.

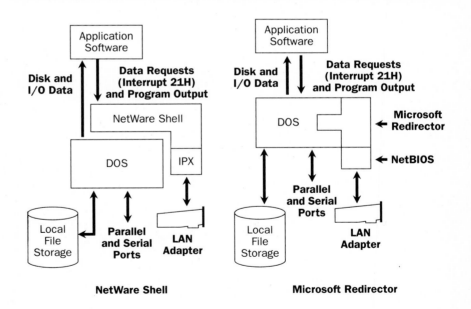

An application program interface (API) is actually a specification describing how application programs, ranging from word processing packages to graphics and spreadsheet programs, interact and request services from the disk or network operating system. The specification describes the *software interrupt* a program issues to identify a request for service, along with the format of the data contained in the request.

For example, when application programs want to access a file on a disk drive, they build a block of data containing the parameters for the request and pass it to DOS by putting its address in a register and generating an *interrupt 21 hexadecimal*. In response to the interrupt, DOS reads the address register and then the data block. All "well-behaved" programs follow this process. Only "ill-behaved" programs go around the DOS services to interrogate the disk drive hardware directly.

In the case of the transport-layer software, the standard API provides the redirector (and certain classes of application programs that make direct calls to the transport-layer software) with a way to send and receive requests to and from the network.

Some operating systems provide only one API for the transport-layer software, typically the NetBIOS API using software interrupt 5C hex.

- Novell has a unique API for its SPX (Sequenced Packet Exchange). SPX is an enhanced set of commands implemented on top of IPX (Internetwork Packet Exchange) transport-layer software and allowing more functions, one of which is guaranteed delivery. An optional Novell module accepts calls from application programs using the NetBIOS 5C hex interrupts and translates them to IPX.

- Microsoft LAN Manager networks can use another API called Named Pipes for special node-to-node applications, and particularly for access to communications and database servers.

The communications portion of the transport-layer software follows a standard protocol—perhaps NetBIOS, TCP, or Novell's SPX—to move information from one network node to the other. Some products, such as LAN Manager, can load instructions conforming to different network protocols on demand, so that the application program can take advantage of transport-layer software using one of two or three protocols depending on the source or destination of a particular packet of information.

Because the driver software is unique to each hardware card, adapter manufacturers usually provide the driver software or include code that you link with code from the network operating system to create a complete module. Western Digital, for example, includes with its Ethernet adapter a floppy disk containing driver software compatible with dozens of communications-protocol-and-API combinations.

The client stations' redirector and driver software could take as much as 50k to 70k of RAM, as it does in NetWare stations. Other operating systems, like those from Artisoft and D-Link Systems, have very small modules and load part of the code in memory outside of the 640k used by DOS, taking only 4k to 10k away from DOS applications. Optional operating-system pieces that might also reside in the client PC include a menu to program available services, electronic mail, and station-to-station chatting.

Some programs, such as QEMM from Quarterdeck Office Systems and NetRoom from Helix Software, provide ways to place network redirector and driver software into memory locations outside of those used by DOS. In addition, in mid-1990 Novell released versions of its network shell that can load and run outside of the RAM used by DOS applications.

Application Programs

Because the redirector routes requests for standard operating-system services from local devices to remote devices on the network, application programs don't have to be "the network version" to be able to save and retrieve data files on dedicated subdirectories in a network file server. The programs exchange data with DOS or OS/2 just as they would if the PC didn't have a network connection.

When a file is shared by several people at once, some level of software must arbitrate simultaneous demands for the same data. Having several applications read the same data at the same time is all right, but reading data while another application is trying to write it can lead to inaccuracy at best and a crashed program at worst. If multiple programs attempt to write to the same portion of a data file at the same time, the resulting data corruption can ruin an entire file.

Before the release of DOS Version 3.0 in 1984, local area network software designers had to put routines in each network operating system to control data access. Unfortunately, manufacturers didn't agree on standards for these routines or their use. You had to buy a customized version of a database product to work with a specific LAN operating system. Often, the database management system (DBMS) you wanted was not available for the network operating system you chose.

Microsoft helped alleviate this situation with the introduction of DOS 3.0 and the version that quickly superseded it, DOS 3.1. DOS 3.0 introduced special commands for multiuser applications:

- ATTRIB makes files read-only to protect them from being changed or erased.

- LASTDRIVE is a CONFIG.SYS statement that tells DOS to make more drive designations available for use. These drive designations are linked to resources on a server.

- SHARE is a command that invokes the DOS file- and data-locking capabilities that will be described later.

When Microsoft added these capabilities to DOS, companies that don't use DOS on the network file server, like Novell and Banyan, added emulation of the DOS data-locking services into their operating systems to stay compatible. When DOS on a workstation locks data on a Novell or Banyan server, the unique operating system in the server responds just as if it were DOS.

DOS 3.3 added other functions useful for LANs:

- APPEND is one command that few people seem to use, but it is certainly valuable on networks. APPEND tells DOS where to search for data files in the same way that PATH tells it where to search for program files.

- FASTOPEN is used by a few LAN operating systems, specifically IBM's older PC Local Area Network program (PC LAN), to improve performance. (IBM's PC LAN requires DOS 3.3 so that it can use the FAST-OPEN command.) Issuing the FASTOPEN command causes DOS to cache file names for faster response. People using DOS-based operating systems such as DCA's 10NET will benefit from including FASTOPEN in their servers' AUTOEXEC.BAT file.

- SET HANDLE is another CONFIG.SYS statement that tells DOS to set aside space for more open file names. In many years of LAN testing I have run into only one instance where DOS reported "Out of file handles," but this could be a problem when several workstations run complex applications on the same server.

All of these DOS commands and statements are useful when multiple stations share a server, but some other features of DOS 3.*x* become critical when several stations try to share the same data file.

You can run any application program on a LAN if you don't plan to let people share data files. The only thing that might keep any specific program from running in a LAN environment is a copy-protection scheme.

Normally, the easiest way to use a program on a network is to use ATTRIB to make the program's .COM, .EXE, and .OVL files read-only and to give each user a private subdirectory in which to store data files. In this way, all parties can use the application program and keep their own separate data files. If they want to exchange files, it is easy and fast to copy the files from one subdirectory on the server's hard disk to another.

Licensing limitations usually prohibit multiple stations from running the same copy of a program, so be sure you don't let more than one person use the same program at the same time, even in separate private subdirectories, if you don't own enough licensed copies of the program. In Chapter 10 I'll introduce a category of software *PC Magazine* has tagged "LAN metering programs." These programs regulate the number of client stations that can access programs and files at the same time.

Data Sharing

When you want to share data files among many people at the same time, matters get more difficult. Let's first consider the case where files are shared like library books—one user at a time.

When an application program opens a data file, the program can set certain restrictions on the simultaneous use of the file by other application programs. The options enabled under the DOS 3.0 SHARE function give programmers the ability to open a file for exclusive use (denying any other application the ability to read or write the file simultaneously) or in other modes that allow reading or writing (or both) by other applications under certain conditions. Application programs can open data files under a condition called Deny None, which makes the file available to all applications for all functions at all times.

Many application programs designed before the introduction of DOS 3.0 open data files using what is now termed the Compatibility mode. This mode, originally designed for DOS 2.0 to have backward compatibility, provides no protection against simultaneous users overwriting each other's data in files. That is why the safest way to install an application on a network is to give each user a private subdirectory for data files.

More modern applications use one of the DOS 3.0 SHARE modes to open a file. These are the sharing-mode options available to a programmer:

0 Compatibility

1 Deny Read/Write

2 Deny Write

3 Deny Read

4 Deny None

Programmers can open a file under any of these conditions. Option 2, Deny Write, is a common sharing mode for network operations because it allows one client PC to change the file while others can only read it. If all PCs need the ability to modify files, then all programs use option 4, and the programmers use special techniques to avoid data corruption.

If an application is not designed to create shared data files, the programmer should write the code to open data files in a mode that denies all access to a second program trying to get into a file. This means that the files created by the application are available to stations on a network on a first-come-first-served, one-at-a-time basis, like a book in a library.

Multiple Simultaneous Access

A database management system is the most common example of multiple simultaneous file access on a LAN. A database is made up of files containing records. Programs running in client PCs often must open several files at the same time in order to read records in each file. Simultaneously, programs on other PCs might have one of the same files open to write records. Obviously, if one station tries reading a record while another is writing it, some kind of problem will occur.

The DOS SHARE feature allows an application program to lock a range of bytes in a file for exclusive use. When an application program issues a DOS 21 hex interrupt and a 5C hex function call (don't confuse this with the 5C hex *interrupt*, which calls NetBIOS), it can then tell DOS how many bytes to lock for exclusive use. When DOS locks these bytes, no other program can write or read them. DOS sends an error message back to any application trying to access a locked data segment.

DBMS packages with their own programming languages—such as dBASE IV, for example—let programmers use this DOS data-locking function by providing an internal command called RLOCK. Typically, database programmers invoke the RLOCK command to tell the application program to lock one or more specific records before they are rewritten, but the DBMS converts this into a command telling DOS to lock a range of bytes.

If you are a database programmer writing applications for a multiuser system, either you or the database program must tell DOS which bytes to lock to prevent one application from reading a file while another application writes it. If you have to remember to issue an RLOCK command (as in the older dBASE III), then the program is said to have *explicit* record locking. If the DBMS is "smart" enough that it will automatically tell DOS to lock a range of bytes while the program writes a record (as in DataEase, for example), then the program is said to have *implicit* record locking.

In a multiuser system, you also have to do something about the application that tries to access a range of bytes when it is locked by another program. Some database management programs will return a "Record locked" message to the application program when they run into locked bytes. The application programmer must anticipate getting this message and find a way to handle it.

The options for handling a "Record locked" return vary. A programmer can decide to build a loop that tells the application to wait a short time and try again, to abort the application, or to send a message to the screen asking the user what to do. Some database programs automate this process by automatically retrying the access. This feature is usually combined with a limit on the amount of time the record may be locked.

So a real application, such as a networked database management system allowing several operators to access and update a warehouse inventory, must contain lines of code directing DOS to lock a range of bytes in a file designated as a record or field while it is in use. The creator of the DBMS application also has to put in routines responding to the "locked" signal from DOS and informing an operator who tries to change a field that it is already in use and cannot be modified. Opening files for shared or exclusive use and handling conflicts over simultaneous access to a given range of bytes in a file are problems faced by people writing networked applications.

The most complex situation takes place when several applications have several files open at the same time. Since records in the different files are indexed to each other in some way, you can get into a situation where two applications simultaneously lock data that both of them need to finish their tasks. This is called a *deadlock* or "deadly embrace" in the classic computer literature. There are many techniques (such as time-outs) to break a deadlock, but all of them slow processing.

Some database management programs—Paradox, for example—don't use the DOS file- and byte-locking options. They do the job for DOS in a more elegant way that is also designed to avoid deadlocks. A Paradox application leaves a message in a special log file while it creates or changes a portion of a data file; when it is finished, it erases the message in the log file.

Other applications check this log file. If one application needs to read a record being written by another application, it will wait. If the wait is too long, the person using the second application receives a message indicating which user has the record locked. At this point, it is up to the people using the data to resolve the problem.

This log-file architecture is a more elegant method of sharing data than the one DOS provides. It is much easier on the person writing applications, but it also puts a greater load on the network and the server. Each application accesses the log file before every access to the data file. Applications writing to a data file write an entry in the log file before each data file access and erase it afterwards. That means there are more packets on the network and many more disk access requests for the server to satisfy than under DOS data protection.

Neither method of protecting data is perfect. You should know the advantages and drawbacks of both architectures. But now, at least, networks of PCs have mature methods that allow many people to use the same data at the same time.

The best advice for the average person acting as a network or database administrator is to choose application programs with good technical-support options. You will often need to talk to an expert on the phone or in person to solve problems. The cost of LAN hardware, network software, and installation is just the opening gambit in the network game. You need good support to install, configure, and manage networked applications.

■ Types of Servers

A network can have up to three generic types of servers: file servers, print servers, and communications servers. Any particular network might have several servers of various types. Remember, I'm using the term server in a functional sense as a device playing a role in the network. Here is an outline of the types and subtypes of network servers:

File servers:

>   Database servers
>   CD-ROM servers

Print servers:

>   On a PC
>   Special devices

Communications servers:

>   Gateways to mainframes
>   Facsimile servers
>   Electronic-mail gateways

Sometimes file, print, and communications services reside in one computer on the network, and sometimes the tasks are spread among many PCs. In networks designed by companies such as AT&T, Banyan, and DEC, one PC makes lots of services available to others. On a network using Banyan's VINES, one server can provide shared file access, communication links to a mainframe, and long-distance links between servers using X.25 technology. Figure 8.2 provides a generic view of the servers and client stations in a practical network.

Companies like Microsoft and Artisoft design their network operating systems so that many PCs can act as servers of various types, even while people are using them to run standard applications. In a network using Novell's NetWare, the PCs acting as servers are typically dedicated to that task.

A *file server* makes hard disk storage space (up to a gigabyte or more) available to the client PCs. The file server answers requests for data read and write actions, routed from application programs by the redirector software in each client PC, and mediates simultaneous requests for access to the same data.

Database servers, a subset of the file-server category, include those servers that make expensive hardware such as CD-ROM or optical disk available, as well as "back-end" database processors. The latter machines process special commands—often in IBM's Structured Query Language (SQL)—from database query programs running on networked PCs. They receive simple requests for reports from the client stations and execute the complex code needed to extract and compile the information from a raw database. Because the database-engine software runs in the PC acting as a file server, the query programs don't have to pull files over the network cable for sorting and matching in the client PCs. This architecture reduces the communications load on the network but puts a heavy processing load on the PC with the database.

Figure 8.2

PCs can act in multiple roles on a network. This diagram shows a network with three servers: a file server doubling as a print server, a communications server with a shared modem, and a remote print server. The communications server can also run standard applications as a personal computer, though there is always a trade-off when a computer simultaneously runs applications and provides network services. MS-DOS and OS/2 client stations share the resources.

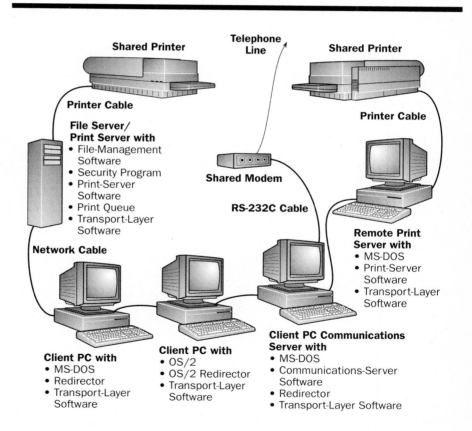

The *print server* accepts print jobs from application programs running on the client stations, stores them on a hard disk, and sends them to a printer when their turn comes up in the queue. A print server can typically address up to five printers simultaneously. The same computer often serves as both file server and print server, although in many LAN architectures any PC on the LAN can act as a print server.

The possible roles of a *communications server* are more diverse than those of the file and print servers. The functions of a communications server range from linking client workstations on the LAN with mainframe computers to sharing a pool of expensive modems or a facsimile board among the client stations. *Fax servers* provide everyone on the network with the ability to share the hardware for incoming and outgoing facsimile transmissions. PCs acting as communications servers are usually dedicated to that task. Communications servers perform one of the most interesting and potentially valuable functions on a LAN because they allow sharing the cost of expensive communications resources.

All of these different types of servers make possible the applications providing the functional and economic rationale for installing a network; the ability to share information and the efficiencies provided by electronic-mail or workgroup-scheduling programs all justify a LAN. Of course, servers need special software—the LAN operating system—to handle the many tasks involved in sharing resources.

The Structure of Server Software

The sharing software in file, print, and communications servers comes in many different modules. Communications servers run software that translates between the network and whatever communications speeds, data alphabets, and protocols the external connections use. File-server software includes sophisticated queues for requests and usually some kind of disk cache. Disk caching loads large segments of the data from the hard disk into RAM to satisfy requests from fast memory instead of from the slower hard disk.

Servers have the same kinds of transport-layer software as workstations. The server also runs software that buffers and queues requests for service from the network stations. The server software typically includes some kind of security protection based on either a password attached to each resource or a table of rights assigned to each named user.

File servers might use DOS to access their files, but only for the sake of simplicity and economy. DOS is not a multitasking operating system, so it must queue requests for service arriving from several clients, and it doesn't provide the fastest access to files. High-performance LAN file-server operating systems, like those from AT&T, Banyan, Digital Equipment Corp., DSC Communications, Microsoft, and Novell, handle multiple tasks at once, and they have very efficient hard-disk file formats that are capable of handling gigabytes of storage.

The choice between DOS and a multitasking operating system as the underpinning of the file server marks a significant difference between two kinds of LAN operating-system products. PCs running a file-server operating system based on DOS keep their ability to run standard applications at the same time. Since it is possible to share files or printers with the network and still run local applications, all PCs on the network can act as combination server/workstation "peers." We call these *peer-to-peer networks*. Multitasking file servers typically are not also used as workstations, although some—particularly LAN Manager servers running over the operating system OS/2—technically can run both file-server software and normal applications.

File-server software in peer-to-peer networks resides in the individual PC's memory and divides or "slices" the processor's time between file services and the standard applications. The RAM left for applications is typically about 400k, and the programs run more slowly than normal, but many people happily share drives and printers on multiple networked PCs using peer-to-peer systems.

Network operating systems have many component modules, but today's software isn't difficult to install, and the default installation parameters usually provide excellent operation. LANs based on multitasking operating systems often have more features and options, so configuring their software is more difficult. Yet with careful attention to the manuals, anyone comfortable with DOS can install and manage these systems.

The Elements of File-Server Software

You can break file-server software down into three major elements:

- The *file-management system* writes and reads data on one or more hard disk drives.

- The *disk cache system* gathers incoming and outgoing data into a cache in RAM memory for faster handling than the physical capabilities of a hard disk would allow.

- The *access system* controls who may use the data and how multiple applications simultaneously access files.

These elements of the file-server software are really sophisticated applications that run over a file-management system. Some products, such as Artisoft's LANtastic and DCA's 10NET, rely on DOS as a file-management system. Microsoft's LAN Manager is an application running over the OS/2 operating system. But in many products, such as Banyan's VINES and the 286 and 386 versions of Novell's NetWare, the application and file-management systems are unique and tightly integrated.

In some products, particularly LAN Manager and some versions of NetWare, the application runs on top of standard multitasking operating systems such as OS/2 or Unix. These multithreaded task managers can handle multiple communications and processing tasks at a time. They have a much firmer footing than DOS to support heavy loads of data requests from client stations.

The multitasking LAN operating systems—those able to let hundreds of nodes access gigabytes of data on a single server—set the pace and direction of the industry and determine how people will connect to, across, and out of their network environments.

Multitasking operating systems like NetWare, OS/2, and Unix provide important options for flexible, secure, and reliable connections. A network of PCs running with one of these operating systems can shove minicomputers out the back door in many organizations.

File-Management Functions

Regardless of whether the file management system is DOS, OS/2, Unix, or the highly specialized system underlying NetWare, its basic function is to move the heads of the hard disk drive and deliver data to the client stations through the network. Specialized programs, however, use techniques for fast and orderly movement far beyond what DOS can handle. Products like Novell's NetWare and Microsoft's High-Performance File System (HPFS) use all of these techniques in an attempt to gain maximum efficiency and throughput.

A technique called *elevator seeking* makes operation of the hard disks more efficient. The heads on a hard disk drive must move in and out on the spinning disk to read and write data. Each large movement takes milliseconds of time. The elevator-seeking software improves efficiency by queuing and ordering requests requiring head movement into orderly steps in the same direction. The order of the requests' arrival doesn't matter; each request is satisfied in the most logical fashion. This allows the drive heads to operate in a sweeping motion, from one edge of the disk to another. Elevator seeking improves disk drive performance by significantly reducing disk head thrashing and by minimizing head seek time.

A *directory-hashing* technique indexes directory entries according to a mathematical formula for fastest retrieval. Two types of directory hashing expedite directory access. The first hashing algorithm indexes the volume directories, while the second indexes the files by volume and subdirectory. Directory hashing reduces the number of directory reads after the server starts operation. NetWare and other file systems take good advantage of directory hashing.

Server operating systems typically cache entire directory structures of volumes attached to the server. During initialization, the operating system reads entire volume directories into memory and continually updates them. First the copy in server RAM is updated; then the operating system updates the physical volume as time permits between servicing user requests. The technique provides fast response, but it carries a potential danger. If a power failure or other problem takes down the server before the volume is updated, the file can be damaged.

Disk Caching

Disk caching, the process of using server RAM to hold the most recent and frequently requested blocks of data from server storage, greatly enhances retrieval times. Hard disk drives can retrieve data in times measured in terms of hundredths of a second. Solid-state RAM can deliver the same data in thousandths of a second. When modern computers handle thousands of requests a second, people using client stations can perceive the difference a disk cache makes in delivering data to the screen.

Application programs typically request data in blocks of less than 1k. Caching file systems, however, will typically pick up at least 4k of data surrounding the requested bytes and place them in RAM. Network administrators can often tune the caching software to use different sizes of data blocks.

Caching doesn't help speed processing of the initial requests for data, but when the responses to subsequent requests for related data can come from the cache, they move more quickly than when they come from the hard disk. In many operations, the cache hit rate—the number of data requests satisfied from the cache—will exceed 80 percent.

File caching also speeds up user writes to network files. Requested writes are cached in flagged file-cache blocks. These blocks are systematically written to disk between the handling of other user requests. But caching file-write actions is usually an option that network administrators must turn on, because a write cache has one significant drawback. If the hard disk or server system suffers a catastrophic failure or power outage, the data waiting in cache to be written is lost. You must balance the potential efficiency improvement in a busy network against the potential loss of data due to a malfunction.

High-Reliability File-System Options

Fault tolerance, the ability to continue operation despite the failure of significant subsystems, is a relatively new factor in local area networking. As more users put their most valuable applications onto networks, fault tolerance has become increasingly important. Some network operating systems, notably the System Fault Tolerant (SFT) versions of NetWare, include capabilities to store data simultaneously on more than one drive for improved survivability. Some companies provide improved survivability options for 3Com and Unix operating systems also.

Novell has offered SFT versions of NetWare for several years with such features as bad-block revectoring, disk mirroring, and disk duplexing. SFT

NetWare is complex and significantly more expensive than the standard version. SFT NetWare carries a retail price of $4,995, compared with $3,295 for the standard version. Implementing a full SFT system can more than double the cost of data storage on a file server and still does not guarantee a crash-proof system.

In *bad-block revectoring*, a technique Novell refers to as *HotFix*, a small piece of software monitors the hard disk drive to detect malfunctions caused by a bad section of magnetic media on the drive. When it detects this problem, the software attempts to recover any available data and to revector the file address map to point to its new location. The software also marks the block of media as bad so that it isn't used again.

The *disk-mirroring* technique requires two disk drives: a primary and a secondary one. Ideally, the secondary disk is identical to the primary one; if not the same, it must be of the same type and larger than the primary disk, although the extra space will not be utilized. All data copied to the primary disk is also sent to the "mirror" disk, although not necessarily to the same physical location. If the primary disk fails, the secondary disk immediately takes up the current task with no loss of data.

Another basic feature of disk mirroring is that data can be read from the mirror disk if a read error occurs on the primary disk. Read-after-write verification and HotFix are active on both disks. Therefore, the bad block on the primary disk will be marked, and the correct data from the mirror disk will be written to a good location on the primary disk. This completes a loop allowing full recovery from read and write errors.

Disk mirroring becomes *disk duplexing* through the addition of a completely separate hard disk controller card. This redundant configuration further improves reliability. Disk duplexing also benefits LAN throughput by allowing a technique called *split seeks*. When simultaneous multiple read requests occur, both drives receive and process them immediately, effectively doubling disk drive throughput and overall system performance. In the case of a single read request, the operating system looks at both disk drives to determine which can respond best. If both are equally occupied, NetWare will send the request to the drive whose current head position is closest to the desired data.

In summary, disk mirroring requires only one controller card and uses a second disk, which can immediately pick up a failed operation with no loss of data. Disk duplexing, with a controller card for each drive, enhances system performance by sending simultaneous writes and read requests to both disks through separate disk channels. It also allows continued operation if a disk controller fails. Disk mirroring and duplexing both provide additional levels of system survivability.

Security Systems

The concept of sharing resources and files carries a lot of appeal in terms of both economy and improved productivity. But too much sharing can become too much of a good thing. Server software must provide some way to differentiate the requests coming from different client stations and to determine whether each person or station has the right to receive the requested data or service. No one wants an unauthorized employee reading personnel or payroll records. You often need to limit the activity of network users to certain files to prevent both mischief and inadvertent damage.

A LAN software package typically uses one of two types of file security plans (Microsoft's LAN Manager makes both techniques available). The first plan gives each shared resource on the network a "network name;" a single name can designate a whole shared drive, a subdirectory, or even a file. You can associate a password with a network name and limit the read/write/create capabilities associated with that password. This scheme, used by DOS-based networks, makes it easy to shift the shared resources, but one user might have to keep track of several passwords. Security is easily compromised when password management is a constant headache.

The other security architecture uses the concept of groups: Each person belongs to one or more groups, and each group has specific access rights. This architecture, used by NetWare and VINES, makes each person responsible only for one personal password. The LAN administrator can easily move people into different groups as they change jobs or leave the organization.

Both types of security architecture typically enable an administrator to allow or deny individuals or groups of users the ability to read, write, create, delete, search, and modify files. For example, you might want to give data-entry clerks only the ability to modify accounting files in order to prevent people from copying your financial files for their own purposes. A few operating systems even include a capability called "execute-only." This function allows a person only to run a program, which can't be copied or accessed in any other way. Appropriate use of various security options safeguards your important information.

DOS-based networks have uniformly poor physical security for the server. Anyone who can get at the server's keyboard can access files on its hard disk. This problem was shared by early releases of LAN Manager but was dealt with in Version 2.0. Servers using multitasking operating systems— NetWare 2.X, NetWare 3.X, Nexos, and VINES—don't allow access to files from the server; you must go through the network's security system to get them.

The encryption of passwords, both when stored on-disk and during transmission, is an important feature in high-security applications. Where previously a technician could easily attach a network analyzer to the cable and capture passwords and data files as they crossed the network, NetWare 3.X now includes encrypted passwords to thwart anyone tapping into the cable.

The Print-Server Functions

Computers acting as print servers make printers available for shared use—in some cases up to five for each print server. Print servers store incoming jobs as files in a special subdirectory called a *print spool* on a hard disk drive. When the full print job has arrived in the print spool, its file waits in a queue for the first available printer (or a specially designated printer).

The drive that holds the print spool could be on another PC acting as a file server, but this arrangement puts a lot of traffic on the network as print jobs move from the PC running the application to the print server, from there to the spool on the file server, and eventually back to the print server for printing. In common practice, either the print-server function is located together with the file-server software or the PC acting as a print server has its own hard disk.

Networking software products such as Artisoft's LANtastic allow any networked PC running DOS to act as a file or print server, or both, and still run application programs. Microsoft's LAN Manager gives the same server abilities to OS/2-based PCs. Novell's NetWare lets you combine file- and print-server functions in the same PC or establish separate print servers. PCs acting as NetWare file servers can't run applications, but the print-server software can reside in a PC used to run application programs.

The biggest advantage in designing a network with separate print servers is the ability to arrange the geography of the network to suit the users. If you combine the print-server and file-server functions, you must locate the shared printers close to the server hardware, primarily because of distance limitations on parallel-port connections. Since the PC acting as a file server for a robust network has many noisy hard disk drives, powerful fans, and probably a bulky uninterruptible power supply, it's usually consigned to a remote location—perhaps even behind a locked door for security. You'll have to plan carefully or have a lot of luck to find a location suitable for the file-server hardware and convenient for people trying to retrieve finished print jobs.

Sharing printers through conveniently located personal workstations acting as print servers seems like a good way to overcome the problem of where to locate printers. While the idea of utilizing a PC simultaneously as a print server and as a personal workstation has appeal, it also has practical limitations. You can only slice a PC so many ways until the people at client stations and the person using the machine for local applications all receive slow service. Hardware interrupts generated by serial- and parallel-port activity and concurrent requests for access to the hard disk can slow down even the fastest PC when it operates as both a server and a personal workstation.

The decision of whether to make a print server part of a file server, part of a client PC, or a dedicated node hinges mainly on how much printing the client PCs will do. If your organization prints no more than 30 to 50 pages of plain text an hour, then combining the print server and file server makes sense. But heavier printing loads and considerations about the printers' physical location might dictate using separate print servers or print servers combined with client workstations.

As the number of print jobs coming from the client stations builds, and as the complexity of application programs increases, only people running lightweight applications find it practical to contribute printer services to the network through their PCs. The common practice is to set up dedicated PCs as network print servers in convenient locations around the office. This architecture takes space and requires the full resources of a PC, complete with hard disk, monitor, and keyboard, for each print server.

Special Print Servers

In late 1990, a new category of products showed up at PC Magazine LAN Labs. At first, we called them *Ethernet peripheral-sharing devices.* This mouthful of words describes their function, but it isn't a phrase likely to stick in the minds of buyers. After much brainstorming, we decided to call them what they are: *special-function servers.*

These products from Castelle, Hewlett-Packard, Intel (Figure 8.3), and Microtest attach to a network cable and make printers available to the client PCs using Novell software, without the need for any other hardware. The Intel and Microtest products also have varying capabilities to act as communications servers. Their size—the Intel and Microtest units are about as big as VHS videotape cartridges—allows you to place special-function servers with their attached printers or modems on any table or rollaway printer stand. And their price, between about $500 and $1,000 list, gives you an affordable alternative to using a PC as a print or communications server.

The processors in these devices use special software contained in read-only memory. They don't need attached monitors, drives, or keyboards. Special-function servers typically use print-server software running on a NetWare file server to receive and store print jobs, but then they take those jobs from the queue, over the network cabling, and send them to the printer. This architecture moves the print job over the cable at least twice—something purists will moan over—but no one can deny the practicality and value of these special-function servers.

While the initial versions of these products worked only on the IEEE 802.3 Ethernet cabling scheme under NetWare, later versions allow various

Token-Ring and LAN Manager combinations. These products will not work with DOS-based LAN operating systems.

Figure 8.3

Intel PCEO's NetPort print server for Novell and Ethernet networks allows users to locate printers anywhere along the network. NetPort™ is a trademark of Intel Corp.

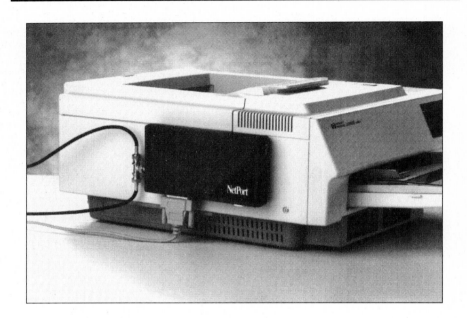

The Communications-Server Functions

The phrase *communications server* covers a variety of tasks. Communications servers can act as gateways to mainframe computers, allowing client PCs to share a costly mainframe communications channel. They can make pools of expensive high-speed modems available for sharing on a first-come-first-served basis. And they can run software such as Action Technologies' Message Handling Service (MHS), which is able to link different electronic-mail systems.

Unlike print servers, the major consideration for communications servers isn't geometry; you can set them anywhere you find a phone line. The major consideration is CPU power. While a print server buffers the print jobs going to the printers, communications servers must provide real-time connections between client PCs and communications channels. This puts a heavy load on the PC acting as a communications server.

Handling the hardware interrupts generated by the serial and parallel ports keeps the CPU in a communications server very busy. Few people will enjoy running application programs on a PC that simultaneously functions as a communications server. So in today's typical network, communications-server software usually runs on a separate PC dedicated to the task.

I'll talk a lot more about communications servers in all their forms in Chapter 12. For now, you just need to recognize the important role that communications servers play in linking LANs to each other and to other resources such as mainframe computers, nationwide networks, and facsimile services.

■ The Network Operating System Is a System

Network operating systems contain many pieces and parts. Often, you can select options and configurations—such as transport-layer software or application program interfaces—that are uniquely suited to your organization. But such interactive systems need careful management. In the next chapter, we'll consider the most popular network operating systems and give some emphasis to their practical capabilities and limitations.

CHAPTER

9

The Best LAN Operating Systems

- Industry Trends and Evolutions

- The NetWare Family

- VINES

- LAN Manager

- Digital and AT&T

- POWERserve

- LANtastic

- Choosing Server Hardware

- Choosing Networking Software Products

This chapter provides detailed overviews of the best-selling and most technologically advanced network operating systems. We'll describe Novell's NetWare in its various flavors, Banyan's VINES, Microsoft's LAN Manager, Artisoft's LANtastic, and operating systems from Digital Equipment Corp., AT&T, and Performance Technology.

These descriptions won't simply tout the benefits of each product. The PC Magazine LAN Labs crew and I have spent enough time with each of these products to see their limitations as well as their assets.

We'll begin with a quick look at industry trends and the impact of competition on the LAN operating systems.

■ Industry Trends and Evolutions

Here are some things you should know.

- The major LAN operating systems are all fast enough for practically any organization's needs.

- Compatibility and interoperability between operating systems are available and improving.

- NetWare has by far the largest market share.

- Every other manufacturer, Banyan and Microsoft included, has only a small slice of the pie.

- Microsoft's LAN Manager, Version 2.0, is a worthy challenger to NetWare.

- DOS-based products, such as LANtastic, have a bright future.

The size of the market and the potential for profits make for hot competition among LAN operating-system vendors. Novell, which has had as much as 70 percent of the market share in PC-based networks, is no longer the only game in town. Even though the current crop of network operating-system companies have not yet taken away much of Novell's market share, the group, with Microsoft leading the way, are throwing more marketing and development dollars into their products.

In 1989, network operating-system companies fueled the growth of networks by announcing and delivering products conforming to open standards instead of proprietary protocols. AT&T, Digital, and 3Com led the industry in providing interoperable products for open standards. Instead of trying to lock-in and control each account with unique communications standards, they lured buyers with software that worked according to nationally and internationally accepted standards.

In the 1990s, the companies in this market continue to promise buyers more compatibility and interoperability. This trend has gone so far that now companies not only support open standards, they also deliver software for each other's proprietary protocols. AT&T runs Microsoft's LAN Manager over the Unix operating system instead of its native OS/2; Novell's Portable NetWare runs over DEC's VMS, Unix, and OS/2. 3Com created Demand Protocol Architecture (DPA) for Microsoft's LAN Manager, supporting many different protocols, including NetWare, DECnet, and others. The DPA software loads and unloads protocol stacks to address different servers as needed for each transaction.

In the practical sense, support for multiple protocols means that an administrator can configure a networked PC so that the DOS F: drive is a VINES file server, the G: drive is a NetWare file server, and the H: drive is a LAN Manager server. The person using this PC doesn't need to know anything about the operating systems to access the data on each server. This capability is available today, but the pieces and parts must be carefully integrated so they mesh without binding.

Improved interoperability and flexibility are prime marketing and technology goals for networking-software companies in the '90s. Just as you can mix and match Ethernet adapters from different vendors, so will you have the means of easily mixing elements of network operating systems and linking servers running different operating systems on the same network, all supplying services to the same clients.

Performance and Other Important Factors

We've learned a lot about network performance in four years of testing at PC Magazine LAN Labs, but we have also learned that some important factors are more difficult to measure: Reliability, technical support, compatibility, and management features are more important than throughput to the average user. In terms of speed, all of the operating systems described in this chapter perform well enough to meet almost any computing needs.

Under a heavy network load equaling the activities of one hundred typical workstations, a typical file server delivers a 50k file to a client PC in 1.4 seconds—about the same performance as a PC AT's hard disk supplies. Under a lighter network load you'll get better file retrieval times from these systems than you will from the hard disks usually found in 80286-based desktop machines of the late 1980s.

Another conclusion I've drawn from our testing is that a PC acting as a file server is an interactive and relatively homogeneous system. It's difficult to comment on the importance of one part of the system without commenting on other system parameters.

For example, with today's drives, disk controllers, software, and LAN adapters, the speed and type of the processor don't seem to make much difference after you get to a 20-MHz 386. This will change in the next few years with the introduction of more applications that run part of their code on the server, but it will change slowly.

Investing in an expensive server with a Micro Channel or Extended Industry Standard Architecture interface does you little good if your hard disks and controller aren't adequate to the task. But the amount of processing power and the interface bus you buy will make a difference in the coming years if you run more tasks in the server and install fast hard disk systems.

RAM, RAM, and More RAM

Network operating systems consume RAM both in the client PCs and in every PC that acts as a server. On the client side, many companies such as Artisoft have created compact programs, while other companies have successfully found ways to put the redirector and driver software elements into memory above the 640k block of RAM used by DOS. In the mid-1980s, the client PC redirector software used more than 100k, but client nodes now need only 50k to 70k. MS-DOS, Version 5, introduced the ability to load network software above 640k, and companies such as Helix Software provide utilities such as NetRoom with similar capabilities. NetRoom also allows placing drivers in the area called *extended memory*, above 1 megabyte.

Even as the RAM requirements for client PCs shrink, the servers need more memory than ever. For example, NetWare 3.X works in a server with 2.5Mb of RAM, but it prefers 4Mb, and while LAN Manager operates in 4Mb, Microsoft suggested we use 10Mb when we installed it on our computers.

Client/Server Computing

The hot buzzword in the LAN operating-system market is *client/server* computing. In the client/server architecture, certain disk-intensive tasks stay on the file server. The concept of client/server computing was explained in the previous chapter. This technique lowers network traffic congestion, but it increases the load on the server's processor.

As you load more jobs onto the file server, it requires more RAM and processing power. As you gain power in the server, you can add more features in the LAN operating systems—and the cycle repeats itself. New software, usually chasing the power of the new hardware, will increase the importance and presence of network operating systems in an increasing web of computer interconnections.

With such factors as interoperability, compatibility, and manageability in mind, let's turn to the specific operating systems you can buy today. We'll start with the winner of many acquisition decisions, Novell's NetWare.

■ The NetWare Family

In 1982, in a small office by the steel plant in Orem, Utah, Ray Noorda, Judith Clarke, Craig Burton, and programmers from a company called Superset foresaw what PC networking could become. Their competition at the time was from companies mainly interested in selling hard disks, like Corvus Systems, but Novell has always been directed toward providing software for integrated computing systems.

When times were tough and the financial backers put pressure on Ray Noorda to turn a quick profit, he kept Novell headed toward the longer-term goals of providing software, systems tools, and support. NetWare 3.11 is at least the eighth major revision of a product that services more than four million people on over 400,000 LANs.

Novell's product strategy has been crystal-clear and consistent: Market an operating system with good features and performance, and do everything possible to create the environment it needs to run. Novell is primarily a software company, but it entered the hardware market several times to develop new products or to drive down hardware prices through competition. Novell never overtly used the strategy of "account control"—raised to a fine art by IBM—to capture business. Instead, it went to great lengths to build outside support and even to stimulate competition. Its philosophy of "NetWare Open Systems" is in step with the trend toward standards today.

The NetWare product family set four milestones for other PC-based network operating systems to meet.

- Novell was the first company to introduce a network operating system for true file sharing as opposed to simply writing private unshared files to a shared hard disk.

- It led the way to hardware independence by providing NetWare with the ability to run on more than 30 different brands of networks and over 100 different network adapters.

- Novell reached companies needing reliability with System Fault Tolerant (SFT) NetWare. SFT NetWare ensures data integrity by including the Transaction Tracking System (TTS), disk mirroring, and disk duplexing.

- Open Protocol Technology (OPT) was the fourth milestone. By providing a protocol-independent architecture for all NetWare services, NetWare supports heterogeneous connectivity.

The Entry Level System (ELS) NetWare products provide solutions for small networks where cost is a concern. ELS Levels I and II let you set up single-server networks that do not need internetwork routing services and the safeguards of SFT NetWare. ELS NetWare offers nearly all the features of its big brother—such as supervisor control, time-accounting capabilities, and file caching—but is limited to eight simultaneous users. One machine on the network acts as a server/workstation and makes its drives and printer available to client PCs.

NetWare 2.X, previously known as Advanced NetWare 286, provides support for medium-size networks (up to 100 users) and internetwork routing services. SFT NetWare adds disk mirroring and duplexing, providing networks with added reliability.

Portable NetWare consists of portable C code for all the NetWare services licensed to computer manufacturers for integration into their operating systems. With NetWare 3.X, previously known as NetWare 386, Novell provides the industry with the platform necessary for building networked applications, in addition to incorporating all the features in previous versions of NetWare.

All of the NetWare products share features such as high-performance disk caching (with elevator seeking and other techniques), strong security, and the ability to use a wide variety of network adapters.

Novell is a serious company that sets goals and has a good track record for meeting them. That is important to keep in mind, because a lot of the appeal of NetWare comes from the promise of continued support and integrated products.

ELS NetWare

In early 1991 Novell stopped selling the Entry Level System (ELS) versions of NetWare for small network installations, but ELS NetWare is still widely used. These products provided neither dedicated-server nor true peer-to-peer operation. The PC acting as a file and print server can also run application programs, but not all networked PCs can contribute resources to the network, as they can under products such as Artisoft's LANtastic.

At a list price of around $1,900 (and a much lower street price) for the software to support eight users, ELS NetWare Level II was slightly more expensive than other operating-system alternatives for small LANs. ELS NetWare Level I, a four-user version of the software with fewer capabilities, sold poorly. People who bought low-end NetWare typically purchased ELS II.

Generally, ELS NetWare takes about 50k to 60k of RAM in each client PC. PCs acting as file and print servers use 1Mb of extended memory for file service, leaving approximately 590k for applications software (all nondedicated server processes run in extended memory).

ELS NetWare II supports Macintosh connectivity, making integration of Macs and PCs across a network less expensive than it would be with most of Novell's other connectivity solutions. This operating system will run on 80286 or 80386 PCs, supporting IBM PCs and compatibles and PS/2 clients running DOS Version 2.0 or later or OS/2.

ELS NetWare provides good security, Macintosh integration, and the opportunity of getting help from the hundreds of companies that specialize in installing and integrating NetWare. But those three points were its only significant advantages over the less costly and much more flexible alternative of using a DOS-based operating system like Artisoft's LANtastic. There was no smooth upgrade path between ELS NetWare and Novell's next-level product, NetWare 2.X. The ELS products were a dead end and Novell replaced them with lower priced versions of NetWare 2.X for small LANs.

NetWare 2.X

In the late '80s and early '90s, shipments of NetWare 2.X (Figure 9.1) formed the basis for Novell's $500 million annual revenue. NetWare 2.X services medium-size networks of up to 100 users. It can work with data files up to 255Mb in size, which is a limitation in certain classes of applications. Theoretically, however, you can attach up to 32 gigabytes of data storage to a single server. The SFT version of NetWare 2.X adds disk mirroring and duplexing, providing networks with added reliability.

Under NetWare 2.X, one computer acts as the server that provides file and print services. The software does allow you to set up remote print servers around the network.

Novell bases all network transport-layer communications on its own Internetwork Packet Exchange (IPX) and Sequenced Packet Exchange (SPX) protocols. IPX, NetWare's native network communications protocol, moves data between server and/or workstation programs running on different network nodes. IPX usually exchanges data with the NetWare shell, but it also works with the NetBIOS emulator available in NetWare, and with programs such as terminal-emulation packages that exchange data with communications servers. SPX is an enhanced set of commands implemented on top of IPX, allowing additional functions—one of which is guaranteed delivery.

Testing at PC Magazine LAN Labs has consistently shown the advantage of SPX/IPX for typical PC applications. Applications running on PCs typically request data in small blocks, often as small as 512 bytes. SPX/IPX is better suited to moving small blocks than the transport protocols of competing operating systems such as Banyan's VINES and Microsoft's LAN Manager. Those products excel in other kinds of tasks such as LAN-to-LAN communications, which use larger blocks.

Figure 9.1

The box containing Novell's NetWare comes with the software for one server and all the client PCs. You order the hardware separately.

If you need NetBIOS service for applications like 3270 terminal emulation, Novell provides a NetBIOS API for SPX/IPX that works well. You simply type "NetBIOS" on the PC needing the NetBIOS service, and DOS loads a 40k program giving SPX/IPX the ability to use the NetBIOS application-program interface. NetWare 2.X is not a peer-to-peer operating system; therefore the workstations on the network cannot share their resources without the addition of third-party products.

Installing NetWare 2.X is not a walk in the park. Value-added resellers have amassed years of experience configuring NetWare 2.X servers for their customers. You need to plan ahead and install all the network hardware you'll want to use in the near future, because just about any changes you make will require several more hours to regenerate the operating system.

NetWare has an excellent security system with many options. The primary security structure assigns people to groups; each group has specific rights. Of course, a group might consist of only one person or it might contain hundreds of people. This structure works well in organizations of any size, and is particularly useful in organizations where people move between jobs and those with high personnel turnover. The network administrator can easily add a person to or delete a person from a group such as Accounts Payable and be certain of effective security. Additionally, administrators can restrict the days and even times when users can log on to the network. Forced periodic password changes require all users to adopt new passwords at selected time intervals.

The only drawback of the security system in NetWare is the need to create and update the data that identifies groups, rights, and users on every file server separately. In large multiserver networks, this becomes a constant task for network administrators. As I'll describe later, Novell has an answer to this problem in NetWare Naming Service.

Probably the biggest shortcoming of NetWare 286 overall is its print-spooling software, which is generally difficult to use and not as fast as competing products. Fortunately, printer-enhancement programs—notably PS-Print from Brightwork Development and LANSpool from LAN Systems—can aid network printing by improving throughput and providing the ability for client stations to make printers available across the network.

Electronic mail can become a tremendous asset to any organization. NetWare does not include e-mail, but Novell does include an important service that third-party e-mail systems can use. It's called Message Handling Service (MHS). MHS is a piece of software that runs on a single PC in the network and transmits users' messages between e-mail and other application packages marketed by many companies.

Until the middle of 1989, Novell's NetWare 2.X had been the standard of comparison for network operating systems. When the rest of the field started closing in on NetWare's speed and security, Novell released a new product, NetWare 386. NetWare 386 takes full advantage of the power in the Intel 80386 and 80486 processors. NetWare 386 and existing NetWare 2.X servers can coexist on the same network, and you don't have to make any changes to the client workstation software to give them access to all NetWare servers.

NetWare 3.X

In NetWare 3.X, Novell provides the industry with a powerful platform for building client/server applications. Two features put NetWare 3.X in a class by itself: increased capacity and a $7,995 price tag. By today's standards, NetWare 3.X is very fast; it doesn't degrade under heavy processing loads, and it provides huge amounts of storage. Potentially, it is a rich environment for the introduction of a new generation of applications.

Many of us can remember the days when we thought a 20Mb hard disk would handle all of our storage requirements. Although it is tough to predict the computer requirements of the future, you won't outgrow the RAM access and disk storage capability of NetWare 3.X anytime soon. By the same token, outfitting a PC today with NetWare's theoretical maximums is not possible. You would find other alternatives before you sat through a PC's memory check of 4 gigabytes of RAM (1G = 1,000Mb).

Specifications

NetWare 3.X is a true 32-bit network operating system designed for use on Intel 80386 and 80486 processors. If NetWare 3.X detects the presence of a 486 processor, it takes advantage of the chip's advanced features by executing longer instructions (more commands per CPU cycle). Three other PC-oriented network operating systems—Banyan's VINES, DSC Communications' Nexos, and Microsoft's LAN Manager—operate the 386 processor in its protected mode. Nexos has a built-in data-management capability that gives it very fast performance in certain applications, and VINES has powerful communications capabilities, but none of these products enjoys the wide support of NetWare.

Novell moved into the minicomputer arena with its new file system. The file system in NetWare 3.X keeps all the old tricks of elevator seeking, I/O queuing, and disk caching, but it adds huge capacity. Sporting a maximum disk space of 32 terabytes (1Tb = 1,000,000 megabytes), NetWare 3.X can handle the data load of the largest organizations. Volumes can span multiple drives, and you can have files as big as 4 gigabytes. That means a single data file may be spread across several hard disks and your application will never know the difference.

Gone are NetWare 2.X's restrictions: 100 users, 1,000 open files. NetWare 3.X allows each server to have up to 250 users and 100,000 open files. If a rare application requires 100 simultaneously open files (for example, multiple data tables, indexes, help files, and drivers), the old NetWare 286 is limited to giving 10 users simultaneous access to that application. Under NetWare 3.X, 250 users can run a hundred-open-file program with capacity to spare. Novell has made provisions for adding still more users in subsequent releases.

The maturity of NetWare 3.X shows in the way it reports error messages. When I mistakenly left the cable from a NetWare 3.X server disconnected and tried to start the operating system, it responded with an on-screen message saying, "The network cable is not connected to the computer." That's a pretty clear error message! Another time, a NetWare 3.X server sent me a special message reporting that it was receiving an unusual number of bad packets from one of the client stations. When I inspected the network connection, I saw a small crack in the T-connector. These are good examples of how NetWare 3.X helps the network administrator succeed.

Novell has announced an interesting upgrade: the NetWare Naming Service. Typically, when you want to use resources on multiple servers in a NetWare network, you must log on to each server. The multiple log-on actions can be automated, but it's a lot of work for network administrators.

The NetWare Naming Service, available in 1991 for NetWare 2.X and NetWare 3.X, gives users a simple way to access multiple NetWare servers, and offers network managers centralized administration. NetWare Naming Service uses the concept of *domains*, a set of servers grouped into a logical unit. By logging on to a domain, users log on to multiple servers transparently.

NetWare 3.X includes two security enhancements: security auditing and encrypted backups. A security auditing function keeps a nonmodifiable audit trail of all security changes occurring on the server. Moreover, as NetWare backs up files over the network, the data is sent and stored in encrypted form, and unencrypted only when it gets back to the server after a restore.

NLMs

NetWare Loadable Modules (NLMs) are applications—often developed by companies other than Novell—that run in the file server. This category includes simple programs like drivers for Micro Channel cards, complex but familiar products like SNA and electronic-mail gateways, and products for network management, security, and workgroup productivity. NLMs allow the powerful server to replace the dedicated network machines you might be using today as SNA gateways, electronic-mail gateways, and communications servers—but not without some risk.

While NLMs offer great functionality, they run in the same machine as the file-server software and at the same time. If the file-server hardware malfunctions, you lose all the functions in it. (In today's most common network configuration, with separate PCs acting as different kinds of servers, if the file server goes down you can still use SNA gateways and some other services operating on separate machines on the network.) What's more, if some task requires, an NLM can access the kernel of the NetWare 3.X operating system. If the NLM crashes, it could potentially bring down the file server.

The Btrieve software, Novell's key-indexed record manager, is the back-end processor for the new client/server computing model and is optimized for the Intel 80386. This data-management service provides a good base for server-based applications and lets you maintain compatibility with the 10,000 existing Btrieve applications.

The remote-console NLM allows system administrators to monitor server information from their workstations. This feature is a network administrator's dream. An administrator can sit at any workstation and monitor any server on the network. In addition, the administrator's computer acts as if it were the server console, allowing an administrator to load and unload NLMs and completely control the server.

The print-services NLM provides the spooling and queuing of print jobs for up to eight printers. It also allows authorized users to access and manipulate print jobs. The print-services NLM supports printers attached to local workstations, and it manages up to 16 printers on the network. This flexibility lets organizations do high-volume printing at the most convenient and secure locations. While the print-spooling NLM performs much better than the older NetWare 2.15 software, it is relatively slow compared with LAN Manager 2.0's Print Manager.

To keep just anyone from adding an NLM to the server, Novell includes the Secure Console option, restricting anyone but the system administrator from adding NLMs or server applications. Another feature that makes the system manager's life simpler is the new Workgroup Manager classification. As the name implies, this person has supervisor privileges for the users assigned to a workgroup.

Programming for NetWare

The hefty NetWare 3.X shipping box includes diskettes with all the programming tools necessary to create distributed applications. The C Network Compiler comes complete with the 286 Watcom C Compiler and Linker, a C graphics library, the Btrieve library, the Express C editor, the NetWare API Library, and a windowing debugger. Programmers can use these tools to create DOS- and OS/2-based workstation front ends for accessing the server applications.

For creating NLMs, Novell provides the C Network Compiler/386. It has all the same functions as the regular compiler but is specific to the 80386 processor and NLMs. Along with these compiler packages, Novell includes NetWare Remote Procedural Calls for 386 and the NetWare Streams specification. Streams is AT&T's name for its method of handling many simultaneous tasks by means of the Unix operating system.

Since programmers can access the kernel of NetWare 3.X, a book called *NetWare Theory of Operations* (included with the software package NetWare Programmer's Workbench) provides warnings to developers about actions inside the kernel, where the slightest mistake could bring down the server. To provide additional guidance, Novell also holds classes for NLM system developers.

Installation

You can install NetWare 3.X faster than you can install, for example, Microsoft's Windows—and with less hassle. To bring the server to life, the system administrator only needs to identify what types of network card and hard disk are installed. I've installed the operating system and had users logged on within about 15 minutes, not counting the time necessary for preparing the hard disk. This is a far cry from the several hours needed to bring up an early NetWare 286 file server. However, I would like to see Novell apply the same effort to simplifying the generation of NetWare shell software for the client PCs. You still have to go through an involved process to create the NetWare shell software.

Upgrading from NetWare 2.X to NetWare 3.X requires you to reformat your hard disk. NetWare 3.X boots from a DOS partition (or floppy disk) and then runs the SERVER.EXE program, which in turn accesses the NetWare partition.

On the client PC side, NetWare 3.X gives OS/2 client stations full IPX/-SPX, NetBIOS, and Named Pipes support. The introduction of Named Pipes paves the way for applications using this powerful peer-to-peer communications architecture.

DOS users will be extremely pleased with the new NetWare shell software. By supporting expanded and extended memory, NetWare frees 34k of conventional memory for applications. Users of client PCs can unload NetBIOS and the workstation software, freeing memory when you don't need the network.

Integration with Microsoft Windows, Version 3.0, makes it easy for users to attach to file servers and printers without exiting Windows. With Windows' NETPOPUP program, workstations receive broadcast messages in a window without disrupting any running applications.

Novell provides companies moving from NetWare 2.X to NetWare 3.X a smooth transition. If you have extra hard-disk space available on another server, simply copy the entire server being upgraded to another one. After installing NetWare 3.X you run the UPGRADE program, which converts all of your NetWare 2.X system information, including passwords, user rights, and mappings, to the new format.

Functions

The most innovative feature of NetWare 3.X is Dynamic Resource Configuration. System administrators and users alike benefit from this artificial intelligence–type feature. NetWare 2.X requires the system manager to allocate specific amounts of memory for directory caching and routing buffers, and to bring the server down any time these values change. With NetWare 3.X, not only can these values change with the server up, the operating system itself determines the optimal values and adjusts them on the fly.

A few other new or enhanced features are also of interest. The Multiple Name Spaces feature allows NetWare 3.X to handle files from different operating systems. NetWare 3.X associates different file names with the same file if it will be used by different operating systems. For example, a Microsoft Excel file used by both the DOS and Apple versions of Excel would have two file entries when stored on the server.

NetWare 3.X provides added data security with file-salvaging and encryption features. One file-salvaging option automatically purges all deleted files, and another maintains all deleted files until NetWare runs out of disk space.

As NetWare needs disk space, it purges on a first-deleted basis, and the system manager can purge all recoverable files at any time. NetWare preserves security by letting only users with proper authorization undelete a file. In addition to encrypting passwords on the server, NetWare 3.X encrypts them on the wire, preventing network analyzers like Novell's LANalyzer from reading what the client PC sends to the server.

The NetWare 3.X Bottom Line

NetWare 3.X is everything users and application developers could ask for in a network OS. For the users, the file system is fast, reliable, and spacious. System maintenance is simple, and you can expand your network in terms of both the number of users and the number of file servers. It also provides programmers with the platform and all the tools for creating next-generation server applications.

There are many good reasons for buying NetWare 3.X: increased throughput, ease of installation, 250 users, 100,000 simultaneous open files, and reduced system maintenance time, to name a few. A change in the price structure in 1991 made it easier for organizations with smaller networks to afford the more powerful NetWare version. Prices range from $3,495 for a 20-user package to over $12,000 for 250 users.

Two other operating systems provide large capacity and sophisticated management capabilities: Banyan's VINES and Microsoft's LAN Manager.

■ VINES

Banyan System's VINES (VIrtual NEtworking Software) is a network operating system that carries a strong flavor of the complexity and features found in traditional minicomputer software. The VINES system is actually a series of applications running over a special version of AT&T's Unix operating system, but the Unix layer is hidden by VINES and is not available for other application programs. A PC running VINES typically performs all server functions, including acting as a communications server. This concentration of functions makes the multiprocessor capabilities of VINES particularly important.

The technical specifications for VINES put it in competition with NetWare 3.X and LAN Manager. At about $6,000 for a full network software package, it is also in the same price range. VINES led its competition in its ability to connect widely separated file servers efficiently through a variety of long-distance communications alternatives. For this reason, VINES finds its best acceptance in large network installations.

You can just about pick the hardware platform that you want to use for your VINES server. Banyan offers its own Network Server, Desktop Network Server, and Corporate Network Server—PCs with different processor and expansion capabilities—which will all run VINES. Any PC using an Intel 80286, 80386, or 80486 processor is a candidate to be a VINES server.

On the software side, you can choose from VINES/386 Micro Channel, VINES/386, or VINES/286. Banyan also markets a special version of the software, shown in Figure 9.2, for a Compaq SystemPro computer with multiple CPUs. The operating system underlying VINES/386 is AT&T's Unix System V, Release 3.2.1. While the 386 products can hold their own, the 286 product might need a hard look. A 286 processor gets a heavy workout running the Unix-derived operating system used in VINES/286. This 286 product is targeted at small or remote workgroups.

Figure 9.2

Banyan markets its VINES operating system in versions for many different CPUs. This is a special version for the Compaq SystemPro using multiple processors.

The client software requires 115k of DOS memory. This number can go down to as little as 20k on a computer with a 386-type processor using a product like Quarterdeck Office Systems' QEMM or Helix Software's NetRoom. These programs can put the networking software into memory above 1 megabyte so that other programs have more space in standard RAM. The memory requirements vary, depending on the specific driver being used and how the system is configured.

Banyan pioneered the use of a valuable feature for networks with many file servers—a feature called *global naming services,* which has been emulated by Novell and Microsoft. Banyan calls its naming service StreetTalk. Street-Talk provides a way of naming resources and users located on various servers and nodes across the network. The VINES software lets you assign each resource a name in the form "Item@Group@Organization" and a password. Every server maintains and updates a universal Access Rights List (ARL) containing the StreetTalk names of the resources and the users allowed access to each resource. The administrator doesn't have to log on to each server and configure resources and user rights. One step does it all. This technique makes it easy to establish a high level of resource security and reduces the administrator's workload.

VINES also has a feature called StreetTalk Directory Assistance (STDA). STDA allows users to find network resources faster by replicating directory information on multiple servers throughout the network. This feature is most useful for extremely large networks with multiple servers.

One feature that sets VINES apart from the popular Novell and Microsoft LAN operating systems is the fact that StreetTalk allows users to access gateway services, mail systems, print queues, fax gateways, and host gateways with a single password. Another advantage Banyan has over the competition is its experience in client/server computing. VINES offered SQL database operations on the server years before other products did.

Banyan is committed to supporting industry standards. In cooperation with Microsoft, Banyan has given VINES the ability to work with SMB, NDIS, NetBIOS, Named Pipes, mailslots, and LAN Manager APIs. Because VINES can work with this acronym-laden list of interfaces, companies writing application software for networks find a common development environment and a larger potential market for their products.

The VINES operating system uses a specially designed version of Unix V to run on computers with multiple processors. Unlike other multiprocessor operating systems that assign specific types of tasks to specific processors (Microsoft's LAN Manager, for example), VINES divides tasks evenly between the processors by finely parsing the stream of work and assigning tasks to the available processors on a first-free-first-tasked basis. VINES can assign tasks to as many as eight 80386 and 80486 processors in a single PC.

VINES provides an all-in-one-box solution for connecting to remote servers and transferring data to other servers, SNA gateways, async services, database servers, and mail servers. Banyan also offers a host of communications products aimed at mini and mainframe computers. These include products for server-to-server communication within the LAN, over a wide-area network, or through an X.25 network, as well as products for 3270/SNA terminal emulation, e-mail, and remote network management.

As a communications server, the computer running VINES has a variety of ways of connecting to IBM mainframes. For example, Banyan's 3174

Emulation/Token-Ring product allows a VINES server to communicate with an IBM computer using the SNA communications protocol over a Token-Ring network or through an IBM 3174 controller or 3745/372X communications processor. This feature lets people use a single IBM Token-Ring network for both PC-to-host and PC-to-server traffic and provides greater throughput when accessing the host.

Additional Token-Ring support comes through a feature called *source-level routing.* This technique allows VINES servers or clients to communicate across IBM Token-Ring bridges to remote VINES servers, so users gain flexibility in configuring Token-Ring networks. Another feature, *Token-Ring bridge emulation,* puts the bridge function inside the server and eliminates the need for dedicated PCs operating as Token-Ring bridges—with some added load on the server's processor.

Overall, Banyan's VINES is a strong contender in the mainstream network operating system market. NetWare and LAN Manager file servers provide faster throughput than VINES file servers for PCs running typical applications, but the throughput of VINES is good enough to support dozens of client PCs on one 386 PC acting as a file, print, and communications server.

As nationwide corporate networks become more common, VINES will play an increasingly important part in the decision process of network administrators.

■ LAN Manager

When AT&T, DEC, HP, IBM, Microsoft, NCR, 3Com, and a score of other companies back a single product, it's a good bet that this product will be important. The product these companies are putting their resources behind is called LAN Manager. LAN Manager is a network operating system jointly developed by Microsoft and 3Com, but many companies sell LAN Manager under their own labels. For example, IBM ships LAN Manager as IBM Server Manager. 3Com shipped the first retail package of LAN Manager Version 1.0 in October 1988, calling it 3+Open LAN Manager.

When choosing a company to buy LAN Manager from, keep in mind that the underlying software is the same, but in most cases each company integrates the software into its product lines in a different way. If you don't have any special needs for an integrated system, then choose the company that will give you the best support.

The original implementation of LAN Manager was not strong enough to compete with NetWare. Lack of security and so-so performance prevented LAN Manager from becoming the big hit that Microsoft and IBM expected. But LAN Manager Version 2.0, released late in 1990, started a whole new ball game. Microsoft came to the plate with a big stick. It took all the criticism the industry tossed out and addressed each issue in Version 2.0. In particular, Microsoft answered complaints about security by producing a product as secure as any of its competitors.

LAN Manager 2.0 is a serious and worthy challenger to the predominance of Novell's NetWare in the PC LAN market. LAN Manager 2.0 performs well; it is compatible with all of the LAN application programs marketed today that follow DOS 3.1 procedures, and it is a great platform for growth. The major drawback is that it gobbles server RAM as a whirlpool sucks ocean water. But the reason it gobbles RAM is the same reason it is a good platform for growth: It works over OS/2.

It is important to understand that in a LAN Manager network, OS/2 is required only on computers acting as servers. Client workstations *can* use OS/2, but workstations using plain old MS-DOS can also be clients in a LAN Manager network. The file-server software uses OS/2 as its file system in the same way that NetWare and VINES use a unique operating system and Unix, respectively, as the file systems on their servers. All of these network operating systems can service both DOS- and OS/2-based client PCs on the same LAN. The interaction of OS/2 and DOS applications across the LAN is a different problem, but it is much more a question of the applications than the operating system.

Because LAN Manager uses the multitasking operating system OS/2 on the server, it avoids the problems inherent in older operating systems like 3Com's 3+Share and IBM's PC LAN that augment or modify DOS to get it to do more than one thing at a time. And because it uses OS/2, LAN Manager carries the promise of supporting distributed computing applications that mutually share the power of the servers and workstations in ways that make sense.

With the exception of a few database development systems that can assign some tasks to the server, you can't buy many real distributed applications using the OS/2 communications capabilities today, but well-known and unknown companies continue to discuss their plans for OS/2 distributed applications. When they come along, it will take a robust and flexible LAN operating system like LAN Manager to support them.

The ability to let a computer act as a file server and run OS/2 applications at the same time is unique to LAN Manager among the high-powered LAN operating systems. This architecture gives LAN Manager a smooth entry into a computing technology called *distributed processing*. Under distributed processing, application programs can borrow free CPU processing power from around the network.

HPFS File System

The single biggest improvement in LAN Manager 2.0 is a speed increase gained from Microsoft's new High-Performance File System (HPFS). Microsoft departed from the original File Allocation Table (FAT)–based system developed for floppy disks over ten years ago. At that time hard disks for PCs were rare. As hard disks became popular in the early '80s, the patches to DOS did not manage large amounts of data efficiently.

Like NetWare 3.X, LAN Manager 2.0 can handle gigabyte-size files and heavy traffic loads. The standard Microsoft offering comes with two versions of HPFS, one for computers based on the Intel 80286 and another for those using i386/i486 chips. Each OEM determines what its customers get.

You need a 386 or 486 processor to gain the performance and local security that HPFS can provide. Although LAN Manager 2.0 will run on a 286-based server, I don't recommend it.

Dual-Processor Capabilities

LAN Manager runs on PCs with dual processors, such as the Compaq System-Pro, by running any server-based application (such as SQL Server) on one processor and 386-specific versions of HPFS and the network I/O subsystem on the other. This explains why file requests are not satisfied faster with two processors than with one. If LAN Manager is the only task running under OS/2, the second processor stands idly by, waiting for something to do.

Developing Applications for LAN Manager

Developers creating applications for OS/2 and LAN Manager have a wide choice of ways to use the LAN to communicate between nodes. The available application program interfaces (APIs) range from those that are unique to PCs, like NetBIOS, to those that are universal across machines from different manufacturers with different operating systems and architectures, like TCP/IP and OSI.

One widely publicized LAN Manager API is called Named Pipes. Named Pipes is a software feature available on every LAN Manager node, including servers and even DOS-based client PCs. It lets a program on one node invisibly communicate with programs running on other nodes. PC-based LANs are able to do this today using the NetBIOS services that almost every LAN operating system provides. Communications servers, some electronic-mail packages, and other services typically use NetBIOS in today's networks. But the Named Pipes API is "higher-level" and much easier for programmers to implement than the NetBIOS interface. Additionally, Named Pipes should be faster than NetBIOS in some applications, because the session between nodes is maintained through multiple transactions instead of through individually addressed blocks of data.

The power of Named Pipes is appealing, but its popularity is not assured. IBM's system designers have developed a competing communications scheme that is universal across their systems, called Advanced Program-to-Program Communications. Additionally, all of the versions of LAN Manager will continue to support the NetBIOS API, and there are a growing number of available application programs that directly address NetBIOS.

Regardless of sideshow arguments about the use of a specific API like Named Pipes, it is clear that Microsoft and 3Com have put a lot of effort into making LAN Manager appealing to software developers. These companies fully support international standards and promote easy-to-use program interfaces.

Buying and Installing LAN Manager

Microsoft's LAN Manager Entry Level System carries a $995 price tag. The only real limitation of this system is that it has a one-server, five-user license. The LAN Manager Advanced System includes a one-server, unlimited-user license and retails for $2,995. You can upgrade the five-user package to unlimited users, or you can upgrade the network by adding an unlimited-user server and keeping the five-user server. The one thing you cannot do is to add a second five-user server into the LAN.

As you plan your LAN, you should know that LAN Manager servers can interoperate with existing servers and workstations using IBM's older PC LAN software. Additionally, IBM and 3Com have demonstrated the compatibility between LAN Manager and the client-station software contained in IBM's OS/2 Extended Edition. If you have PC LAN, you can add a LAN Manager server without changing the workstation software and, if you wish, you can retain any existing PC LAN servers on the network.

The LAN Manager package contains ten manuals and the diskettes. The Entry Level System comes with 5 1/4-inch diskettes, but you can trade those for 3 1/2-inch diskettes if you need them. The LAN Manager Advanced System comes with both sizes of diskettes.

The documentation for LAN Manager is excellent. The *LAN Manager Installation and Setup Guide* is a complete and well-written 80-page book that spells out every detail of the installation. All of the manuals use flow charts, screen diagrams, and step-by-step instructions to lead you through the installation and management of OS/2 and the network.

Installing LAN Manager with OS/2 and HPFS on the server should take between 30 and 45 minutes. OS/2 gives the file-server software disk-caching abilities, hard-disk partitions of up to 4 gigabytes, and a maximum file size of 2 gigabytes. The operating-system software, however, can use only a maximum of 16 megabytes of RAM; this might not be enough to run some database-server software in the file server. The version of OS/2 you get with LAN Manager is licensed for installation only on the network server. If you want to set up OS/2 workstations, you should buy additional copies of the operating system for those nodes.

On the client-station side of things, setup is just as easy—if you have a hard disk. Without one, setting up the LAN Manager 2.0 client software is difficult. The documentation does not explain how to install the software on floppy disks. If you call Microsoft's technical-support line or contact your LAN Manager reseller, those people can explain how to install the workstation software on either 3 1/2-inch or 1.2Mb 5 1/4-inch diskettes. The software will not fit on 360k diskettes.

During the installation, you have three major decisions to make:

- You must decide whether you want to dedicate the computer as a server or give it the ability to function both as a server and as an OS/2 workstation.

- You must choose between one of two security schemes.

- Finally, you have to decide what network protocols you want to use.

The manual explains these decisions, and they are reviewed in the following paragraphs. You should consider them beforehand, because if you make the wrong choice you might have to regenerate both the server and workstation LAN software.

The choice between a dedicated and a shared server is more complex with an OS/2-based system than with a DOS-based system. Getting dual use out of a DOS-based PC usually means that both LAN and local operations run equally poorly. It also means that the server is always in danger of being locked up by a local application or an unthinking three-finger reset.

Under OS/2, the danger of locking up the entire machine is small. The operating system handles multiple access, so the decision between dedicated and shared operation hinges on the extent of competition for the disk drive between local and network programs, the availability of RAM, and security concerns. I typically configure LAN Manager servers for dedicated operation, but using a fast 386-based computer as both a server and a workstation is a reasonable proposition under LAN Manager.

LAN Manager will operate under either of two security arrangements. The first system, called *user-level security*, assigns passwords to resources like disk drives, I/O ports, or anything you designate with a network name. This scheme is typical of DOS-based networks, particularly those using the older Microsoft MS-Net software. It is flexible, yet it can be very specific because each user could theoretically have a unique password for each resource. This scheme can also be a large burden for an administrator.

The second scheme, called *share-level security*, is more typically associated with minicomputer multiuser operating systems. Each user is given membership in one or more groups. The access rights and security restrictions of the group control the individual. This arrangement is generally considered better for larger networks, because it simplifies departmental and workgroup file management. LAN Manager modifies the typical share-level arrangement by letting the administrator specifically deny a user access to a resource that is otherwise available to the group.

Originally, a LAN Manager 1.*x* server provided no local security. Anyone with access to the physical computer could boot from an OS/2 diskette and access all the files on the hard disk. Now, with HPFS386, system administrators have two types of security for the file system. The "local security" option in the setup program restricts any hard-disk access to users with the proper permission. Before users can access the hard disk (even if LAN Manager is not running), they must log on locally. Even without the "local security" option set, HPFS386 stores access permissions for each file and directory in extended attributes with the file. This prevents anyone from looking at data on the disk with the standard HPFS.

The third decision you must make when you install LAN Manager is which protocol software you want to use to transmit messages across the network. Microsoft and 3Com products typically use a protocol called Xerox Network Services (XNS) to transport and acknowledge receipt of data across the LAN. XNS is a widely supported protocol, and network devices such as bridges and routers from many different companies use it. But IBM uses a different protocol under its all-encompassing Token-Ring architecture called Data Link Control (DLC).

To ensure compatibility with IBM Token-Ring installations, Microsoft's LAN Manager and other companies' LAN Manager packages include IBM's DLC protocols as an installation option. DLC messages can travel across IBM Token-Ring bridges. You probably need to take the DLC option only if you plan to use Token-Ring adapters.

Microsoft bases LAN Manager 2.0's interface to network adapters on the Network Driver Interface Specification (NDIS) codeveloped and copublished by 3Com. Every major company in the LAN adapter market has NDIS driver software for its hardware. The industry's broad acceptance of this protocol lets you choose from a huge selection of network adapters.

A LAN Manager server can use up to four network interface cards in its internal bridge. This allows you to mix and match cards and media inside the server to accommodate existing networks and different physical layouts.

Using multiple adapters in a server PC also increases reliability and improves throughput in large networks.

After you answer the final server-installation questions, the LAN Manager installation software copies files to the appropriate drive and modifies the server's CONFIG, STARTUP.SMD, and initialization batch files for each session.

Once you install the server software, you run through similar menus and decisions to create the client-workstation software. One nice feature of the installation software is that it is self-configuring for the video adapter in each station. The amount of memory that LAN Manager uses on a DOS workstation varies according to the protocol and other services you install. In the first version of the software, the protocol driver and redirector take about 150k of RAM. If you add Named Pipes and other services, you can lose over 200k of RAM to networking software on a DOS workstation.

If you run a DOS-based workstation with an 80386 processor, you can use a special device driver to load most of the software into high memory. The exact amount of RAM you save depends on how much memory is taken by video and other high-memory functions.

3Com's Additions to LAN Manager

3Com has done more to customize LAN Manager than any other company even though they no longer sell this operating system. Figure 9.3 shows the Microsoft version of the LAN Manager operating system. An important program 3Com added to LAN Manager is the Connection for NetWare. This software allows DOS-based workstations to attach simultaneously to LAN Manager and both NetWare 3.X and 2.15 servers. DOS clients can access file and print services on all servers without regard to the host operating system. While this program works with all versions of LAN Manager 2.0, 3Com does not license the software separately.

3Com accomplishes the trick of working with both operating systems through a technique it calls Demand Protocol Architecture (DPA). DPA loads an unmodified Novell IPX protocol stack and the NetWare shell on top of the same NDIS adapter driver supporting LAN Manager. DPA doesn't simply emulate the NetWare shell; it uses native NetWare client software to access NetWare servers.

Novell uses the IPX communication protocol to talk to NetWare servers. Cleverly, DPA creates an NDIS-compliant IPX driver by linking an IPX-to-NDIS translation program to the NetWare IPX object file created during shell generation. After the program is linked, the driver loads and unloads through the services of DPA. With DPA, LAN Manager can allow users to use NetWare servers only when needed and then unload the IPX protocol, freeing memory for other DOS applications.

3Com no longer sells LAN Manager. The company has refocused on internetwork connectivity, but their work helped bring the product to a market now served by Microsoft, AT&T, DEC, and others.

Figure 9.3

Microsoft's LAN Manager is a robust network operating system supported by AT&T, IBM, Microsoft, and many other companies.

Administrative Resources

LAN Manager includes several administrative utilities that help users access shared resources and help the administrator regulate the users. These menus conform to IBM's Systems Application Architecture. This means the menus are highly graphic, and many people will find it easier to work their way through them with a mouse than with a keyboard. You can control all the resources and make all the connections in a network using the menus, but in case you like to use batch files to control things, LAN Manager has a command language too.

The popularity of IBM's PC LAN networking software and the related MS-Net products marketed by other companies led to the adoption of the MS-Net command language in the industry. This command language contains commands such as Net Share and Net Use and a concept called Sharenames. Net Share makes a resource available, Net Use links a workstation to the available resource, and a Sharename is a handy way to refer to a resource. For example, Sharename lets you share files by calling them Accounts instead of "SERVER1\D:\DBMS\ACCNTG\PAYABLE\JUNE" or something similar. If you want to use it, LAN Manager uses the same command-language syntax as PC LAN.

LAN Manager makes administering large networks much easier with centralized management features. Network managers can logically group a set of servers together as one domain and administer it as a single server. This allows the network managers to change users' rights, passwords, and time restrictions for all servers at once and not on each individual server. Managers can also safely delegate certain types of management tasks, such as disk backup or print-queue management, to other people. Additionally, a complete set of security utilities allows fine control over end-user access to the system. Through the Remote Administration facility, network managers can do all of these things from any OS/2-based workstation.

Other management tools include a network auditing facility, network statistics and error logging, and automatic scheduling of events:

- The network auditing facility allows managers to monitor the use of any network resource.

- LAN Manager logs error messages and network performance statistics that may be useful in fine-tuning the server. LAN Manager 2.0 includes a self-tuning memory-management facility like the one in NetWare 3.X. This artificially intelligent feature dynamically reallocates memory buffers, allowing the server to give the fastest possible response.

- Remembering to perform certain tasks at a specific time each day or month is monotonous. This is where auto-scheduling comes in. It can send messages and run programs at preset intervals, freeing the administrator for more thought-intensive tasks.

LAN Manager 2.0 supports diskless workstations better than NetWare 3.X. Unlike NetWare, LAN Manager allows each computer to have its own AUTOEXEC.BAT file. This allows system administrators more flexibility for configuring the users on the network. In addition, each user can have a unique log-on batch file. Conversely, NetWare's log-on scripts offer more functionality than normal DOS batch files.

Auto-reconnect is a big convenience for users. If the network goes down, the auto-reconnect feature establishes the network connection when the server comes back up. As long as the workstation wasn't expecting something from the server at the moment of failure, the user doesn't know the server was down. This saves users the effort of logging on again and re-executing the Net Use command for all of the resources they were using.

LAN Manager now has built-in fault tolerance, including drive duplexing, disk mirroring, and a new file-replication system. These features match any offering on the market. File replication lets administrators automatically duplicate specified files across servers at predefined intervals. HPFS manages bad disk space and reroutes the data to other sectors, similar to NetWare's HotFix.

With an uninterruptible power supply (UPS), LAN Manager protects the server from power failures. Unlike NetWare, which uses a special interface, LAN Manager communicates with the UPS through a standard RS-232 port. When the power goes out, the UPS signals LAN Manager, which in turn sends a warning to everyone on the LAN. If the battery drops below "10 percent remaining life" before power is restored, the server is shut down safely.

LAN Manager does an excellent job of handling shared printers through the OS/2 Print Manager. Microsoft and 3Com obviously learned from some of the problems people experienced with shared printing under early versions of MS-Net. LAN Manager's print-job-management capabilities include the standard functions like prioritizing and managing the jobs in the print queue. You can also control form feeds and set the system to hunt for available printers for certain kinds of jobs. LAN Manager includes a PostScript de-spooler that makes it easy to use networked printers for desktop publishing. OS/2's Print Manager will not let anyone without the proper security level modify a print job.

Another interesting sharing feature lets serial devices like modems, scanners, and printers be pooled and shared across the LAN. Thus, these serial devices can be addressed by an application program as if they were attached to a local serial port.

You can administer a LAN Manager server from the server itself or from any workstation running OS/2 on the network. If your network has more than one LAN Manager server, you can create a separate OS/2 management session for each server on the management workstation.

LAN Manager contains good capabilities for monitoring and troubleshooting network operations. A display screen called Net Statistics reports data such as the number of I/O actions, active sessions, and network errors, and even the average response time. LAN Manager sends automatic messages to the administrator when certain problems arise, such as a malfunctioning printer or an excessive number of bad password attempts. A feature called the Alerter service can forward alert messages to another user on the network.

The network administrator has several tracking and recording tools too. The Audit Trail service keeps track of who used server resources and what kinds of actions they took. You can set up the audit log to record when users open files and access I/O ports. A real-time report on the active sessions is available to the administrator; it shows who is connected to the server, how long the connection has been up, and how long the connection has been idle. An administrator can force a session closed to disconnect a user or free up resources.

Performance

NetWare 3.X typically outperforms LAN Manager 2.0 in throughput tests. Still, both operating systems provide such good performance that who finishes first isn't as important as the total capacity and power these operating systems provide. If you assume that this performance is adequate, then network decisions can be based on more important criteria such as application compatibility, support, flexibility, and cost.

LAN Manager is a young product, but the people behind it are skilled and have done their jobs well. It is clearly a powerful network operating system with enough features to please the most jaded administrator of a large LAN. The competition between LAN Manager and NetWare will shake out and sharpen the marketplace; all buyers and most resellers will benefit from the renewed emphasis on standards and the room for innovation that LAN Manager brings.

■ Digital and AT&T

I can't discuss serious network operating systems without describing the approaches taken by two important companies, Digital Equipment Corp. and AT&T. Digital Equipment Corp. has introduced or sponsored many networking concepts, most notably Ethernet. Digital is the second-largest computer company, after IBM, and the current focus of its products and sales is clearly on networking.

AT&T doesn't have a big share of the LAN software market, but many important architectures and products, including Unix, have come from its laboratories, and it is a leader in the design of 10BaseT hardware. The company provides a wide range of services, and is an important integrator and installer of complete network solutions.

Digital and AT&T have many similarities beyond size and the ability to provide everything you need in networking products and services. Most notably, they both have major LAN operating systems based on Unix—although Digital provides alternatives AT&T does not have—and they both sell their own versions of Microsoft's LAN Manager. Both companies also back IEEE 802.3 Ethernet in competition with IBM's backing of IEEE 802.5 Token-Ring as a favored network cabling and signaling system.

After a brief look at Digital's non-Unix networking products, I'll tell you how to use a computer running Unix as a server for a network of PCs. You'll find more information on using the TCP/IP protocols, which are often associated with Unix, in Chapter 13.

Digital's Networking History

Digital Equipment Corp. got its start in the 1950s in an old textile mill in Maynard, Massachusetts. Founder and CEO Kenneth Olsen saw a need for computers that could do things other than the accounting and payroll functions prevalent at the time. Olsen had a vision of computers that would be affordable to engineers and scientists and would not require a sterilized environment to operate.

From its first minicomputer, the PDP-1, to the present-day VAX series of super-minis, Digital has come a long way. The PDP-1 was announced in 1959 and was the first of its kind. It came with an unheard-of innovation, a CRT integrated into the console. The system was housed in a cabinet about the size of a refrigerator, but it required only normal office power and air-conditioning.

The VAX 11/780 computer was introduced in October of 1977 and was Digital's attempt at competing with the king of the hill—IBM. The idea was to provide a more powerful computer that would give current Digital users a path to migrate upwards without totally junking their existing investment in software and peripherals. The VAX 11/780 offered a "compatibility" mode in which software written for the PDP-11 series of minicomputers would run without modification. It also contained a compatible bus structure so that existing peripherals could be used.

In May of 1980 Digital made another significant announcement. Along with Xerox and Intel, Digital introduced the plans for Ethernet to the world. Ethernet provides a way to connect computers in offices and across campuses with economy and speed. The capability let Digital set its target squarely on becoming the largest computer company ever.

With the release of the first VAX computer, Digital also came out with its Virtual Memory System, or VMS. This operating system was written to take full advantage of the 32-bit architecture of the VAX hardware. The VAX 11/780 with VMS was a true multitasking/multiuser hardware/software system.

When it introduced the VAX 11/780, Digital also announced a networking product called DECnet, which became the basis of all Digital networks. DECnet is a network architecture, implemented primarily in software, allowing multiple computers to link using any of several kinds of connections and to share resources such as large disks and printers.

The original DECnet was designed for parallel interfaces and was intended to connect computers located within 20 or 30 feet of each other. Serial interfaces were available for longer distances, but they were much slower than the parallel connections.

With Digital's announcement in 1980 of its Ethernet plans, DECnet took on a new significance. The DECnet protocol layers fit nicely over the Ethernet cable and signaling scheme.

Today, DECnet over Ethernet cabling is Digital's preferred networking solution. Digital's customers represent a huge base of Ethernet connections, which they use to link terminals, minicomputers, and PCs together in networks that are becoming increasingly integrated.

Digital recognizes that integrated multivendor systems are the rule today. In mid-1989, it began selling a full line of completely IBM-compatible PCs that Digital remarkets from Tandy Corp. Perhaps more importantly, the system architecture now has room for many non-Digital products. Technical-support people from Digital have been to Novell's schools, and they will help you put Novell's LAN operating system NetWare on a VAX. The folks from Digital know many different ways to integrate PCs and VAX computers, and to link networks of these computers to IBM mainframes.

Digital's Pathworks

There are several products in the market that provide Digital's minicomputers with the ability to act as servers for networks of PCs running DOS. Digital's minicomputers run on one of two operating systems: VMS or Ultrix. VMS is the most widely used operating system, but Ultrix, a version of Unix, is growing in popularity. Digital markets a product that has gone through several name changes, but is now called Pathworks for VMS. Additionally, Novell markets a completely different product called NetWare for VMS.

The people at Digital Equipment Corporation once had very ambivalent feelings toward Unix. For much of the 1970s and 1980s, a lot of Digital's hardware ran versions of AT&T's Unix operating system instead of Digital's competing VMS. Now, seeking a more flexible stance, the people at Digital offer an implementation of Unix they call Ultrix for their hardware. The Ultrix operating system is an alternative to VMS on hardware as diverse as the $10,000 DECsystem 5100, the $190,000 DECsystem 5800 RISC minicomputers, and a wide variety of older architecture VAX computers. In the middle of 1991, Digital released a version of Microsoft's LAN Manager called Pathworks for Ultrix.

All of the basic capabilities of the AT&T implementation of LAN Manager apply to Pathworks. The software products for the client PCs are called Pathworks for DOS and Pathworks for OS/2. Each client license costs $195 for either operating system. These are typical LAN Manager redirector and NetBIOS products with the ability to use adapters following the NDIS protocols and to take advantage of memory above 640K with HIMEM.SYS.

Digital also includes support for electronic mail programs, including the Simple Message Transport Protocol and Digital's VAXmail. The client package also has TCP/IP capabilities so applications and utilities using TCP/IP will work across the network to the Ultrix software that also includes TCP/IP. The Pathworks for DOS package also provides peer-to-peer networking because it includes DECnet-DOS, a peer-to-peer program built on Microsoft's older MS-NET software.

As one of the strongest proponents of Microsoft Windows, Digital's people believe in graphical user interfaces. Their Pathworks for DOS package includes a VT-320 terminal emulator designed to run under Windows. They have a version of the X Windows System called PC DEC Windows. This product allows a person using a PC to execute and display an Ultrix DECwindows application in one window and a VMS DECwindows application in another.

People with networks of Digital's computers are likely to continue to expand the use of Digital's products while simultaneously linking them to other networking systems. Pathworks for Ultrix provides an excellent way to link PCs running DOS and OS/2 to Digital's RISC and VAX hardware and to other computers running LAN Manager and NFS.

Datability's RAF

PCSA has some competition from a product marketed by a company called Datability Software Systems. This vendor's Remote Access Facility (RAF) consists of client PC software and file/print-server programs for Digital's VAX computers.

RAF provides all of the features you'd expect in a mature network operating system. Applications running on the client PCs have full access to files on the host VAX, complete with file locking and multiple simultaneous access to the same data files.

On the VAX, the RAF host software works like PCSA, translating DOS or OS/2 requests from the client stations into VMS file procedures. As with PCSA, data is stored in VMS file format and is accessible by native VMS programs. But RAF has two advantages over PCSA: price and NetWare compatibility. The RAF host software for each VAX costs about

$300. The PC software, at $495, is a little pricey, but there is room to negotiate for volume purchases.

When you run the RAF client software on a PC, you can also run NetWare. For instance, if you have both NetWare and RAF servers on a network, you could redirect a client PC's F: drive to a Novell file server and its G: drive to a VAX running RAF. Managers of multivendor facilities love this kind of capability.

Overall, the translation between the client PCs' DOS or OS/2 requests and the VMS format on the VAX slows down both PCSA and RAF, so neither system has the throughput of a dedicated NetWare or LAN Manager server. But the ability to mix and match servers (as you can with Datability's RAF) lets LAN administrators blend performance and compatibility into a perfect system for each organization.

Unix Networking

Unix is a multitasking operating system with widespread popularity. On one end of the spectrum, Unix runs on high-powered desktop computers called *graphic workstations,* used for computer-aided design work. By contrast, many organizations use Unix running on a computer with an 80386 processor as a very low-cost way to provide multiuser accounting and database services. Low-cost terminals connect to the computer running Unix and run special Unix application software in the shared processor.

These high-level and low-level activities in the Unix market leave a lot of room in the middle. The middle ground will probably be occupied by Unix computers acting as file, print, and communications servers for networks of PCs.

I've been very impressed by the latest releases of Unix from AT&T and The Santa Cruz Operation (SCO). AT&T, Microsoft, and SCO worked to deliver "merged" versions of Unix that can use the same compilers and provide the same services; this gives people writing and rehosting applications a broad base of operating systems to shoot for. Frankly, SCO Unix is easier to install than OS/2—and less RAM-hungry!

The history of Unix involves both Digital and AT&T. For many years AT&T was the only company that could sell long-distance telephone service and high-speed communications circuits in the United States. Starting in the 1960s, the switches and control units that AT&T used to deliver these services became computerized. As AT&T's engineers and computer scientists worked with the telephone switching systems, they determined that a program-development environment would make their efforts more productive. That's how the Unix operating system was born.

Initially, AT&T turned to companies like Digital Equipment Corp. for computer hardware. The Unix operating system was written for one of Digital's early machines, the DEC PDP-7. The initial work on Unix was done in 1969 and 1970, primarily by Dennis Ritchie and Ken Thompson at AT&T Bell Labs. The Unix system was completely rewritten in 1973 using the newly developed C programming language. AT&T made the operating system available at no cost to colleges and universities because the Federal Communications Commission prohibited this company from selling computer products. This gave Unix a strong technical base, and entry-level computer scientists' early exposure to Unix has certainly contributed to its growing market today.

Improvements to AT&T's Unix made at the University of California at Berkeley brought network support, support for many peripherals, and software-development tools. Specifically, the Berkeley Standard Distribution (BSD) version of Unix added an implementation of the TCP/IP protocols I'll describe in Chapter 12. In Unix System V, Release 3.0, AT&T added networking capabilities and a high-level multitasking feature called Streams.

The increasing momentum of the Unix bandwagon has convinced many companies to offer application software that can run on a larger Unix-based minicomputer system as well as on DOS-based PCs. One example is the Informix database package, which lets you create data tables on a terminal through the minicomputer's multiuser operating system and update them from a PC. Common file areas can be created that look like DOS files to the PC and look like Unix-type files to terminals attached to the host. This provides a means of creating a true distributed database system.

Similarly, there are several ways to turn a computer running Unix into a server for a network of PCs. An early favorite was a program called Network File System (NFS), first offered by Sun Microsystems. NFS gives client PCs—running a program called PC NFS—simultaneous multiple access to data files stored on a computer using the Unix filing system. Many companies marketing Unix products license NFS from Sun. AT&T includes a similar program called Remote File Service (RFS) in AT&T Unix System V, Release 3 and later releases, but RFS has never achieved the acceptance of NFS for PC networking.

LAN Manager over Unix

The latest product marketed by AT&T and Digital is an implementation of Microsoft's LAN Manager running over Unix. I've tested the AT&T product at PC Magazine LAN Labs, and it's a good implementation of LAN Manager.

Like Digital's PCSA, LAN Manager over Unix must translate between DOS and OS/2 requests from the client PCs and the Unix file structure. This translation takes some time, so the throughput is not as fast as what you would expect from a NetWare file server. Nonetheless, the service is fast enough for most applications.

Client PCs use the same software to connect to a file server running LAN Manager over Unix that they would use to connect to servers based on OS/2. You can map drives on DOS- and OS/2-based client PCs to both types of servers simultaneously.

The two major advantages of running LAN Manager over Unix come from the ability to share data files among DOS, OS/2, and PC applications and to allow client PCs running DOS and OS/2 to use communications resources, such as X.25 packet-switched network services, on a Unix host.

Since AT&T and Digital offer both OS/2 and Unix versions of LAN Manager, both companies provide their customers with the ability to mix and match computer architectures while receiving top-notch integration expertise, installation service, and technical support.

AT&T's version of LAN Manager is called AT&T StarGROUP. It supports most of Microsoft's application program interfaces and has a communications platform based on the OSI model.

■ POWERserve

Performance Technology markets a dedicated network operating system called POWERserve. It doesn't have a large share of the networking software market, but it is a fast, flexible, sophisticated, and economical operating system from a good company, so I think you should know about it.

Founded in 1985 by the minds behind Datapoint's ARCnet, Performance Technology specializes in software but also offers some peripheral hardware products. POWERserve, at $2,795, has top-end technical qualities and low-end pricing.

POWERserve uses a standard NetBIOS, allowing applications running on client PCs to communicate with OS/2-, Unix-, and Xenix-based communications servers and other nodes on the network. The software uses the Intel/Microsoft/IBM Server Message Block (SMB) transmission protocol to give compatibility with many other networks. By including a popular and top-notch electronic-mail program, cc:Mail, Performance Technology allows interoperability with other LANs using cc:Mail and Action Technologies' Message Handling Service.

Installing POWERserve is a quick and simple process. You simply type "A:INSTALL" and answer a few questions about your configuration. POWERserve needs at least 2Mb of expanded memory (EMS), although Performance Technology recommends 4Mb to 8Mb. While on 80286-based computers this must be true EMS, i386 machines can use Quarterdeck's QEMM-386 to turn extended memory into expanded memory. POWERserve supports disk sizes up to 512Mb and as many as 255 users.

POWERserve includes a variety of network management tools. The server's console screen provides an easy-to-understand view of the network statistics. It displays performance and activity statistics, a list of active workstations, and cache-queue information.

A program called Navigate, also available as a stand-alone product, is one of the favorite utilities among the PC Magazine LAN Labs crew. It gives any network user an easy way to find and manage files and subdirectories on all of the servers and drives in the network. Through sliding windows, it maneuvers you around the various servers, printers, volumes, and files. Navigate helps both users and administrators become more familiar with the new concepts of networking.

Performance Technology has a large network of resellers across the country. Each reseller has been trained to install and support all of the company's products. While each dealer may have a different price structure for training and support, Performance Technology stands behind its distribution channel.

Performance Technology markets a variety of other network-related products, too. POWERmirror adds system fault tolerance to any Server Message Block or NetBIOS through disk drive mirroring. POWERbridge bridges LANs with dissimilar topologies using the SMB protocols developed by Microsoft and IBM. Other products include tape-backup hardware and software for network drives and a complete line of network cards.

Performance Technology has a winner with POWERserve. Its excellent performance challenges NetWare 3.X on our benchmark tests. Easy installation, strong compatibility with other SMB-based products, the inclusion of cc:Mail, and a low price make POWERserve a good value among network operating systems.

■ LANtastic

Compared with a customized file-handling system such as NetWare's or a multitasking operating system such as Unix, LAN file-server software operating over DOS offers some significant advantages with only a few drawbacks. Servers that run over DOS can make resources available to the network and run normal applications at the same time. You can run your own word processor or spreadsheet on your PC while other people share your printer or hard disk through the network. You have less RAM for your application, however, and it runs more slowly when the network software is loaded.

DOS-based servers typically don't retrieve files as fast as multitasking systems do, but they are less complex to set up and manage. PCs acting as file and print servers don't run applications as quickly as they might normally, but often the people using the machines don't notice the difference.

There are a number of DOS-based LAN operating systems. D-Link Systems and DCA 10NET Communications both market products with good reputations. D-Link offers simple installation and flexibility, while DCA's 10NET is often chosen by large companies and government acquisition committees looking for products with ISO compliance. But Artisoft's LANtastic leads all competing products in sales and popularity. LANtastic has earned a hatful of *PC Magazine* Editors' Choice awards and an Award for Technical Excellence for its performance, services, and value. Its long list of features includes the ability to share CD-ROM players across the network, plus NetBIOS compatibility, electronic mail, and even a voice capability within its e-mail system.

For LANtastic, Artisoft sells both IEEE 802.3-compliant Ethernet adapters and a lower-cost adapter using a proprietary wiring and cabling scheme, shown in Figure 9.4. Frankly, I don't recommend the use of any adapters for proprietary wiring and signaling schemes, including Artisoft's. Its Ethernet adapters are top-quality, and since they are identical to Novell's NE1000 and NE2000 adapters, you can use them with NetWare, LAN Manager, and other network operating systems if you outgrow the capacity of the LANtastic operating system.

Fantastic Features

LANtastic uses a small amount of memory and provides fast throughput. A PC acting as a file and print server loses only 40k of RAM to the operating-system software, and the redirector in client stations takes only 13k. You can load the operating system into expanded memory or place the disk-caching program into either extended or expanded memory. This ability to load into the memory not used by DOS frees up enough room for large applications that require more RAM.

LANtastic's Quick-Install program automatically assigns network resources, account files, and privileges. It modifies the CONFIG.SYS file with the appropriate files, buffers, file-control blocks, and Lastdrives designation, and creates a batch file that activates the network in one command. If you have any difficulties using the Quick-Install program, an on-line help menu stands ready to aid you; it even scrolls automatically to the section you are working in. Additionally, technical assistance is available Monday through Friday, as is an electronic bulletin-board system monitored by a full-time system operator.

Figure 9.4

LANtastic is a small and fast LAN operating system that works over DOS. The vendor, Artisoft, sells its own adapters using proprietary cabling as well as an excellent line of Ethernet adapters.

LANtastic has excellent print-server software, which includes the ability to feed jobs to multiple printers simultaneously. You can print specific jobs with a high-priced laser printer while the spooler searches through the queue for any files that can be printed by one of the network's lower-end devices.

You can also increase the size of the network printer buffers and specify the location of spooled files on the disk. Both of these improvements help make the printing process more practical. Another feature, global clearing of the print queue, allows you to delete the entire contents of the queue at once, rather than one file at a time. This comes in handy when someone doesn't understand the delays in network printing and repeatedly submits the same job for printing.

LANtastic's disk cache gives applications fast, repetitive access to data files. On our benchmark tests, LANtastic outperformed all its competitors, often equaling Novell's popular NetWare 2.X in throughput.

Diskless workstations are common in local area networks, and LANtastic supports them. Through Artisoft's on-board ROM chips, the LANtastic software provides the initializing files a diskless workstation needs to boot up automatically.

LANtastic's security allows you to limit each user's access to the system during certain hours. This is particularly useful in colleges, where a limited number of PCs must be shared by many students. Near the end of the specified period, a warning message displays the amount of time remaining before the user will be logged off the network; the message remains on-screen until the operating system logs off. You can also specify a date for closing an account, which is quite convenient when you are managing temporary personnel.

Amid all of this praise, it's difficult to find some cautionary note that ought to be sounded regarding LANtastic. The only potential problem relates to the fact that LANtastic is optimized for performance and simplicity. It doesn't carry much compatibility baggage, and this limitation would be a stumbling block for anyone wanting a growth path to larger Microsoft and Novell networks. Nonetheless, you can expand a LANtastic network with many servers to satisfy the needs of 100 or more client PCs.

Voice E-Mail

LANtastic's voice e-mail is unique in a peer-to-peer operating system, and its features are comparable to those in the best voice-mail packages on the market.

Artisoft bundles voice-mail capability into its LANtastic network operating system and has kept the price of the voice adapter card (shown in Figure 9.5) to a low $149. While the voice and LAN systems work well together, you're not required to take one with the other. You could use the voice adapter without the network and transmit files of digitized voice via modem, or mail them on disks.

Software developers who want to integrate Artisoft's voice-communications feature into their products can purchase the LANtastic Voice Programmer's Interface for $195. A set of special audio programming commands makes it possible for programs to use the LANtastic Voice Adapter card to record and play digitized sound.

The voice e-mail package helps you create, play, pause, rewind, forward, and erase voice-mail messages. You select the voice-communications route you wish to take—Mail or Chat—from LANtastic's main menu list, create and send your message, and either pick up your handset or turn on your speaker box. The Voice Adapter card distributes the voice data through an RJ-11 phone connection on the card.

Artisoft includes a telephone handset with each Voice Adapter card. While this is the primary tool for recording and playing back messages, a separate output jack on the adapter can feed one of the small amplifier/speaker combinations designed for higher-quality sound.

Figure 9.5

Artisoft's LANtastic Voice Adapter comes with a telephone handset and provisions for adding an amplified speaker.

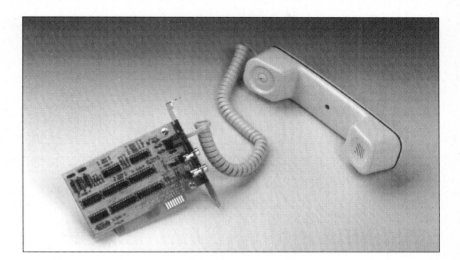

The LANtastic Voice Adapter translates analog sound into a digital format in your PC. The system has an audio bandwidth of 200 to 4,000 Hz—far from high fidelity, but slightly better than the best telephone quality. Being a digital system, it avoids the cumulative noise found in standard analog telephone systems.

Once digitized, your data is treated like any other file stored in the PC. You can send it out through a modem or through the LAN e-mail system. On the receiving end, another voice card translates the digital file back into sound so the person at the receiving machine can hear the message.

You can opt for a voice-compression mode that reduces the size of your voice files by about 50 percent; this can save time when you have a large file of digitized sound to transmit. There is some distortion of the voice pattern when you play back your message after compression, but it's not severe enough to deter you from using the mode.

The Chat mode of the LANtastic operating system lets you conduct a real-time two-way telephone discussion across the network using the voice adapter boards. Unfortunately, there is a significant delay due to the format-conversion process. You'll find the regular office telephone system more responsive, although the Chat mode has some potential for use in training situations.

Using the Mail Services option, you can send a voice message or save an entry to a specified disk file. You can choose from a list of recipients and send multi-address messages. A pop-up e-mail notification alerts each workstation of incoming e-mail; you get separate notifications for digitized sound and for standard data messages.

The screen display that accompanies voice recording and playback in the LANtastic e-mail system deserves special mention. This screen depicts a pointer—like the mechanical pointer on a dictating machine—that shows your location in the recorded message and offers excellent rewind, replay, and editing capabilities.

The voice-communications feature within Artisoft's LANtastic makes the product unique in the LAN market. The ability to send voice inexpensively over LAN cabling may sound futuristic, but it's available today.

CD-ROM Support

Many interesting information sources, including maps, statistical summaries, and compilations of publications, are available on CD-ROM disks. But seldom does one person need sole and prolonged access to all the information contained on a single CD-ROM. CD-ROM information bases beg to be shared through a network. In fact, in terms of productivity, sharing CD-ROM resources is one of the best reasons I know for installing a LAN in the first place. It's possible to add a third-party CD-ROM server (a type of file server) to a LAN running Novell, Banyan, or Microsoft networking software. But LANtastic comes with the ability to share CD-ROM drives across the network as a built-in feature.

Artisoft's menu-driven installation program copies the files from the distribution disk to their proper place in the directory structure. Your next step is to install a CD-ROM drive with the proper device driver, along with a copy of a special program that modifies DOS for the large file sizes used in a CD-ROM—a program called Microsoft CD-ROM Extensions. Fortunately, the PC does not have to be dedicated to the task of acting as a CD-ROM server. As the Microsoft CD-ROM device driver loads, the next available logical-drive letters are assigned to the CD-ROM drives.

After LANtastic is installed, the program's menu lets you initiate an automatic broadcast to the network telling each station which drive letter is assigned to the CD-ROM device. You then assign a network resource name to the shared drive and inform LANtastic that the resource is a CD-ROM drive, whereupon the operating system channels any relevant service requests it receives from application programs to Microsoft CD-ROM Extensions. LANtastic also supports multiple CD-ROM drives by letting you give each drive a different network resource name.

When you want to access a particular drive on a CD-ROM server, you have LANtastic link one of your unused drive letters to the named server and drive. Thus, if you want your D: drive mapped to a drive named DATA-BASE on a CD-ROM server named CDSERVER, you enter the command

```
NET USE D: \\CDSERVER\DATABASE
```

on the DOS command line. The networking software makes the link and directs the database retrieval software to your D: drive to find its data.

LANtastic's CD-ROM capability is easy to install, use, and manage. It adds a significant and unique value to this program.

On the bottom line, LANtastic's voice-chat feature, CD-ROM compatibility, good security, disk cache, high performance, and very reasonable price combine to make the package appealing to anyone looking for a high-quality LAN for 2 to 100 users.

■ Choosing Server Hardware

Throughout this chapter, I've provided information on the amount of processing power and memory needed to run the various network operating systems. Several companies, including Compaq Computer Corp. and NetFrame Systems, market a class of computers designed specifically to act as file servers. They typically have room for many hard disks, and ports to connect printers and plotters. The newest feature of these specialized server machines is the ability to make multiple CPUs available to the network operating system. These "super servers" typically carry a significantly higher price tag than machines with slightly more humble but still very substantial capabilities.

Very few organizations need super servers today. A properly configured computer with an 80386 processor operating at 25 or 33 MHz can act as a file and print server under NetWare, VINES, LAN Manager, or Unix for 100 to 200 client PCs running typical office applications. Proper configuration means a fast hard disk, a disk drive controller capable of caching requests, and an adequate number of network interface adapters to carry the load.

You need multiprocessor capabilities when you add more programs running in the server, because running database-server and communications-server software reduces CPU efficiency. You can run these programs on separate PCs, or you can combine them all into a server with multiple processors. The separate-PC approach has some significant advantages in terms of system reliability and performance.

In general, I recommend that you build your network modularly. Use separate computers acting as servers to create the capacity and throughput you need where you need it. Look carefully before you put all of your processing power in one cabinet. Modern networking-software products make it easier than it used to be to manage separate servers, and the advantages of reliability and scalability inherent in a modular approach are important.

■ Choosing Networking-Software Products

Finding the right network software for your organization isn't as difficult as it might seem. Any of the products I've described in this chapter will serve you well.

Here's what to consider when you make your networking choices:

- What is the maximum number of client PCs you're ever likely to have? If the number is less than 100, look closely at LANtastic.

- Do you need to integrate Apple Macintosh computers into your network? If so, consider NetWare and 3Com's version of LAN Manager.

- Do you need to integrate computers using the VMS or Unix operating system into the network? If so, consider the LAN Manager products from Digital or AT&T.

- Do you need to link LANs across long-distance telephone lines? Banyan's VINES and the LAN Manager family have excellent capabilities for LAN-to-LAN connections.

- Which product comes with the best local technical support? The success of your network operation is directly proportional to the technical support you receive.

Network Management and Control

- Alarms and Acronyms

- Down-to-Earth Management

- Protocol Analyzers

- Gathering Statistics at the Server

- LAN Metering Software

- Network Management Brings Results

The phrase *mission-critical applications*—always spoken in gravely serious tones—is an overused part of marketing pitches for network products. It seems that every company aiming to price its products at the high end of the scale touts their reliability and dependability for "mission-critical applications." Yet the amount of overuse this phrase receives actually signals an important fact: Organizations depend on their networks for productivity, and some companies start to lose money the second a network malfunctions.

Not only do networks represent an investment in wiring, computers, and software totaling thousands of dollars per node, the data that networks hold and deliver is often the production equipment of the business. The local area network system of a modern organization rates as much management attention as the milling and welding machines in an automobile-manufacturing plant or the sales counters of a department store.

Good networks operate invisibly. The servers respond to requests from the client computers quickly and without any special actions on the part of the people using the network's resources. Because designers make these systems transparent, problems of wiring, configuration, design, or deterioration often don't appear or aren't reported until they result in catastrophic failures. The phrase "Your network is down!" is guaranteed to flash-freeze the blood of any network administrator. I want to help you avoid receiving unpleasant surprises from your network.

In this chapter, I describe the techniques and tools of network management and control. I'll deal with four somewhat overlapping levels of network-management systems:

- Networkwide reporting and control

- Wiring-hub reporting and control

- Protocol analysis and traffic counting

- Statistical analysis

The field of network-management systems is confusing primarily because network control and reporting take place at so many levels. The largest networks have a hierarchy of devices and programs at several levels reporting status and problems upstream to a central data-gathering and reporting system. But you don't have to put this hierarchy in place all at once. Some products, such as wiring-hub traffic reporting and control systems, generate excellent reports on their own without the need to exchange information with other devices.

The lowest level of network reporting devices consists of hardware boxes with internal microprocessors and programs in ROM that report on the quantity and quality of data passing a particular point in the network. These devices include LAN wiring hubs, bridges, multiplexers, microwave radios, and telephone modems. Their internal processors and programs gather statistical information and send out status reports to some intermediate level of management software running on a PC. These programs might provide all the analysis a particular network manager needs, or they might send specified items of information on to higher-level management programs.

The LAN operating systems in print and file servers can also send special alert messages and regular status messages on to higher-level management programs running on computers elsewhere in the network. At the highest level, application programs complain to management programs about files they can't find or access. The reports from all these levels of hardware and software must be in some common format so that one top-level system can compile them and present them to people who use them or respond to them.

There are competing grand architectures for network management and control marketed by such companies as AT&T, DEC, Hewlett-Packard, and IBM. But there is also an attempt to standardize network-management protocols and procedures within the International Standards Organization.

■ Alarms and Acronyms

The whole network-management-and-control industry has two factors in common: reliance on the principle of alarms and the use of a bewildering blizzard of acronyms. The concept of alarms is easy to understand; the acronyms take a lot longer to master.

Using performance alarms means that you instruct the software to call for your attention only when something abnormal occurs. Typically, you can easily adjust the limits of abnormality. Abnormal events might be defined in terms of more than 30 consecutive Ethernet packet collisions, an unusually small or large number of packets sent within a period of time, or practically any other parameter you want to know about, from the temperature inside an equipment cabinet to the AC line voltage. The network-management-and-control software packages offer responses to alarm situations that range from silently logging the event to frantically sounding speaker beeps and flashing colored symbols on the screen while sending messages to a printer.

We'll start picking our way through the flurry of concepts and acronyms surrounding these products at the highest level of grand network-management architectures. Picture these architectures as the overarching scheme you might use to plan a network-management control center that looks like a small version of NASA Mission Control. I'm talking about big networks, but big networks are made up of many little networks with many nodes, most of them PCs. Each of the nodes in all of the little networks has to report to the big system. As is typical in the computer industry, there is an ideal solution that everybody talks about, a good system that works today, and a slightly different and unique way of doing things from IBM.

Everybody's Talking ISO CMIP

The management structure everyone talks about is an emerging "open" architecture called the Common Management Information Protocol or CMIP (pronounced "see-mip"). CMIP is an evolving proposal being developed by the International Standards Organization (ISO). Major companies such as AT&T, DEC, HP, and Northern Telecom have released products making up various pieces of a full CMIP network.

The ISO proposals—and emerging companion documents such as the standard being developed by the U.S. National Institute of Standards and Technology—primarily define the functions of network-management software and describe how reports are formatted and transmitted. They also describe the format of the messages sent to devices trying to correct or isolate error conditions.

The functions the CMIP model defines include fault management, configuration management, performance management, security management, and accounting management. The other models agree with these definitions in general terms.

Fault management includes detecting problems and taking steps to isolate them. *Configuration management* provides messages describing active connections and equipment; it is closely tied to fault management because changing configurations is the primary technique used to isolate network faults. *Performance management* includes counting things like packets, disk access requests, and access to specific programs. *Security management* includes alerting managers to unauthorized access attempts at the cable, network, file-server, and resource levels. *Accounting management* involves billing people for what they use.

Digital Equipment Corp. and AT&T have the most complete implementations of CMIP. Digital calls its CMIP-compatible network-management system the Enterprise Management Architecture. AT&T calls its system the Unified Network Management Architecture (UNMA). The first product released under AT&T's UNMA—the first real CMIP product—was called the Accumaster Integrator.

Everybody's Using SNMP

CMIP is a great idea, but companies are still developing products to meet the protocol, and all the existing CMIP-compatible products take a lot of memory and processing power. People have solved the problem of LAN management in several alternative ways.

CMIP:

- 👍 **ISO-standardized**
- 👍 **Interoperable**
- 👍 **Powerful**
- 👎 **Big**
- 👎 **Still evolving**

SNMP:

- 👍 **Inexpensive**
- 👍 **Good enough**
- 👍 **Not processor-hungry**
- 👍 **Widely supported**
- 👎 **Lacking security**
- 👎 **Weak in documentation**
- 👎 **Modified into too many variants**

The control and reporting system used on-line today in many major networks is called the Simple Network Management Protocol (SNMP). SNMP was developed and is used by the same federal-government and university community that brought out TCP/IP and its suite of protocols. Dr. Jeffrey Case at the University of Tennessee is a leader in the development and use of SNMP.

SNMP works well in the large DOD and commercial networks that use TCP/IP, and there are plans to evolve SNMP products into CMIP products. Proteon, for example, has a high-level data-gathering network-management system called OverVIEW that runs on an MS-DOS PC and gathers SNMP reports. Cabletron has an SNMP system called Spectrum using artificial-intelligence modules that can apply complex rules and react to the reports of network events it receives. Even AT&T, a strong supporter of CMIP, has lately acknowledged the importance of SNMP and added support for this management architecture to the AT&T Systems Manager products.

SNMP's drawbacks center around its lack of security, the inconsistent quality of its documentation, and the tendency of some companies to create nonstandard configurations. But industry support for it continues to grow, despite these drawbacks, because SNMP doesn't take as much processing power or memory to run, it's here today, and it works well enough for even the largest network systems.

NetView:

👍 **Powerful**

👍 **True blue**

👎 **Prone to consume CPU power**

👎 **Expensive**

IBM's NetView

IBM unveiled its network-management products in early 1986. It calls its overall system NetView. The architecture relies on PCs running software called NetView/PC on an intermediate level to gather data on the network and report to the NetView program running on a mainframe. Perhaps because the first version of NetView/PC required every network to have a computer dedicated to reporting or because NetView itself takes considerable mainframe resources, NetView/PC did not capture a large part of the market. But IBM's latest version of NetView/PC runs over OS/2 and can collect data from several networks simultaneously. IBM has also announced plans to evolve NetView to become compatible with CMIP in the 1990s.

In mid-1990 IBM significantly raised the prices for all its NetView products. IBM's new pricing made NetView by far the most expensive network-management system to install and operate.

■ Down-to-Earth Management

Since few people need the kind of network-management system that NASA could use to control deep space probes, I'll narrow the focus of this chapter just a bit. I've already discussed some of the statistical and security-related network-management utilities contained in network operating systems like NetWare, VINES, and LAN Manager. These utilities don't tell you much, if anything, about the activities of remote printers, communications gateways, mail servers, database servers, routers, and other devices on the LAN. If you want a full picture of the activity and health of the network you have to go to the lowest common denominator: the physical layer of network cabling.

Reporting and Control from the Wiring Hub

Reporting and control from the wiring hub:

👍 **Practical**

👍 **Effective**

👍 **Complete with on-line disconnect control**

👎 **Requires special hardware and wiring**

As I pointed out in my discussions of 10BaseT and Token-Ring wiring topologies, a central wiring hub is a strong pulse point in the network. Since all of the traffic goes through the hub—even traffic that bypasses the file server and goes directly between client stations and print or communications servers—a microprocessor in the hub can monitor and report on all network activity. The same processor can also give the network administrator certain levels of control over network connections.

The wiring-hub control and management systems, like the Proteon TokenVIEW Plus shown in Figure 10.1, provide a great deal of information. These packages are uniquely independent of the LAN operating-system software, and they fit into most of the grand management-architecture schemes, or soon will.

Figure 10.1

Proteon's TokenVIEW management system includes a Series 70 Intelligent Wire Center, TokenVIEW Manager software, and interconnecting system boards. (TokenVIEW is a registered trademark and Series 70 is a trademark of Proteon, Inc.)

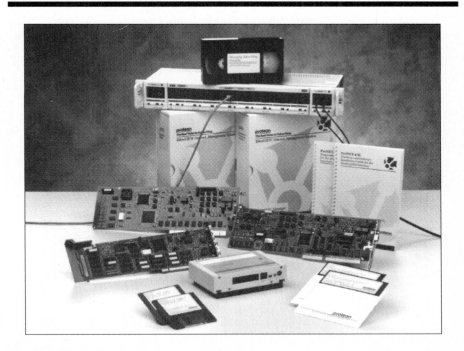

From its central vantage point, a wiring hub sees every node and, as Figure 10.2 shows, can record events, measure the number and quality of packets each node sends, and provide information on network interfaces. The on-board processors in these hubs work with software running in a PC to report on all network nodes and control them when necessary, mainly by disconnecting them.

Figure 10.2

The TokenVIEW Plus software provides a wide variety of information in real time, and it keeps a detailed log of network events. (TokenVIEW is a registered trademark of Proteon, Inc.)

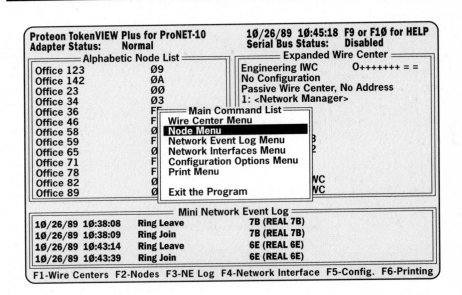

The leading companies marketing wiring-hub reporting and control software include Cabletron, NetWorth, Proteon, SynOptics, and Thomas-Conrad Corp. Other companies, including David Systems and Standard Microsystems Corp., are newcomers to the market.

The cable-hub data-gathering systems use a variety of different wiring schemes. Proteon's system works only with Token-Ring networks. The systems from Cabletron, NetWorth, and SynOptics can interconnect practically all types of cabling. Figure 10.3 shows the NetWorth system. If you want to run similar software on a Macintosh, Farallon Computing has a product called TrafficWatch that reports on and manages networks using Apple's LocalTalk architecture.

These products don't decode the traffic passing through the hubs. More complex devices called *protocol analyzers*, described later in this chapter, handle the complex decoding chore. Protocol analyzers that capture and decode packets provide some of the same information available through wiring-hub reporting and control systems, but you have to work a lot harder to get the information, and you lack the "big picture" view the wiring-hub systems provide.

Figure 10.3

The NetWorth hub-management system provides flexible and powerful software with a variety of alarms, reports, and real-time displays. (EtherNext Series 4000 EtherManager Network Management Software © 1990 NetWorth, Inc.)

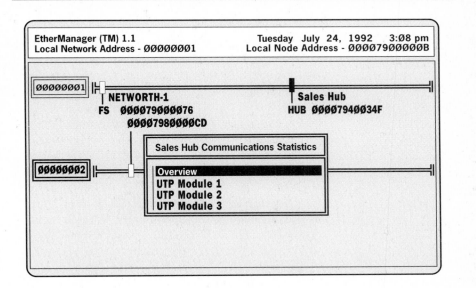

The reporting and control systems that operate at the network cable level don't decode packets, so they present no risk to the security of data or passwords. Protocol analyzers have a role in organizations where people develop sophisticated software and network hardware, but reporting and control systems have a role in almost every network. People who use protocol analyzers in place of network reporting and control systems are using a telescope to view a football game from the sidelines. They can read the quarterback's lips, but they miss a lot of the action.

It is very difficult to break out the added incremental cost for the network reporting and control capabilities in these systems. If you use the wiring hubs or concentrators from Cabletron, SynOptics, and companies with similar products, they include major elements of the network-management features. Additionally, while the initial cost for software and hardware is usually several thousands of dollars, that single cost is amortized over all of the nodes you now have and all that you will add in the future. Since larger networks usually benefit most from reporting and control, the per-node cost is typically very small.

By themselves, these products provide all of the network reporting and control capabilities that many organizations will ever need. But if you think your network will grow with multiple servers, gateways, bridges, and wide-area connections, you will soon find yourself thinking about adding more layers of reporting. Looking for CMIP or SNMP compatibility in all of your network components is a smart idea, but starting to install reporting and control now at the lowest hardware layer is the smartest move of all.

SynOptics LNMS

SynOptics Communications has been the leader in wiring-hub reporting and control systems, so I'll take a few paragraphs to describe this company's popular products. At the same time, Cabletron Systems leads a pack of aggressive challengers to SynOptics. Cabletron's LANview software, combined with its line of Multi Media Access Center intelligent wiring hubs, bridges, and network interface boards, makes this firm a powerful competitor.

SynOptics' LattisNet Network Management System (LNMS) runs in one dedicated PC under Microsoft Windows. It receives status and performance data from several different models of network hubs called *LattisNet concentrators*.

Several pieces of hardware make up a concentrator. SynOptics provides a choice of cabinets, each containing a different number of slots and appropriate power supplies. A single Model 3000 Premises Concentrator can connect to up to 132 nodes. Smaller units provide economical connections for department-size networks or subnetworks at a level price of about $130 to $150 per node.

Each concentrator cabinet accepts the same family of 10- by 14- by 2-inch slide-in modules, which provide connections for the nodes over twisted-pair or fiber-optic cable. Similar modules integrate thin Ethernet and fiber-optic cable with 10BaseT unshielded twisted-pair networks. SynOptics also has connections for the 100-megabit-per-second Fiber Distributed Data Interface (FDDI). These slide-in modules connect and translate between the different wiring and signaling schemes, so network planners can mix and match media to make custom-tailored systems.

Each module in the LattisNet system has an array of status lights providing a visual presentation of the present activity. This visual presentation on the hardware is echoed in the display of the LNMS software too.

The heart of the LattisNet Network Management System is a device called the Network Management Module. This module works in a concentrator and carries its own 80186 processor, which gathers data and sends packets to the special processor board and software running in the PC designated as the system-management console. Because the concentrator must maintain a connection to other concentrators and to the PC running LNMS even if the network is down, the Network Management Module can call those stations by using a modem and a telephone line if it can't make contact over the network. One version of the Network Management Module has an RS-232C port for an external modem, and another version has a built-in modem.

The display screen of the system-management PC running LNMS, created under Microsoft Windows, is certain to become a "must see" stop on every VIP tour of your facility. Even if people don't understand the details of what they are looking at, the LNMS screens are impressive.

For the network manager and troubleshooter, the LNMS screens are valuable tools. The primary system display shows a diagram of the network, portraying each LattisNet concentrator and every module and connection in it. You don't have to enter the details of the network into a database so the program can build the diagram. The software uses the network to interrogate each concentrator, gather its status on a second-by-second basis, and create the screen presentation from that current information base. If a person doing repairs on a concentrator across the campus changes a module or disconnects a cable to one node, you see the change on the screen within 5 seconds. You can supplement the database the program creates to add English names and other descriptive data to each node, but the program does most of the work.

An eye-catching part of the screen presentation is a histogram showing the activity going through each concentrator. This marching display is particularly useful for pinpointing very busy sections of the network that need more connections or perhaps require an intelligent bridge to isolate them from the rest of the network.

While the histogram is eye-catching, other screens are spectacular. If you use a mouse or the cursor-control keys to select a particular concentrator on the network, the screen creates a complete diagram of the concentrator with all of its modules, plus a second-by-second update of the status lights on each module. If you make a similar cursor selection of a single port on the concentrator, you can select displays showing the respective numbers of good, misaligned, undersized, late, and colliding packets. You can display the activity on several nodes at the same time, so you can perform sophisticated tasks like checking the flow of data between a workstation and a gateway.

This screen display gives you a very complete picture of the present status of the network and its subelements. For longer-term analysis, LNMS provides the ability to collect raw statistical data and the programming to create a predefined series of reports. The reports include half a dozen pie and bar charts showing throughput rates and out-of-tolerance operation. These data collections and reports are created as ASCII files, so you can pass them on to more sophisticated database programs.

In the area of control, none of these media-level systems can do anything more than disconnect a node from the network, but LNMS at least gives you the option of doing that politely. You can disconnect a node after a notification message or without notification, or arrange for automatic disconnection if certain criteria (such as a dozen packet collisions in a row) are reached.

SynOptics and Cabletron support the high-level protocol standards and include reporting according to NetView and CMIP protocols.

LAN Traffic Counters

LAN traffic counters:

👆 **No wiring hub needed**

👆 **Simple to install**

👆 **Low cost**

👆 **Excellent information**

👎 **No on-line control**

If you don't have a network wiring hub, but you would like to see the volume of network activity, to see what stations are active, and to receive alerts when certain types of errant packets move across the network, there are alternative products that are easier to install and operate and cost less to buy. We call this category of products *LAN traffic counters*.

LAN traffic counters are software products that typically you can run on any network station, although there are exceptions (the NetWare-specific Monitrix Network Manager from Cheyenne Software, shown in Figure 10.4, and Novell's LANtern Services Manager, shown in Figure 10.5). They provide excellent eye-catching displays of network activity and statistics, and they even measure cable quality, but they can't disconnect errant stations from the network. Some of the traffic counters capture packets, usually without any filtering, but they don't break down the packets or display anything beyond the hexadecimal code they contain.

Figure 10.4

Monitrix, a product of Cheyenne Software, is remarketed by companies like Standard Microsystems Corp. Monitrix monitors, gathers, and presents real-time statistical information on network traffic.

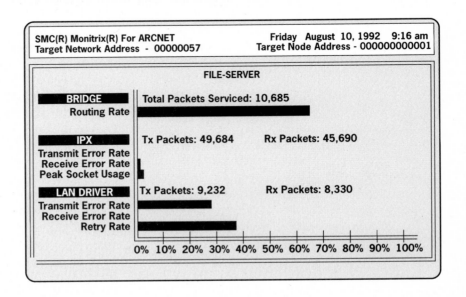

Figure 10.5

The LANtern Services
Manager from Novell uses
Microsoft Windows 3.0 to
provide a comprehensive
view of the network. Here
the screen displays
(clockwise from upper left)
a network map, alarm
thresholds, a segment
map, a trend graph, real-
time traffic statistics, and
overall network statistics.

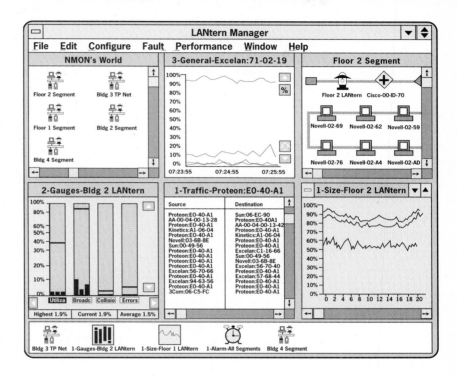

It's interesting to note how wildly these software products vary in price. Emonitor, from Brightwork Development, lists for $295 and is worth every penny; anyone who cares about the operation of an Ethernet or ARCnet network should have Emonitor or its ARCnet equivalent, ARCmonitor, close at hand. Network Inspector, from Tiara Computer Systems, carries a $1,495 price tag—which is more than the LANWatch protocol analyzer from ftp Software.

Some traffic counters are designed specifically for Novell's NetWare. Monitrix runs in the server of a NetWare 3.X or NetWare 2.X network, and Network Inspector contains special diagnostics for NetWare.

Adapters at Work

The key element in all protocol-analysis and traffic-counting tools is the network adapter card that links the computer into the network. The chip sets on such adapters alert the software to each passing packet, translate data formats, and move received data to RAM so the software can work on it. The chip sets also contain cable-testing functions.

The National Semiconductor chip set on a typical Ethernet adapter card can report 17 different errors pertaining to transmission control, reception, and packet format. Some of the most common errors include *runt* packets, which don't contain enough bits, and *dribble* packets, which contain enough bits but don't end on an even byte. The Hewlett-Packard LANProbe in Figure 10.6 shows a display waiting to report these types of errors.

Figure 10.6

The HP 4990S LANProbe monitoring system displays network activity in clear, easy-to-read graphics. The top half of the screen shows network trends, including errors, while the lower half displays statistics on traffic from individual nodes.

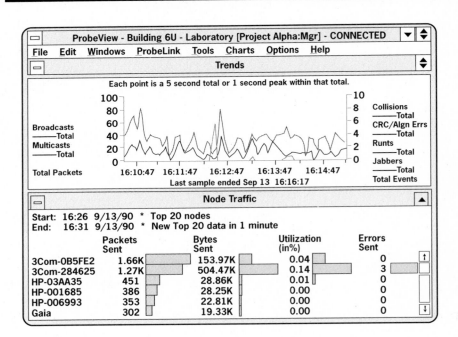

When a transmitting Ethernet adapter detects a collision with another station's packet, it transmits a jam signal of 4 to 6 bytes of arbitrary data to ensure that all stations detect the collision. Any receiving adapter reports the jam signal as a collision to any monitoring software. The LAN traffic counters accept these reports from Ethernet adapters, or similar types of reports from ARCnet or Token-Ring adapters, and convert them to useful charts, graphs, and reports. Figure 10.7 shows how LAN Command displays the information reported by one Token-Ring adapter.

Some programs work with many brands of adapters, and some work with only one brand. When the PC Magazine LAN Labs team tested these products, we found that the type of adapter in use significantly influenced each program's ability to report and capture data under heavy loads correctly.

Figure 10.7

The LAN Command program marketed by Dolphin Software reports many statistics gathered from specific network adapters. This screen shows the identification, configuration, utilization rates, and problems of a specific Token-Ring adapter installed in a node called Server1.

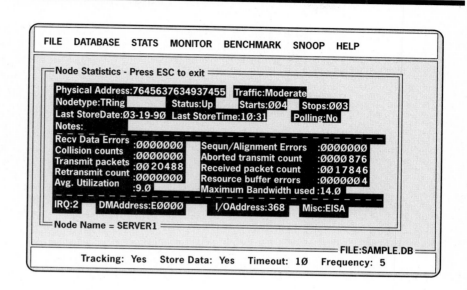

Both wiring-hub traffic-management systems and traffic counters operating over LAN adapters provide a practical and broad view of the network. They measure the force and volume of the river of data coursing through your network. But sometimes you need to sample the quality of the water to get a more detailed picture of what it carries. In networks, you sample the data stream with products called protocol analyzers.

Protocol analyzers:

👍 **Detailed microscopic views**

👍 **Explanations of problems**

👎 **Security risks**

👎 **High costs**

■ Protocol Analyzers

"I'm not sure what it does, but I knew when I saw it that I just had to have one." That feeling, expressed by a fledgling network manager at a Manhattan bank, represents the feelings of many buyers of LAN diagnostic equipment. For some people, protocol analyzers are powerful tools, but for others they are talismans and amulets that confer status and just might ward off network miseries.

Protocol analyzers, like Network General's Sniffer and the SpiderAnalyzer shown in Figure 10.8, carry price tags up to $25,000 and beyond. They have growing competition from alternative products that are more economical and just as useful for typical network managers. You'll want to find the right combination of price and capability for your installation. Let's start with a few simple definitions and explanations. What is a protocol, and why does it need analysis anyway?

Figure 10.8

Spider Systems' SpiderAnalyzer P320R is a portable protocol analyzer with a wide range of protocol-decoding and traffic-monitoring capabilities.

Protocol = Agreement

A protocol is nothing more than a formal agreement about how computers should format and acknowledge information during a communications session. When products from different companies each follow the same protocol, they have the ability to communicate together—theoretically, at least.

In operation, communications software wraps the data message inside leading and trailing data fields whose format is determined by the protocols they follow. These data fields form an envelope for the message while it transits the communications link. Since the sending and receiving systems use the same protocols, they know how to read the envelope's address, route it, deliver it, and even get a receipt, regardless of what it contains. If communications over the link break down, reading the leading and trailing fields and even opening the envelope and decoding the data in the message it frames might give you clues to the problem.

A protocol analyzer is the tool you use to read a protocol-configured packet. Different protocol analyzers exist for all types of communications circuits, including X.25, ISDN, and several specific types of local area network cabling, signaling, and protocol architectures. You can set up analyzers for ARCnet, Ethernet, and Token-Ring networks. These products typically look like portable (or sometimes luggable) PCs. They have screens with flashing displays, and software that can produce graphs and printed reports.

A LAN protocol analysis system, including special software and sometimes special hardware, usually takes a PC's full capabilities to run. You'll often dedicate a PC to this one job. Only Hewlett-Packard packages its high-powered analyzer in a special-purpose computer, which is equipped with a Motorola 68000 processor.

Network protocol analyzers capture data packets flying across a network and use special software to decode them. All LAN protocol analyzers let you filter and sort incoming and captured data for easier processing, and the top units, such as Network General's Sniffer, provide an English-language identification of the protocols in use and an evaluation of any damage or irregularities in the captured data. Figure 10.9 shows the decoding screen display of a Sniffer.

Figure 10.9

This split-screen display from Network General's Sniffer gives both a summary and a detailed view of the packets crossing a network. The bottom window shows a decoded packet, including a comment about the function it performs (writing a data file).

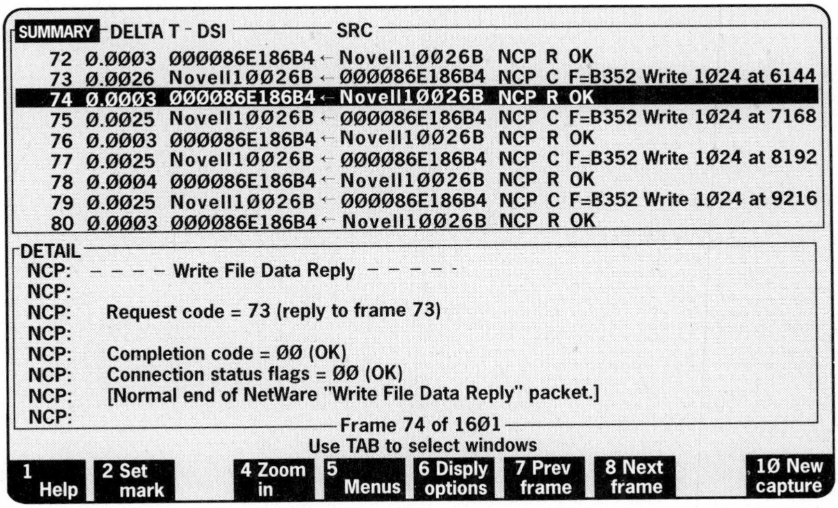

```
┌SUMMARY┬─DELTA T ─ DSI ──────── SRC ──────────────────────────────┐
│   72  Ø.ØØØ3  ØØØØ86E186B4 ←  Novell1ØØ26B  NCP R OK             │
│   73  Ø.ØØ26  Novell1ØØ26B ←  ØØØØ86E186B4  NCP C F=B352 Write 1Ø24 at 6144 │
│   74  Ø.ØØØ3  ØØØØ86E186B4 ←  Novell1ØØ26B  NCP R OK             │
│   75  Ø.ØØ25  Novell1ØØ26B ←  ØØØØ86E186B4  NCP C F=B352 Write 1Ø24 at 7168 │
│   76  Ø.ØØØ3  ØØØØ86E186B4 ←  Novell1ØØ26B  NCP R OK             │
│   77  Ø.ØØ25  Novell1ØØ26B ←  ØØØØ86E186B4  NCP C F=B352 Write 1Ø24 at 8192 │
│   78  Ø.ØØØ4  ØØØØ86E186B4 ←  Novell1ØØ26B  NCP R OK             │
│   79  Ø.ØØ25  Novell1ØØ26B ←  ØØØØ86E186B4  NCP C F=B352 Write 1Ø24 at 9216 │
│   80  Ø.ØØØ3  ØØØØ86E186B4 ←  Novell1ØØ26B  NCP R OK             │
├DETAIL─────────────────────────────────────────────────────────┤
│ NCP:  – – – – Write File Data Reply – – – – ·                   │
│ NCP:                                                            │
│ NCP:    Request code = 73 (reply to frame 73)                  │
│ NCP:                                                            │
│ NCP:    Completion code = ØØ (OK)                              │
│ NCP:    Connection status flags = ØØ (OK)                      │
│ NCP:    [Normal end of NetWare "Write File Data Reply" packet.] │
│ NCP:                                                            │
│              ─────── Frame 74 of 16Ø1 ───────                   │
│                   Use TAB to select windows                     │
├─────┬─────┬─────┬──────┬──────┬──────┬──────┬──────────────────┤
│ 1   │2 Set│4 Zoom│5     │6 Disply│7 Prev│8 Next│       1Ø New    │
│ Help│ mark│ in   │Menus │ options│ frame│ frame│       capture   │
└─────┴─────┴─────┴──────┴──────┴──────┴──────┴──────────────────┘
```

You can use the protocol analyzer to display packets selectively in real time or to capture activity on the network for later study. You might set filter criteria so that the analyzer displays only incoming packets going to or from certain stations, formatted according to specific protocols, or containing certain errors. Setting several filters simultaneously reduces the need for storage capacity in the analyzer. Alternatively, you can let the analyzer capture all the data it can hold—often more than 3,000 Ethernet packets—and then use the same filters to perform a careful analysis of the captured data. Some analyzer software contains an editor so you can delete unimportant data, enter comments, print reports, and even create files in common database formats.

The ease of setting filters and reviewing data is an important criterion for protocol analyzers.

The protocol-analysis capability is powerful, but the function most people use these devices for is much less sophisticated. The screen display you usually see is a graph of current network activity. My experience is that people giving VIP tours of an organization love to bring visitors past the "network control center" so they can see the marching bar graphs showing network and presumably corporate activity. These screens (like the one shown in Figure 10.10) usually include other information, such as the number of bytes or bits per second moving across the network, the percentage of maximum network capacity, the number of bad packets, and some measurement of the peak load experienced since the monitor was activated.

Figure 10.10

Another screen display from the Sniffer shows the number of packets exchanged between the LAN adapters, identified by manufacturer and Ethernet address. Other fields on the screen show the number of good and bad packets, and the sliding bar graph shows the number of frames or packets moved per second.

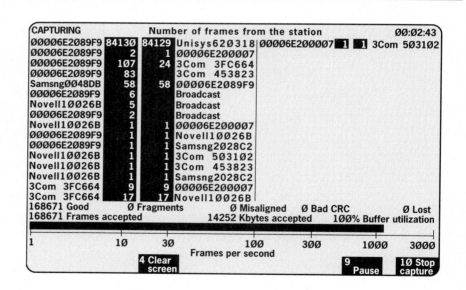

Protocol analyzers contain many other functions. Most have the ability to replace arcane hexadecimal station addresses with meaningful names, giving the whole process a friendlier atmosphere.

Most analyzers can also use a technique called *time domain reflectometry,* or TDR, to test cables for improperly terminated connections. This technique involves sending a signal out on the cable and then watching for and interpreting its echo. The systems can locate the position of open and shorted cable conditions with varying degrees of accuracy. We've tested some products claiming to have TDR capabilities and found that you might be better off witching with a bent willow twig instead. Real TDRs are typically precision devices, often equipped with oscilloscope screens for exact measurement.

Protocol analyzers can generate network traffic too. Some systems, like Network General's Sniffer, contain a traffic generator that loads the network with a stream of good packets. This activity is useful for checking certain behaviors of adapters and routers, but not much else.

An important troubleshooting capability, contained in Novell's LANalyzer, lets you rebroadcast a captured data stream onto the network. Imagine, for example, that a network troubleshooter captures an exchange between a client workstation and a server, and it contains errant responses from the server. The troubleshooter can enter the captured data file, edit out the bad responses, and send the same requests to the server over and over again while trying to isolate the problem. All of this happens without interrupting activity at the client station. This capability has obvious security implications that we'll address a little later, but it is a useful troubleshooting tool.

LAN protocol analyzers aren't unique to any particular type of network operating system. You have to pick a product that works with the network adapters and cables in your system. Also, you should choose a product that has decoders available for the protocols used by your networking software. For example, if you have a NetWare server, make sure the package has IPX/SPX decoding. If you have a LAN Manager server, select a product that can decode NetBIOS and SMB.

Security

As passive monitoring devices, analyzers don't log on to a server, and they aren't subject to server-software security. The ability to copy and decode packets as they cross the network means that anyone with a protocol analyzer can easily find and decode packets carrying passwords used as people sign on to servers; in fact, the protocol analyzer can capture any data sent across the network. NetWare 3.X encrypts passwords for transmission, but no operating system encrypts data files; this is typically the job of add-on encryption hardware or special-purpose software. When you give someone a protocol analyzer, that person gains a wide-open tap on the network.

Packet Decoding

A protocol analyzer can do one thing for you that no other product can: It can decode the contents of captured packets or tokens and display an English-language interpretation of the contents, in addition to displaying the hexadecimal code. If you need that function, odds are you will lay out between $10,000 and $20,000 for the tools to do it.

Buy What You Need

The first consideration for these management products is value. Not only should you get what you pay for, you should use what you pay for, too. LAN protocol analyzers are impressive tools—if you need one, there is no substitute—but if you don't need all their power, then wiring-hub reporting and control programs or LAN traffic counters can give you an excellent view into the operation of your network for a lot less money.

Statistical reporting software:

👍 **Detailed reports**

👍 **Trend tracking**

👎 **No on-line control**

■ Gathering Statistics at the Server

Mountains of statistics are nothing without interpretation and insight, but with those skills managers can use statistics to move mountains. Networks are dynamic operational systems. You can define their operation in terms of certain measurable parameters. Managers can use the measurements of those parameters to plan for growth, determine a baseline for comparison, find problems in early stages, and justify budgets.

A host of modern programs now provide statistical data in both raw and quantified form to LAN administrators. Careful analysis of the data helps administrators create a productive and efficient LAN environment. The products available range from those that check the LAN for circumstances exceeding certain limits to those that soak up every detail of operation they can wring from servers and network adapter cards.

The products producing statistical reports are typically software, although a few have specific hardware components. For the most part, these are third-party, add-on software packages for your LAN. They complement any statistical-reporting and management-control capabilities your network operating system already has.

The factors these programs attempt to measure include

- the amount of disk storage space used by particular applications, persons, or cost centers;

- the amount of activity in specific programs or files;

- the connection time of specific people or client PCs;

- the number of print jobs (expressed in several different ways);

- server workloads over a period of time;

- any of a few dozen more parameters.

Statistical reporting programs are old hat in mainframe and minicomputer systems. Mainframe and minicomputer administrators can generate printouts many inches thick showing performance, storage, and resource management statistics. It's natural then that Banyan's VINES, based on the minicomputer operating system Unix, was the first PC-based LAN operating system to offer strong statistical-management tools.

Novell's NetWare became popular because of hot marketing and fast performance, but to hold onto its lead and gain acceptance in the mahogany-paneled world of big business, NetWare needed the auditing and management-control tools to compete with minicomputers. Novell took some steps to improve reporting under NetWare 3.X, but now several vendors offer complex statistical reporting software for NetWare and other network operating systems.

Almost all of the LAN statistical reporting packages gather operational statistics without a special wiring hub or monitoring hardware. Network General's Watchdog is one exception; it includes a special high-quality Ethernet card for the workstation acting as the statistical report gatherer. Using a simple menu-driven system, Watchdog gives you detailed information about your network in screens like the one shown in Figure 10.11, and it alerts you with a message and sound when thresholds or limits are met.

Figure 10.11

Network General's Watchdog doesn't decode packets as the Sniffer does, but it shows network activity, and it displays an interesting marching bar chart showing the network activity for the past 60 seconds. It gathers this information from its own LAN adapter.

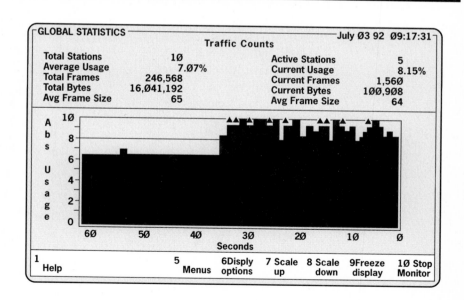

The statistical data you collect with such reporting programs constitutes a day-to-day assessment of your operation. This serves as a baseline to assist in LAN troubleshooting and as a platform for planning growth. The programs allow you to compile and format your LAN information so you can see statistics before and after a problem or change. Such information is valuable for finding problems and for projecting requirements and budgets. Programs that create data files in dBASE or comma-delimited ASCII formats lend themselves to financial-analysis tasks.

Some of the programs alleviate potential problems on a network, such as a virus infection, by watching for the signs of a virus and alerting a LAN manager at the first symptom. The programs warn you when application or data files show any change from the original. An example is TGR Software's SCUA Plus; it alerts you to a possible network virus and helps find any unwanted or disruptive file. Other products notice and alert your LAN manager to network bottlenecks, thus improving efficiency and performance. Several programs are useful in finding out whether you need additional memory on your server, or whether you need to upgrade a software application.

Managing the access rights of users—and other aspects of security within a network—can be a hassle, but some of these packages can add their own simple security schemes to those in the LAN software. Front-end menu products that run on every PC and keep people away from DOS, like Perfect Menu, significantly limit security and access problems.

Just like NetWare

Several of the statistical reporting packages designed for NetWare, like LANtrack (shown in Figure 10.12) and Net Companion (shown in Figure 10.13), have the look and feel of Novell's own utilities. They also integrate tightly with NetWare's internal structure.

The tight integration of third-party products was simplified in mid-1989, when Novell released Version 1.1 of a package called the Professional Development Series. This two-volume set of Novell red binders and software provides system developers with a unique C-language library of NetWare management functions.

Using this library of calls to NetWare, programmers can write code in a few weeks that would have taken months to create before. The release of this program library led to a rapid increase in the number of analysis and management tools available for NetWare. Unfortunately, many of the programs offer only the same set of features.

Some NetWare-specific packages run in the server as an Advanced NetWare 2.X Value-Added Process (VAP) or a NetWare 3.X NetWare Loadable Module (NLM). Monitrix, the network monitoring program illustrated in Figure 10.4, seems to disappear on the file server after you install it. Two differently priced versions of this product are available, a NetWare 2.X VAP and a NetWare 3.X NLM. Server-based VAPs and NLMs are more efficient when reporting server usage because they are near the action on the network server.

Figure 10.12

The LANtrack program marketed by Network Management, Inc. generates reports of events or conditions that exceed its programmed parameters. In this case, it is issuing warnings about a critical shortage of file storage space.

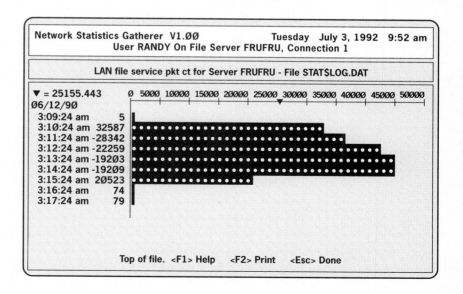

```
LANtrack Maintenance  Ver 1.Ø              Monday  July 2, 1992  3:36 pm
                        User RANDY on file server FRUFRU

FRUFRU/SYS:SYSTEM/TRK$LOG                     1,2Ø9 Bytes         93% of file

Ø5/29/9Ø  ØØ:53:12  FRUFRU     -Server Utilization  [S --> C]
                                 Critical = 95%,  Warning = 9Ø%,  now at = 99%
Ø5/29/9Ø  ØØ:53:12  FRUFRU     -Space free on SYS  [S --> C]
                                 Critical = 1Ø%,  Warning = 15%,  now at = 6%
Ø5/29/9Ø  ØØ:53:2Ø  FRUFRU     -Server Utilization  [C --> S]
                                 Critical = 95%,  Warning = 9Ø%,  now at = Ø%
Ø5/29/9Ø  ØØ:54:ØØ  FRUFRU     -Space free on SYS  [C ... C]
                                 Critical = 1Ø%,  Warning = 15%,  now at = 6%
Ø5/29/9Ø  ØØ:54:ØØ  FRUFRU     -Space free on SYS  [C ... C]
                                 Critical = 1Ø%,  Warning = 15%,  now at = 6%
Ø5/29/9Ø  ØØ:54:55  FRUFRU     -Space free on SYS  [C ... C]
                                 Critical = 1Ø%,  Warning = 15%,  now at = 6%
Ø5/29/9Ø  ØØ:54:55  FRUFRU     -Space free on SYS  [C ... C]
                                 Critical = 1Ø%,  Warning = 15%,  now at = 6%
Ø5/29/9Ø  ØØ:55:45  FRUFRU     -Space free on SYS  [C ... C]
                                 Critical = 1Ø%,  Warning = 15%,  now at = 6%
Ø5/29/9Ø  ØØ:55:45  FRUFRU     -Space free on SYS  [C ... C]
```

Figure 10.13

This screen from ETI Software's NetCompanion program reports on the activity of a specific file server over a period of time. The network manager can select the time span and server being monitored.

```
Network Statistics Gatherer  V1.ØØ          Tuesday  July 3, 1992  9:52 am
                 User RANDY On File Server FRUFRU, Connection 1

        LAN file service pkt ct for Server FRUFRU - File STAT$LOG.DAT

▼ = 25155.443      Ø  5ØØØ 1ØØØØ 15ØØØ 2ØØØØ 25ØØØ 3ØØØØ 35ØØØ 4ØØØØ 45ØØØ 5ØØØØ
Ø6/12/9Ø
3:Ø9:24 am      5
3:1Ø:24 am  32587
3:11:24 am -28342
3:12:24 am -22259
3:13:24 am -192Ø3
3:14:24 am -192Ø9
3:15:24 am  2Ø523
3:16:24 am     74
3:17:24 am     79

             Top of file.  <F1> Help    <F2> Print    <Esc> Done
```

NetWare-specific packages usually specialize in a particular task, or do something unique allowing the LAN administrator to track or trace network usage. For example, some packages link to NetWare's Bindery, a special database containing definitions and information on servers, users, and applications. BindView Plus offers you just such a complete screen picture and printed reports on the NetWare Bindery. Figure 10.14 shows a report on the server generated by The Frye Utilities for Networks.

Figure 10.14

This screen, generated by the Frye Utilities for Networks, marketed by Frye Computer Systems, reports on data gathered from a NetWare file server. The display includes a marching bar chart showing server utilization.

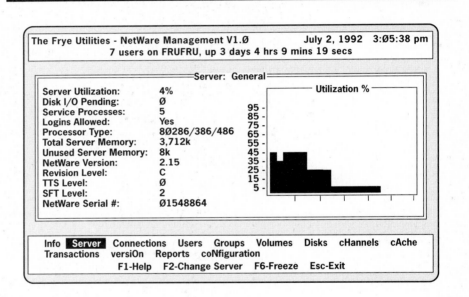

Some products specialize in reporting file-server disk-cache information. Good disk-cache information not only can help your LAN's execution, it also enables you to keep the network running smoothly. Fresh Utilities and LTStat have such a cache-report facility, but their reports show different types of data in varied formats.

TXD, from Thomas-Conrad Corp., has unique features that allow it to perform its statistical reporting tasks even when the network is malfunctioning. If the server is down, this statistical reporting tool runs node-to-node to give you a picture of your system's status. This could be very important if you want to trace an intrusion or problem.

Network statistical reporting packages aren't glamorous. But these packages can help a network manager work more efficiently, plan more effectively, and spot threatening situations before they become problems. You don't have to select only one of these products. You'll want to mix and match the best blend of reporting products for your network needs.

■ LAN Metering Software

LAN metering software:

👍 **Lowers software costs**

👍 **Prevents piracy**

👎 **Adds administrative workload**

LAN metering programs are tools for metering your network activity; they give you important information on how the network and network applications are used. Obviously they overlap with the functions of what I call statistical reporting software, but metering programs have the unique ability to regulate the number of simultaneous users for each application on your network and to establish better security on your LAN at the same time.

Marketing a networked application is a challenging task for many companies. The technology of file sharing isn't a problem anymore; any graduate of a one-semester programming course knows how to write applications that can have simultaneous multiple accesses to the same data file. But LAN piracy is a real threat to the survival of many software companies.

There are two forms of piracy: blatant and subtle. Blatant piracy takes place when someone copies a program from the LAN file server onto a floppy disk and walks out the door with it. But LANs are often the scene of subtler piracy. When a network administrator buys one single-user copy of a spreadsheet program and lets twelve people access it simultaneously, the company selling that product has been pirated out of a lot of money!

Some software companies try to ignore networks and offer no site-licensing agreements. If you want to use their packages legally at multiple PCs, you need to own multiple copies of each program. Particularly in the case of several federal-government computer contracts, this has led to organizations with closets full of shrink-wrapped packages—one for each potential user—while one copy of the program is shared on the network.

Other program vendors, notably Ashton-Tate, have fought the LAN piracy problem with techniques like internal counters that locked out attempts to use more than the authorized number of copies, and "bump disks" that increased the number of authorized users. Network administrators hated these restrictions because they interfered with legitimate backups and server restorations.

Today, most vendors of applications that can work on networks have site-licensing agreements available. Because no one has a perfect solution, the most common licensing agreement is on a "per server" basis. Only the most inexperienced or corrupt administrator would violate this type of license.

Per-server site licenses are expensive for small LANs. Many administrators find that buying a supply of single-copy versions of each program is still the best alternative. But smart network managers also know that it usually isn't economical to have a separate copy of an application program for each person on the network. Seldom does everyone need to use any one application at the same time. Smart network planners and administrators attempt to buy only enough copies of an application to meet the peak demand—but demands have a way of changing.

To cope with occasional excess demand, certain add-in software products (like Connect Computer Co.'s Turnstyle, shown in Figure 10.15) "meter" the number of applications in use. Some of the products can prevent more than a preset number of people from using the program at the same time. They send a message to the user who tries to exceed the limit. Although these programs try to buffer the negative impact of denying access, being locked out of an application usually makes people unhappy. They tend to take out this unhappiness on the LAN administrator.

Figure 10.15

Turnstyle, marketed by Connect Computer Co., monitors the copies of a program in use and limits use to the number of licensed copies. The program called Z has one user and is licensed for two.

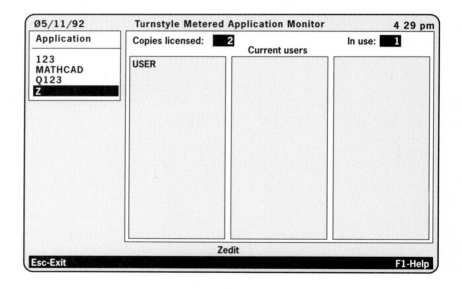

Other products only audit and report on use; they don't lock people out. The reports show when the demand exceeds the legal supply, and you can take action to correct the situation before it becomes a serious problem. With metering-software tools, you can track the number of copies of an application in use and determine the number of copies you should buy for effective LAN management. You can also improve the overall security of the network and compile statistical data.

Metering products vary in price from $100 to $800 and up, depending on the applications and nodes on your network. You can choose among simple packages that report LAN usage, menuing programs that control applications from behind customized screens, and auditing packages that create extensive reports on every type of network activity.

Legal Quandaries

LAN administrators have a moral and legal responsibility to audit or meter the use of all licensed applications. Software companies lose money when people violate their software licenses by letting more than the allowed number of users access the program.

Software companies have taken legal action against large corporate LAN pirates, although most cases are settled out of court. The vendors often learn about licensing violations from disgruntled employees looking for some way to strike at a former employer. Large organizations and independent auditing firms usually have software licensing on their internal audit checklists. If the application being audited is misused, there may be fines and discredit for the accused company. But with the audit and control measures established through metering software, license-abuse problems should never arise.

Because metering programs give you a full picture of who uses what resource when, they provide great support for budget requests and operations reports. You can wow the bean-counters by producing professional-looking reports from most of these programs. Add a few month-to-month statistics, put them on an overhead chart, and you may never have to worry about your budget requests being rejected!

Different Networks

There are metering products for every network environment. Most metering products use a TSR program to control or monitor how each workstation uses applications. All metering programs work well in networks running a file-server operating system like NetWare, VINES, or Microsoft's LAN Manager. These LAN operating systems can initiate the operation of the metering software from a protected script. Some metering programs actually run in the NetWare or VINES server and sit at the site of the action. Unfortunately, they can use up to 500k of server RAM.

Metering programs specifically designed for NetWare include Blue Lance's LT Auditor, Brightwork Development's SiteLock, Network Management's LANtrail, and Triticom's Argus/n. Programs supporting NetWare and a host of other network operating systems include The Aldridge Company's Precursor, Certus International Corp.'s Certus LAN, Connect Computer Co.'s Turnstyle, Net Inc.'s NetMenu, and Saber Software Corp.'s Saber Meter.

Some packages have additional capabilities. For example, SiteLock and Certus LAN 2.0 identify corrupt executable programs that may indicate viruses on your network.

In DOS-based networks, it's more difficult to ensure that the metering software takes full control, because it runs from either DOS batch or AUTOEXEC.BAT files. Determined pirates can circumvent batch files. In a sloppy network, where everyone has the right to create directories and files, the metering program is of little value because anyone can copy an application to a different directory and use it. This is one way of bypassing site licenses to use an application illegally.

A menuing system is a more secure type of metering program that runs particularly well on DOS-based networks. NetMenu and PreCursor are complex menuing tools for LANs. Their menuing capabilities allow you to limit the number of simultaneous users for each application during the menu setup process.

Metering programs help network administrators stay legal and economical at the same time. When you prevent software license abuse and piracy, you prevent harm to your organization and improve your overall management.

■ Network Management Brings Results

Apart from a few dancing histograms and moving bar charts, LAN administrative software may seem to be pretty dull stuff. It can bury you under mountains of statistics and create deskwork when you might crave technical work. Yet these programs can not only save your job by spotting problems, abuses, and trends, but they can also enhance your work by supporting requests for both money and people to help run your LANs.

CHAPTER

11

Workgroup Productivity

- The Scheduling Dilemma

- Electronic-Mail Programs for Productivity

- Get It Right the First Time

It seems that everyone from seminar speakers to industry watchers and computer journalists has an opinion on the definition of *workgroup productivity software*. Obviously, the category includes software that runs on a LAN and makes people more productive as a group. But while some pundits draw the category broadly enough to include any multiuser software, others defend only certain categories of software—such as project-management or document-control packages—as being true workgroup productivity programs. No matter where you draw the lines, these programs use the power of the network to help people work together more effectively, improve efficiency, and cut down on the time needed to perform some important but sometimes irritating tasks.

As an editor of *PC Magazine*, I set a relatively strict definition of workgroup productivity software; in this context, the reviewers exclude standard applications running on a network and focus on packages unique to a network or multiuser environment. I don't think you get much group synergy from using a standard application program on the network, but you can broaden everyone's span of interaction, improve communications, and reduce repetitive tasks by using certain kinds of multiuser network programs. For example, I include group-scheduling or calendaring software in the category but exclude multiuser spreadsheet programs. Scheduling programs, group telephone directories, and electronic mail are an important part of the workgroup productivity category of software.

Among the programs that fit my definition of workgroup productivity software are Higgins, Network Scheduler, Office Works, PackRat, Right Hand Man, Shoebox 3, Syzygy, Tandy Workgroup Companion, and Word-Perfect Office. These packages range in price from $50 to $250 per user; they typically run with a wide variety of networking software and have no sensitivity to the network interface cards or cabling used in the LAN. As Figure 11.1 suggests, these products typically offer many different kinds of functions.

Programs that concentrate entirely on providing electronic-mail capabilities, such as cc:Mail, Da Vinci e-mail, and The Network Courier, are another key part of the network productivity category. Many of the programs that sport a variety of features can interact with these specialized electronic-mail packages and use their services to notify people of meetings, deadlines, and other important events.

■ The Scheduling Dilemma

In many organizations, scheduling three or more busy people for a meeting, along with arranging for such facilities as a conference room and a slide projector, can be a frustrating and time-consuming task, requiring any number of phone calls. If one person or facility is not available when the other people or

Workgroup productivity programs:

👍 **Allow people to share information without disrupting the normal flow of work**

👍 **Provide time-saving and effort-saving ways to coordinate meetings and schedule the use of resources**

👍 **Allow people to discuss problems in real time without leaving their desks**

👎 **Require everyone to cooperate if the programs are to be effective**

👎 **Take RAM away from other applications**

facilities are, a series of negotiations begins. Mathematicians refer to this method of simultaneously handling several unknown factors as "progressive approximation," but whoever has to make all the contacts and coordinate the compromises will call it frustration.

Figure 11.1

The main menu for FutureSoft's workgroup productivity program Right Hand Man allows you to activate functions as diverse as networked electronic mail and a financial calculator. The shared telephone directory and scheduling features are particularly useful in many organizations.

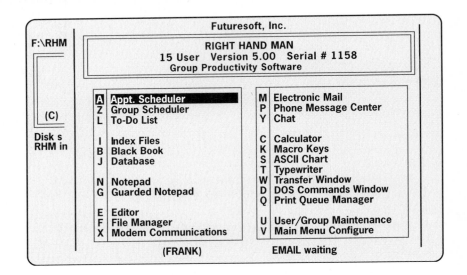

LAN scheduling products simplify this task and often eliminate the frustration. If everyone in the organization uses the scheduling software, one person can access the public calendars of other people and the sign-up sheets for resources; it won't take long to determine when everyone involved is free to attend a meeting. The process does not involve any invasion of privacy: As Figure 11.2 shows, the person planning the meeting doesn't see every detail on a personal calendar, but just enough to find the free time.

Variations in Approach

Scheduling programs vary in how they present free time. Some packages, like Higgins, display graphs of conflicting and open times. Right Hand Man and other programs use a representation of calendar pages, while a few programs use text explanations to outline the scheduling options. Powercore's Network Scheduler offers a series of different views depicting how you and others in the workgroup spend your time.

Figure 11.2

On this Right Hand Man group-scheduling screen, the hours when individuals already have activities scheduled are blocked out. Anyone trying to schedule a meeting can clearly see the available free time. In larger groups, the program will search for and nominate meeting times or show times with the least conflict.

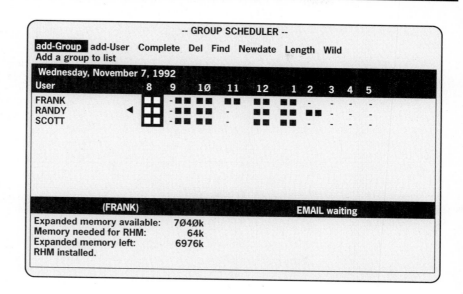

Scheduling programs also vary in how they confirm the proposed events. The simpler packages assume that if the event fits on the calendar, the people scheduled to attend will be there. Other programs ask for confirmation, while some go as far as to tie into electronic-mail programs to create notification and confirmation messages.

Personal calendars are at the heart of the group-scheduling process. The best scheduling software is useless if people don't cooperate by keeping their personal calendars current. Calendars that aren't readily available and easy to use will never be maintained by group members. With this in mind, it seems imperative that these programs allow you to run the personal calendar as a TSR (terminate-and-stay-resident) module and make it easy to use. At the same time, program developers must be conscious that the amount of memory a TSR module consumes is an important consideration.

One problem common to all of these packages is that they don't provide an easy way to schedule individual resources. Since a group of resources—like three conference rooms or three slide projectors—usually has only one manager, it's foolish to make that person repeatedly check into a separate personal-calendar module to confirm the scheduled use of each room or device. The person scheduling the meeting and the person managing the resources should not have to treat each identical projector, VCR, viewing screen, or meeting room as a separate entity.

More than E-Mail

Many of the scheduling products include electronic-mail features. With the notable exception of Higgins, though, the e-mail programs in these packages don't have the wide variety of features found in the special-purpose e-mail programs. Scheduling programs that also handle electronic mail work well in a self-contained homogeneous network, but only a few (Higgins and Right Hand Man among them) can readily communicate with dissimilar mail systems on other networks or on larger computers.

In addition to scheduling capabilities and electronic mail, these packages offer various productivity utilities. The names and telephone numbers of the people you do business with are a valuable resource for your organization. The networked utility we use most at PC Magazine LAN Labs is a shared telephone directory.

When an organization publishes an internal telephone directory or a list of external telephone contacts on paper, a lot of resources are needed to prepare and update it. But the story is different when each user on a LAN contributes to and maintains an electronic telephone directory. The process is quick and simple, and the results are current. And looking up a listing in an electronic phone book certainly beats fumbling with business cards or photocopied lists of names.

Many people on networks in relatively large offices take advantage of multiuser chat programs. These programs substitute an on-screen real-time discussion for a face-to-face meeting or telephone conference call. When two or more people use one of these programs on the LAN, the screen on each PC divides horizontally into separate windows, one for each user. The text that you type appears immediately in the window with your name. It's an ideal way for three or four people to conduct a fast exchange of ideas without getting up from their desks.

Chat programs are included in some integrated packages, such as Right Hand Man. Mustang Software sells a workgroup chat product called Brainstorm that is specifically designed for group problem solving and discussion. People using this program can participate in any of several simultaneous on-screen discussions. The program allows users to create private sessions, import text into the discussion, and take advantage of a variety of different text-manipulation techniques.

Other shared resources available in productivity packages include document indexes and notepads. Many of the packages include personal productivity tools such as calculators and private telephone directories as well.

Workgroup productivity packages can effectively reduce the hassle of managing the daily activities of corporate employees. These packages alone don't provide sufficient justification for installing a network if you haven't already got one, but if you can also take advantage of a network's file- and printer-sharing capabilities, the increased productivity and reduced frustration these programs provide can be a welcome dividend from your LAN investment.

■ Electronic-Mail Programs for Productivity

The editors of *PC Magazine* are e-mail junkies. We make decisions, send magazine copy, and exchange information over electronic mail, and we provide electronic interaction with our readers through our on-line service, PC MagNet, as shown in Figure 11.3.

Figure 11.3

PC MagNet, an interactive on-line service that can be accessed via CompuServe, provides a way for the editors of *PC Magazine* to exchange information and viewpoints with the readers. The menu system makes it easy for readers to download utilities and other useful programs and to participate in editorial forums.

```
 4  Forums - talk to PC Magazine
 5  Electronic Mail
 6  Free -- Participate in a PC Magazine Survey
 7  Search for PC Magazine Reviews
 8  Computer Library Searchable Databases
 9  Consumer Reference Library
1Ø  Other Ziff Services
11  CompuServe Information Service

!4

PC  MagNet                    PCM-7Ø

 1  Editorial Forum      ----  Viewpoints
 2  Utilities/Tips Forum  --  PC Magazine Utilities, Tutor, Advisor
 3  Programming Forum  --  OS/2, Power Programming, Languages
 4  After Hours Forum  ----  Music, Games, Politics, Economics, SF, Film
 5  Practice Forum      ------  FREE!  Learn how to use the forums
 6  File Finder        ---------  Locate files in forum libraries

 7  Type a Letter to the Editor
 8  Upload a Submission to PC Magazine

!
Esc for ATtention, Home to SWitch          Capture Off        On: ØØ:Ø1:Ø9
```

On a practical level, the biggest benefits we get from using electronic mail are that it nearly eliminates telephone tag and that it allows our widespread staff to ignore time zones and office hours. These capabilities do a great deal to improve our individual and group productivity and to reduce frustration. The more people in an organization use e-mail, with its ability to store information and deliver it when the recipient is ready to take it, the less they are controlled by the demands of that real-time communications device, the telephone.

E-mail programs:

👍 **Reduce telephone tag**

👍 **Improve efficiency**

👍 **Work with various computers and operating systems**

👍 **Span great distances**

👎 **Decrease personal contact**

👎 **Create complex installation problems**

Electronic-mail systems break the tyranny that time holds over communications. For most of recorded history you couldn't engage in real-time communications farther than you could project your voice. The time required to communicate severely limited the quantity and quality of communications. The introduction of electronic devices, particularly the telephone, eliminated the time needed to move a message across distances, but telephone communications brought with them the new requirement of synchronicity—the need to beat the game of telephone tag. For most of this century, if no one answered the phone when it rang, the potentially fast-moving message wasn't delivered.

We work around the problem of synchronicity by using answering machines and facsimile machines. Additionally, many organizations have found relief from telephone tag and discovered a whole new way of communicating through electronic mail. Electronic mail breaks the tyranny of time by moving messages across long distances quickly and by storing messages and forwarding them to you where and when you're ready to receive them.

Our surveys of *PC Magazine* readers with local area networks continually show network e-mail as the third most common use of a network—after sharing printers and sharing access to mainframe computers. Once organizations develop the critical mass of users needed to make electronic mail effective, it becomes an indispensable and nearly addictive communications link.

The 80/20 rule of office correspondence says that 80 percent of the words you write are for internal consumption and 20 percent go outside your organization. E-mail makes it much easier to create and distribute the internal 80 percent, and it can invisibly handle distribution to the critically important external 20 percent, too.

Easy to Do, Hard to Do Well

It's easy to write an e-mail software package. The program simply writes files containing messages into specified shared subdirectories and retrieves them on request. You'll find e-mail capabilities in practically every DOS-based LAN operating system, such as Artisoft's LANtastic and DCA's 10NET, and in some unlikely programs such as the PC Tools utilities from Central Point Software.

The Basics of E-Mail and Beyond

The basic functions of electronic mail, illustrated by the menu shown in Figure 11.4, include creating, reading, forwarding, replying to, and issuing receipts for messages. All e-mail packages must do these jobs. Of course, the e-mail programs vary significantly in the utilities, menus, and other amenities they provide for creating and receiving messages.

Figure 11.4

The pull-down menu from the electronic-mail system Da Vinci illustrates the primary functions of an electronic-mail program. Attachments to electronic-mail messages can include binary data files.

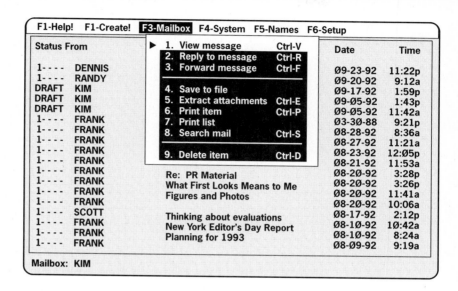

Here are some of the most useful features in an e-mail system:

- a TSR message-waiting module
- a pop-up window for reading messages
- the option of importing text files into messages
- the option of attaching binary files to outgoing messages
- the option of using standard word processing programs to prepare mail
- return receipts for messages
- electronic folders for special subjects
- encryption during transmission
- encryption of stored messages

Electronic-mail programs running on mainframe and Unix-based computer networks defined these functions years ago. Programs competing for success in the LAN-based e-mail market must have additional capabilities to differentiate themselves from the pack. As an example, The Coordinator, marketed by Action Technologies, provides a structured approach to the exchange of communications. As Figure 11.5 shows, The Coordinator helps its users keep track of their electronic-mail correspondence.

Figure 11.5

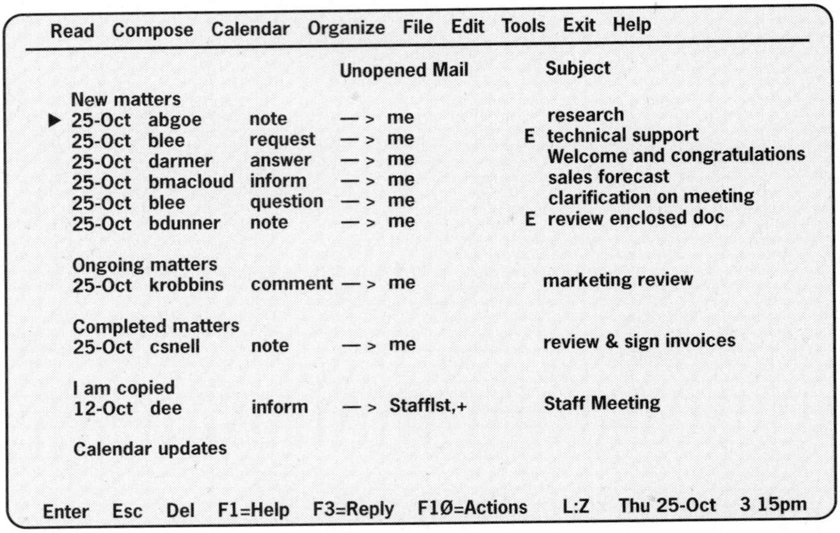

The Coordinator, from Action Technologies, makes it easy to follow the thread of a conversation by categorizing messages according to topic and status. This program even includes a variety of prepared replies such as "Get back to me in seven days," and it reminds you when a reply is due.

```
┌─────────────────────────────────────────────────────────────┐
│  Read  Compose  Calendar  Organize  File  Edit  Tools  Exit  Help │
│  ─────────────────────────────────────────────────────────── │
│                          Unopened Mail        Subject         │
│  New matters                                                  │
│ ▶ 25-Oct  abgoe     note      — >  me          research       │
│   25-Oct  blee      request   — >  me        E technical support │
│   25-Oct  darmer    answer    — >  me          Welcome and congratulations │
│   25-Oct  bmacloud  inform    — >  me          sales forecast │
│   25-Oct  blee      question  — >  me          clarification on meeting │
│   25-Oct  bdunner   note      — >  me        E review enclosed doc │
│                                                               │
│   Ongoing matters                                             │
│   25-Oct  krobbins  comment — >  me            marketing review │
│                                                               │
│   Completed matters                                           │
│   25-Oct  csnell    note      — >  me          review & sign invoices │
│                                                               │
│   I am copied                                                 │
│   12-Oct  dee       inform    — >  Stafflst,+   Staff Meeting │
│                                                               │
│   Calendar updates                                            │
│                                                               │
│  Enter  Esc  Del  F1=Help   F3=Reply  F1Ø=Actions   L:Z   Thu 25-Oct   3 15pm │
└─────────────────────────────────────────────────────────────┘
```

Since LAN redirector and driver software can take as much as 100k of RAM, any additional memory lost to the e-mail service can be significant. cc:Mail and other products include an unload command that will terminate TSR operation—if the e-mail TSR was the last TSR module loaded. Memory-management programs like Helix Software's NetRoom and Quarterdeck Office Systems' QEMM help reduce the impact on RAM by putting the notification software in the memory space above the 640k DOS boundary.

Other important capabilities include message encryption, the ability to set up special-interest bulletin boards where users can post messages pertaining to a specific topic, and the ability to attach binary files to e-mail messages. The best programs, like Higgins E-mail (Figure 11.6) and cc:Mail, include extensive editing capabilities, special utilities to help you easily prepare text for transmission, and the option of using your own text editor to create mail.

Top-notch LAN e-mail programs also include the ability to connect across long distances and exchange messages with dissimilar systems. For the most part, these packages gain this ability through the actions of a program called the Message Handling Service (MHS).

Some packages, such as cc:Mail, Higgins, and The Network Courier, offer their own connections to different electronic-mail systems and services. For example, Higgins offers a $995 add-on module called Higgins To:FAX that interfaces with the Intel Connection CoProcessor. This module sends facsimile copies of outgoing electronic mail, using the CoProcessor's modem for data exchanges with other CoProcessor-equipped machines. Even though some companies sell their own inter- and intranetwork e-mail links, MHS is the most flexible intermediary system.

Figure 11.6

Higgins E-mail provides convenient storage and retrieval of blocks of frequently used text. Strong editing functions and the ability to route, classify, track, and respond to messages easily are features of the best electronic-mail programs.

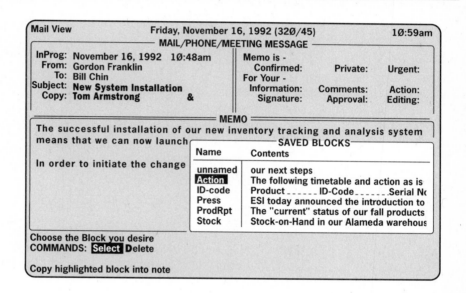

Gateways to fax systems work well for sending fax messages from an e-mail system. The major drawback of e-mail/fax systems is the same one plaguing standalone PC/fax systems: poor ability to receive incoming mail. There is no standard way to address a fax message to a particular recipient; someone must use special software to view each incoming fax and route it to the right person. And incoming fax messages are saved as graphics images, requiring a laser printer with a lot of memory to reproduce them on paper.

The Purpose, Power, and Promise of MHS

MHS was developed by Action Technologies, the same people who market The Coordinator, but Novell now manages development of the program. Some companies, like Mustang Software, bundle it with their e-mail programs, and Novell makes it available at no additional charge to every purchaser of NetWare. (You have to send in a postcard found in the NetWare package.) The growing popularity of MHS comes because writing programs that use it is relatively easy and because it works on practically any network. Figure 11.7 shows a management screen from MHS.

Figure 11.7

The MHS program provides a list of applications on the network with MHS capabilities (upper-right corner). The left side of the screen shows network users. The administrator must link the users with their primary e-mail programs using the window in the lower-right corner.

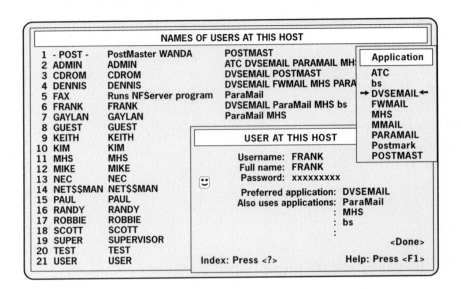

MHS is easy to understand if you think of it as a communications program that runs on a networked PC and controls the serial ports while using extensive scripts and moving data in and out of shared files. The PC acting as an MHS server is dedicated to the task. MHS shares files with application programs such as cc:Mail, Da Vinci e-mail, Higgins, and Ashton-Tate's spreadsheet and analysis software, Framework III. These applications use MHS to connect with distant homogeneous LANs and as a gateway to dissimilar mail systems.

MHS can connect homogeneous LANs over telephone lines, but its real value lies in the MHS gateway interfaces that are available for DEC, IBM, and a growing number of other electronic-mail systems. Neither Action Technologies nor Novell makes the MHS gateway interface software. This comes from yet other companies that specialize in understanding the detailed actions needed to link dissimilar mail systems.

The network administrator installs the MHS software on the one PC destined to be the MHS server. The MHS program requires information about the people who use e-mail, their network e-mail applications, and the off-network electronic-mail services they use. The control program communicates with the network e-mail applications and runs separate software products called *gateways* to access off-network e-mail resources.

Not all networked e-mail packages have MHS capabilities, but when products have the ability to send messages to MHS, they automatically gain the ability to exchange messages with each other. For example, if some people in your organization use Microsoft Windows, they might want to use cc:Mail, a product with excellent Windows compatibility. Other people who don't use Windows might prefer the structured approach to mail handling provided by The Coordinator. The MHS server running on the network will automatically become aware of these programs and route messages between them. Each person with a networked PC could run a different MHS-compatible electronic-mail program and still stay in touch with everyone else, because MHS would move the messages between programs.

MHS servers on geographically separate networks can communicate over modems and dial-up telephone lines. They exchange e-mail messages according to the schedule you create.

Moving messages between applications inside the network is the major service MHS performs without adding other software. Its other important function involves moving messages between e-mail systems on the local network and those in completely different environments. You need to add gateway programs to link MHS to the external environment. MHS controls the operation of these gateways and runs them according to your script.

The gateways run in the same PC that acts as the MHS server. You must program each gateway with the appropriate telephone numbers, communications parameters, account numbers, and access codes. Of course, you also must provide modems or direct computer links between the MHS server and the external system. The designer of the gateway software has to understand the external mail system and the structure of the MHS-compatible files and create the code to translate between them.

A variety of companies market MHS gateways for different mail and facsimile systems. On-Site Information Systems markets an MCI Mail gateway for MHS that it sells in a five-user version for $595. Alcom sells a product that links MHS to a wide variety of services including MCI Mail, Western Union's EasyLink, and telex. The basic Alcom LanFax package sells for $1,495, and add-on gateways are available at an additional cost. The MCI Mail gateway, for example, is $795.

Any package that addresses MHS can link to Digital Equipment Corp.'s All-in-1, IBM's PROFS, MCI Mail, VMSMail, Wang Office, and other services through Soft-Switch, an on-line computer service. Subscribers use the MHS protocol to send mail to Soft-Switch, which then translates and resends the mail to the specified destination system.

Other programs besides electronic-mail packages can take advantage of MHS. Ashton-Tate's Framework spreadsheet has package MHS capabilities, so people can easily exchange spreadsheets even if they don't have a full e-mail system.

The MHS format has a lot of promise, but the software itself shows its age. It's difficult to provide security for messages transiting MHS because the program uses shared-access subdirectories, and even the fairly small population of users at PC Magazine LAN Labs keeps our MHS server busy. The program would benefit from being re-hosted to a multitasking operating system, so you could simultaneously run multiple MHS sessions driving multiple modems and providing security on at least the departmental level. On the other hand, the PC running today's version of MHS doesn't need much CPU power or memory above 640k, nor any disk drives, so you can use the oldest cast-off 4.77-MHz PC as an MHS server without difficulty. You can also create multiple servers on the same network if the load gets heavy.

Getting Your Mail Remotely

People calling in from a PC on the road or from home can use a LAN-based electronic-mail system in three ways. Some e-mail packages, such as Higgins, are available in a special version that looks like the LAN version but runs through a modem and connects to a special communications server for e-mail on the network. These programs will quickly transfer incoming and outgoing messages, including attached non-ASCII files, while leaving a copy of all mail in your network mailbox.

If the e-mail company doesn't sell a special piece of software, you can easily use a modem remote-control program like Carbon Copy, Close-Up, pcAnywhere, or Remote[2] (shown in Figure 11.8) to set up a remote-entry communications server. Callers remotely run the LAN e-mail program on a networked PC, read the screen, create replies, and use the remote-control program's file-transfer abilities to transfer any non-ASCII files. This technique also keeps all the mail on the network while giving you full access. This is the technique the PC Magazine LAN Labs crew uses, and we think it works fine—although we did discover the need for an 800 number on the data-entry telephone line so that people on the road can call in easily.

Finally, MHS has a remote-entry program module. This program calls into the MHS server and lets you exchange mail while you run a single-user version of any MHS-compatible e-mail system.

X.400 for Intermail Communications

MHS and e-mail gateways sold by various companies provide workable ways to link different electronic-mail systems. Nonetheless, programmers must customize each gateway program. In an ideal world, each program would conform to specific standards spelling out how different products can exchange electronic mail.

Figure 11.8

Remote[2] from Digital Communications Associates allows people calling in with a modem to use a networked PC to run programs and easily perform tasks such as checking their electronic mail. Authorized users have specific passwords and associated rights on the network.

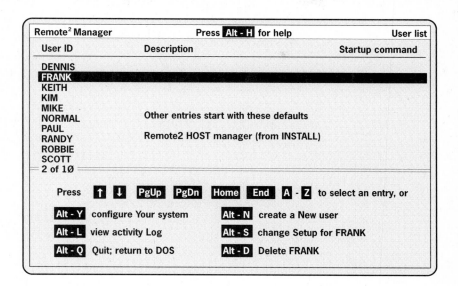

The CCITT has developed a set of rules for e-mail communications. This international committee's X.400 standard describes how to set up mail messages, name users, control access, and configure many other factors. The good news is that many companies are developing new products or interfaces for existing products that conform to the X.400 standard. The bad news is that implementing X.400 will probably take more time and money than most managers of PC-based LANs care to spend.

First adopted in 1984, the X.400 standard receives a lot of lip service, but only a few specialized products support it. In practice, the addressing scheme is burdensome and creates a great deal of processing overhead. Instead of including X.400 services in commercial programs, companies have delivered specialized X.400 gateways.

The first X.400 specification relied on X.25 as an underlying transmission protocol. X.25, the international standard for packet-switched wide-area data communications, is more popular in the rest of the world than in the United States. In the U.S., the first gateway services were provided by X.25 value-added networks such as Tymnet and Telenet. A later evolution of the X.400 standard encourages building X.400 gateway products for use over local Ethernet links as well as long-distance X.25 networks.

At this time, only large organizations whose managers feel obliged to support international standards seem to make good use of X.400 systems.

People with less stringent policies will find good ways to link e-mail systems using gateway options available from various companies and through MHS.

Making the Difficult Look Easy Isn't Easy

Once the system administrator gets all of the e-mail packages, the MHS server, and the gateways set up properly, users can send mail to dissimilar systems by simply including the recipient's name in the mailing list and hitting the Enter key. Anyone on the LAN can use a few keystrokes to post the same message off to people connected to mainframes, the guy in the next office, a colleague on MCI Mail, a friend with just a fax machine, and someone who receives mail only in stamped paper envelopes. But our experience shows that setting up those mail programs and gateway programs can take a lot of consultation and experimentation.

The address strings hidden behind the seemingly innocent "recipient name" block in each application look like cartoon cuss words with strange groups of letters punctuated by @|#: and other symbols. The system administrator or savvy end user must create such an address string for each potential addressee. Each combination of application program, gateway program, and target system contains its own rules, hazards, and shortcuts. The only way to avoid wasted time and high levels of frustration is to make sure you can get good technical support from the e-mail and gateway companies. Once you learn the chants and incantations needed to link your particular combination of systems, you can work magic. Until then, you might as well try to transmute lead into gold.

If your organization plans to install a hundred or more electronic-mail nodes spread across more than one physical network, you'll probably need specialized help getting started. Unless you foresee expansion continuing for years, it isn't worth developing the expertise in-house, so buying the time of an experienced systems integrator or consultant is a smart idea.

E-Mail for Growth

An e-mail program simplifies information-sharing tasks for its users and moves information quickly without the problem of telephone tag. But large systems aren't simple to install and manage properly. Fortunately, links such as MHS and product-specific gateways allow you to mix and match e-mail systems throughout your organization to meet specific needs. Electronic mail is the foundation for a strong and practical information-sharing system in your LAN.

■ Get It Right the First Time

Individuals who use a network invest a lot of their own time and resources in workgroup productivity software. They come to depend on their scheduling programs to keep them on time, and on their electronic mail to keep them up to date. Their LAN-based telephone directories and lists of contacts become valuable corporate resources. Once they learn to use a system and trust it with their information, they won't want to move to new software merely because they've outgrown the old system or because it becomes unsupportable. You should put forth a lot of effort to make sure the workgroup productivity programs you buy will serve your needs for a long time.

I suggest that you involve at least a representative sampling of the people who will use the workgroup productivity tools when selecting the software. In other chapters of this book, I've explained that you can safely shop for such products as Ethernet adapters and the computers you use as servers based on price. But cost should be a small consideration when you look for workgroup productivity software, because the investment you make can pay good dividends. Ease of use, room for growth, and support from a good company are the important factors to consider when you make this purchasing decision.

CHAPTER

12

Linking PCs to Mainframe Systems

- Mainframe and Minicomputer Systems

- TCP/IP for Multiplatform Networking

The computer industry is buzzing with the word *downsizing*. It refers to the process of replacing large, centralized computer installations with networks of PCs. But despite the trend toward downsizing in the development of new applications and systems, organizations have billions of dollars invested in proven programs running on centralized mainframe and minicomputer systems. Replacing these programs is not cost-effective, and there are scientific and engineering applications that will require the power of a mainframe for years to come. Mainframes and minicomputers are going to be around for many years, and increasingly, people will want to use PCs to interact with them.

In this chapter I'll describe how to link PCs—and particularly networked PCs—to dissimilar computer systems. I'll provide specifics on the alternative ways you can connect PCs to IBM mainframe computers, along with general information on using a set of protocols called TCP/IP to connect to a variety of computers from different manufacturers.

■ Mainframe and Minicomputer Systems

A mainframe computer system lives up to its label as a "system." Many different pieces of hardware and software must play together in a successful mainframe system. The system must have at least one central processor, but it isn't unusual for several processors to operate together to share the processing load and to provide backup processing in case one device fails. Such a system might include gigabytes of on-line data storage and even more storage using tape and other archive systems.

Minicomputer systems are more difficult to define. Only a few years ago you could safely define a minicomputer as a computer with over a megabyte of memory. Today, the PCs many people use on their desktops have more processing power and memory than the minicomputer used by a group of people down the hall. I'm not going to attempt a technical definition of a minicomputer because it will immediately be out of date, but characteristically it is a computer running a multiuser operating system and not able to use DOS or OS/2 applications.

People typically interact with modern mainframes and minicomputers through devices called *terminals* with screens and keyboards. While the terminals include their own processors, memory, and sophisticated video capabilities, they aren't PCs and they don't run application programs. The mainframe applications—often written to serve many users simultaneously—run in the mainframe or mini's central processing unit. One terminal can typically have several programs or sessions running on the mainframe at the same time.

Manufacturers offer a variety of connection alternatives for terminals. IBM provides ways for terminals to connect to the central computer system over coaxial cables, through modems, and as part of a local area network.

IBM and the BUNCH

In the 1970s and early '80s there were many mainframe and minicomputer companies. The "BUNCH"—Burroughs, Univac, NCR, Control Data, and Honeywell—gave IBM a run for its money. Digital Equipment Corp. established itself as the major vendor of minicomputers. Other companies such as Amdahl and Telex cloned pieces and parts of the IBM mainframe systems.

Today, Digital stresses the use of its minicomputers as servers. Unisys, built on the structure of Burroughs and Sperry, continues to have success in certain mainframe market areas, but most PC-to-central-computer products are designed for IBM mainframes. If you need to link a PC to a Unisys mainframe, the solution is easy: Chi Corp. has an excellent line of products for PC-to-Unisys links.

IBM 3270

Any explanation of how to hook PCs to IBM mainframe computers has to deal with a lot of IBM equipment numbers and describe the IBM network architecture schemes. IBM's major line of terminals, printers, and other communications devices falls into the general category of the "3270 family" of equipment. Each type of device has a specific model number, many of which begin with the digits 327. They're all designed to work in concert to orchestrate access to the mainframe's computing power, for users of both PCs and other equipment. Well over 2 million 3270-family terminals were in use in 1990.

IBM's Systems Network Architecture (SNA) is its grand scheme for connecting its myriad 3270-family products. It includes a flexible suite of network protocols that can be configured in several different ways. Here's how the 3270 family of products fits into various SNA setups.

In a classic 3270 system, each 3278 or 3279 terminal connects to a 3174 or 3274 *terminal cluster controller* through coaxial cable. The cluster controller acts as a concentrator by gathering messages from the terminals for more efficient transmission to the mainframe.

Groups of cluster controllers attach via a telecommunications line (which can run a few hundred feet locally or even across the country, through leased telephone lines and modems) to another, larger device called a *communications controller* or a *front-end processor* (FEP). The common IBM front-end processors are models 3705 and 3725. Other companies, such as ITT Courier, Lee Data, and Memorex Telex, make products that are "plug compatible" and compete with IBM's 3270 devices.

In a relatively recent evolution of the classic plan, IBM gave the 3174 terminal controller, the 3725 FEP, the 3745 communications controller, and other devices the ability to become nodes on a Token-Ring network. This architecture requires relatively expensive adapters and more memory on the 3270 hardware. Because the IBM Token-Ring Interface Coupler mainframe hardware has the acronym TIC, this architecture is usually called a "tick" or "tick connection."

PUs and LUs

In IBM's SNA connection scheme, each terminal or printer connected to the controller is called a *physical unit*, or PU. Different kinds of PUs have different capabilities. The front-end processor expects to send certain kinds of data to and get specific kinds of responses from each type of PU.

Each PU holds one or more *logical units*, or LUs; these address and interact with the host in an SNA network. It is actually the LU—typically a program—that does the work that's transmitted over the communications link. IBM's Virtual Telecommunications Access Method (VTAM) software, which runs in the mainframe, works with the Network Control Program (NCP) in the front-end processor to recognize, configure, and communicate with the LUs.

During operation, the 3278/9 terminals send messages called *scan codes* to the cluster controller each time a key is pressed. The cluster controller echoes the keystrokes back to the terminal so that they are confirmed and displayed on the screen. Data from the mainframe host goes in steps through the front-end processor, to the cluster controller, and into a display buffer in the terminal.

Data coming to the terminal for screen presentation is handled in blocks called *fields*; these can vary in length from a few characters to a whole screen. The size and characteristics of a field depend on what the terminal finds in the display buffer. Characteristics like blinking, reverse video, seven-color displays, and underlining are defined by modified characters containing extended-attribute bytes. These bytes give different meanings to incoming characters to let them represent functions not ordinarily handled in the 8-bit data alphabet the 3270 terminals use.

Easy Transfers

Simple file transfers between a PC and mainframe are often performed using an IBM editing utility on the mainframe called IND$FILE. This method of moving data is effective, but it's slow. Companies like Linkware Corp., Mackensen Corp., Micro Tempus, VM Personal Computing, and others sell software for both the PC and the host that speeds file transfers between them.

Making mainframe data easily available to PC applications is another task for paired PC/host software. Companies as diverse as Lotus Development Corp. and Martin Marietta market software for the PC that extracts data from mainframe systems for PC applications.

One Screen for All and All Screens for One

Today, people have PCs on their desktops. Personal computers offer a flexibility and responsiveness the mainframe systems can't touch. But many people with PCs also need access to mainframe systems. People from system programmers to administrative assistants make good use of multiple mainframe sessions. Some people continually monitor mail systems (such as IBM's popular PROFS) in one session while using a scheduling program in a second session and a major mainframe application in a third one. People developing applications often have multiple sessions active to receive error messages and to simulate several users.

But people don't want screens and keyboards for both terminals and PCs on their desktops, and there are many ways that application programs running in a PC could use information distilled by a mainframe application. So the logical thing to do is to make the PC act like a terminal. Some of the most successful and long-lived PC add-on products, such as DCA's IRMA terminal emulator, give PCs the ability to serve as terminals for IBM mainframes.

Before a PC and an IBM mainframe can communicate and transfer data with each other, some major obstacles must be circumvented. For example, the PC's keyboard doesn't have as many keys as a 3270 terminal does, and the terminal has several special graphics characters that aren't in the PC's screen repertoire. The PC also lacks an appropriate communications interface, and it uses the ASCII data alphabet instead of IBM's standard mainframe alphabet, the Extended Binary Coded Decimal Interchange Code (EBCDIC).

There are currently three basic ways to overcome these difficulties: by adding a plug-in card combined with software and/or hardware and making the PC act like a 3270 terminal when attached to a cluster controller, by connecting a protocol converter between the PC and the mainframe that translates the mainframe's data into a form usable by the PC, or by using a network to link the PC and the mainframe.

Connecting the PC to a 3174 or 3274 terminal cluster controller through coaxial cable is a popular technique because it is simple and requires no action at the mainframe end. The technique of using a separate computer called a *protocol converter* to interface the PC and the mainframe has lost its appeal because it is expensive, and today's powerful PCs can handle the terminal-emulation tasks very well. Knowing the subject of this book, you can guess that I'll focus on using a LAN to link PCs and mainframes.

Regardless of the connection scheme, these terminal-emulation products let you touch a key to toggle between local DOS programs and mainframe processes. You don't even have to consider finding desk space for both a PC and a mainframe terminal.

Terminal-Emulation Functions and Features

The terminal-emulation portions of the different products on the market differ mainly in the variety of IBM terminals they ape. Some products act like simple character-mode terminals, while others let the PC, driven by mainframe programs, display excellent color graphics screens. All of them give you the option to remap the PC's keyboard so that various keystroke combinations send the messages expected from the special function keys on IBM terminals.

A PC acting as a terminal operates in one of several modes. A CUT (Control Unit Terminal) can have a single session with the mainframe. In the DFT (Distributed Function Terminal) mode, the 3270 terminal can have up to five concurrent sessions with the mainframe. IBM has another, related mode it calls MLT (Multiple Logical Terminal), allowing multiple sessions with CUT-mode terminals through IBM's 3174 terminal cluster controller.

An application program interface, or API, looks for inputs from other programs. When an API is available, people who write applications like accounting, inventory, and communications programs can use simple commands to move data through the network to the mainframe and interact with mainframe applications. The API converts the relatively simple commands that have been written in C or some other high-level programming language into the complex actions needed to move, verify, and store data.

IBM has defined several APIs for use with mainframe applications. Some of them require software running on both the PC and the mainframe, but others work locally in the PC. For instance, IBM's 3270-PC API and the High-Level-Language Application Program Interface (HLLAPI) run only on the PC; Advanced Program-to-Program Communications (APPC) requires software on both the PC and the mainframe, but it allows for a high degree of integration between PC and mainframe applications.

These products also have the ability to record and replay macros. A *macro* is a set of recorded keystrokes stored and ready to replay. Macros make it easy to use applications that normally require many keystrokes to start. The programs can memorize the keystrokes you use and store them as a macro that you can easily initiate. Attachmate Corp.'s facility for creating macros is particularly handy because you can easily create a macro that will pause, wait for keyboard input, and then continue. This is useful for entering a date, a password, or some other piece of information.

3270 Under Windows

The topic might sound dry, but products providing 3270 terminal emulation under Windows are exciting to see because they display the full activities of several mainframe programs simultaneously in small windows you can easily read.

On DOS machines, the character-based environment forces the emulation programs to produce sterile but functional screens. When you run multiple sessions, you typically have to page through full-screen displays. Attachmate's Extra!, a DOS-based emulator, provides multiple windows on the same screen, but each one provides only an incomplete view of the session it represents.

Under Microsoft Windows, 3270 terminal emulators can shrink the window displaying a 3270 session almost to postage-stamp size and still provide a usable and readable display. You can monitor the activity in as many mainframe sessions as you're likely to have and still use other local applications. Figure 12.1 shows multiple sessions running under Wall Data's Rumba program.

Figure 12.1

This Rumba screen displays five mainframe computer sessions simultaneously. A quick click of the mouse puts you into any mainframe session or DOS window. The keypad in the lower right corner makes it easy to select special functions available to terminals but not included on the PC's keyboard.

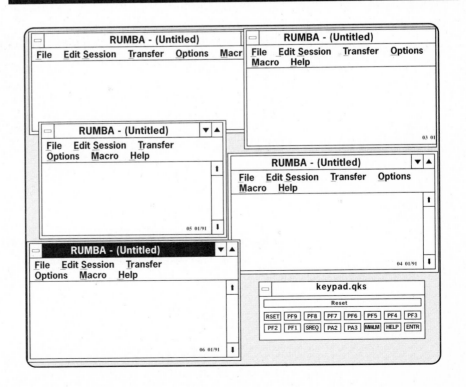

Such 3270 emulators thrive in the Windows environment. They let you make icons to launch mainframe applications, provide interesting icons to show mainframe activity, and use three functions of Windows—DDE, DLL, and the clipboard—to link mainframe and Windows applications.

Chi Corp. made good use of entertaining icons, shown in Figure 12.2, in designing LinkUp 3270 for Microsoft Windows. Using an Old West motif, it has cactus trees to hang data on, Boot Hill to kick off programs, and other entertaining images. Wall Data uses a Rumba dance theme in its product with equal effectiveness; the packaging and icons all show the PC and mainframe working in step. Users of machines like Sun workstations have known for years that there's nothing wrong with being entertained while you work. These packages follow that lead.

Figure 12.2

This screen shows multiple mainframe sessions running under Chi Corp.'s LinkUp 3270 for Windows. LinkUp 3270 features clever icons and toggle switches that appear to move as you turn a feature off and on.

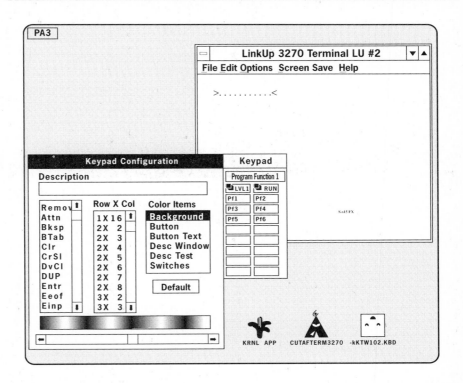

The dynamic data exchange (DDE) capability of Windows allows different applications to share data. The techniques used are called *hotspot* and *hotlink*. Under the hotspot technique, you can control mainframe applications with your mouse. The terminal-emulation program understands cursor movements and mouse inputs over screen elements generated by the host. In other words, you can double-click your mouse on a screen element generated by the host application or mainframe communications software, and the Windows terminal-emulation software will tell the host to take a corresponding action.

Under the hotlinks scheme, a specially written application can accept messages in predefined areas of a display generated by the host computer. For example, Microsoft Excel can hotlink to the host display session and react to the information displayed on the screen.

The 3270 emulation programs running under Windows can also benefit from Dynamic Link Libraries (DLLs). DLLs are a group of functional program elements, such as device drivers, shared by all Windows applications. The sharing action provides for efficient use of memory.

IBM has a product called Windows Connection, Version 2.0, which uses the DLL to call IBM's HLLAPI programming interface. HLLAPI allows the personal computer or workstation program to interact with the mainframe application rather than the user at the keyboard. IBM's Windows Connection creates a pipe between HLLAPI.DLL and a DOS HLLAPI TSR to transfer requests and data between the Windows applications and the DOS sessions.

Another way applications can share data is through the Microsoft Windows clipboard. All of the products in this market include an edit feature, allowing the user to copy portions of the host display to the clipboard in Windows and then paste the same data to another application's Windows session. This differs from DDE in that the clipboard requires user intervention in moving the data between applications.

The graphical interface also helps reduce problems associated with remapping the PC keyboard to emulate the much larger 3270 keyboard. On-screen keyboard maps make it easy to re-align the keyboard and to use the mouse instead of keystrokes to select special "keys."

The Coaxial Terminal Connection

The coaxial adapter card architecture, pioneered by DCA and now offered by a dozen companies, supplies each PC with a direct coaxial attachment (common to IBM 3270 terminals) for the mainframe's terminal cluster controller. The PC runs software that makes it act like an IBM terminal, and the mainframe regards it as such. Data is transmitted via standard IBM 3270 cables. The terminal-emulation software in the PC not only lets you transfer files between the PC and the mainframe, but it typically lets you toggle between mainframe sessions and DOS programs.

Because this type of architecture calls for a dedicated port for each PC on the mainframe's terminal cluster controller, whether or not it is active, connecting a large number of PCs via this method becomes expensive. The performance (measured in terms of throughput and response time) is good, and the installation easy, but the costs for mainframe hardware are high. Additionally, the 3270 coaxial adapter is, like a LAN adapter, another device that you must integrate into each PC. It takes an expansion slot, an interrupt, and some portion of RAM.

LAN Connections

If you use a LAN to connect to a mainframe, you avoid the expense of putting a 3270 coax adapter in every PC, the problems of installing such adapters, and the cost of buying additional terminal cluster controllers for the PCs. There are two distinctly different ways of using a LAN to connect to a mainframe: a direct connection and a gateway. The gateway connection scheme includes several options.

Many gateways use a relatively slow SNA synchronous data link control (SDLC) connection operating at 19.2 kilobits per second (kbps). Connection options such as coaxial attachment or attachment over a Token-Ring network between the gateway and the mainframe create a link that operates at speeds up to 16 megabits per second (mbps).

During our testing of gateway products at PC Magazine LAN Labs, we found that the throughput over the shared 19.2-kbps SDLC line adequately supports a dozen or more PCs acting as terminals. While the overhead created by gateway activity on a typical network is negligible, if the PCs do more than terminal emulation—for example, exchanging files or engaging in program-to-program communications—the throughput over the shared link quickly becomes a limiting factor. You can install more gateways on the network to divide the load, but that means a greater cash outlay for PCs and possibly mainframe hardware. It also means that you'll add to the workload of the network manager.

The LAN gateway alternative significantly reduces the cost of mainframe hardware needed for multi-PC-to-mainframe installations. One PC, usually dedicated to the task, acts as the gateway—a specific type of communications server. This is the only machine that connects directly to the mainframe. The mainframe regards this gateway as a terminal cluster controller and talks to it over one of a variety of communications links.

A LAN gateway product consists of a special card that fits into the gateway station's interface bus, software that runs in the gateway station and links the card to the LAN, and terminal-emulation software that runs on each PC on the LAN. The emulation software and gateway software communicate through the network's communications services software.

If you use NetWare as your network operating system, Novell's IPX/SPX will route the mainframe data between each client PC and the gateway PC. Other networks will use a transport-layer protocol like NetBIOS to carry the data. These communications services work from node to node and are totally separate from the file-server software. You can set up and use a LAN gateway on a network that doesn't even have a file server. Just be sure the gateway product you choose supports the communications services of your network.

In a LAN gateway configuration, the networked client PCs run terminal-emulation software and share the single mainframe connection through the gateway. If you use the network for other tasks, like file- and printer-sharing, the per-PC cost of attaching to a mainframe can be very low. The primary cost factors are the prices of the gateway computer, the gateway/terminal emulation software, and the connection scheme you choose.

Other Gateway Connections

Today, a typical gateway uses a relatively slow SDLC link to connect to the mainframe hardware suite. But there are two other gateway-to-mainframe connection schemes you should consider: Token-Ring (IEEE 802.2) and IBM 3299 multiplex. Figure 12.3 will help you understand the network-to-mainframe connection alternatives.

The Token-Ring gateway—which DCA and others call an 802.2 gateway, with reference to the IEEE standard—links the gateway PC and mainframe over a Token-Ring network. The mainframe element is TIC-equipped, and the PC gateway houses one or more network adapter cards, which connect the gateway to the network stations over Ethernet, ARCnet, Token-Ring, or any other wiring scheme. Another LAN adapter card in the gateway PC makes the Token-Ring connection to the TIC. You might establish a "PC Token-Ring to mainframe Token-Ring" gateway in order to reduce the number of physical units polled by the mainframe.

Attachmate, Banyan, DCA, IBM, and Novell either market separate 802.2 gateway products or include 802.2 gateway capabilities in their direct Token-Ring attachment packages. These are priced in different ways. DCA charges about $3,000 for a 16-session 802.2 gateway (the price includes the terminal-emulation software), while IBM includes both direct and gateway capabilities in its $475-per-station Personal Communications/3270 package.

You have to add the cost of the PC acting as a gateway, but typically even an unloved 4.77-MHz PC can do the job. The cost of the TIC-equipped mainframe components varies widely depending on what equipment you want to use, how you get support, and how you buy the equipment. If you don't have TIC-equipped mainframe components, there is still a gateway alternative that offers a high-throughput link to the mainframe.

Several companies market gateways that emulate IBM 3299 multiplexers. The real IBM 3299 multiplexer is designed to make it easier to connect a group of terminals to a mainframe over several thousand feet of cable. The multiplexer combines the data from eight different coaxial cables onto one cable to reduce the cost of wiring.

Figure 12.3

PCs acting as 3270 terminals can connect to the mainframe through an SDLC gateway, a 3299 coaxial multiplexer gateway, a Token-Ring gateway, and a direct Token-Ring connection. A large mainframe installation might include all of these attachment schemes.

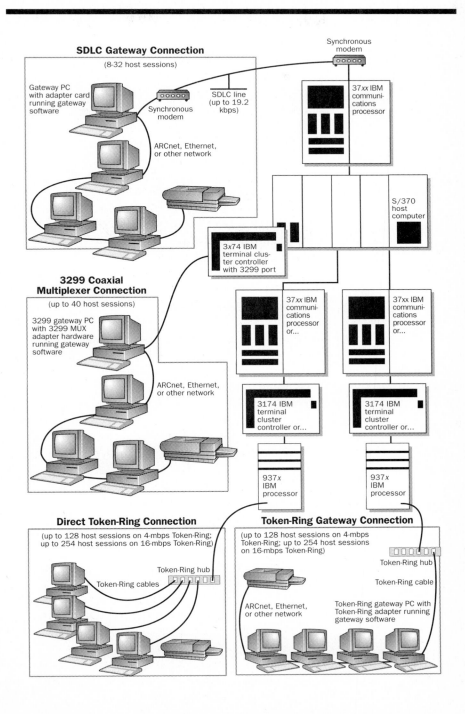

Each of IBM's 3174 terminal cluster controllers has one of its four primary channels configured for an IBM 3299 connection. You can economically upgrade controllers with a microcode change to give 3299 service.

When a gateway PC on a network emulates a 3299 with appropriate software and a special coaxial adapter card, it uses a high-speed connection to the IBM 3174. The gateway can distribute up to forty simultaneous mainframe sessions to its attached PCs running terminal-emulation software. Our testing has shown that the 3299 gateway architecture provides throughput at least as good as the Token-Ring connection, with the potential for significantly lower cost.

The companies that offer 3299 hardware and software are Chi Corp., Data Interface Systems Corp., ICOT Corp., and Novell. These products, including Novell's, work over any network with NetBIOS services. Several companies price such packages on a per-LU basis, which can potentially provide 3299-connected service for $100 per LU or less—plus the cost of a PC for the gateway.

There are many options you can look for in gateway systems, including pooled sessions, sessions divided by groups of users, security controls, and trace/dump utilities. All the companies just listed have good management packages, with varying abilities to audit and retire unused mainframe sessions and control the use of resources.

Installing any LAN gateway requires collaboration between the LAN system administrator and folks with special skills on the mainframe end—the system programmers. People on both sides of the link must set numerous electrical and software parameters to ensure effective terminal operation and file transfer through the gateway. While the software does contain menus to make life easier, the initial installation and configuration of both systems takes the full attention of someone who has complemented a good practical knowledge of MS-DOS with a three- to five-day vendor-run course on the LAN software.

TIC Trick

The method of PC-to-mainframe connection that IBM's sales force most frequently recommends is direct Token-Ring connection. The TIC endows IBM mainframe equipment—including the 3174 terminal cluster controller, several front-end processors, the AS/400 processor, and the 9370 mainframe—with the ability to connect to an IBM Token-Ring network directly. Since PCs can also connect directly to a Token-Ring network, PCs and mainframes can interact as peers on the same network as long as each machine runs the appropriate software. This eliminates the need for gateways, dedicated coaxial-cable connections, and slow-speed communications channels.

The TIC generates fast response times. Our tests show that you can initiate a file transfer from the mainframe to your PC and receive a 50k file through the network in 1 second. The throughput rates we measured for

Token-Ring connection were, in some cases, 80 times as fast as when the same hardware was connected through an SNA SDLC LAN gateway. Graphics screens sent by the mainframe seem to snap into place as soon as you hit the Enter key.

You're right if you suspect there's a catch to this too-good-to-be-true situation. In fact, there are several.

First, you must use Token-Ring network cards and cables. While Token-Ring installations are robust and able to survive cable problems that disrupt other types of networks, the installation is expensive. Not only does the cable itself cost about 40 percent more per foot than thin Ethernet cable, but you also need many times the amount of cable for the same number of nodes. And for every eight nodes you install on a Token-Ring network, you need a $600 hub. Such hubs stack together in a relay rack; you need a room just for the rack and the centralized wiring ducts.

In addition, TIC equipment is not available for older versions of IBM's terminal cluster controllers or front-end processors. If you want to use the TIC architecture, you might have to upgrade to new mainframe communications equipment.

Using the direct Token-Ring connection requires close coordination between the people managing PCs and the people living with the mainframes. The system programmers tending the mainframe must explicitly define each SNA physical unit (that is, each connected PC) in the mainframe software. This means you have to coordinate the addition and deletion of PCs with the mainframe system programmers and wait until they make the changes to their software before the PCs can be serviced.

Lastly, if you use a network gateway to connect PCs and mainframes, only one physical unit is defined; that unit distributes many logical units or sessions to the connected PCs. You can add networked PCs in back of a gateway at any time, and they can immediately use 3270 SNA sessions. If you have been in this business for more than a few years, you know that configuration freedom was one of the driving factors behind the popularity of PCs. While the TIC option may appear simple, it can make management more complex.

PC-to-mainframe products for Token-Ring connections are solely software-based. Since Token-Ring adapter cards supply the electrical connections to the mainframe, the PC-to-TIC products consist of 3270 terminal-emulation programs, various utilities, application programming interfaces, and driver software that carries data to and from the Token-Ring adapter cards. The typical retail price for these packages is between $400 and $500 per station.

More than IBM

So far I've described in detail how you can connect networks of PCs to IBM mainframe systems, particularly those running under IBM's Systems Network Architecture. But while IBM's hardware is widely popular, network designers often need to integrate computers from many different manufacturers into a practical information-management and -transfer system. For that, they need more than IBM's proprietary SNA.

■ TCP/IP for Multiplatform Networking

One of the most difficult problems that system integrators and managers face is connecting different types of computers in a network. As the number of PCs in an organization grows, so does the need to link those PCs to any of several minicomputer and mainframe systems.

In an ideal world, every computer would exchange information freely with every other computer, regardless of the name on the front panel or the processor and operating system inside. In the real world, even computers from the same manufacturer are often unable to exchange data.

There is, however, one Rosetta stone of the computer world that can link a wide variety of mainframe, minicomputer, and PC systems. That common denominator is called TCP/IP, and anyone who deals with PCs every day will appreciate its power. Just imagine a $250 to $500 software package that provides easy file transfers and simple electronic-mail services between PCs and many kinds of dissimilar computer systems.

TCP/IP stands for Transmission Control Protocol/Internet Protocol. Protocols are procedures for communications, described on paper and agreed to by the people who design products. The TCP/IP standards are brought to life in software sold by many different companies.

The DOD Drives Common Protocols

The TCP/IP protocols were developed by the U.S. Department of Defense when DOD scientists were faced with the problem of linking thousands of dissimilar computers. The Defense Advanced Research Projects Agency (DARPA) is a small organization occupying leased office space a couple of miles from the Pentagon in the Virginia suburbs. But its impact on technology in general and on data communications in particular has been huge.

In the mid-1970s, DARPA saw the need to interlink dissimilar computers across the nation to support research efforts. Back then, computers usually used point-to-point leased lines and vendor-specific protocols to communicate. DARPA contracted with several organizations to develop a standard set of nonproprietary protocols that would provide easy communications between computers connected in a multinode network. This open protocol predates the current work of the International Standards Organization by a decade.

The TCP/IP protocols evolved from work done at MIT, with the participation of several companies, and from healthy rounds of industry comments. In 1980, DARPA installed the first TCP/IP modules on computers in its networks. It mandated that all computers attached to the growing nationwide ARPANET network had to use TCP/IP by January 1983. But DARPA's planners didn't expect TCP/IP to flourish just because they said it should.

DARPA and other organizations, such as the Defense Communications Agency, contracted with several companies to deliver TCP/IP modules for the computers and operating systems commonly used by the government. They paid companies like Honeywell, IBM, and Sperry (now Unisys) to develop TCP/IP software for specific computer-and-operating-system combinations used in the government. This seed money was well spent because it motivated these and many other companies to use their own funds to get onto the TCP/IP bandwagon.

DARPA also contracted with Bolt Beranek and Newman to develop software for Unix machines. This contract allowed universities to acquire TCP/IP inexpensively and to work with the protocols in many different environments. Perhaps most importantly, the Defense Communications Agency began a program of testing and certifying software for compliance with the DOD's TCP/IP standard.

The problem with many products that claim to follow a standard (like the EIA-standard RS-232C ports on some printers, for example) is that they are incomplete. The designer of the product leaves out "unneeded" features to save money or adds a little twist to keep the product unique. The Defense Communications Agency checked and certified TCP/IP products to make sure they met the standard and really were interoperable. This testing program ended in 1987, but the result of the effort was hundreds of products—for many dozens of different computers and operating systems—that are certified to meet a specific standard.

Many corporations and almost all Federal-government organizations and universities in the U.S. have taken advantage of the availability and standardization of TCP/IP software. The managers of the TCP/IP program also recognize the International Standards Organization's efforts to develop an extensive set of non-vendor-specific protocols, and they openly support that program. Plans are made for TCP/IP to evolve into something called Transport Class 4 or TP4 under the ISO's program. But few people who manage active networks will jump quickly from a tested and proven network protocol to one that is evolving. TCP/IP has a long and bright future, but best of all, it works well today.

TCP/IP On-Line

In a typical TCP/IP network, a cabling and signaling scheme like Ethernet provides the basic links between dissimilar machines. Ethernet adapters are available for practically every type of computer data bus. The cable delivers data wrapped in an Ethernet packet to each machine. Computers with different operating systems and architectures that strip away the Ethernet packet do not know what to do with data they have received from foreign machines unless they find further instructions. TCP/IP provides those instructions; the packets receive standardized handling when they arrive, regardless of the operating environment on the receiving side.

The TCP/IP module used by each machine must be customized for the computer and its operating system but standardized for the network. TCP/IP modules are available for hundreds of different mainframe and minicomputer systems and for many different PC networks.

National and international networks of dissimilar computers are assembled in basically the same way as Ethernet networks, except that long-distance transmission schemes (such as X.25 packet switching) carry the data instead of having Ethernet carry it. X.25 gateways on a LAN can provide TCP/IP-equipped PCs with both local and long-distance connection capabilities.

Hooking Up

PCs using TCP/IP to communicate with non-PCs usually talk over a local area network. Intelligent Ethernet adapter cards play an important role in the success of TCP/IP on the PC.

But TCP/IP isn't limited to Ethernet. IBM has an active program to provide TCP/IP connections over its Token-Ring adapters. The success of Token-Ring, despite its high cost and cabling hassles, makes the marriage of TCP/IP and Token-Ring increasingly important. The ability to run TCP/IP over Token-Ring and provide seamless connections to IBM hardware is an important IBM marketing lure.

There are two ways networked PCs can use TCP/IP. The first involves loading a TCP/IP software module into every machine on the network. The second configuration uses one machine as a gateway out to the TCP/IP network or high-powered computer.

When your network has a great deal of interaction between different types of machines, it makes sense to give every PC its own TCP/IP module. The penalties you pay for putting the software on every machine are in greater RAM use and increased network overhead.

You can partially overcome these penalties by paying more money for intelligent network-interface cards. Such cards can hold the TCP/IP code in their own RAM and take some of the work away from the PC's processor. TCP/IP software packages that are partially downloaded to intelligent network-interface cards take between 17k and 24k of active RAM. Packages that run on standard interface cards occupy nearly 90k of RAM.

Setting up a TCP/IP gateway is the best solution for a homogeneous network of PCs that sometimes need access to a specific TCP/IP network or machine. The PCs on this kind of network do most of their work together using whatever PC-to-PC communications protocol the network provides. PC applications needing TCP/IP services send data through the gateway. The gateway translates between the PCs' network-protocol environment and the TCP/IP environment. The TCP/IP software typically runs on a machine dedicated to the gateway task.

The throughput of the TCP/IP gateway is more limited by the speed of the connection to the TCP/IP network than by its own translation activities. The connection between the gateway and the TCP/IP system can be through Ethernet coaxial cable, public data networks like Tymnet or Telenet, or private networks like the DOD's ARPANET, or by other means. If a TCP/IP gateway connects two Ethernet networks, it is called an Internet router. Since these networks are so common in TCP/IP installations, the phrase *TCP/IP router* is frequently encountered.

TCP/IP Network Particulars

The heart of the IP portion of TCP/IP is a concept called the *Internet address*. This is a 32-bit number assigned to every node on the network. There are various types of addresses designed for different-size networks, but you can write every address in base 10 using this form: 128.22.5.13. These numbers identify the major network and subnetworks a node is on. The address identifies a particular node and provides a path that gateways can use to route information from one machine to another.

Although data-delivery systems like Ethernet or X.25 bring their packets to any machine electrically attached to the cable, the IP modules must know each others' Internet addresses to communicate. A machine acting as a gateway between different TCP/IP networks will have a different Internet address on each network. Internal look-up tables and software based on another standard called the Address Resolution Protocol are used to route the data between networks through a gateway.

Another piece of software works with the IP-layer programs to move information to the right application on the receiving system. This software follows a standard called the User Data Protocol (UDP). It is helpful to think of the UDP software as creating a data address in the TCP/IP message that details exactly what application the data block is supposed to contact when it reaches the address described by the IP software. The UDP software provides the final routing for the data within the receiving system.

The TCP or Transmission Control Protocol portion of TCP/IP comes into operation once the packet is delivered to the correct Internet address and application port. Software packages that follow the TCP standard run on each machine, establish a connection to each other, and manage the communications exchanges. A data-delivery system like Ethernet makes no promises about successfully delivering a packet. Neither IP nor UDP knows anything about recovering packets that aren't successfully delivered. But TCP structures and buffers the data flow, looks for responses, and takes action to replace missing data blocks. This concept of data management is called "reliable stream" service.

Conceptually, software that supports the TCP protocol stands alone. It can work with data received through a serial port, over a packet-switched network, or from a network system like Ethernet. In concept, it doesn't need or even know about IP or UDP, but in practice TCP is an integral part of the TCP/IP equation and is most frequently used with IP and UDP.

Above TCP/IP

TCP/IP delivers data in a standard format and makes that data available for use in higher-level programs. The DOD standardized the protocol specifications for several other programs that take data from TCP/IP and do useful things with it. These protocols include the File Transfer Protocol (FTP), the Simple Mail Transfer Protocol (SMTP), and a terminal-emulation and communications program called TELNET. The specifications for these protocols are carefully described in DOD standards publications MIL-STD-1780, -1781, and -1782. In addition, efforts are underway to standardize the Net-BIOS interface that was originally developed by IBM and Sytek. Figure 12.4 shows the relationship between the protocols in the TCP/IP suite.

Programs supporting the FTP protocol give people the ability to log on to dissimilar machines across a network, use a standard command to list available directories and files, and exchange files with the remote machine. FTP can perform some simple data-translation tasks, like converting data between the standard ASCII alphabet and IBM's EBCDIC. FTP is controlled either through responses to command-line prompts or by commands passed from an application program.

Figure 12.4

This diagram is patterned after the typical ISO seven-layer protocol stack used to identify network structure. It shows the upward path through software and hardware that makes TCP/IP a viable means of data transfer among dissimilar machines linked in a network.

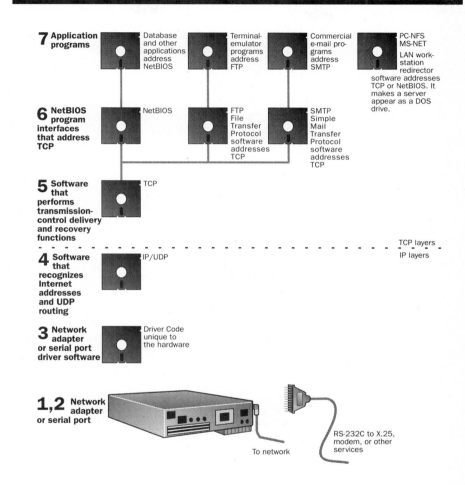

The Simple Mail Transfer Protocol lives up to its name. Programs supporting this protocol do little more than follow a strictly defined script used to enter and retrieve e-mail messages. Several companies market SMTP programs for different kinds of computers. The real advantage of this protocol is that the commands that save and retrieve e-mail messages are the same regardless of what machine acts as the host.

The TELNET protocol describes the operation of a communications program that knows how to call for services from the TCP and IP software. The main purpose of software that implements the TELNET protocol is usually to convert the computer it runs on into a minicomputer terminal. Most of the companies include at least a DEC VT-100 terminal emulator in their TELNET packages. Some companies let you run special versions of popular terminal-emulation programs like Walker Richer and Quinn's Reflection on top of their TELNET software. This combination provides sophisticated emulation of Hewlett-Packard and other terminals.

Almost all of the products that support these higher-level protocols are designed to communicate with a large host computer. You can't get on a network and communicate between two PCs acting as peers using FTP, SMTP, or TELNET. But some companies (such as ftp Software) include host programs that let a single PC become a host and conduct multiple simultaneous sessions with other PCs running FTP, SMTP, or TELNET software.

Many companies provide software conforming to these higher-level standard protocols, but the standardization of the NetBIOS interface is potentially more important to PC system integrators than the availability of the other protocols. Developers of PC software know how to write for NetBIOS. Workgroup productivity applications ranging from electronic mail to personal scheduling are available with NetBIOS interfaces. The introduction of NetBIOS into this suite of applications is a new development, and not many manufacturers have NetBIOS packages available.

Unfortunately, our tests show that the NetBIOS interfaces marketed by some companies do not play well together. At PC Magazine LAN Labs, we got a few of the NetBIOS products to exchange messages between different vendors' implementations, but only with a great deal of trial and error.

File-Server Software

There are no federal standards for higher-level file-server software like NetWare or Microsoft's LAN Manager, but several of the companies marketing TCP/IP software have drivers that can be compiled into the NetWare operating system. Microsoft provides developers with most of the code needed to market TCP/IP drivers for the different OEM releases of LAN Manager.

Sun Microsystems markets file-server software called NFS for computers running the Unix operating system. The NFS software package allows machines wearing many different nameplates to interact as file servers and clients through TCP/IP.

Our experiences at the LAN Labs show that PCs fit into TCP/IP networks very gracefully. Many companies will sell you TCP/IP software for the PC and for specific PC network environments. TCP/IP software provides a fast and efficient way to exchange data with computers of different architectures running different operating systems.

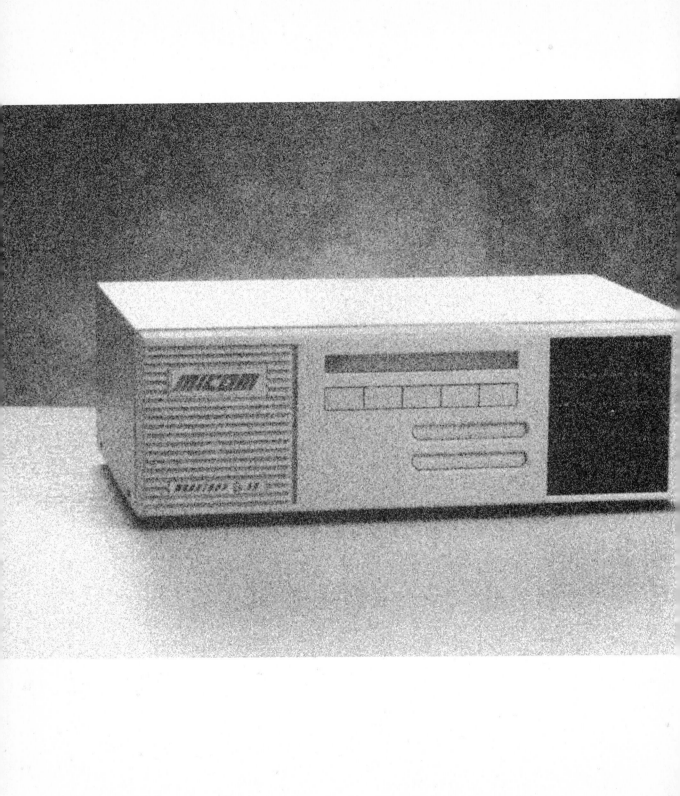

CHAPTER

13

Linking LANs

- Fat Cables and Spaghetti Links

- Extending and Segmenting the Network

- The Linking Media

- ISDN

- X.25: Versatile, Efficient, International, and Necessary

- Linking LANs: A New Frontier

In the first chapter I introduced the idea that information is the raw material, inventory, and processed product of many modern organizations. Computer networks are the production line, the warehouse, and even the retail point of sale for the information products generated by many organizations and businesses. These networks act as local, regional, and even international distribution systems for modern commerce. They form a commercial infrastructure for businesses, countries, and multinational economies.

If local area networks are like the in-house production lines of manufacturing plants, then computer networks using leased telephone lines, metropolitan-area networks (MANs), and wide-area networks (WANs) are the equivalent of the trucking, rail, barge, and air freight systems needed to support smokestack industries. Like those transportation systems, MANs, WANs, and private networks have different capacities, economies, and even regulatory problems.

Some manufacturing companies own their own trucks and boxcars, while others contract for all transportation services. Similarly, some organizations own their MAN and WAN facilities, while others lease these specialized services from commercial suppliers. The suppliers include long-haul carriers like AT&T and MCI, specialized companies such as Tymnet and Telenet, and others such as the local telephone exchange and cable television companies.

When managers of smokestack industries leave the control of transportation systems totally to specialists, they risk inefficiency and unpleasant surprises. Because computer communications systems are so important to the operation of many modern companies, these systems too call for the attention of high-level management. Unfortunately, well-designed networks aren't highly visible, and generally networks are cloaked in technical jargon, but they are both critically important and expensive to run. Managers of organizations relying on computer networks need a generalized understanding of these networks to supervise the information-system professionals effectively.

This chapter is aimed at the general manager who wants a tutorial and reference in wide-area networks and at the computer-support professional who simply needs to link LANs across a campus, across town, or across an ocean. I'll describe the devices used to extend local area networks and the systems used to link LANs together over long distances. We'll revisit some of the concepts from earlier chapters such as connections between dissimilar electronic-mail systems, network management, and TCP/IP. I'll also introduce products called bridges, routers, and brouters—products that are easier to use than to explain!

■ Fat Cables and Spaghetti Links

Local area networks have a wide bandwidth; they can pass millions of bits of data per second. The concept is easy to understand if you picture a LAN as a fat cable that can move a lot of data quickly. Because the signals needed to represent the 0's and 1's on a fast LAN are closely spaced, the equipment cannot tolerate signal degradation or noise in the data stream.

Unfortunately, as copper cables travel over longer distances they accumulate electrical noise. As the pulses of electricity or light representing the data bits travel long distances through copper or fiber-optic cables, they lose their sharpness and degrade in strength. Induced noise and signal degradation are the two primary factors that limit the fat LAN cable's coverage to several kilometers under the best conditions.

Typically, longer communications links must move data more slowly because of the induced noise and degraded signals. Modern techniques allow the transmission of data at high speed over long distances through the use of multiplexers, repeaters, and other special equipment, but the equipment is expensive, so the combination of signaling speed and distance work together to increase costs. You can buy and install your own cable to run data at 10 megabits per second for less than $1 per foot at distances of several thousand feet. But you'll have to pay about $15,000 per year to lease a 1.5-megabit-per-second link from New York to San Francisco, and you may need to spend several thousand dollars more up front for the equipment to interface your computers to the leased line.

Still, many organizations need to move a lot of data over distances greater than a few thousand feet, so managers need to learn the techniques of extending and linking LANs. The techniques you use to link LAN segments depend on the distance and speed you need, the network communications protocols you use, and your business philosophy regarding leasing or owning facilities.

■ Extending and Segmenting the Network

The first category of products I'll describe—repeaters, bridges, and routers—enables you to extend and segment your network's fat or high-speed cable. You can easily understand why you might want to extend the LAN cable; you might need to span 40 stories in an office building or two miles of a college campus. Devices called *repeaters* enable you to extend your network cable to several thousand feet by retiming and regenerating packets or frames so they can continue over such long distances, but the reasons for segmenting a LAN might not be as clear.

Workers in all organizations interact in groups of common interests. Most communications follow specific paths and take place within the workgroup. However, people need ways to communicate between workgroups too. The simplest scheme is to put all the people in all the workgroups on the same cable and let them communicate and interact as business requires. But this arrangement quickly consumes the available resources of the cable. It doesn't make sense to clog the LAN cable serving the accounting department with all the traffic generated in the engineering department simply because engineers sometimes need to share budget programs with accountants. Organizations with busy networks need a device that can link workgroup LANs while exercising discretion over which traffic passes between them.

This kind of discretionary device is known as a *bridge*. Unlike a repeater, which passes all data between cable segments, a bridge links cable systems while only passing certain specified traffic between them. A *router* is a more complex linking device with greater ability to examine and direct the traffic it carries. While the names, concepts, and uses of bridges and routers are relatively simple, selecting one of these products involves enough options to keep a committee busy for a long time. Figure 13.1 shows the basic concepts behind these three LAN linking devices.

Each of these devices functions at a different level of the ISO's OSI model. The repeater looks only at packets or frames generated by adapters operating at the physical level. Bridges use the specific station addresses generated by firmware in the data-link layer. Routers use information provided by software following specific network-layer protocols. As Table 13.1 shows, a fourth type of device, the LAN gateway discussed in Chapter 12, operates at higher levels of the OSI model to translate data formats and open sessions between application programs.

One word of warning: I'm going to give you the classic descriptions of these devices and a number of explanations and examples. But companies keep bringing out products that go beyond the classic descriptions. The concepts are clear, but the practical products make the classic definitions fuzzy in actual use.

Repeaters

The differences among the products you can use to extend your local area network cable are sometimes subtle, but they are all based on the concept of the multiple layers of communications protocols. Typically people refer to the ISO's OSI model, but Digital Equipment Corp. and IBM have communications models and network equipment that don't exactly fit the ISO model.

Repeaters:

☞ **Repeaters can interconnect different types of media such as coax, fiber-optic, and twisted-pair cables**

☞ **Repeaters extend a network's geographical coverage to the maximum allowed by the media-access protocol**

☞ **Repeaters are relatively inexpensive and easy to install**

☞ **When you link LAN segments through repeaters, you can have a very busy LAN**

☞ **A problem on one LAN segment can disrupt all segments**

Figure 13.1

In simple terms, a repeater moves all traffic in both directions between LAN segments. A bridge only moves traffic between LAN segments that really needs to go between the segments. A router makes decisions about the path traffic will take between LAN segments.

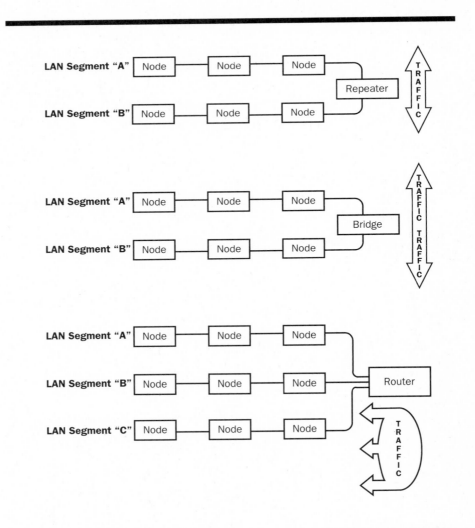

A repeater, like the one shown in Figure 13.2, is typically a humble little box, about the size of a small PC, that connects between two segments of network cable, retimes and regenerates the digital signals on the cable, and sends them on their way again. These functions are typical of those described in the physical layer of the ISO model, so it's common to say that a repeater is a physical-layer device.

Table 13.1

Linking Devices in the
Network Layers

LAYER	FUNCTIONS	LINKING DEVICE
7 Application	Applications move files, emulate terminals, and generate other traffic.	Gateway
6 Presentation	Programs format data and convert characters.	Gateway
5 Session	Programs negotiate and establish connection between nodes.	Gateway
4 Transport	Programs ensure end-to-end delivery.	None
3 Network	Programs route packets across multiple interLAN links.	Router
2 Data Link	Firmware transfers packets or frames.	Bridge
1 Physical	Firmware sequences packets or frames for transmission.	Repeater

Figure 13.2

The PCnic LANrepeater
links separate LAN
segments to allow
extension of the Ethernet
LAN cable beyond the
single 500-foot span
described in the IEEE
802.3 specifications.
(Copyright © 1990 IMC
NetWorks Corp. All rights
reserved.)

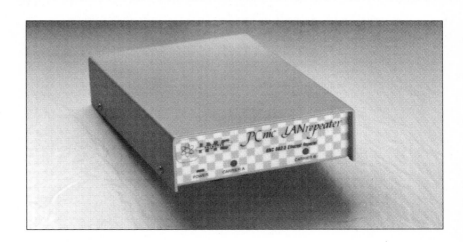

The actions of a repeater allow you to increase the geographical coverage of your LAN. For example, the Ethernet standard specifies that a signal may travel over a maximum cable length of 500 meters for a single segment, but with repeaters interconnecting five segments, a signal on an Ethernet network could reach a maximum distance of 2,500 meters of cable. The slightly different IEEE 802.3 standard allows for up to four repeaters connecting five cable segments, to a maximum of 3,000 meters (1.8 miles), with a total cumulative delay of 950 nanoseconds introduced by the transmission media.

Certain repeaters, such as the Cabletron LR-2000 shown in Figure 13.3, can interconnect cable segments using different physical media such as thin Ethernet coaxial cables and fiber-optic cables. Similarly, repeaters for Token-Ring networks can translate between electrical signals on shielded or unshielded twisted-pair wiring and light pulses on fiber-optic cabling. In modern installations you'll often find repeater modules housed in the central wiring hubs of 10BaseT and fiber-optic-cable systems. But repeaters don't provide a feature called *traffic isolation*. They dutifully send every bit of data appearing on either cable segment through to the other side, even if the data consists of malformed packets from a malfunctioning Ethernet adapter or packets not destined for use off the local LAN segment.

Figure 13.3

The Cabletron LR-2000 is one of a family of repeaters that can move packets between different media such as unshielded twisted-pair wire, coaxial cable, or fiber-optic cable.

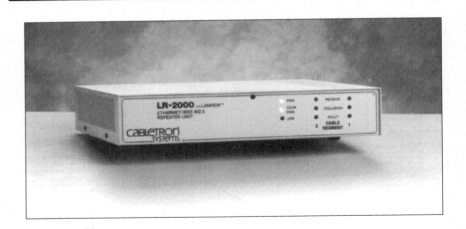

Modern repeaters have features such as light-emitting diodes to display network operation, and they are available in a variety of physical configurations including standalone or rack-mount. Costs range from just under $1,000 for simple Ethernet equipment to well over $2,000 for Token-Ring devices.

LAN bridges:

👍 **Bridges are easy to install**

👍 **Bridges are important network-management points**

👍 **Modem bridges can recognize redundant links between LAN segments and shut them down until they are needed as backup routes**

👎 **Bridges examine each piece of traffic, so they must be fast; therefore the hardware is relatively expensive**

👎 **Bridges can only link similar networks (NetBIOS to NetBIOS or IPX to IPX)**

👎 **The communications link between remote bridges is typically slower than the LAN cable, so it can limit the operation of many types of applications**

Bridges

While repeaters always link elements of a local area network, bridges can link local cable segments, and they can also link the fat cable of a LAN to networks of thinner media such as leased telephone lines. The two main purposes of a bridge are to extend the network and to segment traffic. Like repeaters, bridges can send packets and frames between various types of media. But unlike repeaters, bridges forward traffic from one cable system only if it is addressed to devices on the other cable system; in this way, they limit the nonessential traffic on both cable systems. A modern bridge reads the destination address of the network packet and determines whether the address is on the same segment of network cable as the originating station. If the destination station is on the other side of the bridge, the bridge sequences the packet into the traffic on that cable segment.

The functions of bridges are those associated with the media-access control (MAC) sublayer of the data-link layer (layer 2) in the ISO model. For example, they can read the station address of an Ethernet packet or of a Token-Ring frame to determine the destination of the message, but they cannot look deeper inside the packet or frame to read NetBIOS or TCP/IP addresses. They're often called MAC-layer bridges.

As Figure 13.4 illustrates, bridges are categorized as *local* and *remote*. Local bridges link fat cable segments on a local network. Remote bridges link fat local cables to thin long-distance cables in order to connect physically separated networks. The important point is that you only need one local bridge to link two physically close cable segments, but you need two remote bridges to link two cable segments over a long interconnecting span of media.

How Bridges Learn

As with many aspects of internetworking, it's reasonably simple to generalize: Bridges only relay messages from one cable destined for a station on the other cable. But if you ask, "How does it know?", you uncover a pretty complex subject.

The simplest bridges use a routing table, created by the network manager and contained in software, to decide whether to pass or hold data messages. But people move their computers and change their offices and jobs frequently. Making someone update the routing table in the network bridges every time a computer is moved down the hall creates too much administrative overhead, so bridges typically have software with a learning algorithm.

A bridge, like the CentreCOM products from Allied Telesis shown in Figure 13.5, learns about the stations on the network by sending out a broadcast message that creates a reply from all stations. The bridge listens to all traffic on the attached cable segments and checks the source addresses of all packets and the locations of the sending stations. The routing software builds a table of the stations and the cable segments and then decides when to forward messages and when to drop them.

Figure 13.4

A local bridge directly connects two LAN cable segments. Remote bridges operate in pairs, connecting the LAN cable segments using an intermediary interLAN link such as a leased telephone line.

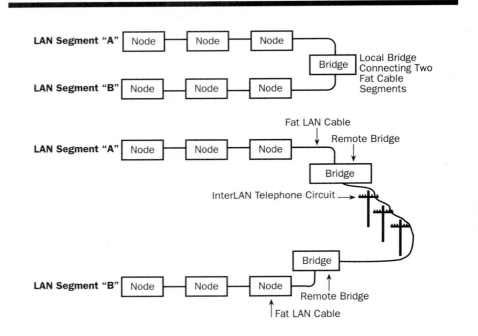

This function is relatively simple when a bridge links only two segments of a network, but it becomes much more complex as networks grow in size. For example, consider the case of a company with networks on the first, third, and fifth floors of a building. These networks could be connected in one of two ways: in *cascade* or through a *backbone*. If the segments are cascaded, then, as Figure 13.6 shows, the first-floor LAN is bridged to the third-floor LAN, and the third-floor LAN is bridged to the fifth-floor LAN. The cascaded bridge topology loads the intermediate LAN segment with traffic destined for the third LAN segment, but it requires only two bridges.

The backbone bridge topology links bridges dedicated to the various LAN segments through a separate backbone cable. The backbone cable is often a fiber-optic link, which allows for relatively great distances. A less common *star* topology, not shown in the diagram, uses a single multiport bridge to link multiple cables and is typically used with lighter traffic loads.

It's possible that, either through error, through a desire for redundancy, or through independent connections to some common point like a mainframe computer, the first- and fifth-floor LAN segments become connected

LAN bridges:

👍 **Bridges let you extend the geographical coverage of your network to the maximum allowed by the media-access protocol**

👍 **Bridges learn the location of stations on the network, and they don't pass unneeded traffic between segments**

by a redundant path. In theory, packets could be recirculated by the bridges and an overload condition called a *broadcast storm* could result. Engineers have developed several intelligent algorithms to detect multiple paths and shut them down.

Figure 13.5

The Allied Telesis family of CentreCOM bridges includes various network-management options.

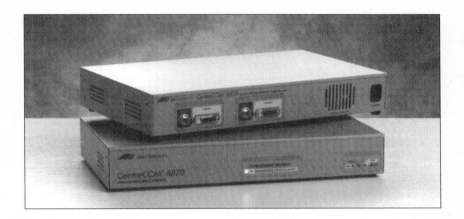

Logical Algorithms for Bridges

Software operating in each bridge determines the most efficient path between network segments and adopts it as the primary route. If the primary route fails, the bridges will use the next-best alternative path. This redundancy is particularly valuable when network segments are connected by long-distance circuits that are subject to interruption.

The software in all of the bridges on the LAN must follow one of several logical algorithms to decide which path to use. The IEEE has adopted a standard, originally developed by Digital Equipment Corp. and Vitalink Communications Corp. and adopted by the IEEE 802.1 Network Management Committee, for a technique called the Spanning Tree Algorithm. Products supporting this algorithm are used primarily by local bridges; the technique isn't economical for use over leased telephone circuits connecting remote bridges. The logic in the Spanning Tree Algorithm lets you link two LAN spans with two bridges for reliability while avoiding the problems of multiple packets being broadcast by both bridges.

Remote bridges, like the Cabletron units shown in Figure 13.7, use different techniques called source routing and protocol-transparent routing. *Source routing* is a technique used primarily on Token-Ring networks and backed primarily by IBM. In the source-routing system, the source node sends test frames over the network until they arrive at the destination station. Each network

bridge along the way adds its own address. The destination station sends the
test frames it receives back to the source station. The source station uses the
information to determine the fastest path and sends the entire message over
that path.

Figure 13.6

The cascaded bridge
topology requires fewer
routers and less
connecting equipment
than the backbone bridge
topology. But the cascaded
topology must move all
data from LAN segment A
through segment B to get
to segment C. The
backbone topology
reduces the overall traffic
load because it can
discriminate between
types of traffic going to
various segments.

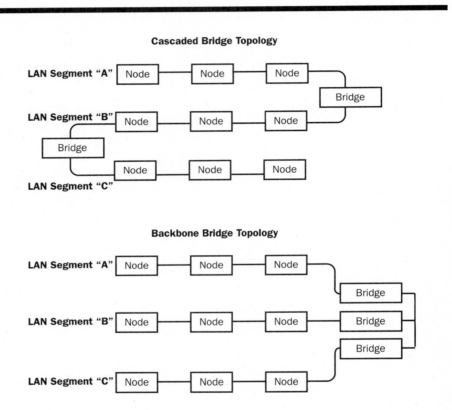

The source-routing technique assures that messages take the fastest
path, and it balances traffic on long-distance links, but it generates network
traffic and requires a lot of processing work at the nodes.

The *protocol-transparent routing* technique puts the workload on the
bridges. Each bridge maintains a map of the entire network and forwards the
packet to the correct network segment. If the bridge hasn't yet learned the
location of the destination station, it forwards the packet to all the LAN segments until the destination replies. This is known as *forward-if-not-local*
logic. Routers use the opposite, *forward-only-if-known-remote* logic.

Figure 13.7

Cabletron Systems' family of remote bridges can use various types of interLAN media to establish links between LAN segments on different floors of a building, in different parts of the country, and on different continents.

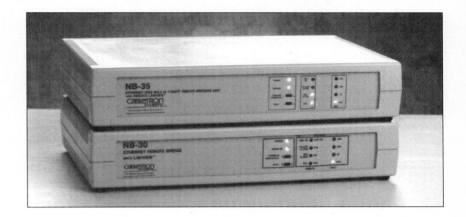

The IEEE 802.1 Network Management Committee and the 802.5 Token-Ring Committee have developed ways to use both source routing and protocol-transparent routing on the same network.

No Translation Services

Like repeaters, bridges can only link similar networks, but bridges and repeaters concentrate on different similarities. A bridge doesn't deal with the physical-layer hardware and drivers handled by repeaters. You can use a repeater to link one Ethernet network to another Ethernet network, despite the type of cabling they use, because the Ethernet packets and the media-access control protocols are the same. But bridges can link LAN segments using completely different LAN adapters and media-access protocols as long as the networks use the same communications protocol; for instance, NetBIOS to NetBIOS, IPX to IPX, or DECnet to DECnet.

Bridge Requirements

Bridges often run inside PCs. Companies like Eicon Technology Corp., Gateway Communications, and Novell sell kits of hardware and software that link LAN segments through several different kinds of thick and thin LAN connections. The price of these kits depends on what kinds of media you're linking. The software and hardware needed to create an Ethernet-to-Ethernet bridge cost less than $1,000. Bridges linking a LAN to an X.25 network, like the G/Remote Bridge marketed by Gateway Communications, shown in Figure 13.8, run around $2,000 to $3,000 plus the cost of a PC.

Figure 13.8

This G/Remote Bridge package from Gateway Communications contains all the software and adapters needed to convert two networked PCs into remote bridges that can transfer data at 64 kilobits per second over various types of interLAN circuits.

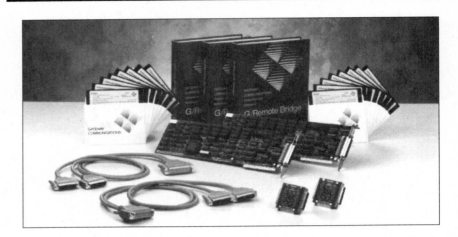

Persoft sells an Ethernet-to-Ethernet bridge product called Intersect. This $1,495 package consists of a software diskette and two Ethernet cards. After it's installed in a dedicated PC, Intersect uses the Spanning Tree Algorithm to detect loops and dynamically learn the location of network nodes.

Unlike other kinds of network communications servers I've described in this book, bridges have a lot of work to do, and they need all the computing power a fast PC can supply. If you set up a bridge in a PC, make sure it has at least an 80286 processor running at 10 MHz, and don't plan on using the computer for any other tasks.

Many companies, including BICC Data Networks, Hughes LAN Systems, Netronix, Racal InterLan, Retix, and 3Com Corp. offer bridges that have their own processors and don't need a PC. These devices, often about the size of a small pizza box, vary widely in price. Depending on the type of connections they make, these bridges can cost anywhere from just over $3,000 to about $10,000.

Bridges can be important elements in network-management systems. Because bridges read the destination and source of every packet, they can collect statistics and report on and control traffic conditions exceeding specific criteria. Many bridges can generate reports in the format of the CMIP or SNMP network-management systems described in Chapter 10.

Routers:

👍 **Routers use protocols, specifically the Spanning Tree Algorithm, to ignore redundant links until they are needed**

👍 **Routers act as a fire wall between LAN segments, preventing problems on one segment from harming other segments**

Routers

Just as bridges improve on the functionality of repeaters, so routers improve on bridges. Routers read the more complex network addressing information in the packet or token and may add more information to get the packet through the network. For example, a router might wrap an

Routers:

👍 **Routers make better use of expensive interLAN circuits than bridges**

👍 **Routers don't care about the MAC-layer protocols used on each LAN segment. They can translate between Ethernet, Token-Ring, and other LAN media-access signaling schemes**

👎 **Routers spend a lot of time working on each packet or frame and can slow down throughput, but the slow speed of the interLAN circuit is often a bigger factor**

👎 **Routers have a relatively demanding level of effort for installation, configuration, and operation**

👎 **Routers are often two or three times as expensive as bridges**

Ethernet packet in an "envelope" of data containing routing and transmission information for transmission through an X.25 packet-switched network. When the envelope of data comes out the other end of the X.25 network, the receiving router strips off the X.25 data, readdresses the Ethernet packet back, and sequences it on the attached LAN segment.

Routers make very smart interconnections between the elements of complex networks. Routers can choose among redundant paths between LAN segments, and they can link LAN segments using completely different data-packaging and media-access schemes. Primarily because of their complexity, however, routers move data more slowly than bridges.

Routers work at the network layer (layer 3) of the ISO model. Unlike bridges, routers don't know the exact location of each node. Instead, a router only knows about subnetwork addresses. It reads the information contained in each packet or frame, uses complex network addressing procedures to determine the appropriate destination, and then repackages and retransmits the data. The router doesn't care what kinds of hardware the LAN segments use, but they must run software conforming to the same network-layer protocol. Some of the products sold by vendors include routers for DECnet, IP, IPX, OSI, and XNS. Telebit Corp.'s NetBlazer, shown in Figure 13.9, combines an IP router with other functions.

Newport Systems Solutions has a unique router that operates as a Net-Ware Loadable Module (NLM) inside a NetWare 3.X server. This configuration puts a heavier processing load on the server's CPU, but it take traffic off the network cable and saves the cost of a separate computer acting as a bridge or router. The product is available with various communications options at a cost ranging to slightly over $5,000. Remember, you need a compatible router at each end of the long-distance link.

Some companies, like Cisco Systems, Proteon, and Wellfleet Communications, sell multiprotocol routers that allow you to combine protocols like IP and DECnet in the same network. The Wollongong Group sells an effective router combining the popular NetWare IPX protocol and the IP portion of the TCP/IP protocol. However, there are no standards for these implementations, and you'd better be ready to buy all your multiprotocol routers from one company.

Routers aren't transparent like bridges. Stations on a LAN segment must specifically address packets or frames to a router for handling. Typically, you won't consider dealing with the complexities of routers until you have LAN segments of 20 or more nodes, or segments using complex protocol suites like TCP/IP.

The addressing scheme used by routers allows administrators to break the network into many subnetworks. This architecture allows many different topologies including a highly reliable ring of leased circuits, as shown in

Figure 13.10. Routers only receive specifically addressed packets or frames from originating stations or from other routers. They don't read every packet or frame on every attached LAN segment as a bridge does. Because they don't pass or even handle every packet or frame, routers act as a safety barrier between network segments. Bad data packets or broadcast storms simply don't make it through the router.

Figure 13.9

Telebit's NetBlazer is an integrated communications server designed to act as an IP router; it can use both leased and dial-up telephone-line connections for simultaneous interLAN communications. This product can be configured with up to 3 Ethernet connections, 26 modem connections, and one 56-kilobit-per-second leased line.

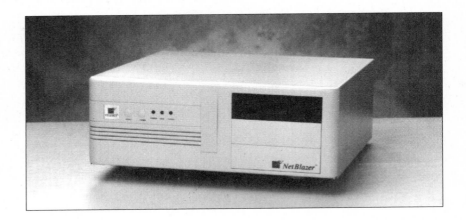

When it relays a packet between LAN segments, a router decides the path the data packet will follow by determining the number of hops between internetwork segments. Usually the router software chooses the route with the least hops. A router that always picks the shortest route typically uses a routing table a programmer has created for a specific network. This kind of device, known as a *static router,* works fine in many networking systems.

Some administrators want to give the router more options. A category of devices called *dynamic routers* can examine factors such as the cost of sending traffic over specific links and the amount of traffic on specific links and decide to send packets or frames over a different route. Of course, the more thinking a router does before it forwards a packet or frame, the longer it takes to get the data to its destination. The throughput you get from a local router depends on the complexity of its routing tables and the CPU power available to run its software. The throughput of remote routers is typically limited by the speed of the media linking them together.

Brouters

I warned you that real products make the formal definitions fuzzy, and there is no better example of this than the devices called *brouters,* marketed by several companies including Halley Systems. A brouter is designed to combine the easy installation, simple management, and multiprotocol capabilities of a bridge with the data-handling functions of a router. Typically, a brouter will route one protocol, like IP or XNS, and will bridge all other traffic. Brouters are particularly useful if you have a mix of networks—using, for example, IP and Digital Equipment Corp.'s LAT protocol—that prevents you from routing the data. It's difficult to give you a rule of thumb for choosing a brouter instead of a bridge or router, but typically you'll look at a brouter when you try to mix several homogeneous LAN segments in with two very different segments.

Figure 13.10

Routers in a large interLAN network can use the interconnecting circuits as alternative routes for traffic. If the circuit between LAN segment A and segment B breaks down, the routers can send traffic around the long way to retain connectivity.

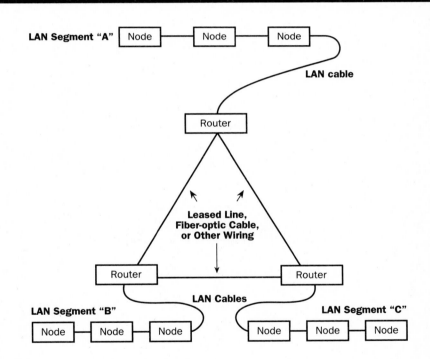

Data Compression and Routers

As I'll describe later in this chapter, you'll have to pay thousands of dollars a month to lease a circuit to link LAN segments; the cost is driven by the speed of the data you want to send across the link. Therefore it makes sense to invest in equipment at both ends of the link that can use the expensive circuit to maximum efficiency.

Because routers strip off the LAN MAC-layer address information before they send a packet from one LAN to the other, they reduce the total number of bits going across the interLAN communications link. The remote router at the receiving end adds the correct MAC-layer address back onto the packet before moving the data into its local LAN segment. Because of this action, routers send the information across the interLAN circuit more efficiently than bridges.

As an example, the Ethernet MAC-layer address is 18 bytes, or 3 percent of the maximum-size packet carried under NetWare's IPX. Since most packets on a LAN of DOS-based PCs are very small, the address can constitute over 50 percent of many packets. Simply removing the MAC-layer address can provide a significant reduction, percentagewise, in the amount of transmitted data. Additionally, companies such as Newport Systems Solutions include software using compression algorithms that can compress certain kinds of data to improve throughput by as much as a factor of four.

Remote Control and Routers

You must pay for what you get in terms of the throughput in an interLAN connecting circuit. Because the interLAN link is typically much slower than the typical LAN cable, it isn't appropriate for some kinds of data-intensive computing activities such as indexing and searching a large database file. If a database program running in a PC on one LAN segment tries to perform a complex search of a database file held on a file server on a different LAN segment, the program could try to pull megabytes of data over the interLAN link. This activity is likely to be both slow and, if you pay for service according to the number of packets moved, expensive.

Another alternative is to use what I call LAN remote-control software. Such programs, like Close-Up/LAN from Norton-Lambert Corp., D-Link Screen Monitor from D-Link Systems, NETremote Plus from Brightwork Development, and R2LAN from DCA, let one computer remotely control another across the network. In effect, the screen and keyboard of the controlling PC are placed in parallel with the screen and keyboard of the controlled PC.

If someone needs to use an application like a database program that would normally try to move a lot of data across the interLAN link, it makes sense to use a remote-control program to run the application on a PC on the other LAN segment instead. In this way, you avoid moving many small packets; only the keystrokes and screen images traverse the interLAN link. These activities typically don't generate enough traffic to saturate even a relatively slow 19.2-kilobit-per-second interLAN link, so there is capacity left for other LAN-to-LAN tasks.

On the other hand, not all LAN remote-control programs are appropriate for remote control across routers or bridges. Some packages simply blast the entire screen image across the network every few milliseconds.

This technique is acceptable on a fat LAN cable, but it puts too much data on an interLAN link. You should use programs (such as those named above) that send only the changed screen elements across the link between controlled and controlling PCs.

Some LAN remote-control products have timing or licensing constraints that limit their ability to function across a remote router or bridge. Make sure that the product you choose is licensed for use on multiple LAN segments.

Gateways

Gateways:

☞ **Gateways are economical to operate and don't put a heavy load on the interLAN communications circuits**

☞ **Gateways perform specific tasks efficiently, like exchanging e-mail or files, and people don't need any training or software following special protocols to use them**

☞ **Gateways are task-specific. They don't do everything and aren't efficient for many types of applications**

If you have to link very different kinds of networks, such as a network of IBM mainframe computers and a network of PCs, you might elect to use a device called a *gateway*. Gateways function at the high end of the OSI model; they totally repackage and sometimes even convert the data going between the two networks. Routers add addressing information to the packets or frames they move and don't change the content of the message. Gateway programs often do change the format of the message to make it conform to the application program at the receiving end.

I described PC-to-mainframe gateways in Chapter 12, but the most common LAN-to-LAN gateways are those used by the electronic-mail systems described in Chapter 11. These gateway programs move electronic-mail messages from the format and coding of one program, sometimes through an intermediate common format, into the format of the receiving program.

The X.400 messaging standard is becoming an increasingly important part of LAN-to-LAN connectivity. X.400 is an international standard aimed at providing a global system for exchanging electronic mail. The standard describes a rather complex model of programs called *message transfer agents* (MTAs); these work together to move a message from someone using one kind of e-mail program, called a *user agent* (UA), to someone using a different type of user agent. The UAs and the MTAs all communicate according to one of three protocols. X.400 is one of the best examples of the complexity that evolves from the design of a committee, but many people have made X.400 work for high-level interLAN connectivity.

Novell, in partnership with Retix and Touch Communications, produces a NetWare MHS-to-X.400 electronic-mail gateway. The gateway moves electronic-mail messages from any MHS-compatible electronic-mail program into an X.400 service. Companies such as MCI and U.S. Sprint provide X.400 environments as subscription services.

A unique company called Soft-Switch, Inc. makes its sole business the movement of electronic-mail messages using X.400 and other proprietary protocols. The company supplies hardware and software products to construct electronic-mail backbone systems and corporate e-mail networks. It markets one package called Softswitch, a high-performance electronic-mail software package that can be integrated into an existing IBM mainframe computer system to support a huge network of interactive PC-and-mainframe e-mail programs.

The primary advantage of using a gateway (like an e-mail gateway) to link LANs at a very high level is that the interLAN communications circuit doesn't have to carry a lot of data. The MHS system works well with dial-up telephone lines and 2,400-bit-per-second modems. Because the computers acting as gateways do so much processing, the interconnecting circuits do not have to carry nearly as much data.

WAITS

In a *PC Magazine* article published in the middle of 1990, I christened a new category of products called *Wide Area Information Transfer Systems* or WAITS. WAITS programs use PCs to move files economically and efficiently between LANs. They can be viewed as a type of gateway, primarily because they are applications and completely insensitive to any underlying protocols.

Automated, unattended operation is key to the WAITS concept. Typically, PCs running WAITS software contact each other and move information at scheduled times, although most allow the option of simply moving files when they are ready. They usually connect over dial-up telephone lines because they don't need high data rates, but they can use any interconnecting circuits.

XcelleNet Wide Area Network Management System, marketed by XcelleNet, is certainly the most sophisticated WAITS product. XcelleNet uses an OS/2-based multitasking master station to interrogate and control remote nodes running under any of several other operating systems. For really big operations, several XcelleNet master stations in the same location can coordinate their operations across the LAN.

Commtech International markets a product called XChange Plus, with the ability to transfer files automatically over a number of different circuits including dial-up or leased lines.

WAITS products can solve the interLAN communications problems for many people who only need to move files between networks and don't need more sophisticated computing tasks involving multiple layers of protocols. These products are inexpensive to install and invisible to the people who benefit from receiving the latest updated data with very little fuss or recurring expense.

■ The Linking Media

So far, we've described the logic and devices used to move frames and packets between LAN segments. If the LAN segments are physically close together, then bridges and routers are useful to extend the fat cable, to control the LAN traffic, and to perform administrative management functions. But many organizations need to link LAN segments over distances farther than a few thousand feet. In these cases, the fat cable ends and some kind of interconnecting communications circuit must carry the data using one of several types of signaling schemes. I'm going to start out describing the transmission circuits you can use to link LANs, and then I'll introduce the signaling schemes associated with each type of media.

Remember that it is difficult and expensive to send data quickly over long distances. In all of the decisions you make regarding linked LANs, you'll have to balance throughput against distance and cost. Because the cost of the internetwork segment is typically the driving factor in the equation, it's often advisable to make a significant investment in network hardware that makes the best use of the long-distance media.

The internetwork media available to link LAN segments includes telephone lines, satellite networks, microwave radio, fiber-optic networks, and perhaps cable television coaxial systems.

Telephone-Line Systems

Stated a little simplistically, there are two types of telephone lines: those going to the public dial network (dial-up lines) and those leased for long-term dedicated use. When you dial a long-distance telephone number, the computers in the telephone switches route your call and set up a temporary dedicated connection. Leased lines provide a full-time dedicated connection that does not pass through the system of switches.

As usual, real products blur the simple definitions by offering, for example, circuits in the dial-up network that virtually appear to be dedicated lines. These virtual private networks (VPNs), offered by AT&T, U.S. Sprint, and other long-distance companies, allow the telephone carriers to make optimal use of the switched telephone system while providing users with service equivalent to full-time leased lines.

You can use dial-up telephone lines to link LANs. The MHS electronic-mail system is an e-mail gateway with the ability to use dial-up lines to transfer messages. Using the latest high-speed modems meeting the CCITT V.32bis signaling standard and V.42bis data-compression standard, you can move electronic-mail messages at a respectable throughput of 50 kilobits per second or better over a standard dial-up telephone line.

The easiest way to link LANs over a dial-up telephone line is to have your PC's modem dial a call to a PC acting as a client on the distant LAN and remotely control the distant PC from your computer. Modern modem remote-control software works well with LAN software, and you can use the file-transfer utilities in these packages to exchange files with data compression and error detection. However, you tie up at least one person and a lot of hardware making this link, you run up high telephone bills, the connection is temporary, and you can do only certain things by remote control. This solution offers limited functionality, and the operation is not transparent to the user.

Competition in the long-distance telephone industry within the United States has driven down the price of dialed long-distance service, so making dialed calls to link LANs on a temporary basis is a practical alternative for many organizations. In the U.S., it is often practical and economical to dial up a link between two routers or bridges for several hours a day to update databases or application programs on LANs. But in many other countries, calling long distance is still expensive, and in some cases the circuits can't pass high-speed data effectively.

Leasing Lines

Selling leased telephone lines has been an important business for the long-distance telephone industry since the 1930s, but in the United States the process got more complex after Bell Telephone System's divestiture and the Federal Communications Commission's Computer II decision, which defined the roles of the various companies in the industry.

In the U.S., a person who wants to lease a single full-period telephone line across state boundaries might have to coordinate the efforts of three different companies to get the long-distance circuit, the "tail" circuit from the long-distance vendor's equipment to the customer's premises, and the necessary terminating equipment. Even with this need for coordination, it is often possible to install a leased line within a few days, or a few weeks at the most, after the companies get their service orders.

People in countries outside the U.S. can often get the complete long-distance service package from one vendor—typically a government monopoly—but in many cases they have to wait months for the service to appear.

Leased lines for digital data transmission are available in various grades of service. The grade of service relates to how fast you want to move data over the line. Leased data lines are specially configured or "conditioned" for data transmission in several speed ranges.

In the U.S., companies selling long-distance services are often called *interexchange carriers* because their circuits carry service between the major telephone exchanges. The companies that sell the service between buildings and homes and the exchanges are called the *local carriers*. In countries outside of North America, there is often no differentiation between these carriers. AT&T is a regulated interexchange carrier whose rates or "tariffs" are subject to the supervision of the Federal Communications Commission. Other long-distance carriers, like Lightnet, MCI, and U.S. Sprint, do not have to file a schedule of public tariffs, but their rates are almost always competitive with AT&T's published tariff rates.

T1 Service

You can lease point-to-point circuits certified for data rates ranging from 2,500 bits per second to over 45 megabits per second. The basic unit of measure for data service, used both by engineers to specify service and by salespeople to price service, is the *T1* channel. A T1 channel can carry 1.544 megabits of data per second, and it conforms to certain technical characteristics for signaling and termination of the circuits.

You can establish your own circuits following the T1 channel specifications to move data across a campus or within a large building, but network designers and managers typically think of T1 as a service traversing hundreds or thousands of miles over leased long-distance facilities. AT&T and other carriers will charge you about $11,000 per month for a dedicated T1 circuit spanning 1,000 miles. A T1 line only 500 miles long still costs about $8,000 a month, but T1 service over 2,000 miles costs about $19,000, or somewhat less than twice the price of the 1,000-mile service. Generally, the formula is cost = base monthly rate + (monthly charge per mile × the number of miles).

If your organization needs even faster service, it isn't cheap. What is termed a *T3* link, providing 45-megabit-per-second service, costs over $100,000 per month on a 1,000-mile path.

In addition to the leased-line charge, you might also pay several hundred dollars a month for the connection from the interexchange carrier to your facilities and for the termination equipment.

You can use the entire capacity of a T1 circuit to link two LAN segments, but the terminating equipment typically gives you the option of breaking the circuit into several parts. For planning purposes, a channel for one voice conversation takes 64 kilobits per second. So if you lease a T1 circuit between different branches of your organization, you could, for example, use 768 kilobits of the 1.544-megabit capacity to carry 12 voice connections between the PBX telephone systems at each end and still have another 768 kilobits per second available to link the LAN segments through a router or bridge at each end.

Years of testing at PC Magazine LAN Labs shows that an average PC on an average network (for example, a PC with a 10-MHz 80286 processor using Ethernet to access a server running Novell's NetWare 2.X on an 80386 processor) enjoys a throughput of about 750 kilobits per second. Since only a few PCs are likely to send data over the interLAN link at any one time, half of a T1 channel will meet the needs of many organizations.

As a footnote: Because AT&T encodes certain supervisory information in the data stream, that company has typically provided 56-kilobit-per-second service to its customers—although it is evolving to 64-kilobit service. You should also know that equipment is available from several companies to compress a voice conversation into a 32- or even a 16-kilobit-per-second channel, making the space on the T1 link even more economical for voice as well as for data transmission. Even 8-kilobit-per-second voice channels are available, but the voice quality is clearly inferior to that of the faster 16- or 32-kilobit services, and few organizations find this voice compression option desirable.

As the demands of your organization change, even on an hourly basis, you can adjust the amount of T1 capacity you give to voice and to data traffic. There are some problems with shifting between voice and data because the two services have different tolerances for error and delay, but many organizations find it efficient to balance their use of T1 channels between voice and data.

Fractional T1

A packaging scheme called *fractional T1* makes it economical to lease circuits for data-communications service slower than the full 1.544-megabit-per-second T1 channel. The basic rate of service for fractional T1 is a channel speed of 64 kilobits per second. Interexchange carriers commonly sell fractional T1 service at rates of 384, 512, and 768 kilobits per second. A 1,000-mile 512-kilobit-per-second service costs about $7,000 per month, plus the fees for terminating circuits and equipment.

Reliability

Redundancy provides reliability. Experienced network administrators know that the long-distance links are the major cause of internetwork outages. Routers, bridges, and other network devices seldom fail, but the leased long-distance circuits linking them often do. You typically don't have to pay the fee for the circuit during the malfunction, but this is little consolation for the people who can't move the data that is the lifeblood of their business.

If you buy a couple of full or fractional T1 circuits from different interexchange carriers, your network routers can automatically use whatever links are available in the event of a failure. Some routers even use the dial-up telephone lines to back up the leased lines. The data-transmission rate over the remaining or alternative route might be slower than the primary route, but some internetwork connectivity is far better than no connectivity.

Connecting to High-Speed Channels

When you connect a remote bridge or router to a high-speed T1 or fractional T1 communications channel, an adapter board in the bridge or router changes the network traffic into a stream of data meeting one of several standards for connection and signaling. The output might follow the EIA RS-232, RS-449, or CCITT V.35 standards. Somehow, you need to connect that output to a device called a *multiplexer* that interfaces with the high-speed communications line.

The job of a multiplexer is to subdivide the available single fast communications channel into multiple channels of voice and slower data communications. Companies such as Network Equipment Technologies, Newbridge Networks, StrataCom, Timeplex, and Verilink Corp. provide multiplexer equipment. The Micom Marathon 5K shown in Figure 13.11 combines the capabilities of a multiplexer with other LAN connectivity products in one box.

Figure 13.11

The Marathon 5K from Micom Communications Corp. is an example of a product that defies typical definitions. It is a high-quality statistical multiplexer that can mix voice, data, and fax signals on a single fractional T1 circuit. You can insert optional bridge or router modules into the same chassis to make it a router/multiplexer combination.

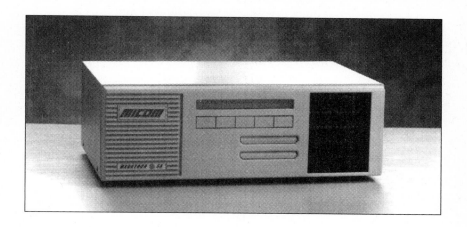

You'll hear people talk about a *channel service unit* (CSU), the side of the equipment connected to the communications channel, and a *data service unit* (DSU), the side of the equipment connected to the bridge or router. As Figure 3.12 shows, the DSU converts all the incoming data into the proper format for transmission over the T1 or fractional T1 circuit. The CSU terminates the high-speed circuit and keeps the signals in phase and properly timed. Some bridge products contain a DSU, so all you need is an inexpensive CSU.

The cost of typical DSU/CSU equipment starts at about $2,500 and climbs to many times that amount for sophisticated multiplexers with numerous network-management and reporting functions.

Figure 13.12

This diagram shows a complex and a simple termination for a T1 or fractional T1 circuit. The top diagram shows a system mixing voice and LAN data on the same T1 link through the services of a multiplexer. The bottom diagram shows a router with a built-in DSU connecting directly to the CSU used to terminate the T1 or fractional T1 circuit.

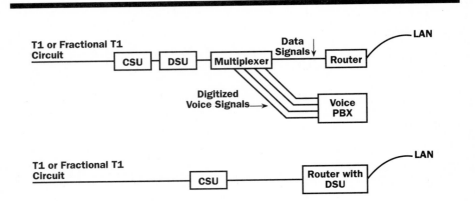

Here are a few facts to remember about T1 circuits:

- T1 is a way of packaging service in increments of 1.544 megabits per second.

- T1 service is provided by many kinds of companies, but primarily by the long-distance or "interexchange" carriers.

- Fractional T1 delivers service in 64-kilobit-per-second increments.

Satellite Communications

The interexchange carriers like AT&T, MCI, and U.S. Sprint use ground-based copper and fiber-optic circuits for nearly all of their connections. But instead of leasing long-distance circuits from the telephone carriers, many organizations, including companies like K-Mart Corp. and Wal-Mart Stores, use their own private satellite radio systems to carry data between their widely separated enterprises. Chrysler Corp. is said to have the largest private satellite network in the world, linking over 6,000 locations.

Companies such as Alascom, AT&T, Comsat World Systems, Contel ASC, and GTE Spacenet Corp. offer a wide variety of satellite services for private industry and governments, ranging from on-call emergency backup services to point-to-point data services, at rates from 19.2 kilobits per second to multiple T1 rates.

Communications satellites are typically in a geosynchronous orbit around the Earth's equator, so from the ground they appear to be stationary in the sky. Each satellite has a number of transponders that relay communications signals. A transponder takes in a weak signal broadcast from an Earth station, cleans it up and amplifies it, and rebroadcasts the signal back to Earth. Because of the satellite's 23,300-mile (35,810-kilometer) vantage point, the rebroadcast signal can cover most of Europe, North America, or

South America—depending on the antennas used on both the satellite and ground sides of the link.

This large area of coverage is one of several potential advantages that leased satellite communications circuits have over terrestrial leased circuits. Satellite communications companies don't charge for their circuits according to distance as the terrestrial companies do. The people in the industry say that satellite circuits use "distance-insensitive" pricing, while prices for terrestrial circuits are "distance-sensitive." The satellite companies charge for access to the transponder and possibly add charges based on the amount of bandwidth, a measure of the data transmission rate you use. You should note that leased terrestrial links are typically usage-insensitive; you pay the same monthly charge for the terrestrial lines regardless of how much or how little data you move through them.

The general rule of thumb is that satellite links can't compete on a cost basis with leased terrestrial links under distances of 500 miles. At distances over 500 miles, the satellite links become increasingly competitive with leased lines.

Another advantage of satellite service for many organizations is ease of installation. You don't have to worry about the coordination between the interexchange carrier and the local carrier or the time needed to install service. For satellite communications, a *very small aperture terminal* (VSAT) with an antenna size of 1.2 to 2.8 meters can be installed on a rooftop or in a parking lot within a few hours. Obviously, such systems are also relatively portable and allow you to avoid telephone-line installation charges for temporary operating locations.

Moreover, satellite services can offer reliability that terrestrial services can't match. The signal paths to and from the satellite are unaffected by all but the heaviest precipitation, and as long as your Earth station is operational, natural disasters can't take out your circuits. Even the terrestrial carriers use satellite circuits to back up their copper-wire and fiber-optic links.

So if you need to link a LAN in your organization's Chicago headquarters to LANs in branch offices in London and Houston, you could equip each location with a small Earth-station antenna and radio system on the roof or in the parking lot, bring a wire from the Earth station into the building, connect it to the network's remote bridge or router, and let the packets or frames fly through space.

Reality is a little more complex than the concept. There are two significant drawbacks to using satellite to link LANs: relatively slow throughput and a factor called *satellite delay*.

Typically the low-cost VSATs can transmit only at 19.2 kilobits per second, so they are a slow link between LANs. This speed is fast enough for many kinds of applications, but there are some jobs that need faster interLAN links.

Satellite circuits:

- Satellites cover a large segment of the Earth for a fee that is relatively insensitive to distance
- Installation is simple for service of 19.2 kilobits per second
- Satellite communications are reliable even in the event of many natural disasters
- Satellite circuits typically are not economical for distances under 500 miles
- Higher speeds require larger antennae
- Satellite delay significantly reduces the response time for many applications

If you want faster service from a satellite, even up to multiple T1 speeds, you'll need a larger and more expensive antenna. The exact size of the antenna depends on the distance from the satellite's position on the equator and other factors, such as the surrounding radio-frequency environment, but T1 service typically requires a 3- to 4-meter antenna, and the installation might require special permits and planning.

Because of the distance from Earth to the satellite and back again, it takes 0.27 seconds for the signal to make the round trip, even at the speed of light. This satellite delay can be significant to people using certain kinds of applications over interLAN circuits. Satellite circuits are fine for automated updates performed by electronic-mail systems, file transfers done by database or accounting programs, and other program-to-program tasks. But if someone in the loop is entering keystrokes into a program and trying to receive immediate replies, then the slow speed of typical satellite circuits and the delay imposed by the extraterrestrial signal paths probably limit the acceptability of this transmission alternative.

Because of the need to conserve the power and resources of the satellite transponder, satellite links typically operate in a star topology. In this configuration, shown in Figure 13.13, the transponder receives a number of incoming signals, combines them, and beams them back toward the Earth in one economical data stream. One Earth station serves as a hub, exchanging data with a number of smaller stations situated almost anywhere within the signal footprint of the satellite.

The hub station has a larger antenna than the others, so it can receive the signal from the satellite with less noise and handle a fat data stream with an acceptable level of errors. Many cities have satellite "parks," like New York's Teleport, where several companies share a few large antennae. When several organizations share a single large Earth station, they share the burden of the installation and maintenance problems.

Satellite circuits aren't a perfect interLAN solution for every organization, but they offer some unique features and geographic flexibility that no other service can match.

MANs and FDDI

So far, in this chapter I've explained how you can lease high-speed services in 64-kilobit increments from terrestrial carriers and satellite carriers. But other companies will sell you circuits to interconnect your facilities within metropolitan areas. For planning purposes, you can think of a metropolitan area as a circle with a 100-kilometer (62-mile) circumference.

As I've described before, there is a technically ideal way to link LANs and there are the practical alternatives. The IEEE 802.6 committee is developing a standard, the technically ideal solution, for *metropolitan-area networks* or MANs. But organizations as diverse as railroads and cable television companies will also sell you local circuits to link your LANs.

Figure 13.13

In this example, the New York LAN segment serves as a hub, using fractional T1 radio circuits of 256 and 768 kilobits per second to move data between the satellite and the four ground stations.

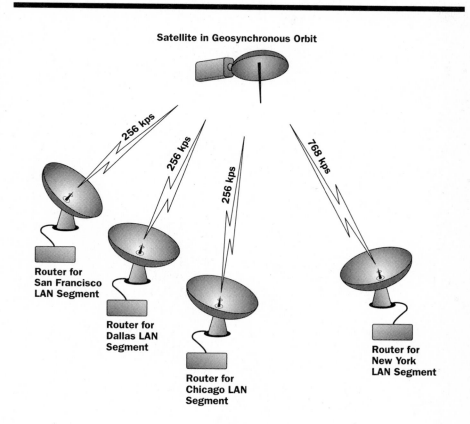

The IEEE 802.6 committee is working on a standard called the Distributed Queue Dual Bus (DQDB). The DQDB topology includes two parallel runs of cable—typically fiber-optic cable—linking each node (typically a router for a LAN segment) on the system. This dual-cable system provides high reliability and high signaling rates, typically in the vicinity of 100 megabits per second. Each ring of cable is independent and moves small 48-byte packets around the ring from node to node; this packet size is specified in other draft standards, such as a high-speed ISDN that will evolve in the mid-1990s.

The DQDB system allocates system capacity to each node in 125-microsecond segments. The IEEE 802.6 MAN is designed to be a metropolitan utility serving a large number of organizations across a large area. In the U.S.,

IEEE 802.6 MANs will probably be installed and run by the local telephone companies. In the early 1990s, IEEE 802.6 DQDB will be something you'll hear a lot about but see little of. The standards for DQDB are still evolving, and the installation of equipment will take years.

You are more likely to see a service called Fiber Distributed Data Interface (FDDI) providing a backbone of communications services across town. In the grand scheme, FDDI networks will act as traffic-gathering points to feed the larger DQDB network. FDDI systems have a sustained throughput of about 80 megabits per second and are limited to smaller areas than DQDB. FDDI operates over distances limited to about 100 kilometers of cable in each ring, and the nodes can't be farther than 2.5 kilometers apart. FDDI systems can be economically installed using existing equipment by organizations that need them, or by companies that want to sell a service to anyone in the extended neighborhood.

The FDDI architecture uses two rings of fiber—the primary ring and secondary ring—to carry data, as shown in Figure 13.14. The rings are in a physical hub topology similar to the one described in the IEEE 802.5 Token-Ring architecture. All nodes attach to the primary ring, but since the secondary ring is designed primarily to provide a backup connection in case of primary-ring failure, some nodes—called *Class B stations*—might not attach to the secondary ring for reasons of economy.

Some organizations, such as Advanced Micro Devices (AMD), promote using FDDI to deliver data to desktops instead of limiting it to internetwork links. There are movements underway to use shielded and even unshielded twisted-pair media for FDDI. While in 1990 it cost just under $4,000 for the interface needed to link a PC to FDDI, AMD hopes this price will fall to well under $1,000 by the middle of the decade.

You're probably more likely to use products like the ISOLAN FDDI/ 802.3 bridge marketed by BICC Data Networks or the Raycom 5600 Series FDDI System to use FDDI to link LAN segments instead of desktops. These products are bridges that attach to both rings of an FDDI network, provide full FDDI fault-isolation capabilities, and move data between Ethernet LAN segments. Because the FDDI interLAN segment has so much data-carrying capacity, you don't need to pay for the sophistication of routers intended to make the most efficient use of the interLAN circuits. But like all FDDI products, these bridges are expensive. For example, the retail price for the ISO-LAN FDDI/802.3 Managed Bridge is over $22,000.

FDDI is an excellent technology for metropolitan network coverage. The ability of fiber-optic cable to ignore electrical interference and to be relatively inert makes it possible to pull cable in all sorts of unlikely places. Railroads are laying FDDI cables along their rights-of-way, while innovative companies are pulling glass fiber through the steam pipes under major office buildings and, in Chicago, in the abandoned tunnels under the city, once used to cart coal to building basements.

Figure 13.14

The FDDI hub topology uses a primary ring for data and a secondary ring as a backup. In this simplified diagram, one node is not on the secondary ring and cannot benefit from its redundancy. On the other hand, a node with a single connection has a low cost for installation and equipment.

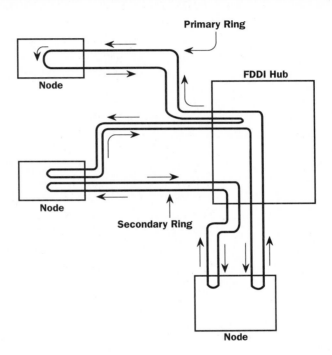

Other Carriers

If your organization needs to connect LANs in a metropolitan area, you might look for communications circuits from unlikely carriers. A few cable television companies have installed two-way coaxial cables and can carry data at high speed. Railroads often have excess microwave radio or fiber-optic channels installed along their routes. I've even seen television stations with excess capacity on their private microwave systems. These organizations and others might be able to sell you a service that can link your LANs.

Specialized companies in many metropolitan areas offer circuits for MAN connectivity. For example, Metropolitan Fiber Systems sells fiber-optic MAN circuits in Baltimore, Boston, Chicago, Houston, Los Angeles, Minneapolis, New York, San Francisco, and other cities. Diginet Communications sells circuits in Chicago and Milwaukee, and Bay Area Teleport sells circuits—primarily carried over microwave radio—throughout central

California. The Teleport Communications Group offers fiber-optic service throughout the New York City commercial area.

Finally, you can be your own carrier within a metropolitan area, particularly if you have at least one office with a top-down view of the skyline. Several companies, including M/A-Com, Microwave Networks, and Motorola Microwave sell microwave radios operating at 23 GHz that you can literally set on a desktop and point out the window toward the distant LAN. These products can only span line-of-sight distances, for a maximum of 3 to 5 miles, but they can provide throughput of 1.544 megabits per second, and since you'll typically buy the equipment for around $10,000 per set, there are no monthly leased-line charges.

■ ISDN

We've looked at interLAN circuits you can lease over terrestrial lines, satellite links, and MAN systems like FDDI. The next interLAN connectivity alternative, the Integrated Services Digital Network (ISDN), uses copper wires to move data down the hall, across town, or across the country. ISDN is more than just circuits; the ISDN specification also covers what kinds of signaling goes over those circuits.

ISDN is one of the best-funded and broadest-reaching programs to come out of the high-technology industry in the latter portion of the twentieth century. The goal of the program is to link every home and organizational desktop with high-speed digital data services carried over copper telephone wires. This movement has the potential to influence how people in Western Europe, Japan, and North America work, study, communicate, and conduct commerce.

The banners waving on the front lines of ISDN carry the colors of some of the largest international corporations, including AT&T, Hitachi, NCR, Northern Telecom, Siemens, government-controlled telephone monopolies, and every U.S. Regional Bell Operating Company (RBOC). The market for end-user equipment alone is estimated at over $5 billion in sales during 1994. The cost of switches and services will add further billions of dollars annually.

Today, ISDN is most important to you if your organization is around Atlanta, Boston, Chicago, Houston, Huntsville, St. Louis, Sunnyvale, Washington, and many cities served by U.S. West. Service is available in other areas, but these are ISDN "hot spots."

Of the Regional Bell Operating Companies, U.S. West, Ameritech, Bell South, and Southwestern Bell have taken leadership positions in ISDN. You can order ISDN service from U.S. West in Olympia, Washington, and Great Falls, Montana, but you will have a hard time getting ISDN service from NYNEX in New York City outside of a few neighborhoods. But all of the

---

ISDN:

👍 **The ISDN architecture of all-digital telephone lines should make it easy to interlink computers with 64- to 128-kilobit-per-second service over long distances**

👍 **The ISDN plan is backed by some of the largest corporations in the world, so it should come true**

👎 **The telephone companies are so hypnotized by digital voice service that they have almost ignored PC-to-PC service**

👎 **The price of ISDN PC adapters and clear-channel data service is far above other interLAN connectivity alternatives**

👎 **Despite its strong backers, ISDN is available only in a few metropolitan areas and from corporate PBX systems**

Bell Operating Companies have made a commitment to ISDN, and the number of service areas is growing every month.

The need to equip the computerized switches of the long-distance telephone carriers with sophisticated software to pass the ISDN calls limits national and international ISDN services today. Pressure from RBOCs and from the increasing number of users of ISDN services should make national service practical within 12 months.

ISDN Technology

This international Integrated Services Digital Network program sets standards for the complete digitization of the telephone systems in Western Europe, Japan, and North America. The plan calls for converting the present analog signaling circuits and systems to digital circuits and systems circulating 0's and 1's instead of analog voice frequencies.

This isn't as radical as it sounds. Modern phone systems are already mostly digital. When you hit the keys on a Touch-tone phone, you program a sophisticated computer in the telephone company's central office and tell it to connect your phone to the desired destination. Your local telephone company's central office computer communicates digitally with computers from other companies, both nationally and internationally, to move your voice.

Digital computer-based telephone switches are the rule in most communities in North America. Many organizations have PBXs that convert analog voice signals to digital 0's and 1's right in the telephone. Many of us use all-digital phone systems already.

Since you've come so far in this book, you should be quick to ask, "If digital switches are so common, then why do I have to use a modem to change my PC's digital signals to analog tones for the telephone lines?" The answer is that modern telephone systems are only modern up to the dial central office. From the dial central office to homes and businesses, they drop back to technology that Alexander Graham Bell would recognize instantly. This local wiring, the "local loop," was designed for analog telephones and signals. Special line cards in the dial central office's telephone switch translate between the digital signals in the switch and the analog signals in the phone line. You must convert your PC's new-technology digital signals into old-technology audio tones with a modem so they can be converted back to digital signals, in different form, at the switch.

Advertisements from long-distance telephone carriers aside, most of the noise you hear on a telephone call comes from the analog local loops on each end. Make these local loops digital and the noise disappears. Of course digital square waves get clipped and distorted, but you can fix digital signal problems by regenerating the signals at intermediate stops. Analog noise is additive throughout the system.

Using digital local loops means you need digital phones at each end. Does that mean you have to throw out your existing phones to use ISDN? Yes, probably. You could use an adapter to integrate an old-style analog phone into ISDN service, but you would miss the convenience of the ISDN services I'll describe a little later. But even on a digital local loop, your PC still needs a modemlike adapter to use ISDN. The unique signaling scheme and voltage levels of ISDN create the need for a digital-to-digital ISDN adapter in each PC.

By the way, when your phone is digital it needs a source of local power. If you don't have a back-up power source for the phone, when the lights go out, so does the phone service.

When you make the local loops digital, you eliminate the bandwidth problems that force us to use sophisticated and high-priced computer-controlled modems to move data at anything over 300 bits per second. Using data compression and sophisticated signaling techniques, modern modems advertise throughputs of up to 48 kilobits per second over dial-up lines, but not with every file and certainly not with everybody's modem. If you make the local loop digital, you can easily send over 140 kilobits per second over the telephone lines.

Sometimes it's easy to make the local loops digital, and sometimes it's very hard. If the premise (home or office) is within 6 to 10 miles of the dial central office, as in most cities and towns, copper cables link the premise and the central office. Copper cables can carry high-speed data, but presently devices called *loading coils* designed to minimize distortion of the analog signals make it impossible to send digital signals over the copper cables. Converting the cabling for digital signaling can be as easy as clipping off the loading coils.

For premises farther from the dial central office, engineers use other techniques, including radio repeaters, to carry the voice signals. These repeaters don't have digital capabilities and are expensive to replace.

For these and other reasons, ISDN will grow first in the cities and in new communities installing telephone systems for the first time. Since the initial market for ISDN services comes from organizations in the cities, the availability of service and the demand for service will grow hand in hand.

Who Is Calling?

What does ISDN bring the average telephone user besides higher-quality voice calls? The answer that the telephone industry loves to demonstrate is the ability to know who is calling before you answer the phone.

Because an ISDN telephone call is digital, the phones and switches can pass a lot of information about the call. A key ISDN buzzword is ICLID or *incoming call ID*. The ICLID message goes from the calling phone's ISDN switch to the called phone. ISDN telephone sets typically have an LCD panel showing the number of the calling phone. With a small amount of internal memory augmentation and your own programming, the phone can display the calling person's name, ring differently for calls from certain people, and route incoming calls to other numbers or services based on who is calling.

The next step in the application of this technology is to route the originating number of an incoming call to a local computer, which then displays the credit record, buying history, or other caller-related information before you answer the call. This technique can save valuable minutes in order-taking or other heavy call-handling situations.

Let Computers Talk

The ICLID is an oversold aspect of ISDN. There are other ways to get incoming call information from modern telephone switches without using the ISDN technology. The bright future of ISDN, which few telephone people see, is in serving as the pipe that links millions of PCs, minis, and mainframes across neighborhoods, cities, and oceans on demand. The applications that will use these communications links include executive information systems, electronic mail, database access, printer sharing, and the rest of the growing list of networked workgroup productivity applications on modern LANs. People using PCs and other computers need to communicate easily and at high speed beyond the typical 1,000-foot boundaries of local area networks.

The designers of ISDN developed a standard dividing the available bandwidth into three data channels. Two of the channels move data at 64 kilobits per second. The third channel operates at 16 kilobits per second and provides a path for telephones to send requests to the ISDN switch while moving data from applications at full speed on the data channels.

In ISDN parlance, the 64-kilobit-per-second data channels are called "B-channels" and the slower 16-kilobit-per-second signaling channel is a "D-channel." The typical type of desktop ISDN service is called 2B+D or "basic rate" service. These services are illustrated in Figure 13.15.

A computer looks at the ISDN line as a wide-open pipe for the transfer of data at nearly 150 kilobits per second. People who are used to reading about 10-megabit-per-second Ethernet and 16-megabit-per-second Token-Ring might assume that ISDN is slow in comparison, but LAN schemes like Ethernet and Token-Ring use sophisticated media-access protocols to control the access of each node to the cable. LAN nodes must wait, retry, repeat, and perform many overhead tasks to share the cable. These actions cut the LAN throughput of even the fastest computer to hundreds of kilobits per second instead of megabits.

Figure 13.15

ISDN carries voice and data over standard telephone lines digitally. Several different rates of service, each combining 19.2- and 64-kilobit-per-second signaling, can link subscriber locations and the central telephone equipment. PCs with ISDN terminal adapters and special telephones with RS-232 connections can combine voice and data on the same desktop.

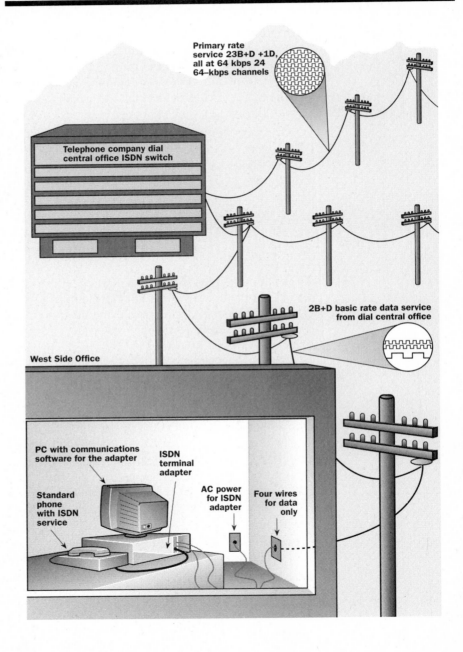

Primary rate service 23B+D +1D, all at 64 kbps 24 64–kbps channels

Telephone company dial central office ISDN switch

2B+D basic rate data service from dial central office

West Side Office

PC with communications software for the adapter

ISDN terminal adapter

Standard phone with ISDN service

AC power for ISDN adapter

Four wires for data only

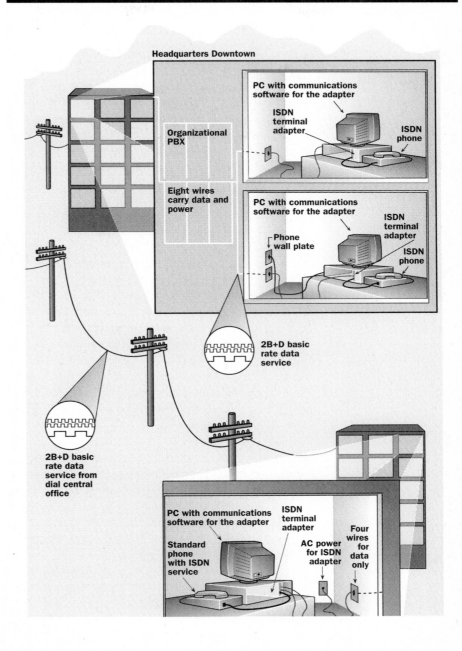

Headquarters Downtown

PC with communications software for the adapter

ISDN terminal adapter

ISDN phone

Organizational PBX

Eight wires carry data and power

PC with communications software for the adapter

ISDN terminal adapter

Phone wall plate

ISDN phone

2B+D basic rate data service

2B+D basic rate data service from dial central office

PC with communications software for the adapter

ISDN terminal adapter

Standard phone with ISDN service

AC power for ISDN adapter

Four wires for data only

Suddenly the ISDN pipe doesn't look so thin. You can move a lot of data quickly over a high-quality ISDN circuit because other nodes don't share or contend for its service.

The Bright Lights

There are companies that realize the potential of ISDN as a communications platform for computer-based applications. Companies like AT&T and NCR have PC adapters for ISDN available for shipping to system integrators and technically sophisticated customers. The packages range from little more than a bare board begging for third-party application software to a tightly integrated and sophisticated product, with software that can make full use of the multitasking features of the OS/2 operating system and the Presentation Manager interface.

In their early versions, these ISDN adapters are not economical for linking individual PCs. Prices of over $1,500 per machine seem to be the norm. In addition, if you get ISDN service from an RBOC instead of from your own PBX, you must pay tariffed service charges. Various regulatory jurisdictions use different rate packages based on connection time, packet counts, and completed call charges.

The pricing of ISDN adapters is more typical of products like SNA and X.25 gateways than PC-to-PC products or LAN interface cards. It seems likely that based on price alone, many people will initially use ISDN connections to link traditional LANs rather than replace them. AT&T and Micom Communications Corp. sell a product they call an ISDN Basic Rate Interface PC card for the reasonable price of about $500, but it only supports a data rate of 19.2 kilobits per second, so it is only marginally useful for most PC or LAN-to-LAN applications.

Right now, the ISDN adapters from different manufacturers cannot communicate with each other. The adapters and application programs use the empty ISDN data channel in unique and proprietary ways. An international CCITT standard called V.120 describes data formats in the fast B-channels, but few companies have spent any money to write software for this standard.

Microcom markets an ISDN LAN bridge that represents a bright spot in the entire LAN-to-LAN and ISDN picture. The Microcom MND/5500 ISDN LAN Bridge uses the V.120 standards and has a retail price under $10,000. If you can get ISDN service and want to use an interesting technology, this product is one of the few in the ISDN arena that makes good sense.

Software Interface

You can get around the signaling problem by buying all your adapters from one company, but the problem of having to use unique application software is more vexing. All of the companies that have visited with us at PC Magazine LAN Labs voice support for a universal application-software interface, but only Hayes Microcomputer Products has tackled the problem. NCR took a smart but potentially limiting sidestep by hosting its ISDN adapters under OS/2.

ISDN Coming to You

If you manage a group of PCs in one of the increasing number of ISDN geographic areas, you need to know how this alternative can serve you to link PCs, mainframes, and existing LANs across the miles, and eventually across thousands of miles, with fast digital service. Today ISDN is economical mainly for linking LANs, primarily on an experimental basis, but in the near future it may replace and displace today's traditional local area network in many installations.

■ X.25: Versatile, Efficient, International, and Necessary

X.25 services:

☞ **X.25 is a widely supported protocol; you have a wide choice of vendors with considerable expertise**

☞ **The vendors of value-added network services have connections available worldwide**

☞ **The value-added X.25 networks often do not offer connection speeds high enough for efficient interLAN service**

You should be aware of a protocol called CCITT X.25, which defines how communications devices like bridges and routers package and route data over a connecting circuit. You can use X.25 data packaging and routing over any of the terrestrial, satellite, or ISDN communications circuits I've described. You can use the data-packaging and data-handling aspects of X.25 over any type of point-to-point circuits, but the protocol is better-known for its packet-switching capabilities.

Packet switching is one of three major switching classes. The others are *circuit switching* and *message* or *store-and-forward switching.* You use circuit switching every time you make a telephone call. The lines the call traverses are dedicated to you and the person you called, and they remain fixed until you hang up. These lines are unavailable to anyone else, even when neither party is talking. In store-and-forward switching, the complete message, like a Western Union telegram, is sent from switch to switch. When the message reaches the destination switch, it is printed out and delivered.

Packet switching breaks messages into small bundles or packets (for instance, 128 characters). These packets are sent out as they are built in a *packet assembler/disassembler* or PAD. A PAD may be nothing more than a special kind of adapter board with its own processing capability and software. A PAD can reside in a PC, and Hayes even builds a PAD into its V-Series of Smartmodems. The packets coming from a PAD are interleaved on a circuit with packets from other sources to make maximum use of the available bandwidth.

To make matters confusing, there are several different packet-switching protocols used in both LANs and wide-area networks. These include protocols as diverse as IBM's Systems Network Architecture (SNA), Token-Ring, and FDDI. The most widely used, internationally agreed-on protocol for packet switching is X.25. The X.25 standard was first adopted as an international standard in 1976 and has been revised and updated every four years since then.

The protocol for X.25 details a specific exchange of packets required to pass information. These packets have structured contents and precede the passing of information. A *call request packet* is sent to the requested host, which can grant permission for the exchange by issuing a *call accepted packet.* The call is set up and information exchanged in the form of packets that contain addressing information. Of course, these packets also contain the actual data that the sender wishes to transmit. The call is ended when a *call clear packet* is sent and a *clear confirmation packet* is received in acknowledgement. Each of the packets in this exchange has a specified structure, and each field is defined. Special *reset* and *restart packets* add to the robustness of X.25. These, along with other prescribed packets such as the *diagnostic packet,* make X.25 extremely versatile and easy to use.

X.25: Good and Stubborn

Several companies, such as AT&T, Telenet, and Tymnet, manage networks of minicomputers spread across the nation and across the world that connect together with high-speed data-communications lines. These companies sell their networks' data-handling and transmission capabilities to subscribers under several different pricing schemes. Outside the U.S., national telephone companies in many countries offer X.25 services, sometimes at lower rates than leased lines or dial-up lines.

Because these networks use software conforming to the X.25 protocols to ensure the accuracy of the data they carry, and because they can offer other associated services, they are called *value-added-networks* or VANs.

Because X.25 packet-switched VANs route each packet to any destination on the fly, they create the ability to link thousands of locations simultaneously. You see this best in on-line services like CompuServe, where people calling in from locations around the world simultaneously communicate with the central database computers.

When you use X.25 VANs to link LANs, you gain error-free simultaneous connections to multiple locations. This capability should make X.25 VANs perfect for LAN-to-LAN connections. Unfortunately, traditional and short-sighted policies in the management of these networks lead to two problems: limited throughput and what I call a "centralized connection" mentality.

Artists often depict an X.25 network as a "cloud" with connections in and out. They use the cloud to obscure the complexity of the minicomputers inside the VAN and their interconnections. There are two types of connections going into the "cloud." The first is a high-speed leased line that can carry 19.2, 56, or 64 kilobits per second, or even 1.544 megabits per second, from the computer to the cloud, using full X.25 protocols. This is an expensive connection, usually reserved for the busy host computer. The other type of connection is a dial-up telephone line that does not provide full X.25 data handling between the computer and the network.

Unfortunately, X.25 vendors haven't installed modern V.32bis modems on many dial access ports so that people can call in at 9,600 bits per second or better. They have few ports that can handle even a maximum speed of 2,400 bits per second. It isn't practical to make interLAN connections at only 2,400 bits per second.

The limitation on connection speed is made worse by the double error-checking used when Novell IPX packets travel over X.25. Both IPX and X.25 have built-in error correction. Novell designed IPX with the "Did you get what I sent?" concept in mind. Therefore, a lot of X.25 packets consist of IPX confirmations to packets that X.25 already confirmed, at least at the X.25 network level, so you need all the throughput you can get to carry the overhead. While the X.25 confirmation is redundant to the higher IPX confirmation, the additional X.25 packet information is needed for the VAN routing.

The other problem with using X.25 VANs to link LANs comes from the traditional use of VANs to make one-to-many connections. In the past, multiple clients used VANs to get to one host. The fee structure and programming of the networks reflect and perpetuate this scheme, but this isn't the best structure for LAN-to-LAN connections.

Despite the limitations on speed and on connection options, X.25 networks are appropriate for many LAN-to-LAN applications. Pressure from users should force the managers of these systems to implement more features for the LAN-to-LAN market.

Public versus Private X.25 Networks

X.25 packet-switching networks provide effective solutions for many applications. For example, X.25 works well where multiple protocols must be handled, low delay is required, or users need to connect to multiple hosts for short periods of time.

A familiar example of an X.25 network application is the processing of credit-card charges you see in stores daily. The electronic transaction from the card reader is frequently carried over an X.25 network. This permits short messages (which include your account number, store identification, and the amount to be charged) to be sent to the proper bank and receipt of the transaction to be acknowledged by the bank. The X.25 network allows this to occur without the use of costly, dedicated connections from each store to each bank that issues credit cards.

Packet-switching services can be obtained by building private networks or through the use of public data networks. As the name implies, a private network is one where network resources are usually dedicated to a small number of applications or a restricted set of users, as in a corporate network. The network resources include the access circuits, the network interfaces between the user and the packet switches, the packet-switching nodes (PSNs) and the trunk circuits that connect them, and the control systems for the network.

Private network access is typically handled through dedicated circuits. With public data networks, network resources are owned by a third party (such as Tymnet or Telenet) and leased on a usage basis to many users, serving many applications. Access to public networks is typically through dial-up circuits.

The decision to use a private or public network is primarily based on economics and, to some extent, on desired network performance.

In public networks, costs to a user are determined by the amount of time the user is connected and by the number of packets the user sends and receives. Although various cost algorithms are employed, generally the more you use, the more you pay. In private networks, user costs are driven by the initial capital investment and network operations costs.

Usage must also be viewed in terms of traffic volume and transaction size. For example, comparing interactive transactions and large transmissions (such as file transfers) over a range of traffic volumes yields "regions" where private and public packet networks are each more cost-effective.

Traffic Mix

From a performance perspective, public networks are sufficient for many uses, but specific applications may require a specialized, customized network. In these cases, a private network provides the flexibility to incorporate the necessary performance capabilities.

■ Linking LANs: A New Frontier

The number of organizations that need to expand their information-processing systems by linking LANs across tens or thousands of miles is growing. Some companies, particularly the aggressive manufacturers of routers and bridges, are responding to this lucrative market for data-transport services. Other companies, particularly the local telephone exchange carriers, are looking the wrong way and might miss tremendous opportunities for new business.

In the mid-1990s, new technologies will provide circuits for interLAN connections. These include

- higher-powered satellites that can provide higher data rates with smaller Earth-station antennae

- digital cellular radio systems

- more powerful private-branch-exchange telephone systems with direct links to LANs.

No book can tell you everything you need to know about linking LANs. You'll need help both from the companies making the routers and bridges and from the companies that sell long-distance circuits. But I've given you enough information in this chapter to form a basis for sound choices and decisions about the architecture you will use to connect LAN segments.

■ Glossary

access method   A protocol that determines which device in a local area network has access to the transmission media at any instant. CSMA/CD is an example of an access method. IBM uses the same term for specific kinds of communications software that include protocols for exchanging data, constructing files, and other functions.

access protocol   The traffic rules that LAN workstations abide by to avoid data collisions when sending signals over shared network media; also referred to as the *media-access control (MAC) protocol.* Common examples are carrier sense multiple access (CSMA) and token passing.

ACK   A positive acknowledgment control character. This character is exchanged between system components when data has been received without error. The control character is also used as an affirmative response for setting up a communications exchange. ACK is also used as the name of a message containing an acknowledgment.

acoustic coupler   The portion of a modem that physically holds a telephone handset in two rubber cups. The cups house a small microphone and speaker that "talk" and "listen" to the telephone handset.

ADCCP (Advanced Data Communications Control Procedures)   A bit-oriented ANSI-standard communications protocol. It is a link-layer protocol.

A/D converter   A device that converts analog signals to digital.

address   A unique memory location. Network interface cards and CPUs often use shared addresses in RAM to move data from each card to the PC's processor. The term can also refer to the unique identifier for a particular node in a network.

Address Resolution Protocol (ARP)   A protocol within the Transmission Control Protocol/Internet Protocol (TCP/IP) suite that "maps" IP addresses to Ethernet addresses. TCP/IP requires ARP for use with Ethernet.

Advanced Communications Function (ACF)   An IBM program package to allow sharing computer resources through communications links. It supports SNA.

Advanced Communications Service   A large data communications network developed by AT&T.

AFP (AppleTalk File Protocol)   Apple's network protocol, used to provide access between file servers and clients in an AppleShare network. AFP is also used by Novell's products for the Macintosh.

alphanumeric   Characters made up of letters and numbers; usually contrasted with graphics characters made up of dots in terminal emulation.

analog   Commonly refers to transmission methods developed to transmit voice signals. These methods were designed only for the bandwidth of the human voice (up to about 3 kHz); this limits their capability to pass high-speed digital signals.

ANSI (American National Standards Institute)   An organization that develops and publishes standards for codes, alphabets, and signaling schemes.

API (application program interface)   A set of standard software interrupts, calls, and data formats that application programs use to initiate contact with network services, mainframe communications programs, or other program-to-program communications. For example, applications use APIs to call services that transport data across a network.

APPC (Advanced Program-to-Program Communications)   An IBM protocol analogous to the OSI model's session layer; it sets up the necessary conditions that enable application programs to send data to each other through the network.

APPC/PC   An IBM product that implements APPC on a PC.

AppleTalk   An Apple networking system that can transfer data at a rate of 230 kilobytes per second over shielded twisted-pair wire. Superseded by the term *LocalTalk*.

application layer   The highest (seventh) level of the OSI model. It describes the way that application programs interact with the network operating system.

applications processor   A special-purpose computer that enables a telephone system to furnish special services such as voice mail, messaging services, and electronic mail.

ARCnet (Attached Resources Computing)   A networking architecture (marketed by Datapoint Corp. and other vendors) using a token-passing bus architecture, usually on coaxial cable.

ARPANET (Advanced Research Projects Agency Network)   A network originally sponsored by the Defense Advanced Research Projects Agency (DARPA) to link universities and government research centers. The TCP/IP protocols were pioneered on ARPANET.

ARQ A control code that calls for the retransmission of a block of data.

ASCII (American Standard Code for Information Interchange) The data alphabet used in the IBM PC to determine the composition of the 7-bit string of 0's and 1's that represents each character (alphabetic, numeric, or special).

ASR (automatic send/receive) A term left over from teleprinters that punched messages on paper tape. Now, it is sometimes used to indicate any terminal that has a storage capability.

asynchronous A method of transmission in which the time intervals between characters do not have to be equal. Start and stop bits are added to coordinate the transfer of characters.

attenuation The decrease in power of a signal transmitted over a wire, measured in decibels. As attenuation increases, the signal decreases.

automatic number identification (ANI) A feature that passes a caller's ten-digit telephone number over the network to the customer's premises so that the caller can be identified.

background program (background mode) A program that performs its functions while the user is working with a different program. Communications programs often operate in background mode. They can receive messages while the user works with other programs. The messages are stored for later display.

balun (BALanced UNbalanced) An impedance-matching device that connects a balanced line (such as a twisted-pair line) and an unbalanced line (such as a coaxial cable).

bandwidth The range of frequencies a circuit will pass. Analog circuits typically have a bandwidth limited to that of the human voice (about 300 Hz to 3 kHz). The square waves of a digital signal require a higher bandwidth. The higher the transmission rate, the greater the bandwidth requirement. Fiber-optic and coaxial cables have excellent bandwidths. Also, in common usage, *bandwidth* refers to the upper limit of the rate that information can be transferred over a network.

base address The first address in a series of addresses in memory, often used to describe the beginning of a network interface card's I/O space.

baseband   A network that transmits signals as a direct-current pulse rather than as variations in a radio-frequency signal.

basic-rate interface (BRI)   The ISDN standard governing how a customer's desktop terminals and telephones can connect to the ISDN switch. It specifies two B-channels that allow 64-kilobit-per-second simultaneous voice and data service, and one D-channel that carries call information and customer data at 16 kbps.

baud   A measure of transmission speed; the reciprocal of the time duration of the shortest signal element in a transmission. In RS-232C ASCII, the signaling element is 1 bit.

BBS (bulletin board system)   An electronic message system.

BCD (binary-coded decimal)   A coding scheme using a 6-bit (six-level) code.

B-channel   A "bearer" channel that carries voice or data at 64 kilobits per second in either direction and is circuit-switched.

benchmark test   A program used to measure system speed or throughput.

Bindery   A database maintained by Novell's NetWare operating system that holds information on users, servers, and other elements of the network.

Bisynchronous Communications   Also abbreviated as BSC, this protocol is one of the two commonly used methods of encoding data for transmission between devices in IBM mainframe computer systems. Data characters are gathered in a package called a *frame,* which is marked by 2 synchronization bits (bisync). The more modern protocol is SDLC.

bit   The smallest unit of information. In digital signaling, this commonly refers to a 0 or a 1.

block   A number of characters transmitted as a group.

BNC connector   A small coaxial connector with a half-twist locking shell.

boot ROM   A read-only memory chip allowing a workstation to communicate with the file server and to read a DOS boot program from the server. Stations can thus operate on the network without having a disk drive.

bps   Bits per second.

bridge   An interconnection device, sometimes working within a PC and sometimes within a special-purpose computer, that can connect LANs using similar or dissimilar data links such as Ethernet, Token-Ring, and X.25. Bridges link LANs at the data-link layer of the OSI model. Modern bridges read and filter data packets and frames, and they pass traffic only if the address is on the same segment of the network cable as the originating station.

broadband   Refers to a network that carries information riding on carrier waves rather than directly as pulses, providing greater capacity at the cost of higher complexity.

broadcast   To send a message to all stations or an entire class of stations connected to the network.

brouter   A device that combines the functions of a bridge and a router. Brouters can route one or more protocols, such as TCP/IP and XNS, and bridge all other traffic. Contrast with *bridge, router,* and *gateway.*

buffer   A temporary storage space. Data may be stored in a buffer as it is received, before or after transmission. A buffer may be used to compensate for the differences between the speed of transmission and the speed of processing.

buffered repeater   A device that amplifies and regenerates signals so they can travel farther along a cable. This type of repeater also controls the flow of messages to prevent collisions.

bus topology   A "broadcast" arrangement in which all network stations receive the same message through the cable at the same time.

byte   A group of 8 bits.

C   A programming language used predominantly by professional programmers to write applications software.

cache   An amount of RAM set aside to hold data that is expected to be accessed again. The second access, which finds the data in RAM, is very fast.

call packet   A block of data carrying addressing and other information that is needed to establish an X.25 switched virtual circuit (SVC).

carrier signal   A tone or radio signal modulated by data, usually for long-distance transmission.

CCITT X.25 Recommendation   An international standard defining packet-switched communication protocols for a public or private network. The recommendation is prepared by the Comite Consultatif Internationale Telegraphique et Telephonic (CCITT). Along with other CCITT recommendations, the X.25 Recommendation defines the physical-, data-link-, and network-layer protocols necessary to interface with X.25 networks. The CCITT X.25 Recommendation is supported by most X.25 equipment vendors, but a new CCITT X.25 Recommendation is published every four years.

CCS 7   A network signaling standard for ISDN that incorporates information from databases in order to offer advanced network services.

central office (CO)   The telephone-switching location nearest to the customer's premises. It serves the businesses and residences connected to its loop lines.

channel   A path between sender and receiver that carries one stream of information (a two-way path is a *circuit*).

character   One letter, number, or special code.

CICS (Customer Information Control System)   This IBM software runs on a mainframe and makes a variety of services available for application programs. It furnishes easy ways for programs to enter mainframe files and find data within them.

circuit switching   A method of communicating in which a dedicated communications path is established between two devices, the bandwidth is guaranteed, and the delay is essentially limited to propagation time. The telephone system uses circuit switching.

clear packet   A block of data containing a command that performs the equivalent of hanging up the telephone.

client/server computing   A computing system in which processing can be distributed among "clients" on the network that request information and one or more network "servers" that store data, let clients share data and programs, help in printing operations, and so on. The system can accommodate standalone applications (word processing), applications requiring data from the server (spreadsheets), applications that use server capabilities to exchange information among users (electronic mail), and applications providing true client/server teamwork (databases, especially those based on Structured Query Language, or SQL). Before client/server computing, a server would download an entire database to a client machine for processing. SQL database applications divide the work between machines, letting the database stay on the server.

cluster controller   A computer that sits between a group of terminals and the mainframe, gathering messages and multiplexing over a single link to the mainframe.

CMIP (Common Management Information Protocol)   An OSI-based structure for formatting messages and for transmitting information between data-collection programs and reporting devices. This was developed by the International Standards Organization and designated as ISO 9596.

CMOT (CMIP Over TCP/IP)   An Internet standard defining the use of CMIP for managing TCP/IP networks.

coax or coaxial cable   A type of network media. Coaxial cable contains a copper inner conductor surrounded by plastic insulation and then a woven copper or foil shield.

codec (coder/decoder)   A device that transforms analog voice signals into a digital bit stream (coder) and digital signals into analog voice (decoder) using pulse-code modulation.

collision   An attempt by two units to send a message at one time on a single channel. In some networks, the detection of a collision causes all senders to stop transmissions, while in others the collision is noticed when the receiving station fails to acknowledge the data.

common carrier   A transmission company (such as a telephone company) that serves the general public.

communications controller   A programmable computer dedicated to data communications and serving as the "front end" in the IBM SNA network.

concentrator   See *wiring hub*.

contention   The condition when two or more stations attempt to use the same channel at the same time.

control character   A character used for special signaling; often not printed or displayed, but causing special functions such as the movement of paper in a printer, the blanking of a display screen, or "handshaking" between communicating devices to control the flow of data.

COW interface (character-oriented Windows interface)   An SAA-compatible user interface for OS/2 applications.

cps   Characters per second.

CPU (central processing unit)   The functional "brain" of a computer; the element that does the actual adding and subtracting of 0's and 1's that is essential to computing.

CRC (cyclic redundancy check)   A numeric value derived from the bits in a message. The transmitting station uses one of several formulas to produce a number that is attached to the message. The receiving station applies the same formula and should derive the same number. If the numbers are not the same, an error condition is declared.

crosstalk   The spillover of a signal from one channel to another. In data communications it is very disruptive. Usually, careful adjustment of the circuits will eliminate crosstalk.

CRT (cathode ray tube)   A video screen.

CSMA (carrier sense multiple access)   A media-sharing scheme in which stations listen in to what's happening on the network media; if the cable is not in use, a station is permitted to transmit its message. CSMA is often combined with a means of performing collision detection, hence *CSMA/CD*.

current loop   An electrical interface that is sensitive to current changes rather than voltage swings; used with older teleprinter equipment.

cursor   The symbol indicating the place on the video screen where the next character will appear.

customer premises equipment (CPE)   A general term for the telephones, computers, private branch exchanges, and other hardware located on the end user's side of the network boundary, established by the Computer Inquiry II action of the Federal Communications Commission.

D/A converter   A device that changes digital pulses into analog signals.

Data Access Protocol   A specialized protocol used by Digital Equipment Corp.

datagram   A packet of computer-generated information that includes a complete destination address provided by the user, not the network, along with whatever data the packet carries.

data-link control   A communications layer in SNA that manages the physical data circuits.

data-link layer The second layer of the OSI model. Protocols functioning in this layer manage the flow of data leaving a network device and work with the receiving station to ensure that the data arrives safely.

data packet In X.25, a block of data that transports full-duplex information via an X.25 switched virtual circuit (SVC) or permanent virtual circuit (PVC). X.25 data packets may contain up to 1,024 bytes of user data, but the most common size is 128 bytes (the X.25 default).

data set 1. A file, a "set" of data. 2. The name the telephone company often uses for a modem.

DB-25 The designation of a standard plug-and-jack set used in RS-232C wiring: 25-pin connectors, with 13 pins in one row and 12 in the other row.

DCE (data communications equipment) Refers to any X.25 network component that implements the CCITT X.25 standard.

D-channel The "data" channel of an ISDN interface, used to carry control signals and customer call data in a packet-switched mode. In the basic-rate interface (BRI), the D-channel operates at 16 kilobits per second; in the primary-rate interface (PRI), the D-channel is used at 64 kbps.

DDCMP (Digital Data Communications Message Protocol) A byte-oriented, link-layer protocol from Digital Equipment Corp., used to transmit messages over a communications line.

DDD (direct distance dialing) Use of the common long-distance telephone system.

DECnet A communications protocol and line of networking products from Digital Equipment Corp., compatible with Ethernet and a wide range of systems.

delay Commonly, a pause in activity. Delay can also be a kind of distortion on a communications circuit. Specifically, it is the property of an electrical circuit that slows down and distorts high-frequency signals. Devices called *equalizers* slow down the lower frequencies and "equalize" the signal.

demodulation The process of retrieving data from a modulated carrier wave; the reverse of *modulation*.

dial-up line A communications circuit established by dialing a destination over a commercial telephone system.

digital   In common use, on/off signaling; signals consist of 0's and 1's instead of a great multitude of analog-modulated frequencies.

disk duplexing   A fault-tolerant technique that writes simultaneously to two hard disks using different controllers.

disk mirroring   A fault-tolerant technique that writes data simultaneously to two hard disks using the same controller.

DISOSS (Distributed Office Supported System)   An integrated package of electronic-mail and document-preparation programs from IBM, designed for IBM mainframe computer systems.

distortion   Any change to the transmitted signal. Distortion can be caused by crosstalk, delay, attenuation, or other factors.

Distributed Systems Architecture (DSA)   A Honeywell architecture that conforms to the Open Systems Interconnection model proposed by the ISO. It supports X.25 for packet switching and X.21 for packet-switched and circuit-switched network protocols.

DQDB (Distributed Queue Dual Bus)   A proposed IEEE 802.6 standard for metropolitan-area networks (MANs).

driver   A software program that interfaces between portions of the LAN software and the hardware on the network interface card.

DTE (data terminal equipment)   Refers to any end-user device that can access an X.25 network using the CCITT X.25 standard, LAP/LAB, and X.25 PAP.

duplex   1. In communications circuits, the ability to transmit and receive at the same time; also referred to as *full duplex*. Half-duplex circuits can receive only or transmit only. 2. In terminals, a choice between displaying locally generated characters and echoed characters.

EBCDIC (Extended Binary Coded Decimal Interchange Code)   The data alphabet used in all IBM computers except the PC; it determines the composition of the 8-bit string of 0's and 1's representing each character (alphabetic, numeric, or special).

echoplex   A method of transmission in which characters are echoed from the distant end and the echoes are presented on the terminal; this provides a constant check of the communications circuit to the user.

echo suppressor A device used to eliminate the echo effect of long-distance voice transmission circuits. This suppressor must be disabled for full-duplex data transmission; the modem answer tones turn the suppressor off automatically.

ECMA (European Computer Manufacturers' Association) A trade association that provides input to international standards-forming organizations.

EDI (electronic data interchange) The communication of orders, invoices, and similar transactions electronically between organizations.

elevator seeking A method of optimizing the movement of the heads on the hard disk in a file server.

EIA (Electronic Industries Association) An organization of U.S. manufacturers of electronic parts and equipment. The organization develops industry standards for the interface between data-processing and communications equipment.

802.X The Institute of Electrical and Electronics Engineers (IEEE) committee that developed a set of standards describing the cabling, electrical topology, physical topology, and access scheme of network products; in other words, the 802.X standards define the physical and data-link layers of LAN architectures. IEEE 802.3 is the work of an 802 subcommittee that describes the cabling and signaling for a system nearly identical to classic Ethernet. IEEE 802.5 comes from another subcommittee and similarly describes IBM's Token-Ring architecture.

EISA (Extended Industry Standard Architecture) A PC bus system that serves as an alternative to IBM's Micro Channel Architecture (MCA). The EISA architecture, backed by an industry consortium headed by Compaq, is compatible with the IBM AT bus; MCA is not.

EMA (Enterprise Management Architecture) Digital Equipment Corp.'s company-specific architecture, conforming to ISO's CMIP.

emulation Simulation of a system, function, or program.

equalization Balancing of a circuit so that it passes all frequencies with equal efficiency.

Ethernet A network cable and access protocol scheme originally developed by Xerox, now marketed mainly by Digital Equipment Corp. and 3Com.

EtherTalk 1. The Apple Ethernet adapter for the Macintosh II computer. 2. The software driver used by the Macintosh to communicate with Ethernet adapters.

facsimile (fax)   The transmission of page images by a system that is concerned with patterns of light and dark rather than with specific characters. Older systems use analog signals; newer devices use digital signals and may interact with computers and other digital devices.

fault   A physical or logical break in a communications link.

fault management   One of the five basic categories of network management defined by the International Standards Organization (ISO). Fault management is used for the detection, isolation, and correction of faults on the network.

fault tolerance   A method of ensuring continued operation through redundancy and diversity.

FCC   Federal Communications Commission.

FDDI (Fiber Distributed Data Interface)   A specification for fiber-optic networks operating at 100 megabits per second. FDDI uses wiring hubs, and the hubs are prime candidates to serve as network monitoring and control devices.

FEP (front-end processor)   A computer that sits between groups of cluster controllers and the mainframe, concentrating signals before they are transmitted to the mainframe.

fiber optics   A data-transmission method that uses light pulses sent over glass cables.

field   A particular position within a message frame. Positions are labeled as the control field, flag field, and so on. Bits in each message have a meaning for stations on the network.

file lock   See *locking*.

file server   A type of server that holds files in private and shared directories for LAN users. See *server*.

flow control   A convention used to regulate communications between two nodes. Hardware and software techniques are available.

foreign exchange   A telephone line that represents a local number in a calling area quite removed from the telephone's actual termination. If your office is in the suburbs but many of your customers are in the city, you might have a foreign-exchange line with a city telephone office.

four-wire circuit   A transmission arrangement where two half-duplex circuits (two wires each) are combined to make one full-duplex circuit.

frame   A data packet on a Token-Ring network. Also denotes a data packet on other networks such as X.25 or SNA.

frequency-agile modem   A modem used on some broadband systems that can shift frequencies to communicate with stations in different dedicated bands.

frequency converter   In broadband cable systems, the device that translates between the transmitting and receiving frequencies.

frequency-division multiplexing   A technique for combining many signals on one circuit by separating them in frequency.

frequency-shift keying   A transmission method using two different frequencies that are shifted to represent the digital 0's and 1's; used in some common modems.

FTAM (File Transfer Access and Management)   An OSI protocol that provides access to files stored on dissimilar systems.

FTP (File Transfer Protocol)   A protocol that describes how one computer can host other computers to allow transferring files in either direction. Users can see directories of either computer on the host and perform limited file-management functions. Software for the FTP client function is usually a part of TCP/IP packages for the PC; some vendors also provide FTP host software for the PC. See *TFTP*.

full duplex   The ability for communications to flow both ways over a communications link at the same time.

functional-management layer   A communications layer in SNA that formats presentations.

gateway   A device that serves as a shared point of entry from a local area network into a larger information resource such as a large packet-switched information network or a mainframe computer.

GOSIP (Government OSI Profile)   The U.S. government's version of the OSI protocols. GOSIP compliance is typically a requirement in government networking purchases.

ground   An electrically neutral contact point.

half duplex   1. Alternating transmissions; each station can either transmit or receive, not both simultaneously. 2. In terminals, describes the condition when a terminal displays its own transmissions instead of a remote-end echo. 3. The configuration option in some modems allowing local character echo.

handshaking   Exchange of control codes or specific characters to control data flow.

HDLC (High-level Data Link Control)   A comprehensive standard developed by the International Standards Organization (ISO). It is a bit-oriented link-layer protocol.

high-speed modem   A modem operating at speeds from 2,400 to 9,600 bits per second.

HLLAPI (High-Level-Language Application Program Interface)   A scripting language (that is, a set of verbs) that allows programmers to build transparent interfaces between 3270 terminals and applications on IBM mainframes.

HotFix   A Novell program that dynamically marks defective blocks on the hard disk so they will not be used.

Hz (hertz)   Cycles per second.

ICMP (Internet Control Message Protocol)   The TCP/IP process that provides the set of functions used for network-layer management and control.

IEEE 802   A large family of standards for the physical and electrical connections in local area networks, developed by the IEEE (Institute of Electrical and Electronics Engineers).

IEEE 802.1D   An IEEE media-access-control-level standard for interLAN bridges linking IEEE 802.3, 802.4, and 802.5 networks.

IEEE 802.2   An IEEE standard for data-link-layer software and firmware for use with IEEE 802.3, 802.4, and 802.5 networks.

IEEE 802.3 1Base5   An IEEE specification matching the older AT&T StarLAN product. It designates a 1-megabit-per-second signaling rate, a baseband signaling technique, and a maximum cable-segment distance of 500 meters.

IEEE 802.3 10Base2   This IEEE specification matches the thin Ethernet cabling. It designates a 10-megabit-per-second signaling rate, a baseband signaling technique, and a maximum cable-segment distance of 185 (nearly 200) meters.

IEEE 802.3 10BaseT   An IEEE standard describing 10-megabit-per-second twisted-pair Ethernet wiring using baseband signaling. This system requires a wiring hub.

IEEE 802.3 10Broad36   This IEEE specification describes a long-distance type of Ethernet cabling with a 10-megabit-per-second signaling rate, a broadband signaling technique, and a maximum cable-segment distance of 3,600 meters.

IEEE 802.4   This IEEE specification describes a LAN using 10-megabit-per-second signaling, token-passing media-access control, and a physical bus topology. It is typically used as part of networks following the Manufacturing Automation Protocol (MAP) developed by General Motors. This is sometimes confused with ARCnet, but it is not the same.

IEEE 802.5   This IEEE specification describes a LAN using 4- or 16-megabit-per-second signaling, token-passing media-access control, and a physical ring topology. It is used by IBM's Token-Ring systems.

IEEE 802.6   This IEEE standard for metropolitan-area networks (MANs) describes what is called a Distributed Queue Dual Bus (DQDB). The DQDB topology includes two parallel runs of cable—typically fiber-optic cable—linking each node (typically a router for a LAN segment) using signaling rates in the range of 100 megabits per second.

impedance   An electrical property of a cable, combining capacitance, inductance, and resistance, and measured in ohms.

IND$FILE   A mainframe editing utility, commonly used to make PC-to-mainframe file transfers; a logical unit in an SNA network that addresses and interacts with the host.

interface   An interconnection point, usually between pieces of equipment.

Internet   A collection of networks and gateways including ARPAnet, MILnet, and NSFnet (National Science Foundation net). Internet uses TCP/IP protocols.

interrupt   A signal that suspends a program temporarily, transferring control to the operating system when input or output is required. Interrupts may have priority levels, and higher-priority interrupts take precedence in processing.

I/O   Input/output.

I/O bound   A condition where the operation of the I/O port is the limiting factor in program execution.

IP (Internet Protocol)   A standard describing software that keeps track of the Internet address for different nodes, routes outgoing messages, and recognizes incoming messages.

IPX (Internet Packet Exchange)   NetWare's native LAN communications protocol, used to move data between server and/or workstation programs running on different network nodes. IPX packets are encapsulated and carried by the packets used in Ethernet and the similar frames used in Token-Ring networks.

IRQ (interrupt request)   A computer instruction that causes an interruption of a program for an I/O task.

ISDN (Integrated Services Digital Network)   As officially defined by the CCITT, "a limited set of standard interfaces to a digital communications network." The result is a network that offers end users voice, data, and certain image services on end-to-end digital circuits.

ISO (International Standards Organization)   A Paris-based organization that developed the Open Systems Interconnection (OSI) model.

jam signal   A signal generated by a card to ensure that other cards know that a packet collision has taken place.

jumper   A plastic-and-metal shorting bar that slides over two or more electrical contacts to set certain conditions for operation.

k   Used in this book to represent a kilobyte (1,024 bytes).

kernel   The heart of an operating system, containing the basic scheduling and interrupt handling, but not the higher-level services, such as the file system.

LAN Manager   The multiuser network operating system codeveloped by Microsoft and 3Com. LAN Manager offers a wide range of network-management and control capabilities.

LAN Manager/X (LM/X)   LAN Manager for the Unix environment.

LAN Server   IBM's proprietary OS/2-based network operating system. LAN Server is compatible with LAN Manager, codeveloped by Microsoft and 3Com.

LAP-B   Link access procedure (balanced), the most common data-link control protocol used to interface X.25 DTEs with X.25 DCEs. X.25 also specifies a *LAP,* or link access procedure (not balanced). Both LAP and LAP-B are full-duplex, point-to-point bit-synchronous protocols. The unit of data transmission is called a *frame;* frames may contain one or more X.25 packets.

leased line A communications circuit reserved for the permanent use of a customer; also called *private line*.

light-wave communications Usually, communications using fiber-optic cables and light generated by lasers or light-emitting diodes (LEDs). The phrase can also refer to systems using modulated light beams passing through the air between buildings or other adjacent locations.

link layer The second layer in the OSI architecture. This layer performs the function of taking data from the higher layers, creating packets, and sending them accurately out through the physical layer.

local Refers to programs, files, peripherals, and computational power accessed directly in the user's own machine rather than through the network.

local area network (LAN) A computer communications system limited to no more than a few miles and using high-speed connections (2 to 100 megabits per second).

local area transport (LAT) A DECnet protocol used for terminal-to-host communications.

local loop The connection between a customer's premises and the telephone company's central office.

LocalTalk The 230.4-kilobit-per-second media-access method developed by Apple Computer for use with its MacIntosh computer.

locking A method of protecting shared data. When an application program opens a file, *file locking* either prevents simultaneous access by a second program or limits such access to "read only." DOS Versions 3.0 and higher allow an application to lock a range of bytes in a file for various purposes. Since DBMS programs interpret this range of bytes as a record, this is called *record locking*.

low-speed modem A modem operating at speeds up to 600 bits per second.

LU 6.2 (Logical Unit 6.2) In IBM's SNA scheme, a software product that implements the session-layer conversation specified in the Advanced Program-to-Program Communications (APPC) protocol.

MAC (media-access control) See *access protocol*.

mainframe A large centralized computer.

MAN (metropolitan-area network)   A public high-speed network (100 megabits per second or more) capable of voice and data transmission over a range of 25 to 50 miles (40 to 80 kilometers).

MAP (Manufacturing Automation Protocol)   A token-passing bus LAN originally designed by General Motors and now adopted as a subset of the IEEE 802.3 standards.

mark   A signaling condition equal to a binary 1.

MAU   See *medium attachment unit* and *Multistation Access Unit.*

MCA (Micro Channel Architecture)   The basis for IBM Micro Channel bus, used in high-end models of IBM's PS/2 series of personal computers.

media   Plural of *medium*; the cabling or wiring used to carry network signals. Typical examples are coax, fiber-optic, and twisted-pair wire.

media-sharing LAN   A network in which all nodes share the cable using a media-access control (MAC) scheme. Contrast with *circuit switching* or *packet switching.*

medium attachment unit (MAU)   A transceiver that attaches to the AUI port on an Ethernet adapter and provides electrical and mechanical attachments to fiber-optic, twisted-pair, or other media.

medium-speed modem   A modem operating between 600 and 2,400 bits per second.

message switching   A routing technique using a message store-and-forward system. No dedicated path is established. Rather, each message contains a destination address and is passed from source to destination through intermediate nodes. At each node, the entire message is received, stored briefly, and then passed on to the next node.

MHS (Message Handling Service)   A program developed by Action Technologies and marketed by that firm and Novell to exchange files with other programs and send files out through gateways to other computers and networks. It is used particularly to link dissimilar electronic-mail systems.

MIB (management information base)   A directory listing the logical names of all information resources residing in a network and pertinent to the network's management.

midsplit A type of broadband cable system in which the available frequencies are split into two groups, one for transmission and one for reception. This requires a frequency converter.

modem (modulator/demodulator) A device that translates between electrical signals and some other means of signaling. Typically a modem translates between direct-current signals from a computer or terminal and analog signals sent over telephone lines. Other modems handle radio frequencies and light waves.

modem eliminator A wiring device designed to replace two modems; it connects equipment over a distance of up to several hundred feet. In asynchronous systems, this is a simple cable.

modulation A process of varying signals to represent intelligent information. The frequency, amplitude, or phase of a signal may be modulated to represent an analog or digital signal.

multiple name spaces The association of several names or other pieces of information with the same file. This allows renaming files and designating them for dissimilar computer systems such as the PC and the Mac.

multipoint line A single communications link for two or more devices shared by one computer and more than one terminal. Use of this line requires a polling mechanism. It is also called a *multidrop line*.

Multistation Access Unit (MAU) IBM's name for a Token-Ring wiring concentrator.

NAK A control code indicating that a character or block of data was not properly received. The name stands for *negative acknowledgement*. See *ACK*.

Named Pipes A technique used for communications between applications operating on the same computer or across the network. It includes a relatively easy-to-use API, providing application programmers with a simple way to create interprogram communications using routines similar to disk-file opening, reading, and writing.

N connector The large-diameter connector used with thick Ethernet cable.

NCP 1. (NetWare Core Protocol) The data format of the requests NetWare uses to access files. 2. (Network Control Program) Special IBM software that runs in a front-end processor and works with VTAM on the host computer to link the application programs and terminal controllers.

NDIS (Network Driver Interface Specification)   A device driver specification codeveloped by Microsoft and 3Com. Besides providing hardware and protocol independence for network drivers, NDIS supports both DOS and OS/2, and it offers protocol multiplexing so that multiple protocol stacks can coexist in the same host.

NetBIOS (Network Basic Input/Output System)   A layer of software originally developed by IBM and Sytek to link a network operating system with specific hardware. It can also open communications between workstations on a network at the transport layer. Today, many vendors either provide a version of NetBIOS to interface with their hardware or emulate its transport-layer communications services in their network products.

NetVIEW   IBM's company-specific network-management and control architecture. This architecture relies heavily on mainframe data-collection programs and also incorporates PC-level products running under OS/2.

NetWare   A popular series of network operating systems and related products made by Novell.

network   A continuing connection between two or more computers that facilitates sharing files and resources.

network-addressable unit (NAU)   In SNA, a device that can be the source and destination of messages.

network layer   The third level of the OSI model, containing the logic and rules that determine the path to be taken by data flowing through a network; not important in small LANs.

NFS (Network File System)   One of many distributed-file-system protocols that allow a computer on a network to use the files and peripherals of another networked computer as if they were local. This protocol was developed by Sun Microsystems and adopted by other vendors.

NLMs (NetWare Loadable Modules)   Applications and drivers that run in a server under Novell's NetWare 386 and can be loaded or unloaded on the fly. In other networks, such applications could require dedicated PCs.

NMP (Network Management Protocol)   An AT&T-developed set of protocols designed to exchange information with and control the devices that govern various components of a network, including modems and T1 multiplexers.

NNTP (Network News Transport Protocol)   An extension of the TCP/IP protocol that provides a network news transport service.

node   A connection or switching point on the network.

ODI (Open Data-link Interface)   A standard interface for transport protocols, allowing them to share a single network card without any conflicts.

OfficeVision   IBM's set of applications designed to bring a uniform user interface to the company's various lines of computing products. OfficeVision works in conjunction with IBM's Systems Application Architecture.

on-line   Connected to a network or a host computer system.

ONMS (Open Network Management System)   Digital Communications Associates' architecture for products conforming to ISO's CMIP.

Open Systems Interconnection (OSI) reference model   A model for networks developed by the International Standards Organization, dividing the network functions into seven connected layers. Each layer builds on the services provided by those under it.

OpenView   Hewlett-Packard's suite of a network-management application, a server platform, and support services. OpenView is based on HP-UX, which complies with AT&T's Unix system.

OPT (Open Protocol Technology)   Novell's strategy for complete protocol independence. NetWare supports multivendor hardware with this approach.

OSF (Open Software Foundation)   A consortium of industry leaders working to standardize the Unix operating system.

OSI   See *Open Systems Interconnection.*

OS/2 (Operating System/2)   An operating system developed by IBM and Microsoft for use with Intel's microprocessors. Unlike its predecessor, DOS, OS/2 is a multitasking operating system.

OS/2 Extended Edition   IBM's proprietary version of OS/2; it includes built-in communications and database-management facilities.

OverVIEW   Proteon's architecture for products conforming to SNMP.

packet   A block of data sent over the network transmitting the identities of the sending and receiving stations, error-control information, and a message.

packet filter   A feature of a bridge that compares each packet received with specifications set by the network administrator. If the packet matches the specifications, the bridge can either forward or reject it. Packet filters let the administrator limit protocol-specific traffic to one network segment, isolate electronic-mail domains, and perform many other traffic-control functions.

packet switching   A transmission technique that maximizes the use of digital transmission facilities by transmitting packets of digital data from many customers simultaneously on a single communications channel.

PAD (packet assembler/disassembler)   An X.25 PAD. A hardware-and-software device, sometimes inside a PC, that provides users access to an X.25 network. CCITT Recommendations X.3, X.28, and X.29 define the PAD parameters, terminal-to-PAD interface, and PAD-to-X.25 host interface.

PAP (packet-level procedure)   A protocol for the transfer of packets between an X.25 DTE and an X.25 DCE. X.25 PAP is a full-duplex protocol that supports data sequencing, flow control, accountability, and error detection and recovery.

parallel transmission   Simultaneous transmission of bits down parallel wires; for example, *byte parallel transmission* requires eight wires. See *serial transmission.*

parity   In ASCII, a check of the total number of 1 bits (as opposed to 0's) in a character's binary representation. A final eighth bit is set so that the count, when transmitted, is always even or always odd. This even or odd state can easily be checked at the receiving end; an incorrect parity bit can help reveal errors in the transmission.

passive head end   A device that connects the two broadband cables of a dual-cable system. It does not provide frequency translation.

PBX (private branch exchange)   A telephone system serving a specific location. Many PBX systems can carry computer data without the use of modems.

PDS (Premise Distribution System)   AT&T's proprietary buildingwide telecommunications cabling system.

peer-to-peer resource sharing   An architecture that lets any station contribute resources to the network while still running local application programs.

physical layer   The lowest layer of the OSI model. It consists of network wiring and cable and the interface hardware that sends and receives signals over the network.

PING (Packet Internet Groper)   An exercise program associated with TCP/IP and used to test the Internet communications channel between stations.

pipe   A communications process within the operating system that acts as an interface between a computer's devices (keyboard, disk drives, memory, and so on) and an applications program. A pipe simplifies the development of application programs by "buffering" a program from the intricacies of the hardware or the software that controls the hardware; the application developer writes code to a single pipe, not to several individual devices. A pipe is also used for program-to-program communications.

polling   A method of controlling the transmission sequence of communicating devices on a shared circuit by sending an inquiry to each device asking whether it wishes to transmit.

presentation layer   The sixth layer of the OSI model, which formats data for screen presentation and translates incompatible file formats.

Presentation Manager   The portion of the operating system OS/2 providing users with a graphical-based rather than character-based interface. The screens are similar to those of Microsoft Windows.

primary-rate interface (PRI)   In ISDN, the specification for the interface at each end of the high-volume trunks linking PBX and central-office facilities or connecting network switches to each other. The primary rate consists of 23 B or "bearer" channels (operating at 64 kilobits per second) and a D or "data" channel (also functioning at 64 kbps). The combined signal-carrying capacity is 1.544 megabits per second—equivalent to that of a type T1 channel.

print server   A computer on the network that makes one or more attached printers available to other users. The server usually requires a hard disk to spool the print jobs while they wait in a queue for the printer.

print spooler   The software that holds print jobs sent to a shared printer over a network when the printer is busy. Each file is saved in temporary storage and then printed when the shared printer is available.

PROFS (Professional Office System)   Interactive productivity software developed by IBM that runs under the VM/CMS mainframe system. PROFS is frequently used for electronic mail.

propagation delay   The delay between the time a signal enters a channel and the time it is received. This is normally insignificant in local area networks, but it becomes a major factor in satellite communications.

protocol   A specification that describes the rules and procedures that products should follow to perform activities on a network, such as transmitting data. If they use the same protocols, products from different vendors can communicate on the same network.

PSDN   Packet-switched data network.

PU (physical unit)   In an SNA network, usually a terminal or printer connected to the controller.

PVC   See *VC (virtual circuit)*.

public data network   A commercially owned or national-monopoly packet-switched network, publicly available as a service to data-processing users.

pulse-code modulation (PCM)   A common method for digitizing voice signals. The bandwidth required for a single digitized voice channel is 64 kilobits per second.

query language   A programming language designed to make it easier to specify what information a user wants to retrieve from a database.

queue   A list formed by items in a system waiting for service. An example is a *print queue* of documents to be printed in a network print server.

RAM (random access memory)   Also known as *read-write memory*; the memory used to execute application programs.

record locking   A feature that excludes other users from accessing (or sometimes just writing to) a record in a file while the first user is accessing that record.

redirector   A software module loaded into every network workstation; it captures application programs' requests for file- and equipment-sharing services and routes them through the network for action.

repeater   A device that amplifies and regenerates signals so they can travel on additional cable segments.

restart packet   A block of data that notifies X.25 DTEs that an irrecoverable error exists within the X.25 network. Restart packets clear all existing SVCs and resynchronize all existing PVCs between an X.25 DTE and X.25 DCE.

reverse channel   An answer-back channel provided during half-duplex operation. It allows the receiving modem to send low-speed acknowledgments to the transmitting modem without breaking the half-duplex mode. This is also used to arrange the turnaround between modems so that one ceases transmitting and the other can begin.

RF (radio frequency)   A generic term referring to the technology used in cable television and broadband networks. It uses electromagnetic waveforms, usually in the megahertz (MHz) range, for transmission.

RFS (Remote File Service)   One of the many distributed-file-system network protocols that allow one computer to use the files and peripherals of another as if they were local. Developed by AT&T and adopted by other vendors as a part of Unix V.

ring   A network connection method that routes messages through each station on the network in turn. Most ring networks use a token-passing protocol, which allows any station to put a message on the network when it receives a special bit pattern.

RJE (Remote Job Entry)   A method of submitting work to an IBM mainframe in a batch format. Though superseded by the 3270 system, it is still widely used in some installations.

RJ-11/RJ-45   Designations for commonly used modular telephone connectors. RJ-11 is the 8-pin connector used in most voice connections. RJ-45 is the 8-pin connector used for data transmission over twisted-pair telephone wire.

RO (receive-only)   Refers to a one-way device such as a printer, plotter, or graphics display.

ROM (read-only memory)   Memory containing preloaded programs that cannot be rewritten or changed by the CPU.

router   An interconnection device that is similar to a bridge but serves packets or frames containing certain protocols. Routers link LANs at the network layer of the OSI model. Modern routers handle multiple protocol stacks simultaneously and move packets or frames onto the right links for their destinations. For example, an X.25 router will wrap an Ethernet packet back into an Ethernet system.

RPC (Remote Procedure Call)   A set of software tools developed by a consortium of manufacturers and designed to assist developers in creating distributed applications. These tools automatically generate the code for both sides of the program (client and server) and let the programmer concentrate on other portions of the application.

RS-232C   An electrical standard for the interconnection of equipment established by the Electrical Industries Association; the same as the CCITT code V.24. RS-232C is used for serial ports.

RS-449   An EIA standard that applies to binary, serial synchronous, or asynchronous communications systems.

RU (request unit or response unit)   A message that makes a request or responds to one during a session.

SAA (Systems Application Architecture)   A set of specifications written by IBM describing how users, application programs, and communications programs interface. SAA represents an attempt to standardize the look and feel of applications and the methods they use to communicate.

SDLC (synchronous data link control)   The data-link layer of SNA, SDLC is a more efficient method than the older bisync protocol when it comes to packaging data for transmission between computers. Packets of data are sent over the line without the overhead created by synchronization and other padding bits.

serial port   An I/O port that transmits data 1 bit at a time; contrasted with a *parallel port*, which transmits multiple bits (usually 8) simultaneously. RS-232C is a common serial signaling protocol.

server   1. A computer with a large power supply and cabinet capacity. 2. Any computer on a network that makes file, print, or communications services available to other network stations.

session   The name for the connection between a mainframe terminal (or a PC emulating a mainframe terminal) and the mainframe itself when they are communicating. The number of sessions that can be run simultaneously through a LAN gateway is limited by the gateway software and the hardware configuration.

session layer   The fifth layer of the OSI model, which sets up the conditions whereby individual nodes on the network can communicate or send data to each other. The functions of this layer are used for many purposes, including determining which side may transmit during half-duplex communications.

SFT (system fault tolerance)   The capability to recover from or avoid a system crash. Novell uses a Transaction Tracking System (TTS), disk mirroring, and disk duplexing as its system recovery methods.

SMB (Server Message Block)   A distributed-file-system network protocol that allows one computer to use the files and peripherals of another as if they were local. Developed by Microsoft and adopted by IBM and many other vendors.

SMTP (Simple Mail Transfer Protocol)   A protocol that describes an electronic-mail system with both host and user sections. Many companies sell host software (usually for Unix) that will exchange SMTP mail with proprietary mail systems, such as IBM's PROFS. The user software is often included as a utility in TCP/IP packages for the PC.

SNA (Systems Network Architecture)   IBM's scheme for connecting its computerized products so that they can communicate and share data.

SNADS (SNA Distribution Services)   An IBM protocol that allows the distribution of electronic mail and attached documents through an SNA network.

SNMP (Simple Network Management Protocol)   A structure for formatting messages and for transmitting information between reporting devices and data-collection programs; developed jointly by the Department of Defense, industry, and the academic community as part of the TCP/IP protocol suite.

space   The signal condition that equals a binary 0.

SPX (Sequenced Packet Exchange)   An enhanced set of commands implemented on top of IPX to create a true transport-layer interface. SPX provides more functions than IPX, including guaranteed packet delivery.

SQL (Structured Query Language)   A formal data sublanguage for specifying common database operations such as retrieving, adding, changing, or deleting records. SQL is pronounced "sequel."

STA (Spanning Tree Algorithm)   A technique based on an IEEE 802.1 standard that detects and eliminates logical loops in a bridged network. When multiple paths exist, STA lets a bridge use only the most efficient one. If that path fails, STA automatically reconfigures the network so that another path becomes active, sustaining network operations.

StarLAN   A networking system developed by AT&T that uses CSMA protocols on twisted-pair telephone wire; a subset of 802.3.

start bit   A data bit used in asynchronous transmission to signal the beginning of a character and indicate that the channel is in use. It is a space signal lasting only for the duration of 1 bit.

star topology   A network connection method that hooks up all links to a central node.

stop bit   A data bit used in asynchronous transmission to signal the end of a character and indicate that the channel is idle. It is a mark signal lasting at least for the duration of 1 bit.

store and forward   See *message switching.*

Streams   An architecture introduced with Unix System V, Release 3.2, that provides for flexible and layered communication paths between processes (programs) and device drivers. Many companies market applications and devices that can integrate through Streams protocols.

strobe   An electrical pulse used to call for the transfer of information.

SVC   See *VC (virtual circuit).*

sync character   A character (two or more in bisync) sent from a transmitting station for synchronizing the clocks in transmitting and receiving stations.

synchronous   Refers to a transmission system in which characters are synchronized by the transmission of initial sync characters and a common clock signal. No stop or start bits are used.

T1   A 1.544-megabit-per-second communications circuit provided by long-distance communications carriers for voice or data transmission. T1 lines are typically divided into 24 64-kilobit channels.

tap   A connector that couples to a cable without blocking the passage of signals down the cable.

TCAM (Telecommunications Access Method)   An IBM system for controlling communications.

T-connector   A coaxial connector, shaped like a T, that connects two thin Ethernet cables while supplying an additional connector for a network interface card.

TCP (Transmission Control Protocol)   A specification for software that bundles and unbundles sent and received data into packets, manages the transmission of packets on a network, and checks for errors.

TCP/IP (Transmission Control Protocol/Internet Protocol)   A set of communications protocols that has evolved since the late 1970s, when it was first developed by the Department of Defense (DOD). Because programs supporting these protocols are available on so many different computer systems, they have become an excellent way to connect different types of computers over networks.

Telex   An international messaging service, marketed in the United States by Western Union.

TELNET   A terminal-emulation protocol. Software supporting TELNET usually comes as a utility in a TCP/IP package, and all TELNET programs provide DEC VT-100 terminal emulation. Many companies either provide or allow other add-in emulators.

10Base2   IEEE's specifications for running Ethernet over thin coaxial cable.

10Base5   IEEE's specifications for running Ethernet over thick coaxial cable.

10BaseT   IEEE's specifications for running Ethernet over unshielded twisted-pair wiring.

terminal adapter (TA)   An ISDN phone or a PC card that emulates one. Devices on the end of a basic-rate interface line are known as *terminals*.

terminator   A resistor used at each end of an Ethernet cable to ensure that signals do not reflect back and cause errors. It is usually attached to an electrical ground at one end.

TFTP (Trivial File Transfer Protocol)   A simplified version of FTP that transfers files but does not provide password protection or user-directory capability. It is associated with the TCP/IP family of protocols.

thick Ethernet   A cabling system using relatively stiff, large-diameter cable to connect transceivers. The transceivers connect to the nodes through flexible multi-wire cable.

thin Ethernet   A cabling system using a thin and flexible coaxial cable to connect each node to the next node in line.

3174, 3270, and so on   Appear at the end of the alphabet in this glossary.

3+Open   A family of 3Com networking products built around the LAN Manager file/print server. 3+Open includes connectivity, messaging, and network management services.

TIC (Token-Ring Interface Coupler)   An IBM device that allows a controller or processor to attach directly to a Token-Ring network. This is an optional part of several IBM terminal cluster controllers and front-end processors.

time-division multiplexing (TDM)   A method of placing a number of signals on one communications circuit by allocating the available time among competing stations. Allocations may be on a microsecond basis.

time domain reflectometry (TDR)   A method of sending a radio pulse down a wire or cable to detect a shorted or open condition. High-priced devices can pinpoint a fault within inches; lower-priced devices often provide widely varying results when they try to pinpoint the distance to a fault.

T interface   A standard basic-rate interface using four copper wires.

token passing   An access protocol in which a special message (token) circulates among the network nodes, giving them permission to transmit.

Token-Ring   The wire and the access protocol scheme whereby stations relay packets in a logical ring configuration. This architecture, pioneered by IBM, is described in the IEEE 802.5 standards.

TOP (Technical and Office Protocol)   An implementation of OSI standards in office and engineering environments. TOP, developed by Boeing and other firms, employs Ethernet specifications.

topology   The map or plan of the network. The physical topology describes how the wires or cables are laid out, and the logical or electrical topology describes how the messages flow.

TP-4 (Transport Protocol 4)   An OSI layer-4 protocol developed by the National Bureau of Standards.

transceiver   A communicating device capable of transmitting and receiving.

transmission control   The layer in SNA that controls sessions and manages communications.

transport layer   The fourth layer of the OSI model. Software in this layer checks the integrity of and formats the data carried by the physical layer (1), managed by the data layer (2), and perhaps routed by the network layer (3).

tree   Refers to a network arrangement in which the stations are attached to a common branch or data bus.

TTS (Transaction Tracking System)   A log of all file activity in NetWare.

twisted-pair Ethernet   See *IEEE 802.3 10BaseT.*

twisted-pair wiring   Cable comprised of two wires twisted together at six turns per inch to provide electrical self-shielding. Some telephone wire—but by no means all—is twisted-pair.

Type 3 cable   An unshielded twisted-pair wire that meets IBM specifications for use in 4-megabit-per-second Token-Ring networks.

UDP (User Datagram Protocol)   A TCP/IP protocol describing how messages reach application programs within a destination computer. This protocol is normally bundled with IP-layer software.

U interface   A standard basic-rate interface using two copper wires.

Unix   A multitasking, multiuser operating system for minicomputers that was developed by AT&T and has enjoyed popularity among engineering and technical professionals. Unix is finding new uses as the basis of file-server operating systems for networks of PCs.

UNMA (Unified Network Management Architecture)   AT&T's company-specific architecture conforming to the ISO's CMIP.

UUCP (Unix-to-Unix Copy Program)   A standard Unix utility used for information exchange between two Unix nodes.

VAN (value-added network)   A privately owned packet-switched network whose services are sold to the public. See *PDN.*

VC (virtual circuit)   An X.25 VC is a PAP logical connection between an X.25 DTE and an X.25 DCE. X.25 supports both *switched VCs* (SVCs) and *permanent VCs* (PVCs). SVCs are analogous to dial-up lines; that is, they allow a particular X.25 DTE to establish a connection with different X.25 DTEs on a per-call basis. By contrast, PVCs are analogous to leased lines because they always connect two X.25 DTEs.

VINES (Virtual Networking Software)   A Unix-based network operating system from Banyan Systems.

virtual circuit   A temporary connection path, set up between two points by software and packet switching, that appears to the user to be available as a dedicated circuit. This "phantom" circuit can be maintained indefinitely or can be ended at will.

voice channel   A transmission path usually limited to passing the bandwidth of the human voice.

VTAM (Virtual Telecommunications Access Method)   An IBM standard for software that runs on the host mainframe computer and works with the Network Control Program to establish communications between the host and the cluster controllers. Among other things, VTAM sets the pacing and LU characteristics.

WAN (wide-area network)   A type of network that connects computers over areas potentially as wide as the entire world.

wideband   Refers to a channel or transmission medium capable of passing more frequencies than a standard 3-kHz voice channel.

wideband modem   A modem that operates at over 9,600 bits per second.

wiring hub   A cabinet, usually mounted in a wiring closet, that holds connection modules for various kinds of cabling. The hub contains electronic circuits that retime and repeat the signals on the cable. The hub may also contain a microprocessor board that monitors and reports on network activity.

X.25   A CCITT standard that describes how data is handled in and how computers can access a packet-switched network.

X.400   The CCITT designation for an international electronic-mail distribution system.

X.500   The CCITT designation for a directory standard to coordinate the dispersed file directories of different systems.

XNS (Xerox Network Services)   A multilayer protocol system developed by Xerox and adopted, at least in part, by Novell and other vendors. XNS is one of the many distributed-file-system protocols that allow network stations to use other computers' files and peripherals as if they were local.

X/Open   A consortium of computer-industry vendors, chartered to specify an open system platform based on the Unix operating system.

X Window   A network-based windowing system that provides a programmatic interface for graphic window displays. X Window permits graphics produced on one networked workstation to be displayed on another.

3174   A new version of the 3274 terminal cluster controller.

3270　The generic name for the family of interoperable IBM system components—terminals, printers, and terminal cluster controllers—that can be used to communicate with a mainframe by means of the SNA or bisync protocols. All of these components have four-digit names, some of which begin with the digits 327.

3274/3276　The most commonly used cluster controller. This device links as many as 32 3270-type terminals and printers to a mainframe front-end processor.

3278　The most commonly used terminal in the 3270 family. It features a monochrome display and offers a limited graphics set.

3279　A color terminal that is part of the 3270 family.

3287　The current series of printers in the 3270 equipment family.

3705　A common front-end processor, typically used to link several 3274s to a mainframe.

3725　A common front-end processor, intended for linking groups of cluster controllers to a mainframe.

3745　A new communications controller that combines the functions of a cluster controller and a front-end processor. The 3745 can interface simultaneously with as many as 8 Token-Ring networks, 512 terminals or printers, and 16 1.544-megabit-per-second communications lines.

■ Appendix

Data PBX Equipment

Hardware

AISwitch Series 180
Applied Innovation, Inc.
651-C Lakeview Plaza Blvd.
Columbus, OH 43085
800-247-9482; 614-846-9000
fax: 614-846-7267

- Price: $4,185-$20,510
- Number installed to date: 200
- Date announced: 1984
- Product classification: Data PBX
- Max number of switched lines: 256
- Type of lines switched: RS-232C
- Switch technology: TDM

AISwitch Series 90
Applied Innovation, Inc.
651-C Lakeview Plaza Blvd.
Columbus, OH 43085
800-247-9482; 614-846-9000
fax: 614-846-7267

- Price: $1,995-$4,980
- Number installed to date: 50
- Date announced: 1988
- Product classification: Data PBX
- Max number of switched lines: 64
- Type of lines switched: RS-232C
- Switch technology: TDM

MDX
Equinox Systems, Inc.
14260 Southwest 119th Ave.
Miami, FL 33186
800-328-2729; 305-255-3500
fax: 305-253-0003

- Price: $800
- Date announced: 1986
- Product classification: Data PBX
- Max number of switched lines: 8
- Type of lines switched: RS-232C
- Switch technology: Electronic matrix

Instanet6000 Series 20 CommServer
MICOM Communications Corp.
PO Box 8100
4100 Los Angeles Ave.
Simi Valley, CA 93062-8100
800-642-6687; 805-583-8600
fax: 805-583-1997

- Price: $5,000
- Number installed to date: 450
- Date announced: 1986
- Product classification: Data PBX
- Max number of switched lines: 250
- Type of lines switched: RS-232C
- Switch technology: Data switch

Q-NET Resource Manager
Microscience Corp.
8601 Dunwoody Place, Suite 136
Atlanta, GA 30350
800-234-3595; 404-998-6551
fax: 404-998-7399

- Price: $7,995-$13,795
- Date announced: 1985
- Product classification: Data PBX
- Max number of switched lines: 128
- Type of lines switched: RS-232C
- Switch technology: TDM

1032 MainStreet
Newbridge Networks, Inc.
593 Herndon Pkwy.
Herndon, VA 22070-5421
800-332-1080; 703-834-3600
fax: 703-471-7080

- Price: $6,365
- Number installed to date: 1,800
- Date announced: 1986
- Product classification: Data PBX
- Max number of switched lines: 48
- Type of lines switched: RS-232C
- Switch technology: Electronic matrix

The Pipe
Quasitronics, Inc.
211 Vandale Dr.
Houston, PA 15342
800-245-4192; 412-745-2663
fax: 412-228-2122

- Price: $2,695
- Number installed to date: 3,000
- Date announced: 1985
- Product classification: Data PBX
- Max number of switched lines: 16
- Type of lines switched: RS-232C;
  RS-449; Centronics parallel
- Switch technology: Electronic matrix

Data PBX Series
Rose Electronics
PO Box 742571
Houston, TX 77274
800-333-9343; 713-933-7673
fax: 713-933-0044

- Price: $2,390-$5,375
- Date announced: 1988
- Product classification: Data PBX
- Max number of switched lines: 16-64
- Type of lines switched: RS-232C

SDC 660
Sequel Data Communications, Inc.
5246 Greens Dairy Rd.
Raleigh, NC 27604
919-790-0300
fax: 919-790-0323

- Price: $95-$100 per port
- Number installed to date: 310
- Date announced: 1986
- Product classification: Data PBX
- Max number of switched lines: 60
- Type of lines switched: RS-232C;
  RS-449

Gateway Data Switch
SKP Electronics
1232-E S. Village Way
Santa Ana, CA 92705
714-972-1727
fax: 714-972-4964

- Price: $8,995
- Date announced: 1990
- Product classification: Data PBX
- Max number of switched lines: 1,000
- Type of lines switched: PICK-based
  systems
- Switch technology: Electronic matrix

DX90

Tek-Com Corp.
2343 Bering Dr.
San Jose, CA 95131
800-346-6597; 408-435-9515
fax: 408-435-9514

- Price: $4,600-$40,000
- Date announced: 1987
- Product classification: Data PBX
- Max number of switched lines: 336
- Type of lines switched: RS-232C

DATOS LAN

Telecommunications Data Services
17993 Cowan
Irvine, CA 92714
800-634-8513; 714-474-7744
fax: 714-474-8540

- Price: $30,000-$67,500
- Date announced: 1988
- Product classification: Data PBX
- Max number of switched lines: 150
- Type of lines switched: RS-232C;
  RS-449

INCS-64

Western Telematic, Inc.
5 Sterling
Irvine, CA 92718
800-854-7226; 714-586-9950
fax: 714-583-9514

- Price: $2,115
- Date announced: 1989
- Product classification: Data PBX
- Max number of switched lines: 64
- Type of lines switched: RS-232C;
  RS-449
- Switch technology: Electronic matrix

Electronic Mail and Associated Products

Coordinator II (V.2.01)

Action Technologies, Inc.
2200 Powell St., 11th Floor
Emeryville, CA 94608
800-624-2162; 415-654-4444
fax: 415-547-2190

- Provides messaging, communication, and conversation coordination on PC networks. Based on IBM SAA/CUA specifications. Implements Novell and ATI's MHS. Windowing system lets users work with calendars, set reminders, compose messages, read mail, and write letters simultaneously. Tracks conversations, traces forward and backward through communications, sorts and files mail. Schedules individual and group activities.

Message Handling Service (MHS) (V.1.2)

Action Technologies, Inc.
2200 Powell St., 11th Floor
Emeryville, CA 94608
800-624-2162; 415-654-4444
fax: 415-547-2190

- Family of software products that delivers messages through store-and-forward networks of micros. Messages submitted by applications to MHS are routed and transferred through WANs that may include LANs, standalones, and various media. Consistent with X.400 recommendations. Sends multiple attached documents through MHS gateway and sends one message to several users simultaneously.

Office Minder (V.1.10)
Advanced Concepts, Inc.
4129 N. Port Washington Ave.
Milwaukee, WI 53212-1029
800-222-6736; 414-963-0999
fax: 414-963-2090

• Includes e-mail with MHS support, telephone messaging, scheduling, project management, resource management, electronic Rolodex, and reminder alarms. Consists of Message Minder, Schedule Minder, Project Minder, and Address Minder. Stores messages, incoming and outgoing mail, personal schedules, long term projects, names, addresses, and phone numbers. Contains built-in calendar.

Framework III Electronic Mail
Ashton-Tate
20101 Hamilton Ave.
Torrance, CA 90502-1319
213-329-8000
fax: 213-538-7996

• Provides communication between Ashton-Tate's Framework III spreadsheet package users and users of compatible mail packages. Uses MHS (message handling service) electronic mail standard message format. Links unlimited number of LANs using MHS hubs.

PMX/StarMail
AT&T Computer Systems
100 Southgate Pkwy.
Morristown, NJ 07960
800-247-1212; 201-898-8000
fax: 201-644-9768

• LAN-based electronic mail system for AT&T's StarLAN Network. Provides network with message server and

user interface of Access Plus. Provides UNIX-to-DOS connectivity.

Desk Executive
Boston Business Computing, Ltd.
3 Dundee Park
Andover, MA 01810-3743
508-470-0444
fax: 508-474-9244

• Performs VAX All-In-1 functions on PC. Provides menu management, word processing, file cabinet, electronic mail, and time management. Integrates with All-In-1. Interface to VMSmail available.

UpFront
BT Tymnet, Inc.
2560 North 1st St.
PO Box 49019
San Jose, CA 95161-9019
800-872-7654; 408-922-0250
fax: 408-922-7030

• Links PC to Dialcom on-line service for electronic mail, fax, telex, mailgram, cablegram, PC forms, and file transfer. Provides macro/tutorial capabilities for messaging and information/newswire applications. Includes full-screen editor and message filing capabilities.

Mail Call
Cappcomm Software, Inc.
26 Journal Sq., Suite 1003
Jersey City, NJ 07306
800-262-4522; 201-795-1500
fax: 201-795-0244

• Enables PC to send/receive electronic mail to/from DEC VAX All-In-1, and VMS mail. Provides flexible communication scripts. Connects to

VAX when exchanging mail. Customization available.

cc:Mail LAN Package
CC:Mail, Inc.
2141 Landings Dr.
Mountain View, CA 94043
800-448-2500; 415-961-8800
fax: 415-961-8400

• Electronic mail system for PC LANs. Supports WAN connectivity with any combination of server-to-server, LAN-to-LAN, and remote PC-to-LAN messaging, as well as connection to other e-mail systems. Provides notification of new mail, distributed mail server software, single common post office, encrypted compressed messages and user directory files, paper mail terminology and tools, automatic conversion among popular graphic displays, and remote PC access. Includes notification of new mail messages provided by bell tone and either flashing desktop icon or pop-up dialog box.

tPost LAN (V.5.0)
Coker Electronics
1430 Lexington Ave.
San Mateo, CA 94402
415-573-5515

• Electronic mail package for LANs and multi-user systems with built-in gateway to remote LANs and standalone field PCs. Includes function key-driven routines, private and public distribution lists, attachments, remote command execution, e-mail-to-fax option, and forms option.

ConneXion-1
Connex Systems
9341 Courtland Dr.
Rockford, MI 49351
800-748-0212; 616-866-5678
fax: 616-866-1250

• Electronic mail and file distribution systems. Exchanges short notes or complete files with central office and with one another. Includes fax component and point-and-shoot interface allowing multiple file sending to outgoing e-mail.

Network Courier MCI Mail Link (V.2.1)
Consumers Software, Inc.
73 Water St., 7th Floor
Vancouver, BC
CD V6B 1A1
800-663-8935; 604-688-4548
fax: 604-682-1378

• Provides users with access to MCI from any LAN. Sends messages, spreadsheets, faxes, and any type of file. Sends and receives messages through remote electronic mail systems (REMS) account to IBM PROFS, DEC VAX-mail, All-in-1, Wang Office, 3Com 3+ Mail, and Compuserve. Requires Consumers Software's Inter-Network.

Cross+Point (V.5.24)
Cross Information Co.
1881 9th St., Canyon Center, Suite 212
Boulder, CO 80302-5181
303-444-7799
fax: 303-444-4687

• Electronic mail system with groupware, computer conferencing, or thought processing. Includes bulletin board, on-line messaging, and windowing. Includes encryption and pop-up notification and fax/e-mail interface to many PC-fax boards. Handles internetworking for LAN-to-LAN communications.

LANsmart Electronic Mail Program
D-Link Systems, Inc.
5 Musick
Irvine, CA 92718
714-455-1688
fax: 714-455-2521

• Allows users to send and receive mail on LANsmart Network. Includes full-screen editor and access security. Interfaces to other text editors and word processors. Runs in background.

Da Vinci eMAIL for DOS (V.1.6)
Da Vinci Systems Corp.
PO Box 17449
Raleigh, NC 27619
800-326-3556; 919-881-4320
fax: 919-787-3550

• Memory-resident electronic mail program. Provides pull-down menus, mouse support, and security. Any number of files can be attached to any message. Receivers are notified of incoming messages by pop-up and tone.

Office Works (V.2.0)
Data Access Corp.
14000 Southwest 119th Ave.
Miami, FL 33186
800-451-3539; 800-331-3960; 305-238-0012
fax: 305-238-0017

• Group productivity program. Supports activities surrounding phone messages, document control, name/address database maintenance, e-mail, and management/scheduling of time.

DaynaMail (V.1.0)
Dayna Communications
50 S. Main St., 5th Floor
Salt Lake City, UT 84144
801-531-0600
fax: 801-359-9135

• Electronic mail application. Provides message handling and addressing and allows communication between Mac and PC. Based on MHS protocol, permits wide-area communications with other MHS-compatible applications.

Gallery Mail
Daystrom Technologies Corp.
405 Tarrytown Rd., Suite 414
White Plains, NY 10607
914-896-7378

• E-mail system for use on Novell network. Shares NetWare user profiles so administrators need not maintain separate lists within third-party packages. Includes icon-based Network Menu Development System and Network File Manager.

All-In-1 Desktop for MS-DOS (V.1.0)
Digital Equipment Corp.
146 Main St.
Maynard, MA 01754-2571
508-493-5111
fax: 508-493-8780

• Allows MS-DOS-based PC users to access All-In-1 applications on VAX. Includes individual and group calendaring, group conferencing, electronic mail, facility for launching application from within All-In-1, auto-dial function, phone book, facility for logging phone numbers called and length of calls, and decision-support tools.

Edge Office
Edge Systems, Inc.
1245 Corporate Blvd., Fourth Floor
Aurora, IL 60504-6420
708-898-0021
fax: 708-898-5406

• Consists of integrated modules including Event Notification, File Cabinet, Telephone Book, Telephone Message Notepad, Electronic Mail, Time Manager, Reverse Polish Notation Calculator, ASE editor, and Document Routing.

Higgins Mail
Enable Software, Inc.
Northway Ten Executive Park
Ballston Lake, NY 12019
800-888-0684; 518-877-8600
fax: 518-877-5225

• Electronic mail subsystem for Enable's Higgins package, which may be upgraded to complete office functions. User interface remains unchanged and all stored messages and keyword filing remain in place after upgrade takes place.

ASAP Electronic Mail
Epic Systems Corp.
5609 Medical Circle
Madison, WI 53719-1228
608-271-9000
fax: 608-271-7237

• E-mail system. Includes personal calendar, to-do lists, sign in/out, log, and bulletin board. Auto-dials remote locations to deliver and receive mail.

FidoNet
Fido Software
164 Shipley St.
San Francisco, CA 94107
415-764-1688

• Store-and-forward electronic mail system. Includes error-correction protocol, time-of-day event scheduling, message routing language, and automatic message routing. Provides eight file transfer protocols.

Right Hand Man (RHM) (V.5.1)
Futurus Corp.
3131 North I-10 Service Rd., Suite 401
Metairie, LA 70002
800-327-8296; 504-837-1554
fax: 504-837-3429

• RAM-resident group productivity package for entire networks or single users. Provides access to 60 different windows. Allows user to customize data bases and store them in RAM until needed. Includes e-mail, appointment scheduler with alarms, macro keys notepad, and calculator with tape and editor. Twenty other modules are available.

=M=C=D=
FYI, Inc.
PO Box 26481
Austin, TX 78755
512-346-0133

• Multiline BBS with electronic mail, conferences, realtime chat, and on-line data bases. Includes full text-indexed data bases that may be searched using full boolean logic to link search terms. Provides for Xmodem uploading and downloading of large files via electronic mail or conferences. Provides for realtime chat with up to eight users simultaneously.

The Major BBS (V.5.11)
Galacticomm, Inc.
4101 Southwest 47th Ave., Suite 101
Ft. Lauderdale, FL 33314
305-583-5990
fax: 305-583-7846

• Multiuser bulletin board system. File upload and download, teleconferencing, classified ads, system information, electronic mail, user information display/edit, shopping, and entertainment/games. Supports up to 64 simultaneous users. Optional extended editions include File Library, Entertainment, Shopping Mall, and MenuMan. Provides X.25 option.

PC-Mailbox MultiUser
GE Information Services
401 N. Washington St.
Rockville, MD 20850
800-433-3683; 301-340-4000
fax: 301-340-4251

• Allows user of GEIS' Quik-Comm system to write, edit, deliver, print, and file electronic mail messages for multiple Quik-Comm users. Supports communication via GEIS' Telex Access, Quik-Gram Service, Quik-Comm System to FAX Service, Quik-Comm System Cross-Community capability, and Quik-Comm System Connector Services.

SolutionPac Office Series (VM Edition)
IBM
Old Orchard Rd.
Armonk, NY 10504
800-426-2468; 914-765-1900

• Includes electronic mail, text, notes, calendar, decision support, relational data base, and query functions for fixed function displays and intelligent workstations.

Officepower
ICL Business Systems
9801 Muirlands Blvd.
Irvine, CA 92718
714-458-7282
fax: 714-458-6257

• Multifunctional office management system. Word processing, electronic filing, electronic mail, appointment calendars, telephone and address dictionaries, phone message log and routing, full-function math, accounting, and electronic spreadsheets. Optional PC, Mac, UNIX integration with GUI.

LAN: Mail Monitor
LanQuest Group
1251 Parkmoor Ave.
San Jose, CA 95126
408-283-8900
fax: 408-283-8989

• LAN electronic mail. Includes local and remote. Built-in editor sends messages and attaches DOS files. Includes auto-transmit, form letters, and encryptions. Available in English, French, and German.

PostMark E-Mail
LANsmith Corp.
406 Lincolnwood Pl.
Santa Barbara, CA 93110
800-522-4567; 805-687-1271
fax: 805-687-2401

• Combines its MHS-compatible e-mail system with ASCII-standard word processor. Performs standard e-mail functions and group discussions.

TeleVision
LCS/Telegraphics
150 Rogers St.
Cambridge, MA 02142
617-225-7970
fax: 617-225-7969

• Sends images through electronic mail systems. Mouse-driven, icon-activated program. Uses data compression and encoding techniques to send text and graphics.

Notes
Lotus Development Corp.
55 Cambridge Pkwy.
Cambridge, MA 02142
617-577-8500
fax: 617-225-1299

• Gives you high-powered groupware with strong e-mail. The high price and heavy RAM usage may turn you away, but its unique detailed features lure you on.

Promulgate/PC
Management Systems Designers, Inc.
131 Park St., NE
Vienna, VA 22180
703-281-7440

• Electronic mail gateway that allows 3+Mail and 3+Open Mail users to transparently exchange messages with UNIX-based systems. Requires 3Com EtherLink card.

Electronic Envelope
MCTel, Inc.
5070 Parkside Ave., Suite 1300
Philadelphia, PA 19131
215-879-3819

• Prepares binary files for data transmission over public and private electronic mail systems. Prepares binary data including graphics, spreadsheets, and special word processing formats like MultiMate and WordStar for transmission over telecommunication networks through formatting binary data to make it appear to electronic mail system as ASCII text.

BBS-PC!
Micro-Systems Software, Inc.
12798 W. Forest Hill Blvd., Suite 202
West Palm Beach, FL 33414
407-790-0770

• Electronic bulletin board. Supports electronic mail, binary, or ASCII file transfers. Includes message reformatting to caller's terminal, permanent user records, and message transfer system that creates files accessible only by addressee or sysop. Supports message threading. DOS gateway.

Postmaster E-Mail
Modem Controls, Inc.
432 N. Clark St., Suite 202
Chicago, IL 60610
800-266-8765; 312-321-0018
fax: 312-321-1276

• Electronic mail system for Novell NetWare LANs. Operates TSR in less than 1,500 bytes of RAM. Provides 100-line message editor. Attach documents. Optional message handling service (MHS) compatibility.

Brainstorm (V.2.0)
Mustang Software, Inc.
PO Box 2264
Bakersfield, CA 93303
800-999-9619; 805-395-0223
fax: 805-395-0713

• Groupware network productivity tool for idea sharing. Functions as topic-oriented message system for LAN users. Provides topic threads for reviewing others' feedback. MHS WAN support available.

Wildcat! (V.2.1)
Mustang Software, Inc.
PO Box 2264
Bakersfield, CA 93303
800-999-9619; 805-395-0223
fax: 805-395-0713

• BBS system. Offers electronic mail, file transfer, questionnaires, and bulletins. Provides customizable display files and security for 50 levels of users. Messaging capabilities include ability to reply, forward to third parties, send carbon copies, request return receipt, and print. Net/multiline available. Versions available supporting 1-250 lines with or without Pro! series utilities.

Total Office Manager (TOM)
Network Technology, Inc.
215 Kingswood Dr.
Fayetteville, GA 30214
404-461-2622; 404-461-6883

• Office automation system designed to simplify the operation of Advanced NetWare LAN. Consists of menu system supporting network functions. Electronic mail, calendar, sign-out sheet, notepad, printer reassignment, card file, terminal emulator, and MHS support.

Notework
Notework Corp.
72 Kent St.
Brookline, MA 02146
617-734-4317
fax: 617-734-4160

• Pop-up e-mail program. Includes pop-up telephoning, messaging, and file transfer. Allows user to print, export, and confirm receipt of messages, customize editing commands, attach files to notes, notify others of incoming calls, and send urgent messages.

CONEXUS
OMM Corp.
4200 Wisconsin Ave., NW, Suite 106
Washington, DC 20016
202-234-2117

• Integrated electronic mail, teleconferencing, and bulletin board system. Supports remote or local access for 900 individual private accounts. Allows multiple levels of security. Includes OMM's MIST+.

Flash-Com
Omni Computer Systems, Inc.
PO Box 162
Chestnut Hill, MA 02167
617-522-4760
fax: 617-522-2793

• Electronic mail and mailing list management. Interfaces with word processing, text editor and modeling software, built-in forms creation, management, and file handling. Interfaces with over 20 other carriers.

Para-Mail (V.2.16)
Paradox Development Corp.
7544 Trade St.
San Diego, CA 92121
619-586-0878

• Allows users to exchange mail over NetWare networks using message handling service e-mail interface. Includes text editor, search-and-paste, internal filing and encryption of messages, support for multiple attachments, conversion tracking, message classification by importance of message, and built-in electronic note pad. Supports X.400, X.25, and MCI Mail communications protocols. Includes optical scanning package.

CliqMail
Quadratron Systems, Inc.
141 Triunfo Canyon Rd.
Westlake Village, CA 91361
805-494-1158
fax: 805-494-1721

• Electronic mail. Component of QSI's Q-Office. Provides network capability between users and hardware. Sends message, document, or file to a person or list of persons in directory, independent of UNIX machine. Annotates received documents. Adds attachments or other documents.

RetixMail for IBM PC
Retix
2644 30th St.
Santa Monica, CA 90405
800-255-2333; 213-399-2200
fax: 213-458-2685

• Provides X.400 world-wide messaging for PC LAN. Uses Microsoft Windows interface and allows user to transfer messages and files between PCs on same LAN and to remote LANs via private line or X.25 public network connections. Makes remote connections with mini or mainframe electronic-mail services that support X.400.

X.400 Gateway
Retix
2644 30th St.
Santa Monica, CA 90405
800-255-2333; 213-399-2200
fax: 213-458-2685

• Provides communications connectivity between TCP and OSI electronic mail networks. Exchange of mail messages between X.400-based electronic mail services and UNIX systems' mail applications is transparent. Conforms to government's Gosip standard and complies with Defense Communications Agency's OSI migration strategy.

MessageNet
S & H Computer Systems, Inc.
1027 17th Ave., South
Nashville, TN 37212
615-327-3670
fax: 615-321-5929

• Electronic mail system. Sends messages via telex, US Post Office, cablegram, telegram, EasyLink, or MCI Mail. Includes menu-driven address book, integrated word processor, interoffice mail facility, filing, and archival system for outgoing and incoming messages.

QuickTalk

SilverSoft, Inc.
1301 Geranium St., NW
Washington, DC 20012
202-291-8212

• Calls up electronic mail system and enters text directly into word processor or spreadsheet. Uploads or downloads file while in background. Converts up to 40 different strings of characters while reading in file or text.

OfficeNet

Source Data Systems, Inc.
950 Ridgemount Dr., NE
Cedar Rapids, IA 52402-7222
319-393-3343
fax: 319-393-5173

• Includes word processing, electronic mail, scheduling and calendars, spreadsheet, file management, phone list, notepad, and calculator functions.

SEAdog (V.4.5)

System Enhancement Associates
21 New St.
Wayne, NJ 07470
201-473-5153

• Sends and retrieves electronic mail using telephone equipment. Supports multiple PCs. Transfers text, spreadsheets, programs, and data base files. Includes real-time conference support, off-line text editor, and user interface.

CompletE-MAIL/MHS

Transend Corp.
884 Portola Rd.
Portola Valley, CA 94025
415-851-3402
fax: 415-851-1031

• LAN-based e-mail system. Supports mail handling service standard. Creates, exchanges, and manages messages, DOS files, and electronic files. Intuitive, icon-based windowing user interface. Incorporates word processor or imports data from user's word processor.

3+Open Mail (V.1.1)

3Com Corp.
3165 Kifer Rd.
Santa Clara, CA 95052-8145
800-638-3266; 408-562-6400
fax: 408-970-1112

• Electronic mail for 3+ Open network. Delivers messages and attachments to multiple users and groups. Supports remote access and internetwork mail routing. Provides electronic filing options, registered mail, batch operations, and auto mail waiting notification. Exchanges messages among DOS, Mac, and OS/2 users on Ethernet, Token Ring, and LocalTalk networks. For use with 3Com's X.400 mail gateway. Supports unlimited mailboxes on server.

LAN Office

Wang Laboratories, Inc.
One Industrial Way, Mail Stop 014-A1B
Lowell, MA 01851
800-835-9264; 508-459-5000

• Includes electronic mail, time management, directory services, note services, user profile customization, and menu modification. Compatible with Banyan Vines, Novell Advanced NetWare, 3Com 3+ Share, and IBM PC LAN Program.

WordPerfect Office (V.3.0)
WordPerfect Corp.
1555 N. Technology Way
Orem, UT 84057
800-321-4566; 801-225-5000
fax: 801-222-4477

• Office automation package for LANs. Includes shell menu for integration of programs, clipboard, electronic mail, notebook with auto-dial feature, scheduler, file manager, calculator, calendar, macro editor, and program editor. Includes Novell's wide-area message handling service (MHS). Includes WPScheduler, WPNotebook, and WPFile Manager.

LAN Fax Gateways and Related Products

NetFax Board
All The Fax, Inc.
917 Northern Blvd.
Great Neck, NY 11021
800-289-3329; 516-829-0556

• Price: $995
• Date announced: 1990
• Group compatibility: CCITT Group 3
• Document transmit rate: 9,600 bps
• System compatibility: IBM AT (16-bit)
• Size of board: Full-length board
• Standard features: Includes software to attach files, graphics, and cover letters to faxes; requires user to exit current application before sending fax.

PagePower (V.2.1)
AT&T Computer Systems
100 Southgate Pkwy.
Morristown, NJ 07960
800-247-1212; 201-898-8000
fax: 201-644-9768

• Graphics package that allows users to share fax resources across LANs. Allows user to create images and send to PCs or fax machines. Supports AT&T Fax Connection board and scanners. Provides file transfer communication utilities for AT&T StarLAN Network and AT&T modems. Converts formatted word processing files to fax without requiring files to be saved as ASCII.

FaxPress 2000
Castelle
3255-3 Scott Blvd.
Santa Clara, CA 95051
800-359-7654; 408-496-0474
fax: 408-496-0502

• Price: $4,395
• Number installed to date: 1,000
• Date announced: 1989
• Shareable devices: CCITT Group 3 facsimile; printer
• Network compatibility: Ethernet; IBM Token Ring; ARCnet
• IEEE standard: IEEE-802.3; IEEE-802.5
• CPU compatibility: IBM PC, XT, AT, PS/2 Model 30
• Interfaces supported: Serial; parallel

PC Race 24/96
Data Race, Inc.
11550 IH 10, W, Suite 395
San Antonio, TX 78249
512-558-1900
fax: 512-558-1929

- Price: $995
- Number installed to date: 1,000
- Date announced: 1987
- Group compatibility: CCITT Group 3
- Document transmit rate: 9,600 bps
- Required facilities: Dial-up
- Standard features: Hayes-compatible, 2,400-bps modem
- System compatibility: IBM (8-bit)
- Size of board: Full-length board
- Integral modem included: Yes

GammaFax CPD
GammaLink
133 Caspian Court
Sunnyvale, CA 94089
408-744-1430
fax: 408-744-1549

- Price: $1,395-$1,690
- Date announced: 1990
- Group compatibility: CCITT Group 3
- Document transmit rate: 9,600 bps
- System compatibility: IBM (8-bit) PC, XT, AT
- Standard features: Direct inward dialing (DID); DFX daughterboard with touch-tone capabilities and ECM

Facsimile Server
Interpreter, Inc.
11455 West 48th Ave.
Wheat Ridge, CO 80033
800-232-4687; 303-431-8991
fax: 303-431-9056

- Price: $3,900-$7,695
- Date announced: 1989
- Shareable devices: CCITT Group 3 facsimile
- Network compatibility: Ethernet
- IEEE standard: IEEE-802.3
- CPU compatibility: IBM PC, XT, AT
- Interfaces supported: Serial; parallel

PDI9624N PureFax
PureData, Inc.
200 W. Beaver Creek Rd.
Richmond Hill, ON
CD L4B 1B4
416-731-6444
fax: 416-731-7017

- Price: $1,495
- Date announced: 1989
- Group compatibility: CCITT Group 3
- Document transmit rate: 9,600 bps
- Required facilities: Dial-up
- System compatibility: IBM (8-bit) PC, XT, AT; Toshiba; Samsung laptop(s)
- Size of board: Full-length board
- Integral modem included: Yes

NetFax Manager

OAZ Communications, Inc.
1362 Bordeaux Dr.
Sunnyvale, CA 94089
408-745-1750
fax: 408-745-1808

- Price: $2,795
- Date announced: 1989
- Group compatibility: CCITT Group 3
- Document transmit rate: 9,600 bps
- Required facilities: Dial-up
- System compatibility: IBM (8-bit) PC, XT, AT
- Size of board: Full-length board
- Integral modem included: Yes
- Standard features: Polling; remote terminal ID; transmit terminal ID; background send/receive; 2400-bps modem; electronic mail compatible

ISDN Adapters and Equipment

PCTA Model 1000

AT&T Computer Systems
100 Southgate Pkwy.
Morristown, NJ 07960
800-247-1212; 201-898-8000
fax: 201-644-9768

- Price: $500
- Date announced: 1990
- Compatibility: ATbus
- Line access standard: Basic Rate Interface (2B+D)
- Reference point: S/T Interface
- Central Office switch supported: AT&T 5ESS
- Command set: Hayes AT; Hayes ISDN Extended

PC/ISDN Platform

AT&T Computer Systems
100 Southgate Pkwy.
Morristown, NJ 07960
800-247-1212; 201-898-8000
fax: 201-644-9768

- Price: $1,395
- Date announced: 1990
- Compatibility: ATbus
- Line access standard: Basic Rate Interface (2B+D)
- Rate adaption standard: DMI 2
- Central Office switch supported: AT&T 5ESS
- Additional features: Circuit switched data; packet switched data

PC53

Dale, Gesek, McWilliams & Sheridan, Inc.
1025 Briggs Rd., Suite 100
Mt. Laurel, NJ 08054
609-866-1212
fax: 609-866-8850

- Price: $3,600
- Date announced: 1990
- Compatibility: ATbus
- Line access standard: Basic Rate Interface (2B+D)
- Reference point: S/T Interface
- Central Office switch supported: AT&T 5ESS; Northern Telecom DMS-100
- Additional features: Packet switched data

ISDN tel/adapter
DigiBoard
6751 Oxford St.
Minneapolis, MN 55426
800-344-4273; 612-922-8055
fax: 612-922-4287

- Price: $1,495
- Date announced: 1989
- Compatibility: ATbus
- Line access standard: Basic Rate Interface (2B+D)
- Reference point: S/T Interface
- Physical interfaces supported: RS-232C; RJ-11
- Rate adaption standard: DMI 2
- Central Office switch supported: AT&T 5ESS
- Additional features: Packet switched data

ISDN PC Adapter
Hayes Microcomputer Products, Inc.
PO Box 105203
Atlanta, GA 30348
404-449-8791
fax: 404-441-1238

- Price: $1,599
- Date announced: 1990
- Compatibility: ATbus
- Line access standard: Basic Rate Interface (2B+D)
- Reference point: S/T Interface
- Physical interfaces supported: RJ-11
- Rate adaption standard: V.120
- Central Office switch supported: AT&T 5ESS; Northern Telecom DMS-100
- Command set: Hayes ISDN Extended
- Additional features: Circuit switched data; packet switched data; built-in diagnostics

I-Cubed
ICL Networks Industry (ISDN Systems Group)
777 Long Ridge Rd., PO Box 10276
Stamford, CT 06904
800-446-4736; 203-968-7222

- Price: $1,695 (includes phone)
- Date announced: 1989
- Compatibility: ATbus; EISA; MCA-bus
- Line access standard: Basic Rate Interface (2B+D)
- Reference point: S/T Interface
- Physical interfaces supported: RJ-45
- Rate adaption standard: V.120
- Central Office switch supported: AT&T 5ESS; Northern Telecom DMS-100; Siemens EWSD
- Additional features: Circuit switched data; packet switched data; dialing directory; voice call setup

PRImate-PC
ISDN Technologies Corp.
1940 Colony St.
Mountain View, CA 94043
415-960-1025
fax: 415-960-1029

- Price: $15,600
- Number installed to date: 25
- Date announced: 1990
- Compatibility: ATbus
- Line access standard: Primary Rate Interface (23B+D)
- Physical interfaces supported: RS-232C; RS-449

SV35

Meridian Networx, Inc.
14044 Ventura Blvd., Suite 303
Sherman Oaks, CA 91423
818-501-7410

- Price: $2,500
- Compatibility: ATbus
- Line access standard: Basic Rate Interface (2B+D)
- Physical interfaces supported: RS-232C; V.35
- Rate adaption standard: V.110
- Central Office switch supported: AT&T 5ESS
- Additional features: Packet switched data

Datavoice SO

Meridian Networx, Inc.
14044 Ventura Blvd., Suite 303
Sherman Oaks, CA 91423
818-501-7410

- Price: $1,995
- Compatibility: ATbus
- Line access standard: Basic Rate Interface (2B+D)
- Physical interfaces supported: RJ-11
- Rate adaption standard: V.110
- Central Office switch supported: AT&T 5ESS
- Additional features: Packet switched data

ISDN PCTA

NCR Corp.
1700 S. Patterson Blvd.
Dayton, OH 45479
800-544-3333; 513-445-5000
fax: 513-445-2008

- Price: $1,695
- Date announced: 1990
- Compatibility: ATbus
- Line access standard: Basic Rate Interface (2B+D)
- Reference point: S/T Interface
- Physical interfaces supported: RS-232C; RJ-11
- Rate adaption standard: V.110; V.120
- Central Office switch supported: AT&T 5ESS
- Command set: Hayes AT

NTI-2001/PRI

The NTI Group
3265 Kifer Rd.
Santa Clara, CA 95051
408-739-2180
fax: 408-739-4847

- Price: $950
- Date announced: 1990
- Compatibility: ATbus
- Line access standard: Primary Rate Interface (23B+D)
- Central Office switch supported: AT&T 5ESS

PC Snet

OST, Inc.
14225 Sullyfield Circle
Chantilly, VA 22021
800-OST-9678; 703-817-0400
fax: 703-817-0402

- Price: $1,695
- Date announced: 1990
- Compatibility: ATbus
- Line access standard: Basic Rate Interface (2B+D)
- Reference point: S/T Interface

- Physical interfaces supported: RS-232C
- Command set: Hayes AT
- Additional features: Packet switched data

B101
Teleos Communications, Inc.
2 Meridian Rd.
Eatontown, NJ 07724
908-389-5700
fax: 908-544-9890

- Price: $1,295
- Date announced: 1987
- Compatibility: ATbus
- Line access standard: Basic Rate Interface (2B+D)
- Reference point: S/T Interface
- Physical interfaces supported: RJ-11
- Rate adaption standard: V.120
- Central Office switch supported: AT&T 5ESS; Northern Telecom DMS-100; Siemens EWSD
- Command set: Hayes AT
- Additional features: Packet switched data

PC-Squared
Vadis, Inc.
1201 Richardson Dr., Suite 200
Richardson, TX 75080
214-690-2481
fax: 214-996-0370

- Price: $1,180
- Date announced: 1989
- Compatibility: ATbus; MCAbus
- Line access standard: Basic Rate Interface (2B+D)
- Reference point: S/T Interface
- Physical interfaces supported: RJ-11

- Rate adaption standard: DMI 2; V.120
- Central Office switch supported: AT&T 5ESS; Northern Telecom-DMS-100
- Additional features: Circuit switched data; packet switched data; voice call setup; dialing directory; built-in diagnostics

NETWORK-OPERATING SYSTEMS

LANsoft
ACCTON Technology Corp.
46750 Fremont Blvd., Suite 104
Fremont, CA 94538
415-226-9800
fax: 415-226-9833

- A DOS-based LAN with peer-to-peer networking capabilites so users can share disks, drives, and peripherals in a LAN environment.

LANtastic
Artisoft, Inc.
575 E. River Rd., Artisoft Plaza
Tucson, AZ 85704
602-293-6363
fax: 602-293-8065

- LAN OS. Interconnects PCs using network adapter cards. Shares programs, data, printers, CD-ROMs, and other resources.

Axcess and CocoNet
Atlantix Corp.
5401 N.W. Broken Sound Blvd.,
Suite 100
Boca Raton, FL 33431
800-262-6526; 407-241-8108
fax: 407-241-8074

• Ethernet LAN designed to integrate PCs running UNIX, DOS, and OS/2. Users can share files, disks, printers, tapes, and distributed processing power within networked operating environment. Includes Redirector, Server, and other network utilities. Provides password protection, access control, and e-mail. Supports ARCnet, StarLAN, and twisted-pair Ethernet cards.

Lan Manager/X (LMX)
AT&T Computer Systems
100 Southgate Pkwy.
Morristown, NJ 07960
800-247-1212; 201-898-8000
fax: 201-644-9768

• UNIX System V equivalent of LAN Manager for OS/2. Allows DOS, OS/2, and UNIX applications to coexist on a single network. Enables users connected to an LMX host to run applications written for UNIX System V and DOS.

VINES (V.4.10)
Banyan Systems, Inc.
120 Flanders Rd.
Westboro, MA 01581
508-898-1000

• Virtual networking software. Network OS. Builds department/corporate-wide networks. Shares printers, tape units, disk drives, and communications controllers. Provides file sharing, e-mail, network administration, time/date sync, global naming, and security. Supports record and default file locking. TCP/IP options. Includes VAN-Guard Security and StreetTalk data base that tracks user ID and network services on large networks with multiple servers.

Network-OS (V.6.3B)
CBIS, Inc.
5875 Peachtree Industrial Blvd.
Bldg. 100, Unit 170
Norcross, GA 30092
404-446-1332
fax: 404-446-9164

• LAN OS. NetBIOS DOS 3.1 compatible. Allows user to use APPC technology. Provides step-by-step installation guide. Menu-driven user interface. Multitasking. Conformant to Open Systems Interconnect model (OSI). User transparent. Includes multiple nondedicated servers.

OS/2 Standard Version (V.1.2)
COMPAQ Computer Corp.
PO Box 692000
Houston, TX 77269-2000
800-231-0900; 713-370-0670
fax: 713-374-1402

• Implementation of OS/2 multiprocessing OS. Includes high-performance file system (HPFS), presentation manager graphical interface, and on-line help utility. Includes ability to begin MS-DOS applications from desktop manager and windowed system editor.

ReadyLink
Compex, Inc.
4055 E. La Palma Ave., Suite C
Anaheim, CA 92807
714-630-7302
fax: 714-630-6521

• A low-cost, DOS-based network operating system interconnected through network adapter cards. Shares drives, disks, and other peripherals.

PC/NOS
Corvus Systems, Inc.
160 Great Oaks Blvd.
San Jose, CA 95119-1347
800-426-7887; 408-281-4100
fax: 408-578-4102

• Distributed LAN OS. Operates without file server. Includes multi-threaded file access, resource sharing, built-in sync communications, virtual console, transparent print spooling, spool queue management, messaging, multilevel security, and EMS support. Supports ARCNET, Ethernet, Token Ring, NetBIOS, and Omninet networks. Supports async gateway communications.

LANsmart (V.2.0)
D-Link Systems, Inc.
5 Musick
Irvine, CA 92718
714-455-1688
fax: 714-455-2521

• Network OS for D-Link LAN. Runs all multiuser applications that use DOS 3.1 file/record locking or NetBIOS standard. Uses disk cache to eliminate the number of I/O operations. Includes message transfer, on-line chat, system administrator programs, modem pool

support, and mainframe connections. Optional e-mail, screen monitor, remote boot, remote access program, and ALS.

DataLAN
Datapoint Corp.
9725 Datapoint Dr.
San Antonio, TX 78229-8500
800-334-9968; 512-699-7000
fax: 512-699-7920

• IBM NetBIOS-compatible LAN OS. Uses NetBIOS application program interface, which allows it to work with all popular NetBIOS-compatible hardware topologies including Ethernet, Token Ring, and ARCnet.

10NetPlus LAN Operating System
Digital Communications Associates, Inc.
7887 Washington Village Dr.
Dayton, OH 45459
800-358-1010; 800-782-1010
513-433-2238
fax: 513-434-6305

• Uses SMB protocols and interfaces to NetBIOS and OSDI transport software for communications. Includes windowing and systems monitor capability.

GV LAN OS (V.1.1)
Grapevine LAN Products, Inc.
15323 Northeast 90th St.
Redmond, WA 98052
206-869-2707
fax: 206-869-2506

• LAN OS. Provides print spooling. Supports e-mail and resource sharing of all peripherals on network. Supports multiuser data and program sharing.

OS/2 Extended Edition (V.1.3)
IBM
Old Orchard Rd.
Armonk, NY 10504
800-426-2468; 914-765-1900

• Includes functions of OS/2 Standard Edition along with advanced RDBM and Communications Manager, which provides intersystems communications, terminal emulation, and LAN requestor support. Includes Remote Data Services SAA function that provides multiuser database support in LAN environment. Includes Dialog Manager that conforms to SAA, and Procedures Language that allows user to write command procedures in a clear, structured way. Provides SNA Gateway, which supports 254 workstations on single LAN. IBM no. 15F7-143, -144.

Net/30 (V.2.0)
Invisible Software, Inc.
1165 Chess Dr., Suite D
Foster City, CA 94404
415-570-5967
fax: 415-570-6017

• LAN OS for use with Invisible Software's LAN boards. Supports file sharing, print spooling, file/record locking, e-mail, menu system with on-line help, security, network management, diskless workstations, and DOS.

EasyNet NOS/2 Plus
LanMark Corp.
PO Box 246, Postal Station A
Mississauga, ON
CD L5A 3G8
416-848-6865
fax: 416-848-0830

• LAN OS. Provides remote spoolers, developer's toolkit, NetBIOS status utility program, SAA CUA interface, and security, print, and spooler sub-systems.

LAN Manager (V.2.0)
Microsoft Corp.
One Microsoft Way
Redmond, WA 98052-6399
800-426-9400; 206-882-8080
fax: 206-883-8101

• Advanced network OS. Provides foundation for client-server computing and tools for distributed administration of LANs. Includes 386/486 microprocessor support. Takes advantage of OS/2's multitasking functions, interprocess communications, and built-in memory protection. Uses OS/2 high-performance file system (HPFS) to speed network throughput. Includes facilities that let multiple servers be administered as single server. Provides fault tolerance, reduced memory requirements for PC/MS-DOS, peer services, and specific security measures including password aging and password validation delay.

ChosenLAN (V.3.58)
Moses Computers, Inc.
15466 Los Gatos Blvd., Suite 213
Los Gatos, CA 95032
408-358-1550
fax: 408-356-9049

• LAN OS. Supports Moses Computers' PromiseLAN in all configurations using Moses adapter boards or IBM standard network boards. Uses IBM SMB protocol. Allows server computer to share or assign its network resources, including application programs and peripherals across multiple users. Provides file and record locking and print spooling. Supports interface with word processing, spreadsheet, and data base programs.

LAN Manager (V.2.01)
NCR Corp.
1700 S. Patterson Blvd.
Dayton, OH 45479
800-544-3333; 513-445-5000
fax: 513-445-2008

• LAN OS. Available in two versions including Entry Level Server Kit and Unlimited Server Kit. Provides a single vendor, open system, industry standard platform that accommodates development of a new generation of network applications based on a client/server architecture model to access single data file without compatibility concerns. Includes network management, administration, and diagnostic tools.

NetWare vLAN+/vNET/EtherNext
NetWorth, Inc.
80101 Ridgepoint Dr., Suite 107
Irving, TX 75063
214-869-1331

• LAN operating system. Provides print spooling, e-mail, modem pool support, remote access, and IBM mainframe connection. Supports NetBIOS.

NetWare
Novell, Inc.
122 East 1700 South
Provo, UT 84606
800-453-1267; 801-379-5900
fax: 801-429-5775

• LAN OS. Various levels for enterprise-wide and workgroup computing.

Provides user transparent connectivity, internetworking capabilities, multiple remote connections, LAN to host communications, data protection, resource accounting, security, and programming tools.

PowerLAN
Performance Technology
7800 IH 10, W
800 Lincoln Center
San Antonio, TX 78230
512-349-2000

• LAN operating systems for MS-DOS and UNIX. Products to integrate client PCs with NetWare and UNIX servers on the same network.

LifeNet
Univation, Inc.
513 Valley Way
Milpitas, CA 95035
800-221-5842; 408-263-1200
fax: 408-263-1474

• LAN OS for PCs. Fault tolerance system provides transaction processing, transaction logging, and file recovery. Includes tutorial maker, pop-up phone message, and calendaring.

Web
WebCorp
3000 Bridgeway
Sausalito, CA 94965
415-331-1449

LAN Metering Software

PreCursor (V.4.0)
The Aldridge Co.
2500 City West Blvd., Suite 575

Houston, TX 77042
800-548-5019; 713-953-1940
fax: 713-953-0806

• Hard-disk multiple-menu system. Creates user interface for running programs. Tracks computer usage for time management, time billing, or security. Provides log-on and file management utilities including backup, tag, and sweep operations. Integrated optional mouse support.

StopCopy Plus

BBI Computer Systems
14105 Heritage Lane
Silver Spring, MD 20906
301-871-1094
fax: 301-460-7545

• Software protection package. Menu driven with transparent residence. Offers unlimited metering and multiple layering.

StopView

BBI Computer Systems
14105 Heritage Lane
Silver Spring, MD 20906
301-871-1094
fax: 301-460-7545

• Screen security program. Provides hacker inhibitory code (HIC) to thwart tracing. Offers custom loading routines, multiple layering, and unlimited metering.

LT Auditor (V.2.03)

Blue Lance
PO Box 430546
Houston, TX 77243
713-680-1187
fax: 713-622-1370

• Audit trail utility for LAN management. Consists of RAM203, which monitors activity of all network workstations, and Lantight, which is used by LAN supervisors to configure LT Auditor and to produce audit reports. Generates File Access and LAN Access Reports. Includes network troubleshooting and self-diagnostics. Auto-archive. External ASCII translation.

SiteLock (V.3.0)

Brightwork Development, Inc.
766 Shrewsbury Ave.
Jerral Center West
Tinton Falls, NJ 07724
800-552-9876; 201-530-0440
fax: 201-530-0622

• Provides total network software control for NetWare LANs. Provides virus protection by verifying protected files before proceeding and by preventing altered, unauthorized, or possible infected software from running. Limits simultaneous use of software programs to insure compliance with license agreement. File server VAP/NLM module interacts with small TSR on each workstation to provide secure environments.

Certus LAN

Certus International
13110 Shaker Sq.
Cleveland, OH 44120
800-722-8737; 216-752-8181
fax: 216-752-8188

• Controls and monitors what network software is accessed, prevents data loss due to user mistake or intentional misuse, and provides recovery from hard-disk and some file server crashes. Enhances standard LAN security features. Verifies integrity of all programs before they are loaded into memory. Supports all common network OSs and hardware.

Lanscope (V.2.1d3)
Connect Computer Co., Inc.
9855 West 78th St., Suite 270
Eden Prairie, MN 55344
612-944-0181
fax: 612-944-9298

• LAN management system. Provides menuing security, usage tracking, software-usage control, network resource management, printer spooling, user productivity, and network management. Modules include menuing system, Audit Trail, Hot Key Workstation Utilities, and Turnstyle Software Metering.

Turnstyle
Connect Computer Co., Inc.
9855 West 78th St., Suite 270
Eden Prairie, MN 55344
612-944-0181
fax: 612-944-9298

• LAN utility. Software-license metering system that monitors the number of users accessing application. Allows only included number of users in licensing agreement to access application simultaneously. Lets administrator see which programs are being used at any given time. Generates reports on use of metered software.

Direct Net (V.1.0)
Fifth Generation Systems, Inc.
10049 N. Reiger Rd.
Baton Rouge, LA 70809
800-873-4384; 504-291-7221
fax: 504-295-3268

• Menuing system for networks. Organizes software into user-defined menu. Features supervisory utilities, automatic menu building, multiple menu options, usage tracking with report generator, metering, virus detection, password protection, and custom file applications.

LANShell (V.2.01)
LANSystems Inc.
300 Park Ave., South
New York, NY 10010
800-LAN-STEL; 212-995-7700
fax: 212-995-8604

• Menuing system. Combines high-speed execution with low memory overhead (9k of RAM). Supports major network standards and software license metering.

WorkStation Manager
McCarty Associates, Inc.
929 Boston Post Rd.
Old Saybrook, CT 06475
203-388-6994
fax: 203-388-6826

• Provides the ability to design standardized interactive menus that can collect data, test variables, and browse data bases. Includes over 500 help, utility, and sample menus using IBM CUA screen standards.

NetMenu

NETinc.
PO Box 271105
Houston, TX 77277-1105
713-974-1810

• Network menuing program. Controls maximum number of people accessing an application. Allows user to create up to 10 menus in each menu file for use in lieu of DOS command-line entries and to update and modify them while in use.

LANtrail (V.3.0)

Network Management, Inc.
19 Rector St.
New York, NY 10006
800-LAN-USER; 212-797-3800
fax: 212-797-3817

• Audit trail utility for Novell NetWare-based networks. Monitors all network activities. Provides reporting, security tracking, and disk usage tracking for network and local drives. Tracks information on file and directory usage, connection usage, and bindery changes. Generates reports. Filters, condenses, and formats data for administrator.

Saber Meter (V.2.10)

Saber Software Corp.
PO Box 9088
Dallas, TX 75209
800-338-8754; 214-361-8086
fax: 214-361-1882

• LAN administration tool that reports and graphs LAN usage and activity. Provides software-license metering and usage auditing. Monitors access and usage by user and application. Stores audit information in dBASE III format.

Argus/n

Triticom
PO Box 11536
St. Paul, MN 55111
612-937-0772

• Monitors station activity and configuration. Monitors application-level usage in each workstation attached to a NetWare LAN. Conducts automatic hardware inventory of all LAN stations, which simplifies network management and configuration tracking. Designed for system managers to help monitor and control network usage.

Printer Sharing Devices (Data Switches)

Slimline Data Switches

Belkin Components
14550 S. Main St.
Gardena, CA 90248
800-223-5546; 213-515-7585
fax: 213-329-3236

• Price: $79-$99
• Product classification: Manual switch/patch equipment
• Max number of switched lines: 3
• Type of lines switched: RS-232C; Centronics parallel; IEEE-488
• Switch technology: Manual patch

8 Pin miniDIN Data Switches

Data-Doc Electronics, Inc.
4903 Commercial Park Dr.
Austin, TX 78724-2638
800-328-2362; 512-928-8926
fax: 512-928-8210

• Price: $80-$130
• Date announced: 1988

- Product classification: Manual switch/patch equipment
- Max number of switched lines: 2-5
- Type of lines switched: RS-232C; miniDIN
- Switch technology: Manual patch

Manual Data Switches Series 1100
Hadax Electronics, Inc.
11 Teaneck Rd.
Ridgefield Park, NJ 07660
201-807-1155
fax: 201-807-1782

- Price: $75-$300
- Number installed to date: 24,500
- Date announced: 1983
- Product classification: Manual switch/patch equipment
- Max number of switched lines: 4
- Type of lines switched: RS-232C; CCITT V.35; analog telco; digital non-T1; T1; coax; twinax
- Switch technology: Relay

Intelligent Printer Buffer Series
Primax Electronics (USA), Inc.
2531 West 237th St., Suite 102
Torrance, CA 90505
213-326-8018
fax: 213-326-7504

- Price: $80-$184
- Date announced: 1989
- Device type: Printer accessories
- Compatible with: IBM PC
- Description: Combined funtion of buffer and data switches in one unit; one input port, one output port with Centronics interface; 64k-512k

Avalon LAN
Avalon Design and Manufacturing, Inc.
130 McCormick Ave., Suite 113
Costa Mesa, CA 92626
800-247-6166; 714-432-7227
fax: 714-432-7482

- Date announced: 1989
- Product classification: Resource sharing network
- CPU compatibility: IBM PC, XT, AT, PS/2 Model 30, Series 1; NCR
- Tower maximum distance: 4,000 feet between stations
- Interfaces supported: Serial; parallel; twisted pair; RS-449; RS-485
- Network provisions: Printer sharing

CarrierNet
Carrier Current Technologies, Inc.
9600 Southern Pine Blvd.
Charlotte, NC 28217
800-222-0377; 704-529-6550
fax: 704-523-7651

- Price: $199/node
- Number installed to date: 2,500
- Date announced: 1989
- Product classification: Resource sharing network
- CPU compatibility: IBM PC, XT, AT, PS/2 Model 25, 30
- Topology: Bus
- Maximum distance: 1 mile without bridges or repeaters
- Interfaces supported: Serial
- Network provisions: Disk sharing; printer sharing; electronic mail
- Access gateways: Ethernet

Super Spooler II
Consolink
1840 Industrial Circle
Longmont, CO 80501
303-651-2014
fax: 303-678-8360

- Number installed to date: 500
- Date announced: 1989
- Device type: Printer accessories
- Compatible with: IBM PC
- Description: 8-port printer sharing device; includes software; 256k to 1 Mb

MetroLAN
Datacom Technologies, Inc.
11001 31st Place, West
Everett, WA 98204
800-468-5557; 206-355-0590
fax: 206-353-9292

- Price: $1,395-$2,795
- Date announced: 1990
- Product classification: Resource sharing network
- CPU compatibility: IBM PC, XT, AT, PS/2 Model 50, 60, 70, 80
- Apple Macintosh topology: Bus
- Interfaces supported: Serial; parallel; twisted pair
- Network provisions: Disk sharing; printer sharing; communications gateways; file transfer; electronic messaging

NetCommander Series
Digital Products, Inc.
108 Water St.
Watertown, MA 02172
800-243-2333; 617-924-1680
fax: 617-924-7814

- Price: $1,895-$8,650
- Number installed to date: 4,000
- Date announced: 1984
- Product classification: Resource sharing network
- Topology: Star
- Multiaccess management technique: Contention
- Maximum distance: 1,000 feet without bridges or repeaters
- Interfaces supported: Serial; parallel
- Network provisions: Disk sharing; printer sharing; modem; plotter
- Access gateways: Ethernet

ACCESS Easy Network
Exzel Corp.
7721 E. Gray Rd., Suite 102
Scottsdale, AZ 85260
800-833-3897; 602-991-9775
fax: 602-991-2041

- Price: $99
- Date announced: 1990
- Product classification: Resource sharing network
- CPU compatibility: IBM XT, AT, PS/2 Model 30
- Network provisions: Printer sharing

Logical Connection
Fifth Generation Systems, Inc.
10049 N. Reiger Rd.
Baton Rouge, LA 70809
800-873-4384; 504-291-7221
fax: 504-295-3268

- Price: $495(256k)-$595(512k)
- Date announced: 1986
- Device type: Printer accessories
- Compatible with: IBM PC, XT, AT, PS/2 Model 30; Apple Macintosh

- Description: Printer sharing switch; 256k-1 Mb buffer; spools documents; Version 3.0 adds Pop-Up DeskSet software

AURA 1000
Intran Systems, Inc.
7493 N. Oracle Rd., Suite 207
Tucson, AZ 85704
602-797-2797
fax: 602-797-2799

- Price: $89 per node
- Number installed to date: 100
- Date announced: 1990
- Product classification: Resource sharing network
- CPU compatibility: IBM PC, XT, AT
- Topology: Bus
- Network discipline: Baseband
- Multi-access mgmt technique: Contention
- Maximum distance: 4000 feet without bridges or repeaters
- Interfaces supported: Serial
- Network provisions: Printer sharing; electronic mail; file transfer

PLM Series
Kansai International, Inc.
20917 S. Western Ave.
Torrance, CA 90503
800-733-3374; 213-782-8073
fax: 213-782-8559

- Price: $179-$209
- Number installed to date: 200
- Date announced: 1990
- Device type: Printer accessories
- Compatible with: IBM PC, XT, AT, PS/2 Model 30
- Description: Automatic printer-sharing device

ShareNet 5110
McComb Research
PO Box 3984
Minneapolis, MN 55405
612-527-8082
fax: 612-377-8906

- Price: $149
- Date announced: 1987
- Product classification: Resource sharing network
- Topology: Ring; bus; star
- Network discipline: Baseband
- Multiaccess management technique: Contention
- Maximum distance: 4,000 feet without bridges or repeaters
- Interfaces supported: Parallel
- Network compatibility: ShareNet
- Network provisions: Disk sharing; printer sharing; communications gateways

LAWN
O'Neill Communications, Inc.
100 Thanet Circle
Princeton, NJ 08540
800-624-5296; 609-497-6800
fax: 609-497-6801

- Price: $495/node
- Date announced: 1989
- Product classification: Resource sharing network
- CPU compatibility: IBM PC, XT, AT, PS/2 Model 30, 50, 60, 70, 80
- Topology: Wireless
- Network discipline: Spread spectrum radio
- Multi-access management technique: Contention
- Maximum distance: 100 feet between stations
- Interfaces supported: Serial

- Network provisions: Disk sharing; printer sharing; electronic mail; file transfer
- Access gateways: X.25

Data Switches
Rose Electronics
PO Box 742571
Houston, TX 77274
800-333-9343; 713-933-7673
fax: 713-933-0044

AutoLink 4 to 1 Printer Sharing Unit
Support Systems International Corp.
150 S. Second St.
Richmond, CA 94804
415-234-9090
fax: 415-233-8888

- Price: $279
- Number installed to date: 1,000
- Date announced: 1985
- Product classification: Automatic switch equipment
- Max number of switched lines: 4
- Type of lines switched: RS-232C; Centronics parallel
- Switch technology: Electronic matrix

Data Switches
Western Telematic, Inc.
5 Sterling
Irvine, CA 92718
800-854-7226; 714-586-9950
fax: 714-583-9514

- Description: A wide family of printer-sharing devices

TCP/IP and Related Products

Isolink PC/TCP
BICC Data Networks
1800 W. Park Dr., Suite 150
Westborough, MA 01581
800-447-6526; 508-898-2422
fax: 508-898-3739

- A set of programs supporting U.S. Department of Defense standard protocol suite TCP/IP. Provides simultaneous network access through Isolan PC Controller Card. Ethernet interface. Includes file transfer, remote log-in, electronic mail, and remote printing. Troubleshooting capability.

SNMPc Network Management
Castle Rock Computing, Inc.
2841 Junction Ave., Suite 118
San Jose, CA 95134
408-434-6608
fax: 408-432-0892

- Incorporates Simple Network Management Protocol (SNMP) to help user oversee TCP/IP networks by monitoring network performance and status and by reporting on network faults. Provides a hierarchical map of the network that graphically displays each node and network segment. Displays part of the map in main window at all times, which can be scaled and moved at any time. Includes realtime graphical or tabular display of counters that trigger alarms when preset limits of network elements are exceeded. Works in Microsoft Windows environment.

cc:Mail Link to SMTP

CC:Mail, Inc.
2141 Landings Dr.
Mountain View, CA 94043
800-448-2500; 415-961-8800
fax: 415-961-8400

• Provides communication link between cc:Mail users of Simple Mail Transfer Protocol-based mail systems. Enables users to prepare and send messages as if they were sending to someone on same e-mail system. Works as TCP/IP node connected to Ethernet network. Includes all TCP/IP and FTP software required on PC side. Users can communicate with users of UNIX Mail, Internet, Bitnet, IBM PROFS, DEC VMSmail, DEC VAX All-in-One, DG AOS/VS Mail, and HP DeskMate. Transfers binary and text files and fax items as mail attachments.

VistaWare

Datability Software Systems, Inc.
322 Eighth Ave.
New York, NY 10001
800-342-5377; 212-807-7800
fax: 212-463-0459

• Converts PCs into high-end dual protocol LAT and TCP/IP Telnet terminal server capable of accessing DEC VAX and UNIX systems. Provides command interface identical to DEC's DECserver. Provides terminal service for up to four dumb terminals and up to two parallel printers connected to standard terminal ports. Optional Network Protocol Translator (NPT) available.

10Net TCP

Digital Communications Associates, Inc.
10NET Communications Division
7887 Washington Village Dr.
Dayton, OH 45459
800-358-1010; 800-782-1010; 513-433-2238
fax: 513-434-6305

• Collection of programs implementing standard TCP/IP protocol family. Allows PCs to communicate with other PCs and with other computers and OSs from AT&T, Apollo, Cray, HP, DEC and others. Supports TCP/IP protocols for file transfer, terminal emulation, and electronic mail.

PC/TCP Plus

FTP Software, Inc.
26 Princess St.
Wakefield, MA 01880
617-246-0900
fax: 617-246-0901

• Communicates with computers supporting the TCP/IP family of protocols. Contains utilities for file transfer, terminal emulation, mail, NFS file sharing, remote backup, printing, and network testing. Available with FTP's NetBIOS and InterDrive options. XENIX version includes utilities for network debugging. OS/2 version uses NDIS driver to run on many different network interface cards.

ProLINC

Hughes LAN Systems, Inc.
1225 Charleston Rd.
Mountain View, CA 94043
415-966-7300
fax: 415-960-3738

• Connectivity package. Provides simultaneous use of multiple protocols such as NetWare IPX, DEC LAT, TCP/IP, and NFS services through use of Hughes' Multiple Protocol Architecture (MPA). Allows users connectivity to transfer data among dissimilar host and network server systems. Allows user to unload protocols after use.

TCP/IP for OS/2 EE (V.1.1)
IBM
Old Orchard Rd.
Armonk, NY 10504
800-426-2468; 914-765-1900

• Allows OS/2 EE V.1.1 system attached to an IBM Token-Ring, IEEE 802.3 LAN, or Ethernet V.2 LAN to interoperate with other systems in TCP/IP networks. Incorporates Transmission Control Protocol (TCP), Internet Protocol (IP), Internet Control Messaging Protocol (ICMP), TELNET client/server, Simple Mail Transfer Protocol (SMTP) client/server, Trivial File Transfer Protocol (TFTP) client/server, and remote execution client/server. IBM no. 73F6072, 73F6073, 73F6074, 73F6075, 73F6071.

OpenConnect/SMTP
Mitek Systems Corp.
2033 Chennault Dr.
Carrollton, TX 75006
214-490-4090
fax: 214-490-5052

• Simple Mail Transfer Protocol. Provides internetwork mail capability. Allows bi-directional file transfer between users on dissimilar SNA and TCP/IP networks.

Excelan LAN Workplace for OS/2
Novell, Inc.
122 East 1700 South
Provo, UT 84606
800-453-1267; 801-379-5900
fax: 801-429-5775

• Lets OS/2 users run multiple TCP/IP protocol sessions.

SmarTerm 320 (V.1.2)
Persoft, Inc.
465 Science Dr.
Madison, WI 53711
800-EMU-LATE; 608-273-6000
fax: 608-273-8227

• Emulates DEC VT320, 220, 100, 52, and TTY. Includes ASCII, binary file transfer, and Kermit, Xmodem, and PDIP error-free file transfer. Includes background operations, softkeys, pop-up windows, and 132-column support. Includes LAT protocol. Includes telnet with support for multiple sessions and named services for popular PC implementations of TCP/IP, including Wollongong's WIN/TCP and Excelan's LAN Workplace for DOS.

PCS/TCP
3Com Corp.
3165 Kifer Rd.
Santa Clara, CA 95052-8145
800-638-3266; 408-562-6400
fax: 408-970-1112

• Allows PCs to communicate with resources over TCP/IP networks. Compatible with 3Com 3+ OS. Provides network access to TCP/IP hosts. DEC VT100 terminal emulation using Telnet protocol to support virtual circuits between PCs and larger processors.

Facilitates file transfer between dissimilar machines and OSs using FTP.

TCP for NDIS
Ungermann-Bass, Inc.
PO Box 58030
3900 Freedom Circle
Santa Clara, CA 95052-8030
800-873-6381; 408-496-0111
fax: 408-970-9300

• Protocol stack that allows third-party LAN adapter makers to incorporate TCP/IP communications protocols into products.

PC/TCP Ethernet Communication Package for PCs
UniPress Software, Inc.
2025 Lincoln Hwy.
Edison, NJ 08817
800-222-0550; 201-985-8000
fax: 201-287-4929

• Allows communication between PCs and other computers via Ethernet and other LANs. Implements ARPAnet TCP/IP protocol, providing file transfer, remote log-in, and electronic mail. Includes clock setting, listing active users on machine, and verifying that machine is on network.

VENIX/System V
VenturCom, Inc.
215 First St.
Cambridge, MA 02142
800-334-8649; 617-661-1230
fax: 617-577-1607

• Incorporates real-time enhancements. Supports IBM Enhanced Graphics Adapter and TCP/IP networking protocol. Enables PC-compatible machines to communicate in multivendor networks and provides a standardized, portable computing environment.

Telnet Manager
Walker Richer and Quinn, Inc.
2815 Eastlake Ave., East
Seattle, WA 98102
800-872-2829; 206-324-0350
fax: 206-322-8151

• Add-on for WRQ's Reflection package. Designed for PC-to-host connections using TCP/IP networking software. Implements Telenet protocol in TCP/IP protocol suite. Combines the terminal emulation capabilities of Reflection with several session-management capabilities.

WIN/TCP for DOS
Wollongong Group, Inc.
PO Box 51860
1129 San Antonio Rd.
Palo Alto, CA 94303
800-872-8649; 800-962-8649; 415-962-7200
fax: 415-969-5547

• Provides a full suite of TCP/IP utilities for DOS. Fully compatible with NetWare.

3270 Terminal Emulation Products

TruLynx/3270-PC
Andrew Corp.
2771 Plaza Del Amo
Torrance, CA 90503
800-733-0331; 213-320-7126
fax: 213-618-0386

• Emulates IBM 3270 PC control program file-transfer capability. Provides two-level password protection, session outage notification, start, terminate, or suspend. Depends on remote connection status. Allows sessions with VM/SP, MVS/TSO, and CICS. Hot-key switching between conversational and PC sessions. Works in conjunction with DataLynx/3174 and 3274 protocol converters.

Micro/Remote 3270 Emulator

Aton International, Inc.
7654 Beenassi Dr.
Gilroy, CA 95020
408-847-3531

• Emulates a 3270 terminal. Enable an IBM PC to act as an IBM 3275 model 2 terminal. Accesses mainframe-based information. Transfers ASCII/EBCDIC files. Allows a PC printer to emulate an IBM 328X mainframe printer. Requires IBM's bisync communications adapter.

StarGroup Software SNA Gateway

AT&T Computer Systems
100 Southgate Pkwy.
Morristown, NJ 07960
800-247-1212; 201-898-8000
fax: 201-644-9768

• Provides MS-DOS workstations with IBM 3270 terminal emulation and connectivity to SNA hosts via UNIX-based StarGroup LAN. Supports up to 128 sessions and provides a communications base for file transfer, file access, and interactive sessions with SNA hosts. Gateway server uses AT&T's SNA/LINK program to emulate IBM 3274 cluster controllers. Gateway package consists of workstation and server software.

Extra! Connectivity Software: Entry Level

Attachmate Corp.
13231 Southeast 36th St.
Bellevue, WA 98006
800-426-6283; 206-644-4010
fax: 206-747-9924

• Provides 3270 terminal single-session functions. Includes file transfer, screen print, and program interfaces. Connects to mainframe via coaxial cable, LAN, modem, or Token-Ring interface coupler. Low memory usage.

3270 Emulation Program—Entry Level

Avatar Corp.
65 South St.
Hopkinton, MA 01748
800-282-3270; 508-435-3000
fax: 508-435-2470

• Emulates IBM 3270 terminals. Provides file transfer to and from IBM mainframe, ability to configure PC working environment and to redefine a PC keyboard to 3270 functions. Compatible with Avatar's PA100G and IBM's 3278/79 Emulation Adapter.

BLAST 3270

BLAST/Communications Research Group
5615 Corporate Blvd.
Baton Rouge, LA 70808
800-242-5278; 504-923-0888
fax: 504-926-2155

• Remote async data communications program that provides file transfer and terminal emulation through protocol converters to IBM mainframes. Includes keyboard remapping for IBM 3270 emulation and Kermit file transfer protocols.

BlueLynx-DFT/3270 Local (V.2.0)
BlueLynx
215 Paca St.
PO Box 877
Cumberland, MD 21502-0877
800-832-4526; 301-777-3307
fax: 301-777-3462

• Emulates a 3270 Distributed Function Terminal connected to an IBM 3174 or 3274 Control Unit. Includes windowing capabilities that allow user to work with as many as five host sessions and up to two notepad sessions simultaneously.

LinkUP 3270 COAX WorkStation Software
Chi Corp.
31200 Carter St.
Solon, OH 44139
216-349-8600
fax: 216-349-8620

• Provides multi-session 3278/79 terminal functionality for micro-to-mainframe communications. Features printer panel and keyboard remapping utilities. Includes non-SNA, BSC, and SNA emulations. IBM EEHLLAPI and PS/API compatible. IND$FILE and Editor-based file transfer included.

DataTalker 3270 SNA
CLEO Communications
3796 Plaza Dr.
Ann Arbor, MI 48108
800-233-2536; 313-662-2002
fax: 313-662-1965

• Emulates remote 3278/79 terminals and 3174 controller. Supports a cluster of 1-9 PCs. Includes application program interface (API), HLLAPI 3.0, NetView support, and file transfer (IND$FILE) for TSO/CMS/CICS. Supports 32 sessions per cluster. Requires DataTalker PC/8, II, PC, PC Plus, DataSync modem boards.

3270-SNA Emulator
Computer Logics, Ltd.
75 International Blvd.
Rexdale, ON
CD M9W 6L9
800-387-4811; 800-387-3995; 416-674-1111
fax: 416-674-1130

• Allows a PC to communicate with host systems in an SNA/SDLC network environment by emulating 3270 information display system devices.

DI3270 (Rel. 3.3)
Data Interface Systems Corp.
PO Box 4189
Austin, TX 78765-4189
800-351-4244; 512-346-5641
fax: 512-346-4035

• Micro-to-mainframe connectivity system for PCs and PC LANs. Supports all 3X78 and many 3X79 terminal models. Supports SNA/SDLC and BSC protocols. Provides multi-session 3270 terminal emulation for multiple PCs in a LAN running Novell Advanced NetWare or for a standalone PC. Includes monitoring, tracing, and statistical analysis tools.

IRMAX DFT (V.2.1)

Digital Communications
Associates, Inc.
1000 Alderman Dr.
Alpharetta, GA 30201-4199
800-241-4762; 404-442-4000
fax: 404-442-4361

• IBM 3278/79 terminal emulation.
Uses connectivity functions of Distributed Function Terminal, which allow
for five concurrent host sessions, 3287
printer emulation, and support for
DCA 3270 APA Graphics Program. Includes DCA's IRMAlink file transfer
programs. Supports IBM's OfficeVision and Expanded-Memory Specification (EMS).

IBM SNA Gateway

DSC Communications Corp.
1000 Coit Rd.
Plano, TX 75075
800-322-3101; 214-519-3000

• IBM PC emulates remote IBM 3274,
supporting 16 user stations per gateway. Interfaces with IBM mainframes
supporting 3270 SNA protocol.

Access/SDLC/QLLC 3270

Eicon Technology Corp.
2196 32nd Ave.
Montreal, QB
CD H8T 3H7
514-631-2592
fax: 514-631-3092

• A 3270 gateway. Access/SDLC
(3270) connects PCs to mainframes via
leased or switched SDLC lines. Access/
QLLC (3270) connects PCs to mainframes equipped with X.25 (DSP/
NPSI). Supports up to 254 LUs. Includes abbreviated dialing from a 100-

name calling directory, auto log-on capabilities and script files, hot-key to
DOS, and integrated trace facility. Includes keyboard and VT100 keyboard
remapping and 3270 data stream conversion tables. Provides emulation for
3274 and 3174 Control Units, 3278 and
3178 displays, 3279 and 3179 color displays, 3287 printers, and 3270-PC file
transfer.

DynaComm 3270 Synchronous Edition (V.3.0)

Future Soft Engineering, Inc.
1001 S. Dairy Ashford, Suite 203
Houston, TX 77077
713-496-9400
fax: 713-496-1090

• Communications package for Microsoft Windows. Includes high-level
script language, IBM 3270 CCITT
mode terminal emulation, full support
of IBM CMS and TSO file send and receive, reconfigurable user interface,
tabular data manipulation, script building utilities, and support of Microsoft's
dynamic data exchange.

G/SNA Gateway

Gateway Communications, Inc.
2941 Alton Ave.
Irvine, CA 92714
800-367-6555; 714-553-1555
fax: 714-553-1616

• LAN gateway for SNA/SDLC emulates 3274-51C Cluster Controller. Provides 3270 terminal and 3770 RJE
workstation emulation for LAN workstations. Uses IBM NetBIOS or Advanced NetWare IPX. Includes
intelligent coprocessor board, gateway

software, terminal emulation software, cable, and documentation.

PC 3270 Emulation (V.3.0)
IBM
Old Orchard Rd.
Armonk, NY 10504
800-426-2468; 914-765-1900

• Allows PCs to communicate around the ring to a 3725 Communication Controller directly attached to a Token-Ring network to access host applications. TopView compatible.

pcPATH SNA-3770
ICOT Corp.
3801 Zanker Rd.
PO Box 5143
San Jose, CA 95150-5143
800-762-3270; 408-433-3300
fax: 408-433-0260

• Allows IBM PC and compatibles remote operation on IBM SNA networks through 3770 RJE station emulation. Supports up to six host communication sessions and unattended operation through enhanced command file language.

IDEAcomm 3270/AFT
IDEAssociates, Inc.
29 Dunham Rd.
Billerica, MA 01821
800-257-5027; 508-663-6878
fax: 508-663-8851

• Terminal emulation package designed for use with IDEA Courier's IDEA 14000 Series of Advanced Function Terminals. Supports multiple session types in windowed environment including 3270, DEC VT 320, notepads, and DOS. Supports HLLAPI interface,

which enables users to simplify complex or multiple-host application environments at terminal level. Enables user to conduct multiple, bidirectional file transfers without using DOS session. Features pop-up and pull-down menus.

Execulink III
Lee Data
10230 West 70th St.
Eden Prairie, MN 55344
800-533-3282; 612-828-0400
fax: 612-828-5799

• A 3270/PC file transfer program. Supports 3270 and VT100 emulation; multiple sessions; foreground/background operations; multiple text and binary file transfers to and from host systems on TSO, VM/CMS, CICS/VS, IWS; and print spooling. Operates via Series 8000 or Datastar 4000 without any hardware changes.

Relay/3270 (V.4.0)
Microcom, Inc.
500 River Ridge Dr.
Norwood, MA 02062-5028
617-551-1999

• Allows IBM PC running Relay Gold to emulate IBM 3277, 3278, or 3279 model 2 or 3 while connected to a mainframe over phone lines. Existing full-screen 3270 applications run with PC and phone. Supports error-free file transfer between mainframe and PC.

MicroGate 3270/SNA
MicroGate Corp.
9501 Capital of Texas Hwy., Suite 105
Austin, TX 78759
800-444-1982; 512-345-7791
fax: 512-343-9046

• Provides remote 3270 terminal emulation for PCs. Remote PCs can access SNA hosts to conduct on-line 3270 sessions. Includes script language for automating date entry and background IND$FILE file transfer and High-Level Application Program Interface. Supports SyncLink communications cards and modems.

AdaptSNA 3270 (V.4.3)
Network Software Associates, Inc.
39 Argonaut
Laguna Hills, CA 92656
714-768-4013
fax: 714-768-5049

• Enables interactive communications between micro and IBM mainframe using IBM 3270 SNA/SDLC protocol. Emulates 3274 and 3278/9 terminals. Direct print sessions run concurrently with terminal emulation using DSC and SCS data streams. Hot button allows simultaneous PC program execution and mainframing session. Supports four-color printing. Allows customizations. Includes MemoryMizer and memory-conservation function.

NetWare 3270 Multi Workstation
Novell, Inc.
122 East 1700 South
Provo, UT 84606
800-453-1267; 801-379-5900
fax: 801-429-5775

• Provides 3270 terminal emulation. Gives a PC access to an IBM mainframe and provides up to five concurrent 3270 mainframe display/printer sessions and one DOS session. Offers Coax, SDLC, and Token-Ring host connection options. Includes file transfer support, multiple Application Program Interfaces, and keyboard definition utilities.

Packet/3270 (V.5.0.2)
Packet/PC, Inc.
135 South Rd.
Farmington, CT 06032
800-722-3270; 203-678-1961
fax: 203-674-8234

• An SNA 3270 emulator for PCs. Supports 3270 display and printer sessions via async communications and packet networks. Provides all the functionality of IBM SNA/SDLC. Provides applications program interface, end-to-end error detection/retransmission, IND$FILE file transfer, compression, and extended attributes. Includes keyboard mapping capabilities supporting extended keyboards, foreign language keyboards, and APL.

SNA Exchange
Passport Communications, Inc.
2755 Campus Dr., Suite 175
San Mateo, CA 94403
800-767-9583; 415-571-9583
fax: 415-571-7409

• SNA/SDLC communications. Emulates IBM 3274, 3278/9 with multi-sessioning, 3287, and 3777-1 RJE workstations. Toggles between DOS and 3270 functions.

Rexxterm (V.2.3)
Quercus Systems
PO Box 2157
Saratoga, CA 95070-0157
408-257-3697

• Provides VT100 and 3270 terminal emulation, and supports Xmodem,

Ymodem, Zmodem, Kermit, and CompuServe-B file transfer protocols. Uses REXX as scripting language. Includes ASCII file upload capability, built-in editor, data capture buffer, host mode, keyboard reconfiguration, and unlimited dialing directory files.

RabbitStation Remote
Rabbit Software Corp.
7 Great Valley Pkwy., East
Malvern, PA 19355
800-RABBITC; 215-647-0440
fax: 215-640-1379

• Provides users with remote access to IBM mainframe applications and data. Provides concurrent emulation of remote IBM BSC or SNA 3270 control units, displays, printers, and 3770 RJE workstations.

3270-Plus
Sterling Software, Inc.
11050 White Rock Rd., Suite 100
Rancho Cordova, CA 95670-6095
916-635-5535
fax: 916-635-5604

• Allows DOS or UNIX PCs to emulate 3270 terminals or controllers for host connectivity to TSO, CICS, and IMS.

Netway 1000/PC
Tri-Data Systems, Inc.
3270 Scott Blvd.
Santa Clara, CA 95054-3011
800-874-3282; 408-727-3270
fax: 408-980-6565

• Provides multiple zone support for PCs on AppleTalk LAN and 3270 workstations providing terminal emulation, file transfer, and local/remote printing.

Rumba (V.3.0)
Wall Data, Inc.
17769 Northeast 78th Pl.
Redmond, WA 98052
800-433-3388; 206-883-4777
fax: 206-885-9250

• A Windows communication program. Lets a PC act as a distributed function terminal and supports extended data streams. Runs multiple 3270 mainframe sessions while maintaining applications in other windows, and gives data-sharing capability to applications running in Windows. Facilitates file transfers and macro customization. Features Hotlinks, which updates data downloaded from host into windows application, and Hotspots, which allows users of local windows programs to execute mainframe functions or previously created macros by clicking on corresponding menu items. Uses 39k of RAM for the first session and 25k each additional session. EGA or higher video adapter required.

PC 3276 SNA/SDLC Emulation
Wang Laboratories, Inc.
One Industrial Way
Mail Stop 014-A1B
Lowell, MA 01851
800-835-9264; 508-459-5000

• Allows a Wang PC to emulate an IBM 3270 terminal and communications controller.

Zero-Slot LANs

PC-Hooker Turbo
Amica
1800 Busse Hwy.
Des Plaines, IL 60016
800-888-8455; 708-635-5700
fax: 708-635-5724

• Transfers files between two PCs. Transfers can be made through a serial or parallel port. Features include on-line help, view/editor, multiple transfers, DOS utilities, modem capabilities, and auto-install.

LANtastic Z (V.1.0)
Artisoft, Inc.
575 E. River Rd.
Artisoft Plaza
Tucson, AZ 85704
602-293-6363
fax: 602-293-8065

• LAN OS. Interconnects two PCs using existing serial or parallel ports on each PC. Operates in background. Shares programs, data, printers, CD-ROMs, and other resources.

PC-Hookup (V.2.0)
Brown Bag Software
2155 S. Bascom, Suite 114
Campbell, CA 95008
800-523-0764; 408-559-4545
fax: 408-559-7090

• Laptop-to-desktop PC file transfer program. Supports transfer over modem and from direct link by cable. Includes cable that can transfer data between parallel or serial ports.

ChainLink
ConnectWorks Co.
110 Causeway Dr.
PO Box 497
Wrightsville Beach, NC 28480
800-992-LINK; 919-256-2366
fax: 919-256-8614

• PC connectivity package for 2 or 16 users. Includes peripheral sharing, file transfer, network management, e-mail, and chatting capabilities.

Flying Dutchman
Cyco International
1908 Cliff Valley Way, Suite 2000
Atlanta, GA 30324
800-323-2926; 404-634-3302
fax: 404-633-4604

• File transfer program that uses parallel port for data transfer. Files can be sent between 5 1/4- and 3 1/2-inch drives.

Hot Wire
Datastorm Technologies, Inc.
PO Box 1471
Columbia, MO 65205
314-443-3282
fax: 314-875-0595

• File transfer, disk management utility. Allows file transfer between any configuration of IBM-compatible PCs. Point-and-shoot capability. Allows user to maintain files on local disks and on disks of a connected computer. Designed for use with direct connections or modems for short- or long-distance file transfers. Includes macro facility, menu bar with point-and-shoot dual directory display, simultaneous visual display of source and target directory contents, simultaneous logging of multiple disk drives, wildcard search capabilities, and other functions.

Brooklyn Bridge (V.3.0)
Fifth Generation Systems, Inc.
10049 N. Reiger Rd.
Baton Rouge, LA 70809
800-873-4384; 504-291-7221
fax: 504-295-3268

• File transfer and access utility. Connects laptop and desktop micros with any size floppy or hard disks. Accesses remote drives and peripherals. Includes file manager with dual directory display and point-and-shoot menu. Move, remove, copy, and backup DOS utilities. Run utility provides dual independent processing.

File Shuttle (V.4.1)
GETC Software, Inc.
1280 Seymour St., 2nd Floor
Vancouver, BC
CD V6B 3N9
800-663-8066; 604-684-3230
fax: 604-689-1401

• Allows file transfer between PCs at up to 3 Mb per minute using standard parallel printer cable or 115,200-baud using 1-4 modem cable. Includes rocket socket cable adapter.

Printer LAN Plus
Grapevine LAN Products, Inc.
15323 Northeast 90th St.
Redmond, WA 98052
206-869-2707
fax: 206-869-2506

• Allows single PC to function as central node of LAN connecting five PCs. Includes 4-port serial card and serial cables. Supports file access and transfers, print spooling and queuing, and electronic mail. Accesses the network from within an application. Supports 25 separate peripherals and remote communications via modem. Interfaces with GLP's GV LAN OS.

Rapid Transfer Easy File Transfer Kit
Intertech Marketing, Inc.
8820 Six Forks Rd.
NCNB Bank Bldg., Suite 100
Raleigh, NC 27615
800-762-7874; 919-870-8404
fax: 919-870-8343

• Selects files to transfer from menu. Supports wildcards. Sorts file list by name, extension, date, or size. Transfers any kind of file including system or hidden files. Sends single files, groups of files, or whole directories. Copies subdirectory structures to any other subdirectory. Creates and removes directories.

Direc-Link (V.3.0)
Micro-Z Co.
4 Santa Bella Rd.
Rolling Hills Estates, CA 90274
213-377-1640
fax: 213-544-4058

• File transfer program. Supports link between any two PCs. Point-and-shoot operating procedure. Copies and transmits directories, groups of directories, or entire disks. Creates directories. Displays, renames, and deletes files. Supports remote operation and printing, and multiple file transmission.

TRANSit (V.1.1A)
RAD Software
9160 South 300 West, Suite 10
Sandy, UT 84070
800-735-4301; 801-255-3569

• File transfer system. Provides parallel, serial, and modem transfers. Includes serial and parallel cables. Displays detailed system information. Allows installation of transit without floppy disks. Includes erase, copy, move, rename, view, edit, find, and other features.

FastLynx (V.1.0)
Rupp Corp.
7285 Franklin Ave.
Los Angeles, CA 90046
800-852-7877; 213-850-5394
fax: 213-874-5646

• File transfer utility. Transfers data between any two IBM compatible computers. Includes serial and parallel device drivers. Includes an on-line diagnostic program and auto port/auto baud select function. Allows user to access remote printers, and to transfer files or directories within the same system.

LapLink III
Traveling Software, Inc.
18702 N. Creek Pkwy.
Bothell, WA 98011
800-662-2652; 206-483-8088
fax: 206-487-1284

• File transfer program. Connects any two IBM-compatible desktop or laptop computers. Allows user to move clone of LapLink to connected system across universal cable. Copies files, directories, or disks in either direction. Checks all transferring information for validity.

Splits a screen showing files on both computers with a graphical directory-tree-style interface for disk management and directory sorting. Hard disk backup. Supports serial and parallel port connections. Includes cable.

MasterLink (V.5.0)
U.S. Marketing, Inc.
1402 South St.
Nashville, TN 37212
615-242-8800
fax: 615-242-8880

• Allows user to connect two computers over serial cable, allowing them to access each others' shared drives and printers simultaneously. Provides record and file locking. Includes 14-foot serial cable.

LAN Analysis Products

Traffic Monitoring Software

Control Room (V.1.0)
Ashton-Tate
20101 Hamilton Ave.
Torrance, CA 90502-1319
213-329-8000
fax: 213-538-7996

• Allows network administrators to inventory, inspect, and personalize the configuration of hardware and software on a network. Consists of series of panels for customizing keyboard settings, disk settings, general hardware settings, memory usage, machine configuration, expert opinion system, equipment summary, and tasks. Provides a TSR program that loads and implements panel

selections when system is turned on. Includes anti-viral scan.

LAN Director (V.1.02)
Athena Software
PO Box 18362
Boulder, CO 80308
303-428-4550
fax: 303-530-0727

• File management package for LANs.
Combines search utilities, menu-driven
interfaces, and other features in a windowing environment. Lets NetWare users copy files, search according to 11
different selection criteria, attach comments to files and directories, and navigate through directory trees. Supports
NetWare attributes including security
features and long file names. Runs up
to eight servers simultaneously. Provides text editor, pull-down menus, and
support for user-definable menus.

LT Stat+
Blue Lance
PO Box 430546
Houston, TX 77243
713-680-1187
fax: 713-622-1370

• LAN utility that manages disk utilization, security, and system configuration. Generates reports including
server, user and group configuration,
trustee assignment, accounting reports,
effective rights, menu file, NetWare
message and error, log-in scripts, directory, volume and user utilization, duplicate file, and last updated file reports.

Emonitor+ (V.1.31)
Brightwork Development, Inc.
766 Shrewsbury Ave.
Jerral Center West
Tinton Falls, NJ 07724
800-552-9876; 201-530-0440
fax: 201-530-0622

• Diagnostic software designed specifically for use on Ethernet LANs. Analyzes network performance, reports
Ethernet errors, and tests individual
Ethernet cables. Facilitates troubleshooting, and supports remote networks and capacity planning.
(ARCmonitor is also available for
ARCnet networks.)

Monitrix Network Manager (V.2.0)
Cheyenne Software, Inc.
55 Bryant Ave.
Roslyn, NY 11576
800-243-9462; 516-484-5110
fax: 516-484-3446

• Network-management VAP or
NLM. Tracks file servers, network
printers, and individual network nodes.
Provides alarm capabilities to indicate
when disk-drive capacity drops below
certain threshold, when printer goes
off-line, or when a problem is detected
with a network node. Performs diagnostic tests by checking transmission paths
between two network nodes. Offers topology map.

Outrider (V.1.0)
Daystrom Technologies Corp.
405 Tarrytown Rd., Suite 414
White Plains, NY 10607
914-896-7378

• Monitors, logs, and displays current
and average CPU use and free and

maximum disk space available. Allows administrators to track up to four file servers simultaneously.

LAN Command (V.1.1)
Dolphin Software, Inc.
6050 Peachtree Pkwy., Suite 340-208
Norcross, GA 30092
404-339-7877

• Network management and diagnostic software. Manages every component of user's LAN including servers, clients, gateways, bridges, and routers. Provides data base system, monitoring and analysis, and other functions.

NetCompanion (V.1.0)
ETI Software
2930 Prospect Ave.
Cleveland, OH 44115
800-336-2014; 216-241-1140
fax: 216-241-2319

• Integrated network management utility. Includes user management, server management and security, network performance monitoring, queue monitoring, file management, workstation configuration, and general purpose utilities.

VigiLAN
EXPERDATA, Inc.
10301 Toledo Ave., South
Bloomington, MN 55437
612-831-2122
fax: 612-835-0700

• A standalone network management system that gathers network diagnostic data and lets you use a PC remotely or locally to view network statistics.

Direct Net (V.1.0)
Fifth Generation Systems, Inc.
10049 N. Reiger Rd.
Baton Rouge, LA 70809
800-873-4384; 504-291-7221
fax: 504-295-3268

• Menuing system for networks. Organizes software into a user-defined menu. Features supervisory utilities, automatic menu building, multiple menu options, usage tracking with report generator, metering, virus detection, password protection, and custom file applications.

FRESH Utilities (V.2.3)
Fresh Technology Group
1478 N. Tech Blvd., Suite 101
Gilbert, AZ 85234
800-545-8324; 602-497-4200
fax: 602-497-4242

• Assortment of 11 utility programs designed to allow network administrators or users to monitor activity and maximize productivity on a network. Includes on-line help. Enables network administrators to generate reports on the activity of server, groups, users, and queues. Command-line utilities include FTLight, FTLogout, FTDirsiz, and others.

Frye Utilities for Networks—NetWare Management (V.1.01)
Frye Computer Systems, Inc.
19 Temple Pl.
Boston, MA 02111
800-234-3793; 617-247-2300
fax: 617-451-6711

• Collects real-time LAN data and cumulative network data for both text and graphics format presentations. Details the status of components and generates a configuration report of the network setup.

LANWatch (V.2.0)
FTP Software, Inc.
26 Princess St.
Wakefield, MA 01880
617-246-0900
fax: 617-246-0901

• Network analyzer for LANs. Useful for developing and debugging protocols and for installing, troubleshooting, and monitoring networks. Includes an analyzer that increases the amount of data, speed, and ways to manipulate data.

Perfect Menu (V.2.3)
International Computer Group, Inc.
18520 Office Park Dr.
Gaithersburg, MD 20879
800-833-2324; 301-670-7007
fax: 301-330-7274

• Network administration product. Organizes all programs, keeps a log of all programs used and statistically compiles user data. Allows user to design interface environment, create menu selections, pick screen colors, choose program execution, and design default selections.

Lomax Utilities (V.2.1)
J.A. Lomax Associates
659 Adrienne St., Suite 101
Novato, CA 94945
800-225-6629; 415-892-9606

• Nineteen reports providing information on network volume utilization and security. Locates seldom-used files, duplicate files, and outdated files. Monitors security access.

BindView+ (V.3.0)
The LAN Support Group, Inc.
PO Box 460269
Houston, TX 77056-8269
800-749-8439; 713-621-9166

• Management and reporting utility for Novell NetWare LANs. Prints custom-tailored, professional audit and management reports detailing file server configurations. Documents system configuration and user configuration data as safeguard against lost or damaged bindery. Allows customization.

GlobeView
Navtel, Ltd.
6611 Bay Circle, Suite 190
Norcross, GA 30071
800-262-8835; 404-446-2665
fax: 404-446-2730

• Reads, analyzes, and decodes data captured by Navtel's 9400 series protocol analyzers. Allows full access to statistical method of testing.

LANtrack (V.1.0)
Network Management, Inc.
19 Rector St.
New York, NY 10006
800-LAN-USER; 212-797-3800
fax: 212-797-3817

• Real-time server monitoring utility for Novell networks. Alerts network administrators of system abnormalities and to potential problems. Provides for various trackable items including disk, cache, network, system, and volume items. Allows administrators to set thresholds for resource use and to configure a program to alert once limits are reached.

File Manager (V.2.0)
Saber Software Corp.
PO Box 9088
Dallas, TX 75209
800-338-8754; 214-361-8086
fax: 214-361-1882

• LAN file management tool. Combines XTree-like presentation with extended network-specific functionality to provide alternative surface for network users. Allows definition of file viewers, editors and execution options. Features include network orientation, file tagging for file-group operation, support for standard DOS operations, search for string within file or file volume, print files in raw or formatted form, sorted displays by name, extension, date/time or size, SAA pull-down menus with mouse support.

Softbreeze (V.3.1)
SoftShell Systems, Inc.
1163 Triton Dr.
Foster City, CA 94404
800-322-7638; 415-571-9000
fax: 415-571-0622

• Hard disk and OS management tools. Consists of five utilities and programming language. Includes file, document, applications and systems managers, and multitasking/task switching module.

Monitrix for ARCnet
Standard Microsystems Corp.
35 Marcus Blvd.
Hauppauge, NY 11788
800-992-4762; 800-433-5345;
516-273-3100
fax: 516-273-3123

• Network management package. Combines Intelligent Hub physical-level product capabilities with Cheyenne's Monitrix software, allowing network monitoring to be performed in background. Includes clock/calendar physical security, event network alarms, and physical event logging. Maintains statistical data bases, graphical interfaces including bridge, network and node maps, and a connectivity check that detects and isolates communication problems between any two nodes.

SCUA Plus (V.2.01)
TGR Software, Inc.
2 Ravinia Dr., Suite 330
Atlanta, GA 30346
404-390-7450
fax: 404-390-7455

• Access and application management tool. Administration package. Protects users from information loss and theft. Includes selective security, LAN compatibility, audit trails, virus prevention and detection, hard disk management, protection against copyright infringement, and on-line help.

TXD (TC8310) (V.1.01)
Thomas-Conrad Corp.
1908R Kramer Lane
Austin, TX 78758
800-332-8683; 512-836-1935
fax: 512-836-2840

• Analyzes network performance and diagnoses problems on Novell NetWare LANs. Determines internetwork configuration, interrogates all nodes, analyzes critical data from one or all nodes, and reports unusual activity levels with interpretation of what levels represent.

Executes point-to-point communication testing.

Network Inspector (V.1.0)
Tiara Computer Systems, Inc.
1091 Shoreline Blvd.
Mountain View, CA 94043
800-638-4272; 415-965-1700
fax: 415-965-2677

- Provides network monitoring and diagnostic tests designed for Ethernet LANs. Collects statistics about nodes and system and filters packets according to address and type. Allows LAN managers to identify hardware failures, isolate cable breaks, and monitor network use.

NetProbe
3Com Corp.
3165 Kifer Rd.
Santa Clara, CA 95052-8145
800-638-3266; 408-562-6400
fax: 408-970-1112

- Network analyzer designed for pinpointing problems in Ethernet and Token Ring networks. Locates nonresponding workstations, internet route malfunctions, network failures, and overloaded network servers. Requires 3Com's EtherLink, EtherLink Plus, or TokenLink adapter board.

Hardware

LANProbe Distributed Analysis System
Hewlett-Packard Co.
5070 Centennial Blvd.
Colorado Springs, CO 80919
719-531-4000
fax: 719-531-4505

- Price: $17,745
- Date announced: 1988
- Function: Protocol analyzer; LAN monitor
- Packaging: Desktop/standalone
- Protocols supported: Ethernet
- Interfaces supported: RS-232C
- Visual monitors provided: 1 CRT display(s)
- Power provision: AC
- Printer interface provided: Yes
- Disk storage provided: Yes

Sniffer Network Analyzer
Network General Corp.
4200 Bohannon Dr.
Menlo Park, CA 94025
415-688-2700
fax: 415-321-0855

- Price: $12,500
- Number installed to date: 3,000
- Date announced: 1986
- Function: Protocol analyzer
- Protocols supported: Token Ring; Ethernet; ARCnet; StarLAN; LocalTalk; PC Broadband; X.25
- Visual monitors provided: 1 CRT display(s)
- Power provision: AC
- Printer interface provided: Yes
- Disk storage provided: Yes

LANalyzer Network Analyzer
Novell, Inc.
LANalyzer Products Division
2180 Fortune Dr.
San Jose, CA 95131
800-243-8526; 408-434-2300
fax: 408-435-1706

- Price: $9,980-$19,995
- Date announced: 1984

- Function: LAN analyzer
- Packaging: Desktop/standalone
- Protocols supported: Ethernet; Token Ring; DECnet; TCP/IP; StarLAN; AppleTalk
- Visual monitors provided: 1 CRT display(s)
- Power provision: Through interface
- Disk storage provided: Yes

SpiderAnalyzer K320
Spider Systems, Inc.
12 New England Executive Park
Burlington, MA 01803
800-447-7807; 617-270-3510
fax: 617-270-9818

- Price: $10,500
- Date announced: 1989
- Function: Protocol analyzer; LAN monitor
- Protocols supported: Ethernet; DECnet; TCP/IP; ISO; LAT; AppleTalk
- Interfaces supported: RS-232C
- Power provision: Through interface

SpiderAnalyzer P320
Spider Systems, Inc.
12 New England Executive Park
Burlington, MA 01803
800-447-7807; 617-270-3510
fax: 617-270-9818

- Price: $15,600
- Date announced: 1989
- Function: Protocol analyzer
- Packaging: Portable/handheld
- Protocols supported: Ethernet; DECnet; TCP/IP; ISO; LAT; AppleTalk
- Interfaces supported: RS-232C

- Visual monitors provided: Dualmode plasma display
- Power provision: AC
- Printer interface provided: Yes
- Disk storage provided: Yes

LAN Remote Control Software

Network Eye
Artisoft, Inc.
575 E. River Rd.
Artisoft Plaza
Tucson, AZ 85704
602-293-6363
fax: 602-293-8065

- Provides multiwindow, multiprocessing, and OS/2-like capabilities for NetBIOS-compatible networks. Allows network user to view other PC screens, interact with or broadcast to those PCs, and perform different tasks on multiple PCs simultaneously within multiple windows on single controlling PC.

Remotely Possible
Avalan Technology
Timothy Fiske House
747 Washington St.
Holliston, MA 01746
800-441-2281

- Remote control software that supports the mouse. Enables PCs to control and monitor other PCs on NetWare.

Blast PC Plus LAN
BLAST/Communications Research
Group
5615 Corporate Blvd.
Baton Rouge, LA 70808
800-242-5278; 504-923-0888
fax: 504-926-2155

• Combines existing Blast features
such as remote-control access, file
transfer, and terminal emulation with
ability to run over NetBIOS and other
LANs.

NETremote+ (V.4.1)
Brightwork Development, Inc.
766 Shrewsbury Ave.
Jerral Center West
Tinton Falls, NJ 07724
800-552-9876; 201-530-0440
fax: 201-530-0622

• Remote access and user support
software for LAN. Allows network
manager to provide instant support for
users anywhere on LAN or WAN by
seeing a remote user's screen and controlling a remote user's keyboard. Includes built-in diagnostics and async
module allowing user to dial into or out
of network.

Line Plus (V.2.14)
Concept Development Systems
PO Box 1988
Kennesaw, GA 30144
404-424-6240
fax: 404-424-8995

• Supports customers by running their
PC from your office. Provides remote
control of another PC. Supports host-
to-remote, remote-to-host, and wildcard file transfer. Sends software updates. Emulates terminals. Communi-

cates with Compuserve and Dow Jones.
Supports Novell NetWare, PC LAN,
Banyan VINES, and NetBIOS.

R2LAN
Crosstalk Communications
1000 Holcomb Woods Pkwy., Suite 440
Roswell, GA 30076-2575
800-241-6393; 404-442-4930
fax: 404-442-4361

• Allows remote operation of PC on
network via NetBIOS. Applications include support/training, project collaboration, and resource sharing. Supports
async communications servers for off-
LAN access. Includes file transfer, chat
window, error-checking, and host keyboard enable/disable.

D-Link Screen Monitor Software
D-Link Systems, Inc.
5 Musick
Irvine, CA 92718
714-455-1688
fax: 714-455-2521

• Allows real-time monitoring and
broadcasting of screens on network. Users are not aware of being monitored.
Provides remote control of other computers on network.

pcAnywhere IV/LAN
DMA
1776 E. Jericho Turnpike
Huntington, NY 11743
516-462-0440
fax: 516-462-6652

• PC-to-PC remote communications
software for network-based PC users.
Permits one workstation to control another on a LAN, or to control a standalone PC at remote location. Features

bi-directional file transfer, general communications capabilities including VT220 emulation and Xmodem file transfer, gateway function, which allows any modem on any networked workstation to serve as non-dedicated communication server, built-in hardware diagnostics, and simultaneous printing at both host and remote locations.

Map Assist (V.2.0)
Fresh Technology Group
1478 N. Tech Blvd., Suite 101
Gilbert, AZ 85234
800-545-8324; 602-497-4200
fax: 602-497-4242

• Memory-resident program. Allows authorized network users across Novell networks to map DOS drives of other workstations as their own logical drives. Allows user to back-up hard drives and share CD ROMs and WORM drives from any network station.

Remote Console (V.1.1)
Fresh Technology Group
1478 N. Tech Blvd., Suite 101
Gilbert, AZ 85234
800-545-8324; 602-497-4200
fax: 602-497-4242

• Enables console operators to view and operate the console of the Novell file server from any PC. Accesses console of non-dedicated file server. Runs on file server using VAP/NLM technology. Operates across bridged servers and mixed topologies. Supports NetWare 286 2.1x and 386 3x.

NetOp
International Intergroup
1777 S. Harrison St., Suite 500
Denver, CO 80210
303-692-9090
fax: 303-756-0678

• Enables users to remote control up to ten PCs, workstations, or servers at a time. Automatically displays all screens. Supports CGA, EGA, and VGA.

Invisible Control
Invisible Software, Inc.
1165 Chess Dr., Suite D
Foster City, CA 94404
415-570-5967
fax: 415-570-6017

• Combines NetWare 286/386 bindery management, LAN reporting, DOS and Macintosh translation, and communications. Allows administrators to store bindery and server properties in a file for later use, and to remote control other users screens and send keystrokes to that machine. Two users can jointly edit a document, or one user can remotely start a lengthy process and then return to their own processor.

LANSight (V.2.0)
LANSystems Inc.
300 Park Ave., South
New York, NY 10010
800-LAN-STEL; 212-995-7700
fax: 212-995-8604

• Remote control program for LANs and WANs. Provides real-time configuration information from a remote location. Offers distributed processing from remote peripherals. Security integrated into NetWare bindery. Requires EGA, VGA, CGA, or MCGA video adapters.

LANshare
Micronet, Inc.
2356 Parkside Dr.
Boise, ID 83712
208-384-9137
fax: 208-344-3515

• Allows users on any NetBIOS-compatible LAN to view the screen display and to control the keyboard of any other network workstation.

Debuggers for DOS and Windows
MultiScope, Inc.
1235 Pear Ave., Suite 111
Mountain View, CA 94043
800-999-8846; 415-968-4892

• Debuggers include run-time and postmortem debugging. Compatible with Microsoft's CodeView and supports C, Pascal, Modula-2, FORTRAN, and BASIC. Contains character mode interface, watchpoints, procedure display windows, and VCR-style remote control.

RemoteTalk
Network Software Associates, Inc.
39 Argonaut
Laguna Hills, CA 92656
714-768-4013
fax: 714-768-5049

• Sync communications package for PC-to-PC remote control and file transfer. Provides 19,200 bps SDLC over leased or dialed lines.

Close-Up/LAN–The Network Remote
Norton-Lambert Corp.
PO Box 4085
Santa Barbara, CA 93140
805-964-6767
fax: 805-683-5679

• Allows user to share screens and keyboards with one, many, or all people on user's network. Enables users on LAN to share printers, modems, faxes, and computers. Can be used for teaching, training, and conferencing.

TeleMagic (Rel. 11.0)
Remote Control
5928 Pascal Court, Suite 150
Carlsbad, CA 92008
800-992-9952; 619-431-4000
fax: 619-431-4006

• Features auto-dialer, tickler file, built-in word processor, notepad area for each record, OE subsystem, instant record retrieval, and help screens. Lists data in any user-defined format and sequence. Generates labels, letters, lists, envelopes, and invoices. Includes e-mail functions.

EXAC
RTI USA
7603 First Avenue #C2
North Bergen, NJ 07047
201-861-1259; 201-861-0084

• The package includes both broadcast and remote control capabilities. Provides the ability to broadcast any screen impage to an unlimited numbers of monitors. Remote control any workstation in the network, even through network bridges.

EasyMenu
Software Clearing House, Inc.
895 Central Ave.
Three Centennial Plaza
Cincinnati, OH 45202
513-579-0455
fax: 513-579-1064

• Includes remote control submits, background job queuing, sequence control resource locking, audit trails, and dynamic JCL modification. Converts from NCR menu processor.

MECO
Software Engineering of America
2001 Marcus Ave.
Lake Success, NY 11042
800-272-7322; 516-328-7000
fax: 516-354-4015

• For unattended automated operations and central and remote control, including IPLs from PC off-site. Provides surveillance of systems and operations consoles. Provides automatic message analysis and response, and alerts and support procedures. Works across mainframes, multiple-CPU environments, partitions, and PR/SM.

Argus/n
Triticom
PO Box 11536
St. Paul, MN 55111
612-937-0772

• Monitors station activity and configuration. Monitors application-level usage in each workstation attached to a NetWare LAN. Conducts automatic hardware inventory of all LAN stations, which simplifies network management and configuration tracking. Designed for system managers to help monitor and control network usage.

CO/Session LAN
Triton Technologies, Inc.
200 Middlesex Turnpike
Iselin, NJ 08830
800-322-9440; 201-855-9440
fax: 201-855-9608

• Remote control software that allows remote users to access home office LANs to run local applications and exchange files.

Remote Access
Ultinet Development, Inc.
9724 Washington Blvd., Suite 200
Carver City, CA 90232
213-204-0111
fax: 213-287-2447

• Enables user to operate keyboard, screen, and peripheral hardware of another workstation by remote control. Allows configuration of all stations on network as "slave" or "master." Allows several stations to control same screen and keyboard simultaneously. 3Com and NetBIOS compatible.

■ Index

END-USER LICENSE AGREEMENT

READ THIS AGREEMENT CAREFULLY BEFORE BUYING THIS BOOK. BY BUYING THE BOOK AND USING THE PROGRAM LISTINGS, DISKS, AND PROGRAMS REFERRED TO BELOW, YOU ACCEPT THE TERMS OF THIS AGREEMENT.

The program listings included in this book and the programs included on the diskette(s) contained in the package on the opposite page ("Disks") are proprietary products of Ziff-Davis Press and/or third party suppliers ("Suppliers"). The program listings and programs are hereinafter collectively referred to as the "Programs." Ziff-Davis Press and the Suppliers retain ownership of the Disks and copyright to the Programs, as their respective interests may appear. The Programs and the copy of the Disks provided are licensed (not sold) to you under the conditions set forth herein.

License. You may use the Disks on any compatible computer, provided that the Disks are used on only one computer and by one user at a time.

Restrictions. You may not commercially distribute the Disks or the Programs or otherwise reproduce, publish, or distribute or otherwise use the Disks or the Programs in any manner that may infringe any copyright or other proprietary right of Ziff-Davis Press, the Suppliers, or any other party or assign, sublicense, or otherwise transfer the Disks or this agreement to any other party unless such party agrees to accept the terms and conditions of this agreement. You may not alter, translate, modify, or adapt the Disks or the Programs or create derivative works or decompile, disassemble, or otherwise reverse engineer the Disks or the Programs. This license and your right to use the Disks and the Programs automatically terminates if you fail to comply with any provision of this agreement.

U.S. GOVERNMENT RESTRICTED RIGHTS. The disks and the programs are provided with **RESTRICTED RIGHTS**. Use, duplication or disclosure by the Government is subject to restrictions as set forth in subparagraph (c)(1)(ii) of the Rights in Technical Data and Computer Software Clause at DFARS (48 CFR 252.277-7013). The Proprietor of the compilation of the Programs and the Disks is Ziff-Davis Press, 764 Gilman Street, Berkeley, CA 94710.

Limited Warranty. Ziff-Davis Press warrants the physical Disks to be free of defects in materials and workmanship under normal use for a period of 30 days from the purchase date. If Ziff-Davis Press receives written notification within the warranty period of defects in materials or workmanship in the physical Disks, and such notification is determined by Ziff-Davis Press to be correct, Ziff-Davis Press will, at its option, replace the defective Disks or refund a prorata portion of the purchase price of the book. **THESE ARE YOUR SOLE REMEDIES FOR ANY BREACH OF WARRANTY.**

EXCEPT AS SPECIFICALLY PROVIDED ABOVE, THE DISKS AND THE PROGRAMS ARE PROVIDED "AS IS" WITHOUT WARRANTY OF ANY KIND. NEITHER ZIFF-DAVIS PRESS NOR THE SUPPLIERS MAKE ANY WARRANTY OF ANY KIND AS TO THE ACCURACY, OR COMPLETENESS OF THE DISKS OR THE PROGRAMS OR THE RESULTS TO BE OBTAINED FROM USING THE DISKS OR THE PROGRAMS AND NEITHER ZIFF-DAVIS PRESS NOR THE SUPPLIERS SHALL BE RESPONSIBLE FOR ANY CLAIMS ATTRIBUTABLE TO ERRORS, OMISSIONS, OR OTHER INACCURACIES IN THE DISKS OR THE PROGRAMS. THE ENTIRE RISK AS TO THE RESULTS AND PERFORMANCE OF THE DISKS AND THE PROGRAMS IS ASSUMED BY THE USER. FURTHER, NEITHER ZIFF-DAVIS PRESS NOR THE SUPPLIERS MAKE ANY REPRESENTATIONS OR WARRANTIES, EITHER EXPRESS OR IMPLIED, WITH RESPECT TO THE DISKS OR THE PROGRAMS, INCLUDING BUT NOT LIMITED TO, THE QUALITY, PERFORMANCE, MERCHANTABILITY, OR FITNESS FOR A PARTICULAR PURPOSE OF THE DISKS OR THE PROGRAMS. IN NO EVENT SHALL ZIFF-DAVIS PRESS OR THE SUPPLIERS BE LIABLE FOR DIRECT, INDIRECT, SPECIAL, INCIDENTAL, OR CONSEQUENTIAL DAMAGES ARISING OUT OF THE USE OF OR INABILITY TO USE THE DISKS OR THE PROGRAMS OR FOR ANY LOSS OR DAMAGE OF ANY NATURE CAUSED TO ANY PERSON OR PROPERTY AS A RESULT OF THE USE OF THE DISKS OR THE PROGRAMS, EVEN IF ZIFF-DAVIS PRESS OR THE SUPPLIERS HAVE BEEN SPECIFICALLY ADVISED OF THE POSSIBILITY OF SUCH DAMAGES. NEITHER ZIFF-DAVIS PRESS NOR THE SUPPLIERS ARE RESPONSIBLE FOR ANY COSTS INCLUDING, BUT NOT LIMITED TO, THOSE INCURRED AS A RESULT OF LOST PROFITS OR REVENUE, LOSS OF USE OF THE DISKS OR THE PROGRAMS, LOSS OF DATA, THE COSTS OF RECOVERING SOFTWARE OR DATA, OR THIRD PARTY CLAIMS. IN NO EVENT WILL ZIFF-DAVIS PRESS' OR THE SUPPLIERS' LIABILITY FOR ANY DAMAGES TO YOU OR ANY OTHER PARTY EVER EXCEED THE PRICE OF THIS BOOK. NO SALES PERSON OR OTHER REPRESENTATIVE OF ANY PARTY INVOLVED IN THE DISTRIBUTION OF THE DISKS IS AUTHORIZED TO MAKE ANY MODIFICATIONS OR ADDITIONS TO THIS LIMITED WARRANTY.

Some states do not allow the exclusion or limitation of implied warranties or limitation of liability for incidental or consequential damages, so the above limitation or exclusion may not apply to you.

General. Ziff-Davis Press and the Suppliers retain all rights not expressly granted. Nothing in this license constitutes a waiver of the rights of Ziff-Davis Press or the Suppliers under the U.S. Copyright Act or any other Federal or State Law, international treaty, or foreign law.

Get PC Magazine Now...and SAVE!

SPECIAL OFFER FOR READERS OF

GUIDE TO CONNECTIVITY

SAVE

54%
on 22 Issues

SAVE

62%
on 44 Issues

You purchased *PC MAGAZINE GUIDE TO CONNECTIVITY,* with one thing in mind—to get *THE MOST* from your system. Now, to keep vital information coming throughout the year, order *PC MAGAZINE,* the #1 resource for IBM—standard personal computing. 22 times a year, *PC MAGAZINE* delivers it all!

- More in-depth reviews than any other computer publication.

- Benchmark test reports on new products from our own PC Labs.

- A comprehensive productivity section for working faster and smarter.

Send in the SPECIAL SAVINGS CARD below: